Econo

D1614394

Adelino Zanini

Economic Philosophy

Economic Foundations and Political Categories

translated by Cosma E. Orsi

PETER LANG

Oxford · Bern · Berlin · Bruxelles · Frankfurt am Main · New York · Wien

Bibliographic information published by Die Deutsche Bibliothek
Die Deutsche Bibliothek lists this publication in the Deutsche
Nationalbibliografie; detailed bibliographic data is available on
the Internet at ‹http://dnb.ddb.de›.

British Library and Library of Congress Cataloguing-in-Publication Data:
A catalogue record for this book is available from *The British Library*,
Great Britain, and from *The Library of Congress*, USA

Cover design: Adrian Baggett, Peter Lang Ltd

The translation of this work has been funded by SEPS
SEGRETARIATO EUROPEO PER LE PUBBLICAZIONI SCIENTIFICHE

Via Val d'Aposa 7 - 40123 Bologna - Italy
seps@alma.unibo.it - www.seps.it

ISBN 978-3-03911-342-2

© Peter Lang AG, International Academic Publishers, Bern 2008
Hochfeldstrasse 32, Postfach 746, CH-3000 Bern 9, Switzerland
info@peterlang.com, www.peterlang.com, www.peterlang.net

Contents

Introduction[*]

1

The highly problematic relationship between 'political sovereignty' and the 'economic sphere' is the main characteristic of Modernity.[1] It manifests the need for forms of 'political government' adequate to the requirements of civil society, which has always had a critical-osmotic relationship with the State.[2] It is not difficult to identify the theoretical and historical foundations of the connection between the political and economical spheres. More complex, however, is to identify a conceptual development able to maintain their unity, as it should be capable of grasping the *dyskrasìa*, overlapping and displacement, which they generate in the modern era. A line of argument connecting a time span ranging from the mid seventeenth to the mid twentieth century – linking *idealiter* Hobbes and Keynes – is inconceivable, since it can only appear, both historically and conceptually, the fruit of a banal *Historismus*. More appropriate, instead, might be to make reference to a sequence of problematic interlacements, wherein each of the knots represents a *conceptual discontinuity* with which to deal –

[*] Given the high complexity of the Italian text, I would like to express my gratitude to Samantha Ball and Pauline M. Jones for their attentive final linguistic revision (Cosma E. Orsi).

[1] For a definition of Modernity, see M. Berman, *All that is Solid Melts into Air. The Experience of Modernity*, Simon and Schuster, New York, 1982; J. Habermas, *Der philosophischen Diskurs der Moderne. Zwölf Vorlesungen*, Suhrkamp Verlag, Frankfurt am Main, 1985; C. Galli, *Modernità. Categorie e profili critici*, Il Mulino, Bologna, 1988; D. Harvey, *The Condition of Postmodernity*, Basil Blackwell, London, 1990.

[2] The nexus between 'crisis' and 'osmosis' is absolutely evident in Marx's critique to Hegel's *Rechtsphilosophie* and in all his political works. Similarly important is Foucault's work on the topic (see *Sécurité, territoire, population* and *Naissance de la biopolitique*, both published by Gallimard-Seuil, Paris, 2004).

a *próblēma*, therefore, able to create a *theoria*, even when it does not allow an adequate unravelling.

The modern issue *par excellence* is not the inevitable and obvious relationship between the political and the economic spheres; rather, it is represented by the aporias that this relationship generates, where sovereignty and needs do not find a satisfactory re-composition via an adequate representation of social and political interests.[3] Even formulated in a different way, the problem remains the same: between Hobbes and Locke, Schmitt and Kelsen, 'differences' and 'repetitions' arise with reference to the foundation of the 'idea of power', to its legitimate use and to its representation – before and after the crisis of *jus publicum europeum*.[4] However, such a crisis is not an 'event', but rather a 'process'. Hence, particularly in the crucial passage between the nineteenth and twentieth centuries, the picture becomes completely confused any time *das System der Bedürfnisse* escapes the political over-determination of the 'general interest'. From Hegel on, the problem would be posed in the following terms:

> As for the conspicuously good will, which is said to be shown by the classes [*der Stände*] towards the general interest, it has already been remarked (§272, *note*) that the masses, who in general adopt a negative standpoint [*dem Standpunkte des Negativen überhaupt*], take for granted that the will of the government is evil or but little good. If this assumption were replied to in kind, it would lead to the recrimination that the classes, since they originate in individuality, the private standpoint [*dem Privatstandpunkt*] and particular interests, are apt to pursue these things at the expense of the universal interest; while the other elements of the state, being already at the point of view of the state, are devoted to universal ends. [...] The classes, therefore, are specially marked out by their containing the subjective element of universal liberty. In them the peculiar insight and peculiar will of the sphere, which in this treatise has been called the civil society [*bürgerliche Gesellschaft*], is actualized in relation to the state.[5]

---

3   Schmitt's notion of representation, distinct between *Repräsentation* and *Vertretung*, is emblematic: C. Schmitt, *Verfassungslehre*, Duncker & Humblot, Berlin, 1928, p.208.

4   P.P. Portinaro, *La crisi dello jus publicum europaeum*, Edizioni di Comunità, Milano, 1982.

5   G.W.F. Hegel, *Die 'Rechtsphilosophie' von 1820. Mit Hegels Vorlesungs-notizen 1821–1825*, in *Vorlesungen über Rechtsphilosophie 1818–1831*, hrsg.

The irruption of the paradigm of political economy involves the consequences highlighted by Hegel, although its genesis is an imperfect one, as there is no original 'programmatic manifesto' with which to confront this paradigm. After Marx, radical modern thought – either in its authoritarian or democratic form – would give an account of such an irruption in its own way, often in equivocal terms, but theoretically always effective. For example, Carl Schmitt[6] quotes Hegel's *Wissenschaftliche Behandlunsarten* to reaffirm the modern relationship – 'politically unrisky' – between the *bourgeois* and the private sphere. He further observes that, in liberal thought, the *concept of the Political* – which is the theoretical representation/reformulation of the categorial value of Hobbesian *homo homini lupus* – becomes mere economic competition, because the State is reduced to society. The State becomes 'a technical-economic unit of a system of production and exchange', based upon economic calculation.[7] Therefore, so conceived, the concept of the Political would be subjected to the mere economic rationality.

It should be observed that, as there was a political thought before Hobbes,[8] so there has been an economic thought before Smith.[9] However, until that moment, a 'social question' *lato et stricto sensu* – capable of reducing political sovereignty entirely to the economic sphere – did not impose itself as *the* problem of European political society. Only at this point in time did the latter become characterized by needs perceived, organized and collectively claimed, and, as such, able to resurface what, in his critique of Hegel's *Rechtphilosophie*, Marx defined as 'the opposition of the universal as *form*, in the form

von K.-H. Ilting, Frommann-Holzboog, Stuttgart-Bad Cannstatt, 1974, Bd.2, p.769; *Philosophy of Right*, trans. by S.W. Dyde, Batoche Books Limited, Kitchener, 2001, p.243.

6   C. Schmitt, *Der Begriff des Politischen*, Duncker & Humblot, Berlin, 1963, p.62; *The Concept of the Political*, trans. by G. Schwab, Rutgers University, Rahway (NJ), 1976, pp.62–3.

7   Ibid., pp.70–1; *The Concept of the Political*, pp.69–73.

8   Q. Skinner, *The Foundations of Modern Political Thought*, Cambridge University Press, Cambridge, 1978.

9   E.A.J. Johnson, *Predecessors of Adam Smith*, King & Son, New York, 1937.

of universality, and the universal as *content*.[10] From now on – this is the true turning point – the impracticability of political primacy, defined in a caricatural way by Schmitt as 'the struggle for economic thought',[11] would become the expression of a *dyskrasia*, if not a clear separation, often represented as a world neutralized and de-politicized by technique, the only *alter ego* of the Economical.[12]

With more or less accentuated nuances, this image has been reasserted by several thinkers. Hannah Arendt, for example, after having noted that in ancient thought the expression 'political economy' would have been literally nonsense, claimed that:

> It is the same conformism, the assumption that men behave and do not act with respect to each other, that lies at the root of the modern science of economics, whose birth coincided with the rise of society and which, together with its chief technical tool, statistics, became the social science par excellence. Economics – until the modern age a not too important part of the ethics and politics and based on the assumption that men act with respect to their economic activities as they act in every other respect – could achieve a scientific character only when men had become social beings and unanimously followed certain patterns of behaviour, so those who did not keep the rules could be considered to be asocial or abnormal.[13]

It can be easily observed that the crisis of the supremacy of politics over economics can be considered, after Marx, as an element that transversally characterizes some of the most 'radical forms' of modern critical thought. With such 'forms of thought', economic doctrine does not entertain – historically and conceptually – particular relationships. However, we believe that it should deal with the critical issues raised by these 'radical thoughts' because, although they do not

---

10 'Es handelt sich hier um den Gegensatz des "Allgemeinen" als "Form", in der "Form der Allgemeinheit", und des "Algemeinen als Inhalt"' (K. Marx, *Kritik des Hegelschen Staatsrechts*, *MEW*, Dietz, Berlin, 1956 ff., Bd.1, p.267).

11 C. Schmitt, *Römischer Katholizismus und politische Form*, Theatiner Verlag, München, 1925², p.19.

12 Regarding this, Heidegger's reflection on the concept of *Gestell* is fundamental (*Vorträge und Aufsätze*, Verlag G. Neske, Pfullingen, 1954).

13 H. Arendt, *The Human Condition*, The University of Chicago Press, Chicago, 1958, pp.41–2. See also, J. Taminiaux, *La fille de Thrace et le penseur professionnel*, Payot, Paris, 1992.

put in question its analytical articulations, they do challenge its foundations. This is the exact concern of this book: before and after Marx. More specifically, it attempts to explain why the relationship between economic doctrine and political categories can only be understood in its *aporetical character*, which qualifies the relationship – modern *par excellence* – between economics and politics. From the above, the presumption to commensurate economic fundaments and political categories stems.

2

Before and after Marx, therefore – moving from Smith to Keynes, through Schumpeter. Obviously, it is possible to disagree on the chosen path, but such a dispute would be superfluous, because on this point any doctrinal justification would be arguable. It is sufficient to say that what links Smith, Marx, Schumpeter and Keynes is not their macroeconomic approach, but rather their particular sensibility – be it implicit or explicit – towards the relationship between the Economical and the Political in a macroeconomic interpretative framework. Thus, in the works of these authors, it is possible to trace the historical and doctrinal development of the modern relationship between the two spheres. That there was a 'body' of economic thought before Smith is obvious; that, in the last thirty years or more, there have been a post and a new Keynesian schools – to say nothing about the anti-Keynesians – is something that does not affect the theoretical definition of our problem.[14] In particular, it is here argued that Keynes concludes the ascendant course of modern economic thought – without denying the importance of the heterodox economists who

14   See P. Arestis, *The Post-Keynesian Approach to Economics. An alternative Analysis of Economic Theory and Policy*, Elgar, Aldershot, 1992; D.K.H. Begg, *Rational Expectations Revolution in Macroeconomics. Theories and Evidence*, Allan, Oxford, 1982; S.P. Hargreaves Heap, *The New Keynesian Macro-economics: Time, Belief and Social Interdependence*, Elgar, Aldershot, 1992.

came after him and who produced, on the specific issue, an immense body of literature, which is, however, 'only' noble *economic theory*.[15]

With the earlier mentioned term *dyskrasía* we shall refer to the unstable overlapping occurring among ethics, economic and politics, and to their different 'discursive orders'. It is the same overlapping which determines the modern characterization of politics in terms of economics. Regarding this, four conceptual frameworks seem to be relevant. The first, indeed, is the specific overlapping of the three 'orders' which characterize Smith's reasoning. The second is Marx's critique of the alleged economic naturalness of social relations as they are described by classical political economy. The third is Schumpeter's disjunction, intended as the distinction between what is logically founded according to economic rationality and what is not – primarily the exogenous concept of the Political. Finally, we have Keynes' synthesis between uncertainty and political normation. Singularly taken, these four conceptual frameworks have been largely discussed in philosophical and economical literature.[16] However, we believe that conceived as different solutions to the same theoretical problem, they might generate a virtuous circle, thanks to which we might achieve clarification of the reasons why the interrelationship between the concepts of *the Political* and the concepts *the Economical* cannot be but what it is and has been since the eighteenth century. The *conceptual discontinuity* is certainly unquestionable, but it is not our intention to provide an encyclopaedic analysis of the problem. Rather, we are interested in the definition of the theoretical framework, of which Smith, Marx, Schumpeter and Keynes gave four exemplar and inescapable solutions, which cannot be disregarded.

Smith's overlapping operates an essential mediation between Hobbes and Hutcheson's anthropological paradigms. An exquisitely theological-political approach is integrated – via Hume's work – and disarmed, so to speak, in the *mare magnum* of human passions, from

---

15 G. Lunghini, 'Teoria economica ed economia politica. Note su Sraffa', in Id. (ed. by), *Produzione, capitale e distribuzione*, Isedi, Milano, 1975.

16 Although in the last decades the studies on Smith and Keynes' works witnessed interesting revisions, the same cannot be said for those concerning Marx and Schumpeter.

which re-emerges a historical-political idea of government, embodied in the claim that political economy is to be considered 'as a branch of the science of a statesman or legislator'.[17] Smith's claim is absolutely clear, but even more eloquent are the passages which render it possible. In spite of the interpretation which dominated for nearly two centuries, in fact, Smith does not reduce the Political to the Economical. He does not operate between two poles, rather he establishes – and this is why the idea of prudence is central to *The Theory of Moral Sentiments* – an overlapping between ethics, economics and politics. Such an approach reveals itself as highly unstable, as these planes shift one upon the other; but such instability is nothing other than the specific problem that political economy initially posed to Modernity. According to such an approach, the limit intrinsic to the *finitude* of Schmitt's concept of the Political as pure *domination* and *decision*, detached both from the ethical and economic ratio, is simply ineffectual. Centrality and aporiae of Smith's politics – stretching from prudence and justice – are the most eloquent expressions of such ineffectuality.

Marx's critique of the classical political economy invokes *per se* its political character, of which he emphasizes its scientific feature. No historiographical revision seems to be necessary in order to recuperate Marx's political discourse. Its 'form', however, depends *entirely* upon the interpretation one gives to his *Kritik* as a means for refuting the alleged neutrality of capitalist social relations and, therefore, for solving the historically determined overlapping between the economic sphere and its political legitimation. That Marx's interpretation of classical authors, and particularly of Smith, resorts to the stratagem of *anakhronismós*, is a matter of fact. Marx's conclusions, however, do not depend upon this artfulness. Rather, his strategy entails a rational abstraction [*verständige Abstraktion*], that solves the overlapping by enunciating the political character of the main economic categories

---

17   A. Smith, *An Inquiry into the Nature and Causes of the Wealth of Nations*, ed. by R.H. Campbell and A.S. Skinner, in *The Glasgow Edition of the Works and Correspondence of Adam Smith*, Clarendon, Oxford, 1979, vol.2, I, p.428. Cf. D. Winch, *Adam Smith's Politics*, Cambridge University Press, Cambridge, 1978.

'critically' used by Marx – moving from the separation between property [*Eigentum*] and labour [*Arbeit*], the fundamental requirements for triggering the de-realization process of labour [*der Entwirklichungsprozeß der Arbeit*], in which it is the labour itself that poses the condition of its exploitation. From here derives the importance of interpreting surplus-value as *difference*, which is not solely economic in kind, as it cannot be equated to the mere *economic surplus* – as proposed, for example, by Piero Sraffa. The live labour intended as a living subject undergoes a separation, which generates a surplus [*Überschuß*]; and it is the capacity of the subject, his unicity [*der einzige Unterschied*] that produces such a difference. This latter presupposes the existence of labour as subjectivity [*Arbeit als Subjektivität*], and therefore the possibility of overturning the absolute separation [*Absolute Trennung*] that characterizes capitalist social relationships, their 'appearance' generated by the overlapping between the economical and political spheres.

In spite of the convergences upon decisive analytical issues such as money and the economic dynamics, Schumpeter tackles the problem from a completely different point of view. If Marx's attempt was to solve the overlapping between the political and the economic spheres, Schumpeter, although well aware of the link between the two, tries to separate them. As a result, the crucial distinction between *theoretische Ökonomie* and *ökonomische Theorie*, namely between statics and dynamics, generates a long wave, aimed at disjoining – and exactly in his theory of economic development – endogenous and exogenous, economics and politics. In effect, if it is true that Schumpeter interprets the 'economic fact', pertinent to the economic theory, in its inevitable exogenous, and therefore also political condition, it is nonetheless true that his rational intent is to distinguish economic dynamics from that which does not pertain to economic *ratio*.

In Schumpeter's economic theory, the concept of the Political appears to be both scientifically unrepresentable and logically unthinkable – in Wittgenstein's terms – according to a correct economic *ratio*. Nevertheless, for the Austrian economist, such unthinkableness is a problem that cannot be avoided. For this reason, as at the analytical level the disjunction between the Economical and the Political is not accountable either to the rightness of *Naturwissen-*

14

schaft, or to the neoclassical 'distinction', we shall define Schumpeter as 'impolitical'. The impossibility of representing the concept of the Political stems from its 'unthinkableness' and, conversely, from its practical irreducibility to a mere and banal 'apolitical' approach.

Of this very same irreducibility, Keynes' synthesis gives a different account. Economics and politics should go together, having as a common denominator the combination of both the rationality and irrationality of human action. After the rediscovery of *A Treatise on Probability*, it has been possible to understand better the foundations of such a synthesis and to identify its crucial link with the category of uncertainty which characterizes *The General Theory*. In fact, it is this link which allows us to question the epistemological and ethical roots of a baseless *lex naturae*, upon which economic theory has built an improbable, economical, and political *ordre naturel*, demolished by Keynes in his critique of the *laissez faire*.

The uncertainty that characterizes human knowledge – along with the ethical baselessness of social Darwinism, which is often invoked to legitimize human action – leads Keynes to believe that it is impossible to find any 'natural foundation' for economics. Therefore, what is necessary is to reduce both economic uncertainty and ethical baselessness to the minimum. Accordingly, Keynes' reasoning calls for the urgency of identifying *political choices* able to fill those gaps generated by economic decision. The relationship between 'epistemological functionalism' and 'practical normation' is the outcome of the impossibility of providing a 'natural foundation' to any social order. As a result, the normative horizon – the only link between uncertainty and practical rationality – becomes political, since it is commensurate not only to the 'animal spirits' changing psychology, but also to the 'political supply' expressed by the political and economic institutions. The very same institutions with which Keynes *politicus* confronted himself repeatedly: from Versailles to Washington.

In synthesis, these are the conceptual knots according to which it is possible to claim that it is the *dyskrasia* between ethics, economics and politics that enables us to understand the 'destiny' upon which any modern alleged political decision – Schmitt's *Entscheidung* – rests. Of such a 'destiny', however – and this is the point –, the concept of the Political should not be the only one held accountable. No less complicated is the ethical and economic landscape. The crucial problem is represented neither by the dynamics of overlapping, nor by that of disjunction as such, but by the fact that none of the four identified conceptual frameworks which qualify these dynamics are *per se* sufficiently stable. In strict analytical terms, forcibly de-contextualized, it would be too simplistic to observe that there is no a 'measure' to which to relate the inevitable and reciprocal shifting of the ethical, political and economic planes. And this is the reason why, in modern age, there is, at first, an interlacing of competences – aimed at compensating, from time to time, either for the lack of a political decision, or for an inappropriate economic strategy –, followed by a massive and constant 'ethical appeal', aimed at coping with both State and market failures. It is true that such an 'ethical appeal' shows, *a fortiori*, the lack of a modern idea of political sovereignty – indeed, the lack of legitimation of the Nation State is a theme that has been discussed since the beginning of the twentieth century. Thus, it is perhaps possible to assert that our reasoning might appear self-referential. Such self-referentiality, however, is particularly important, because it pushes aside Schmitt's suggestive idea of a *Polarität* among *heterogenen Sphären*. It is not by accident that chapter XXIV of Keynes' *General Theory* is entangled in the very same self-referentiality. Similarly, it is not by accident that, starting from such a problem, some currents of the contemporary economic theory, more open to a dialogue with extra disciplinary influences, have tried to find a viable exit,[18] often suggested by philosophers like John Rawls or

18   There are many possible examples. See, among others, A.O. Hirschman, *Exit, Voice and Loyalty*, Harvard University Press, Cambridge MA., 1970; A. Sen,

Robert Nozick.[19] In spite of all this, if the situation was that described by modern radical thought, perhaps the sky of the theory would be clearer, or simply less clouded. At any rate, the horizon may never be easily discernible.

Choice, Welfare and Measurement, Blackwell, Oxford, 1982; A. Sen and B. Williams (ed. by), *Utilitarianism and Beyond*, Cambridge University Press, Cambridge, 1982.

19 J. Rawls, *A Theory of Justice*, Harvard University Press, Cambridge MA., 1980; R. Nozick, *Anarchy, State and Utopia*, Basic Books, New York, 1974.

Chapter I
Overlapping
Adam Smith: the government of the passions

1. Introduction

With remarkable efficacy, Adam Smith addressed one of the modern issues *par excellence*, namely the relationship between ethical custom, political sovereignty and the economic sphere. This approach helped to establish him as one of the classic authors of Modernity, the main expression of which is the *highly problematic* relationship between the economic sphere and political sovereignty. In his famous obituary to Alfred Marshall, John M. Keynes vividly noted that 'Economists must leave to Adam Smith alone the glory of the quarto [...], and achieve immortality by accident, if at all'.[1] Doubtless, a circumstantial judgement, but one that holds an essential and implicit truth: Smith's relevance as a predominantly economic thinker cannot be dissociated from an age that knew him as a philosopher, for the simple reason that he was a philosopher by education, election and profession.

Although elementary, such an essential truth did not, until recent times, receive great attention and then, it was with mixed reactions.[2] The traditional historiographical account portrays the Scottish thinker as the most significant advocate of a universal *laissez faire*. In brief, the understanding of Smith as an economist entirely devoted to the analysis of the relationship between exchange and division of labour left a narrow margin for any other interpretation. This traditional portrait, however, cannot merely be ascribed to the tyranny exerted by

---

1   *Economic Journal*, 1924, vol.34, 135, pp.311–72, in *The Collected Writings of J.M. Keynes*, ed. by E. Johnson and D. Moggridge, Macmillan, London, 1971, vol.X, p.199.
2   Cf. A. Zanini, *Adam Smith. Economia, morale, diritto*, B. Mondadori, Milano, 1997.

economic critique – either that of Marx and Ricardo, or that of neo-classical authors. Obviously, these accounts cannot be ignored; yet it should be noted that philosophers like Leslie Stephen and Victor Cousin explicitly disregarded Smith's philosophical relevance.[3]

In contrast to the above limiting and, in our opinion, baseless interpretations, acknowledgement can and should be given to the intrinsic complexity of Smith's philosophical thought which, although owing much to its predecessors, is nevertheless original. If we consider carefully Smith's *opus*, it becomes immediately apparent that not only his most accurate reflections, but also those contained in his unpublished lectures reveal a scholar fully aware of his own historical collocation and originality. The same is true of his apparently extrinsic interests such as his studies on language and rhetoric and, above all, the corpus of writings collected in the posthumous *Essays on Philosophical Subjects*. However, only in the last few decades, thanks to *The Glasgow Edition*, has Smith's philosophical magnitude been recognized. After having established the groundlessness of the alleged irreconcilability between the moralist and the economist[4] – namely, the so-called *Adam Smith Problem* – has the completeness of Smith's body of thought finally been rediscovered in all its original, episte-mological, ethical, historical and economical articulations. The obvious conclusion is that his reflection covered both the economical and philosophical fields. Nevertheless, the question of which philosophy are we confronted with is not at all marginal, as the literature is not homogeneous.

With or without the label of *bourgeois*, to argue for Smith as a 'moralist' does not signify that much. What is more challenging is to pose his articulate thought within the multi-faceted Scottish intellectual landscape. In this context, it would be wrong to subordinate the

3   L. Stephen, *History of English Thought in the Eighteenth Century*, Rupert Hall Davies, London, 1962, vol.2, p.65; V. Cousin, *Philosophie écoissaise*, Levy, Paris, 1864, p.159. But see P. Gay, *The Enlightenment: An Interpretation*, Weidenfeld and Nicolson, London, 1967, vol.1, p.14.
4   See R.F. Teichgraeber, 'Rethinking "Das Adam Smith Problem"', *Journal of British Studies*, 1981, vol.20, 2, pp.106–23.

economist to the moralist.[5] However, the re-composition of these two facets of the same identity – which historically have undergone infinite dissections – not only presents no small feat, but also highlights the necessity of clarifying the ways in which it is feasible to examine the foundations of Smith's philosophy – something that evidently cannot be identified *ex post*. If it is true that the structure of his thought 'was that of moral philosophy in the broad classical sense', it does not seem that 'Smith presented his views on ethics, economics, and politics as separate systems', and co-ordinated them 'in a unified philosophy'.[6]

Andrew S. Skinner noted how difficult it is to comprehend the way in which Smith transposes the *micro* ethical dimension – within which moral judgements are formed – into the *macro* one: namely, how difficult it is to understand the mechanisms of transforming the individual ethical dimension 'into rules of behaviour which are perceived and obeyed by society at large'.[7] We are here in the presence of a transposition that is implicit in what David D. Raphael defined as 'morality as social phenomenon'.[8] From the very outset, it is clear that this is a seminal issue, posited at the centre of a critical discussion that, although not recent, is nevertheless still essential for our approach. Max Scheler noted, for example, that because Smith's *moral value* is not related to human action and will, but rather can only be deduced by the spectator – who reacts emotively to the experience and behaviour of others – the ethics of sympathy always seems to assume what it wants to infer.[9] Consequently – Scheler concluded –, we are faced with a presupposed ethical deduction, with a social ethics without foundations. Even clearer was Giulio Preti, who identified the

5   A.W. Small, *Adam Smith and Modern Sociology*, The University of Chicago Press, Chicago, 1907, pp.5, 11, 77, 235. Cf. M. Brown, *Adam Smith's Economics*, Croom Helm, London, 1988, p.39.

6   R.F. Teichgraeber III, *'Free Trade' and Moral Philosophy*, Duke University Press, Durham, 1986, pp.4 and 155.

7   A.S. Skinner, *A System of Social Science*, Oxford University Press, Oxford, 1979, p.63.

8   D.D. Raphael, *Adam Smith*, Oxford University Press, Oxford, 1985, p.5.

9   M. Scheler, *Wesen und Formen der Sympathie*, in *Gesammelte Werke*, hrsg von M.S. Frings, Francke, Bern und München, 1973, Bd.7, pp.17–18.

weakness of *The Theory of Moral Sentiments* (henceforth *TMS*) both in the absence of a transcendental horizon and in the affirmation of an ethicism as established social ethos. Deprived of its moral dynamism, however, ethics loses its universal connotation. As Preti argued, Smith 'ignores the ethical sphere, and his analyses are confined to the sphere of ethical taste, that is, to the *ethos* itself, to the custom – to the custom of an epoch and of a social class [...]'.[10]

We believe that such an approach should be inverted, thoroughly reclaiming Smith's 'ethicism': not as a 'universal value', *ça va sans dire*, but as a philosophical presupposition without which it would be hard to grasp Smith's relevance in the Scottish and European intellectual landscapes. Only an ethical approach can indeed outline the relationship between 'virtue and commerce', its synthetic representation *par excellence*: the Market. This latter cannot be subordinated to the nineteenth century economic language. In spite of what has been maintained by the following economic culture, Smith's idea of Market represents in fact an anthropological correlation, which reveals, through what may be defined as the 'ethical adequacy' of a *middle social agent*, the inefficacy of the moral sense, as well as the aberration of the selfish system. This is the 'mundane value' of Smith's 'ethicism'.

As the entire chapter will gravitate around the 'ethical adequacy' of this social figure, it will be necessary to dwell upon it for a time. In *TMS* reference is made to a prudent man,[11] whose behaviour appears

10   G. Preti, *Alle origini dell'etica contemporanea. Adamo Smith*, La Nuova Italia, Firenze, 19772, pp.86, 100–13, 146–7, 184; part. pp.100, 131.

11   In this context, there should be mentioned the reasons of those who, in spite of the asserted continuity between the first and the sixth edition of the *TMS* (see D.D. Raphael, A.L. Macfie, 'Introduction', in *TMS*, p.18), argued that the framework of value to which Smith relates the notion of 'prudent man' is entirely changed. However, the arguments advanced, for example, by L. Dickey ('Historicizing the "Adam Smith Problem"', *Journal of Modern History*, 1986, vol.58, September, pp.579–609), who tries to structure a comparison between the different homogeneities (also in linguistic terms), which in the different editions of the *TMS* are not so evident, is not convincing. In fact, these differences do not fit a new system of values, 'a state in which an ideal self and a natural self struggle'. On this topic see T. Raffaelli, 'Human Psychology and the Social Order', *History of Economic Ideas*, 1996, vol.4, 1–2, pp.25–6; Ch.L.

to be socially appropriated. Therefore, our terminological straining is intended to emphasize what *TMS* already shows: the conformity between the behaviour of the prudent man and a social means arising from experience. Certainly, a misunderstanding can occur when the distinction between the acting agent (the *prudent man*) and the judging agent (the *ideal spectator*) is not made sufficiently clear.[12] The reason for such a possible misunderstanding, however, resides in the fact that although in *TMS* the two figures are completely distinct from one another, they are only so at the level of *reflective judgement*. In effects, whilst the former is always empirically determinable, the latter is not. Nevertheless, as it is approved by the ideal spectator, the behaviour of the prudent man becomes the judgmental canon for the propriety of the inferior virtues: habits of economy, industry, discretion and attention – all that constitute prudence. In short, regarding prudence, the basis for a theory of ethical obligation resides *de facto* in the acting of a prudent man respectful of the principles stemming from the natural right.

This explains the overlapping of two distinct figures, which find their synthesis in the middle social agent, and why there is no a theory of moral obligation able to express an *ethical imperative*. A different foundation from the one that is established by the spectator within civil society and to whom it is possible to ascribe a principle, a norm of judgement to which the action could be related, cannot be identified. To be concise, the rule is constituted upon the middle social

Griswold, jr., *Adam Smith and the Virtues of Enlightenment*, Cambridge University Press, Cambridge, 1999, p.28; H. Mizuta, 'Moral Philosophy and Civil Society', in T. Wilson, A.S. Skinner (ed. by), *Essays on Adam Smith*, Clarendon Press, Oxford, 1975, pp.127–30; C. Charlier, 'The Notion of Prudence in Smith's *Theory of Moral Sentiments*', *History of Economic Ideas*, 1996, vol.4, 1–2, pp.271–97; E. Pesciarelli, *La jurisprudence economica di Adam Smith*, Giappichelli, Torino, 1988, pp.45–54.

12   'The spectator is "ideal" in the sense that he excludes all those features of actual spectators which relate to their special interests as particular individuals involved in the actual situation which they are observing [...]' (T.D. Campbell, *Adam Smith's Science of Morals*, Allen & Unwin, London, 1971, p.127). Thus, it is not possible to identify a *normative characterization* in an *ideal* sense. In this context, it should be considered also the relevance of Campell's critique to the *ideal observer theory* (pp.128 ff.).

agent's experience. As Jean-Pierre Dupuy noted, the reason why, in Smith, society is an enclosed system made of 'actors' and 'spectators' is because at any given time the 'actor' can be 'spectator' and vice versa.[13]

Given the above, it is possible to claim that if the 'means' intended as *reflective judgement* can be ascribed only to a perfectly informed spectator, the 'means' intended as *behaviour* can be ascribed to a prudent man. Consequently, if the former is expressed as perfect means according to propriety, the latter is represented as an approximation to the propriety of the inferior virtues.[14] What is reasserted, however, is the same social character of both. The middle social agent cannot be defined according to a utilitarian, statistical or preferential calculation. Whilst the impartial spectator who judges is an *ideal* middle social agent always *in actu*, the prudent man who acts is a *real* middle social agent always *in potentia*. In short, as a behaviour, the perfect means is only potentially *in actu*, because the act of reducing what is social value to the individual, whilst it is easily identifiable, remains just an approximation *vis-à-vis* an acting agent who is prudent only *in potentia*. Nevertheless, the fact that two distinct roles can be attributed to the very same figure generates the paradox underlined by Scheler, and which characterizes an irresolute but not indeterminate dialectical relationship.

At any rate, such a paradox does not invalidate the representativeness of the concept we have utilized; on the contrary, it represents its bases. Not being of a formal nature, *judgement* and *behaviour* do not depend upon different logics: the judgement is never transcendental. There is neither a transcendental instance able to

13   J.-P. Dupuy, 'De l'émancipation de l'économie: Retour sur "le problème d'Adam Smith"', *L'Année sociologique*, 1987, vol.37, p.330. Concerning this self-referentiality, see also Brown, *Adam Smith's Economics*, p.18.
14   The role of propriety is perfectly underlined by T. Phillipson in his 'Adam Smith as civic Moralist' (in I. Hont, M. Ignatieff (ed. by), *Wealth and Virtue: The Shaping of Political Economy in the Scottish Enlightenment*, Cambridge University Press, Cambridge, 1983, pp.189–90), when he observes that for Smith one of the major achievements of the commercial society was its ability of enabling both the layman and the noble to live respecting the requirements of propriety – although this was not the moral ideal *per se*.

qualify the judgement, nor any anthropological instance able *per se* to qualify the behaviour. Rather, both are synthesized by an ethics that includes them. Hence, it is the shift from a morality intended as the phenomenology of any singular human action to an ethics intended as the ensemble of social behaviours that defines the role of the middle social agent. The progressive detachment of Smith's ethics from the moral obligation inferred both from the natural theology and from the moral critique of the selfish system, establishes an approach to the 'exchange' for which the economic dimension is not the only possible one. Within the parameters of this framework, therefore, the perception of the rising capitalistic market as 'natural' cannot be intended as its apology.

It is worth observing that beginning with Mandeville – who embraces Hobbes' selfish system – a market ideology is already perfectly delineated. Our intention, however, is not to illustrate how Smith would have arrived at a definition of an alleged 'mature' market ideology, but rather, to show that, regarding this, his ethics of sentiments is much more effective than the Hobbesian selfish system. Smith's ethics is based upon an anthropological paradigm whose strength resides in the ability of the middle social agent to mediate between the public and the private spheres. From here derives the Illuministic dualism between morality and politics, which generates an *overlapping* between the ethical, economical and political planes. In turn, this overlapping reveals itself as 'unsolvable', but, not accidentally, exactly its *modern* 'inconceivability' would define the space of political economy as a *specific problem* of Modernity.[15] Consequently, Smith the philosopher merges with Smith the economist. In historiographical terms, to think of the latter denying the former would be an evident contradiction. It is in this way that we shall frame Smith's 'discourse', beginning from an analysis of the philosophical and doctrinal contexts.

15   See *infra*, sect. 8.

2. Hobbes' spectrums

The foundations of the Scottish moral philosophy are based on the social primacy of 'natural being'. They could be traced back on the one side to contemporary English philosophical thought and, on the other, to the European juridical tradition mediated by Gershon Carmichael. In this landscape, Samuel Pufendorf played a fundamental role. However, the main actors were Hobbes and Newton. Whilst the former's theory of government was the explicit political target, the latter's physical revolution was conceived as the unavoidable epistemological point of reference for moral philosophy. Certainly more problematic is to evaluate Locke's contribution,[16] without losing sight

16   Locke's influence upon eighteenth century European culture is absolutely well-known (J. Yolton, *John Locke and the Way of Ideas*, Blackwell, Oxford, 1956, pp.1–25). Between the nineteenth and twentieth century, scholars stressed such an influence, overlapping the gnoseological and the political sphere (T. Fowler, *Locke*, Macmillan, London, 1883; Stephen, *History of English Thought*, vol.1, p.29; V. Cousin, *Cours d'Histoire de la Philosophie Morale*, in *Oeuvres*, Hauman, Bruxelles, 1841, vol.2, p.398; E.P. Janet, *Histoire de la science politique dans ses rapports avec la morale*, Levy, Paris, 1913, vol.2, pp.198–9). At a later stage, when the essential problem became the definition of Locke's contribution to the liberal political thought (F. Pollock, *An Introduction to the History of the Science of Politics*, Macmillan, London, 1920; H.J. Laski, *Political Thought in England. Locke to Bentham*, Oxford University Press, Oxford, 1950, pp.47 ff.; S.P. Lamprecht, *The Moral and Political Philosophy of John Locke*, Columbia University Press, New York, 1918, p.143; R.I. Aaron, *John Locke*, Clarendon Press, Oxford, 1952, pp.36, 270; J.W. Gough, *John Locke's Political Philosophy*, Clarendon Press, Oxford, 1950, pp.120 ff.), it seemed legitimate to argue for an alleged unique tradition, ideally able to link together Locke's politics and Smith's economy (regarding the different interpretations of Locke's works, see P. Laslett, 'Introduction', in J. Locke, *Two Treatises On Government*, Cambridge University Press, Cambridge, 1960, pp.35, 46 ff.; N. Bobbio, *Locke e il diritto naturale*, Giappichelli, Torino, 1963, pp.183–93; E.S. De Beer, 'Locke and English Liberalism: The Second Treatise of Government in its contemporary setting', in *John Locke: Problems and Perspectives*, ed. by J. Yolton, Cambridge University Press, Cambridge, 1969, pp.34–44; R. Ashcraft, *Locke's Two Treatise on Government*, Allen & Unwin, London, 1987, pp.286–97). According to this approach, between the English philosophical tradition and the Scottish Enlightenment there would have not

of the diversity and complementarity between the Lockean and Hobbesian systems.[17] Such a controversial issue cannot be addressed here.[18] At any rate, it is important to stress preliminarily that Locke's contribution to the genesis of the Scottish Enlightenment should not

been a clear discontinuity. The most recent historiography has utterly denied such a conclusion. See D. Forbes, 'Sceptical Whiggism, Commerce, and Liberty', in Wilson, Skinner (ed. by), *Essays on Adam Smith*, pp.179–201.

17 The problem, historiographically rather complex, is only apparently secondary in relation to what we are discussing here. See L. Strauss, *What is Political Philosophy? And Other Studies*, The Free Press, New York, 1968; Id., *Natural Right and History*, Chicago University Press, Chicago, 1953; W. Kendall, *John Locke and the Doctrine of Majority-Rule*, University of Illinois Press, Urbana, 1965, p.77. Strenuous critics of Strauss' asserted contiguity are J.W. Yolton ('Locke on the Law of Nature', *The Philosophical Review*, 1958, vol.67, 4, pp.477–98), J. Dunn ('Justice and the Interpretation of Locke's Political Theory', *Political Studies*, 1968, vol.16, 1, pp.72–84), and R. Ashcraft ('Locke's State of Nature: Historical Fact or Moral Fiction?', *The American Political Science Review*, 1968, vol.62, pp.898–915). Regarding this, it is worth noticing Laslett's thesis, which intends to negate any relationship between the *Two Treatises* and Locke's eventual attempt to confute Hobbes' system (see also J. Dunn, *The Political Thought of John Locke*, Cambridge University Press, Cambridge, 1969, p.79). An idea not at all obvious – and we are referring not only to those who advanced the hypothesis of a possible partial overlapping between Hobbes and Locke (R.H. Cox, *Locke on War and Peace*, Oxford University Press, Oxford, 1960, pp.2 ff.), for example in relation to the state of nature –, but also to those who, moving from the idea that the young Locke was influenced by Hobbes (M. Cranston, *John Locke. A Biography*, Longmans, London, 1968, pp.57–67, 208; A.E. Baldini, *Il pensiero giovanile di John Locke*, Marzorati, Milano, 1969, pp.44–9; R.P. Kraynak, 'John Locke: From Absolutism to Toleration', *The American Political Science Review*, 1980, vol.74, pp.53–69), argued that some themes of the *II Treatise*, although indirectly, seem much more pertinent if referred to Hobbes rather than to Filmer. See, N. Bobbio, *Da Hobbes a Marx*, Morano, Napoli, 1965, pp.89–92; R.M. Lemos, *Hobbes and Locke*, The University of Georgia Press, Athens, 1978, p.74.

18 J. Dunn, 'From Applied Theology to Social Analysis: the Break Between John Locke and the Scottish Enlightenment', in Hont, Ignatieff (ed. by), *Wealth and Virtue: The Shaping of Political Economy in the Scottish Enlightenment*, pp.19–136; D. Castiglione, 'Variazioni scozzesi su contratto ed opinione', in M. Geuna, M.L. Pesante (ed. by), *Passioni, interessi, convenzioni*, F. Angeli, Milano, 1992, pp.103–27.

be taken for granted. To think along these lines would risk under-estimating its problematic relationship with regard to Hume and Smith's body of thought – especially when we refer to Smith as a historian of jurisprudence.[19] Hence, to say that Locke's work should be framed against the background landscape of the historical and theoretical process, which in the crisis of the late Scholastic philosophy moves from Pufendorf to Smith via the eighteenth century Scottish philosophy and sociology,[20] seems to be a reductive statement and therefore requires deeper reflection, above all in relation to Hutcheson.

It cannot be denied that, thanks to Carmichael, Locke's ideas played a seminal role in the Scottish Enlightenment. From this per-spective, of particular importance were Carmichael's comments on Pufendorf's *De Officio Hominis et Civis*. As it is known, Pufendorf's interpretation of Grotius's tradition had refocused attention upon the significance of moral reflection, so demonstrating that the study of ethics was nothing other than the study of natural jurisprudence – namely, the study of the duties derived from the knowledge of nature and from the circumstances characterizing the life of each human being.[21] In turn, Carmichael's interpretation simultaneously repre-sented an answer to Leibniz's criticism of Pufendorf and a critique to Pufendorf's same distinction between natural religion and natural jurisprudence. Such a distinction, in effect, implied the attempt to establish the primacy of natural theology intended as the basis for

19 Concerning the presumed influence of Locke upon Smith, see K.I. Vaughn, *John Locke Economist and Social Scientist*, The Athlone Press, London, 1980, p.117; for a different and correct approach, see D. Winch, *Adam Smith's Politics*, Cambridge University Press, Cambridge, 1978, *passim*; Dunn, 'From Applied Theology to Social Analysis: the Break Between John Locke and the Scottish Enlightenment', pp.119 ff. As it is well-known, Locke has been repeatedly indicated as one of the forefathers of *laissez-faire*: see, for example, J.M. Keynes, *The End of Laissez-faire*, in *CWK*, IX, pp.272–7; a different and update opinion can be found, among others, in M. Seliger, *The Liberal Politics of John Locke*, Allen & Unwin, London, 1968, p.179.

20 F. Fagiani, *Nel crepuscolo della probabilità*, Bibliopolis, Napoli, 1983, p.377.

21 J. Moore, M. Silverthorne, 'Gershom Carmichael and Natural Jurisprudence', in Hont, Ignatieff (ed. by), *Wealth and Virtue: The Shaping of Political Economy in the Scottish Enlightenment*, p.76.

natural jurisprudence.[22] Therefore, it is not accidental that thanks to Carmichael, as a result of the reflection concerning natural right, an interpretative relationship between Grotius, Pufendorf, Locke and Hobbes was subsequently established in the Scottish tradition. Indeed, it was due to Carmichael that Locke became highly influential in the development of the Scottish Enlightenment. However, the great distance between Locke and philosophers such as Hume, Smith, Mac-Laurin, and Reid should not be underestimated. It would be sufficient to recall the 'variations' upon crucial issues concerning Locke's doctrine with regard to the link between property and labour, the idea of property as a right,[23] and the concept of labour as value-labour.[24]

It is above all in Hutcheson that it is possible to find ample traces of the Lockean influence. His arrival in Glasgow was accompanied by his solid fame as a modern philosopher, alien to the problem raised by the Scholastic philosophy.[25] In contrast to Carmichael, he established

22   Cf. H. Welzel, *Naturrecht und materiale Gerechtigkeit*, Vandenhoeck und Ruprecht, Göttingen, 1962.
23   As these themes belong to the Scottish tradition, it is worth recalling C.B. Macpherson's interpretation (*The Political Theory of Possessive Individualism: Hobbes to Locke*, Oxford University Press, Oxford, 1962). For a different point of view, see Seliger, *The Liberal Politics of John Locke*, pp.155 ff., 291–3; Dunn, *The Political Thought of John Locke*, pp.214 ff.; J. Tully, *A Discourse on Property*, Cambridge University Press, Cambridge, 1982; Lemos, *Hobbes and Locke*, p.148; Vaughn, *John Locke Economist and Social Scientist*, pp.53–6; C.E. Vaughan, *Studies in the History of Political Philosophy before and after Rousseau*, Russell & Russell, New York, 1960, vol.1, p.176.
24   On the topic, leaving aside the most distant references – J.R. MacCullogh, A. Campbell Fraser, W. Liebknecht –, it is necessary to keep in mind the warning present in modern literature on Locke – from Aaron, Laski, and Gough to the more recent W. Euchner, *Naturrecht und Politik bei John Locke*, Europa Verlag, Frankfurt am Main, 1969; J.D. Mabbott, *John Locke*, Macmillan, London, 1973; J. Gray, *Liberalism*, Open University Press, Milton Keynes, 1986. Fundamental is G. Pietranera's contribution (*La teoria del valore e dello sviluppo capitalistico in Adam Smith*, Feltrinelli, Milano, 1963, pp.18–31), who noted how in Locke there is at best a general principle of the relationship between labour and value, but not a theory able to determine the foundations and measure of value (see also Lemos, *Hobbes and Locke*, p.143; and Vaughn, *John Locke Economist and Social Scientist*, pp.17 ff., 85).
25   F. Restaino, *Scetticismo e senso comune*, Laterza, Bari-Roma, 1974, p.31.

himself as an intellectual outside the academic environment. His ability to rejuvenate moral philosophy – at that time the principal philosophical discipline among those taught in Glasgow – increased both his influence and the intellectual interest around him. A renewal that could occur thanks to the fact that he was fully aware of what should be fought against and what, instead, should be renewed. Whilst the interlacement of conservative political, clerical, and theological interests (which could be traced back to the General Assembly of Presbyterian Church) was to be fought, the theological instrumentation informing the Presbyterian intellectual class – which exerted an immense influence within the Scottish academy and society – was to be renewed.[26]

In Glasgow, Hutcheson was Carmichael's disciple and in 1729 he replaced his master in his academic appointment. His fame was mainly due to the publication of the *Inquiry* (1725). In the *Preface* to the second edition, one of his most important intellectual debts was declared. He wrote: 'To recommend Lord Shaftesbury's writings to the world is a very needless attempt. They will be esteemed while any reflection remains among men'.[27] This statement was an explicit tribute to Shaftesbury, from whom he derived his theory of moral sense. Nevertheless, because Hutcheson embraced Locke's epistemological doctrine, he detached himself from Shaftesbury's innativism. At any rate, in spite of his debt to Locke – this is the crucial point – his ethical perspective could never be said to be Lockean *stricto sensu*.[28]

This is the context within which Smith's reflection was formed. Nonetheless, his points of reference, be they explicit or implicit, referred to the wider European intellectual landscape, as his famous

26 Ibid., p.39. On Hutcheson, see W.R. Scott, *Francis Hutcheson, His Life, Teaching and Position in the History of Philosophy*, Cambridge University Press, Cambridge, 1900.

27 *An Inquiry concerning Order, Harmony, Design* (17262), ed. by P. Kivy, Nijhoff, The Hague, 1973, p.27. Cf. P. Costa, *Il progetto giuridico*, Giuffrè, Milano, 1974, p.144.

28 This topic is dicussed by L. Turco, 'La prima *Inquiry* morale di Francis Hutcheson', *Rivista critica di storia della filosofia*, 1968, vol.23, 1 and 3, section II, pp.308–10.

Letter to the Edinburgh Review confirms.[29] More specifically, Smith's agreement or disagreement with his most proxy authors such as Shaftesbury, Hutcheson and Hume should be framed within the eighteenth century philosophical *milieu*, in which the dispute concerning the relationship between nature and reason – with particular regard to the alternative between self-love and benevolence – was fundamental.

Basil Willey's classical reading[30] has clearly explained and delimited the evolution of such a relationship. If in the first part of the eighteenth century – he noted – nature was usually associated with reason, in the second half of the century it was associated with sentiment. Such a shift called for the primacy of the social affections, which could be understood in the establishment of the pre-eminence of the cult of sensibility, of '*je sens, donc je suis*', with respect Descartes' *cogito*. In short, the emphasis was progressively placed upon impulse and spontaneity. Such a shift not only implied the refusal of Descartes' rationalism, but also – as Paul Hazard noted – it rejected Pascal's tragic *Weltanschaung*. Although in Pascal both the natural sympathetic feeling and the stigmatization of an omnipotent reason[31] were not at all absent, what would typify the eighteenth century ideology and, in particular, the philosophy of moral sense would be the character of an expansive human nature, insensible to the tragic, to the *disproportion* between human and divine nature. As it could not be *naturally* expansive, the Pascalian 'madness of the cross', the ultimate unknowingly, represented instead a condemnation from which humans could never be redeemed through the serenity of the morality intrinsic to the nature of things. The idea of the universe as a 'great chain of being', which in the eighteenth century would reach its apex with the notion of an expansive nature, would escape both the

---

29 See *A Letter to the Edinburgh Review of 1755–56*, in A. Smith, *Essays on Philosophical Subjects*, ed. by P.D. Wightman, J.C. Bryce and I.S. Ross, in *The Glasgow Edition of the Works and Correspondence of Adam Smith*, Clarendon, Oxford, 1980, vol.3, pp.242–54 – henceforth *EPS*.

30 B. Willey, *The Eighteenth Century Background*, Chatto and Windus, London, 1940.

31 B. Pascal, *Pensées*, 14, 253, 274 (*Oeuvres*, éd. par L. Brunschvicg, Hachette, Nendeln, 1977, vol.12, pp.26–7; vol.13, pp.186, 199).

rationalism *lato sensu* and any form of pessimism, either anthropological or cosmic.

As Arthur O. Lovejoy noted, such a conclusion represents an apparent paradox.[32] In relation to the optimistic anthropological paradigm, in fact, the 'great chain of being' implies a denial of any form of anthropocentrism. Any link of the chain exists *per se*; the finalism, according to which the creation is the instrument for the good of man, is lost. Because any link is only intermediate, any pretence of human perfection also fades. Accordingly, human beings are far from being the best product of nature. All this is true, but if the apparent paradox leads to the definition of an ethics of prudent mediocrity, conservative in Pangloss' terms, it would be difficult to understand the role played by optimism and moral sense in the history of ideas unless we were aware that, although 'this is the best amongst the possible worlds', it is, and will remain, contingent. Leibniz's thesis – Lovejoy concludes –, does not affirm that the present world is absolutely good, but, more humbly, it asserts that any other possible world would be worse. In these respects, Jaakko Hintikka's disagreement towards Lovejoy's argumentation seems to fade away when we observe that Leibniz's thesis, for which ours is the best possible world, is not at all optimistic, as if this is the best possible world, it is not only improbable, but also inconceivable, that the world could be better than it actually is.[33]

The rejection of the Renaissance anthropocentrism neither leads to Montaigne's 'miserable and weak creature', nor to Pascal's *disproportion*. [34] It is necessary here to evaluate more than carefully Locke's measured emphasis.

And when we consider the infinite Power and Wisdom of the Maker, we have reason to think, that it is suitable to the magnificent Harmony of the Universe, and the great Design and infinite Goodness of the Architect, that the *Species* of

32 A.O. Lovejoy, *The Great Chain of Being*, Harvard University Press, Harvard, 1936.
33 J. Hintikka, 'Was Leibniz's Deity an Akrates?', in *Modern Modalities*, ed. by S. Knuuttila, Kluwer Academic, Dordrecht and London, 1981, pp.85–108.
34 M. De Montaigne, *Essais*, II, XII (*Oeuvres complètes*, éd. par R. Barral et P. Michel, Seuil, Paris, 1967, pp.182 ff.); Pascal, *Pensées*, 72 (*Oeuvres*, XII, p.70).

Creature should also, by gentle degrees, ascend upward from us downwards [...].[35]

The 'idea of man' as an 'intermediate link' in the great chain of being ceases to be thinkable as if he were situated at the centre of the universe, because the individual's will is subjugated to 'uneasiness' and a restlessness of need. From one natural need follows another, from one restlessness follows another. Will and freedom coincide only if reason finds the strength of *liberum arbitrium*. The latter – Locke adds – does not reduce our freedom, but implies its possible perfection. This leads to the apology of civil society tailored upon human nature.

Such a parable is evident in Shaftesbury.

> A *human Infant* is of all the most helpless, weak, infirm. And wherefore shou'd it not have been thus order'd? Where is the loss in such a Species? Or what is *Man* the worse for this Defect, amidst large Supplies? Does not this *Defect* engage him the more strongly to Society, and force him to own that he is purposely, and not by accident, made rational and *sociable*; and can no otherwise increase or subsist, than in that *social* Intercourse and Community which is *natural State?* [36]

Here, 'defect' is tantamount to an inescapable reciprocity, an uneasiness, a relentlessness, which, in order to concern mankind, should be acknowledged as irrepressible by each individual. The

35   J. Locke, *Essay*, III, VI, 12 (ed. by P.H. Nidditch, Clarendon, Oxford, 1975).
36   Shaftesbury, 'The Moralists', II, IV, in *Characteristicks*, John Darby, London, 1732, II, pp.308–9. A similar argumentation – in which a late Stoic influence is clearly perceptible (Seneca, *Ad Lucilium Epist.*, II, XV, 95; *De ira*, IV, 31, 7; Marcus Aurelius, *Meditations*, II, 1; VIII, 7, 34; IX, 1; X, 6) – is typical in Pope's *Essay on Man*, I, I, 33–34; II, 69–70; I, VIII; III, I, 7–21 (*The Poems of Alexander Pope*, ed. by J. Butt, Methuen, London, 1965). It should also not be forgotten that the later acquisition of the 'historical sense' and the 'temporalization' of the chain of being as redemption of the 'principle of hope' would allow the apology of progress: see Condorcet's *Esquisse* (*Oeuvres*, éd. par F. Arago, M.F. O'Connor, Firmin Didot, Paris, 1847–1849, vol.7). In particular, concerning the disappearing of the contraposition between nature and society in Condorcet – a disappearing that is implicit in the concept of *civilisation*: J. Starobinski, *Le remède dans le mal*, Gallimard, Paris, 1989 –, see B. Baczko, *Lumières de l'utopie*, Payot, Paris, 1978.

perfection contemplated by the optimistic anthropological paradigm seems to point out that the completeness of the social whole consists of the existence of any hypothetical degree of imperfection affecting its 'natural parts', and concerning, therefore, the human being intended as a solitary individual facing the universe.

In other words, even before recognizing the identity between nature and society, we should understand the ability of society, intended as human *negotium*, to govern the inequalities that nature anyway implies. Optimism, rather than a vulgar naturalism, expresses the belief that natural inequalities lead individuals to recognize themselves in a social whole, which, in turn, becomes a 'natural mirror'. Pascal's *disproportion* loses its tragic cogency; the image of a cosmic solitude of human being vanishes. The individual should not imagine himself somewhere else other than where he is: neither should he return to his senses, nor be doomed to drown in the unknown abyss of a hundred thousand parts of a poppy seed. The *disproportion* between man and nature is now governed by a reciprocal identification between nature and society. Pope interprets such a disproportion as follows:

> The state of Nature was the Reign of God:
> Self-love and Social at her birth began,
> Union the bond of all things, and of Man
> [...]
> Order is Heav'n's first law; and this confest,
> Some are, and must be, greater than the rest,
> More rich, more wise; but who infers from hence
> That such are happier, shocks all common sense.
> Heav'n to Mankind impartial we confess,
> If are equal in their Happiness:
> But mutual wants this Happiness increase,
> All Nature's difference keeps all Nature's peace. [37]

Because needs and imperfections express an ineluctable reciprocity among individuals, the interrelationship between 'mutual

---

37 Pope, *Essay on Man*, III, IV, 147–50; IV, 49–56. Leibniz's influence upon Pope is well known. On this issue it is important to recall what G. Deleuze wrote in *Le pli. Leibniz et le Baroque*, Minut, Paris, 1988.

wants' is synthesized by a paradox: in fact, from them descends happiness and its possible increase. Beyond Locke's reasoning, a suspension of needs seems unnecessary: in the great chain of being, from 'mutual wants' naturally follows human happiness. The differences are not only naturally given and therefore equally distributed, but also, they are given as a result of a sociality that implies them. The very same existence of nature and society is possible because of the different 'thickness' of the links, indissolubly joined one to another. Their presence *de facto* sanctions the organization of the moral world. It is worth recalling here that in the *Encyclopédie* moral and natural equality coincide. The foundations of both rest upon an understanding of human nature common to all human beings.[38] Such an identification not only removes the individual from his historicity, withdrawing what is not comprehensible and irreducible in each singular existence – as noted by Georg Simmel –,[39] but also projects the individual towards a possible ethical freedom with regard to inequality, blocking, at least in appearance, its spread and the consequences stemming from it.

It is in this way, for example, that in Shaftesbury's political naturalism, the existence of an innate moral affection that informs any human consciousness is explicitly and constantly invoked against Hobbes' anthropological pessimism. Surely, Shaftesbury's political naturalism was mediated by his many implicit references to Spinoza. The English dispute about the original characteristics of human nature – by anticipating the more intricate debate between French *philosophes* and by intermeshing with it – implied a strategic confrontation between Hobbes and Spinoza.[40] And if, in the French debate, the difference between the two authors was more tangible and

---

38 'Égalité', in *Encyclopédie ou dictionnaire raisonné des sciences, des arts et des métiers*, Impr. des Editeurs, Livourne, 1770–1779, vol.5, p.381; cf. also 'Droit naturel' (ivi, p.107), 'Libertè naturelle' (vol.9, p.426), 'Société' (vol.15, p.255).

39 G. Simmel, *Grundfragen der Soziologie (Individuum und Gesellschaft)*, de Gruyter, Berlin, 1917; see also his 'Lecture XVI' in *Kant. Sechzehn Vorlesungen gehalten an der Berliner Universität*, Duncker & Humblot, München-Leipzig, 1924.

40 B. Spinoza, *Epist.* L to J. Jelles, 2.6.1674, in *Opera*, hrsg. von C. Gebhardt, C. Winters, Universitätsbuchhandlung, Heidelberg, 1924–1925, Bd. 4, p.239.

– as Franz Borkenau noted – one might say that the ineffectuality of the optimistic anthropological paradigm gave sway to the rise of metaphysics, in England such a debate was interwoven with the deistic disputes, in which Hobbes and Spinoza were but the same 'damned target'.[41] Consequently, one should not underestimate the reasons underlying Shaftesbury's political naturalism and how they had their convergence point in the critique to the alleged Hobbesian paradox. Recuperating the Stoic argument against the Epicurean school, and especially that of Epittetus against Epicurus,[42] Shaftesbury argued: 'Is there then such a thing as *natural Affection*? If not, why all this Pains, why all this Danger on our account?'. Hobbes himself ought to have hidden such a sentiment: 'It is not fit we shou'd know that *by Nature* we are all *Wolves*. Is it possible that one who has really discover'd himself such, shou'd take pains to communicate such a Discovery?'.[43]

With more than a reference to Spinoza, under accusation here is the 'false' definition of a state of nature within which man would be moved exclusively by his own interests. From such a definition – Shaftesbury noted – the plea for political absolutism inevitably follows, because if the differences expressed by Nature are intended as a pretext to reinforce a state of this sort, to think of society would not only be impossible, but also, and necessarily, a waste of time. On the

---

41 The reference is above all to S. Clarke, *A Demonstration of the Being and Attributes of God*, James Knapton, London, 1705 (cf. R.L. Colie, 'Spinoza in England (1665–1730)', *Proc. of the American Phil. Society*, 1963, vol.107, 3; L. Simonutti, 'Filosofia della natura e ateismo', in A. Santucci (ed. by), *Filosofia e cultura nel Settecento britannico*, Il Mulino, Bologna, 2000, vol.1, pp.61–88). This can certainly be observed despite the role of J. Toland's *Letters to Serena* (1704) (Frommann, Stuttgart, 1964, pp.131 ff.). For an overview, L.G. Crocker, *An Age of Crisis: Man and World in Eighteenth Century French Thought*, The John Hopkins Press, Baltimore, 1959; C. Signorile, *Politica e ragione I*, Marsilio, Padova, 1968; F. Borkenau, *Der Übergang vom feudalen zum bürgerlichen Weltbild*, Darmstadt, Wissenschaftliche Buchgesellschaft, 1971; C. Giuntini, 'Scienza newtoniana e teologia razionale: Bentley, Clarke e l'ideologia delle Boyle Lectures', in *Il newtonianesimo nel Settecento*, Istituto della Enciclopedia Italiana, Roma, 1983, pp.19–35.
42 Cicero, *De off.*, I, 44, 158; Epictetus, *Ench.*, I, 20, 6–11.
43 Shaftesbury, 'Sensus Communis', II, I, *Characteristicks*, I, pp.92–3.

one side, under accusation is 'that noteworthy art by which we are all dominated, and rendered docile and meek'; on the other, the assumption that necessitates such an art. The ironic, rather than the theoretical accent, seems to prevail here; but no less explicit is the critique of the anthropological assumptions informing despotic power, because if absolutism reigns sovereign, there can be no common good. Within this framework, Hobbes' political anthropology is overturned by Shaftesbury's positive statement, according to which the Publick spirit 'can come only from a social Feeling or *Sense of Partnership* with Human Kind'. 'And thus Morality and good Government go together. There is no real Love or Virtue, without the knowledge of *Publick Good*. And where absolute Power is, there is no Publick'.[44]

As a result, for a society to exist there is no necessity for a compact: not only because the natural instinct is social, but also because any reference to a hypothetical wild state of nature, which precedes and necessitates the compact, would be contradictory. If, within the natural sentiment, the sense of what is right and wrong were not innate, no civil institution would have been able to adopt it as positive rule: 'It is ridiculous to say – Shaftesbury claims – there is any Obligation on Man to act sociably, or honestly, in a form'd Government; and not in that which is commonly call'd the *State of Nature*. [...] The Civil Union, or Confederacy, could never make *Right or Wrong* if they subsisted not before. [...] The *Natural Knave* has the same reason to be a *Civil one*'.[45] Hence, we either have to consider the existence of many conflicting states of nature 'or, if one, it can be only *that* in which Nature was *perfect*, and her Growth *compleat*'.[46] In this framework, a compact to allow civil society to exist would be senseless.

It would be certainly possible to underline the many weaknesses of Shaftesbury's critique of Hobbes and the selfish system. However, it is exactly the claim that society is the result of a natural affection that radically differentiates him from Hobbes. Shaftesbury's position stems from the identity between individual and collective interest: 'It

44   Ibid., III, I, *Characteristicks*, I, pp.106–7.
45   Ibid., *Characteristicks*, I, p.109.
46   'The Moralists', II, IV, *Characteristicks*, II, p.316.

is already shown, that in the Passions and Affections of particular Creatures, there is a constant relation to the Interest of a *Species*, or *common Nature*'.[47] More than a simple connection between nature and society, an intrinsic and ultimate relationship expressed by the very sense of the human community is here established: 'for a Creature whose natural End is Society, *to operate as is by Nature appointed him towards the Good of such his* Society, or Whole, is in reality *to pursue his own natural and proper* Good'.[48] The primacy of sentiments over reason makes explicit the foundation of an innate natural affection, clearly expressed, for example, in the words of Richard Cumberland: 'For the *Whole* is nothing else but the *Parts consider'd jointly, and in their proper Order and Relation to each other*; and, consequently, the Good of the Whole is nothing else but Good communicated to all the Parts, according to their natural mutual Relation'.[49]

Following Shaftesbury, Hutcheson – undoubtedly not as a simple disciple – interprets the moral sense as an original instinct, not subject to human rationality and will. Through much more refined theoretical argumentations closely connected to the implications and suggestions stemming from the European jurisprudence, he presents human beings as the holders of a natural and immediate impulse to exist in society with their fellows:

> One can scarce deny to mankind a natural impulse to society with their fellows, as an immediate principle, when we see the like in many species of animals; nor should we ascribe all associating to their indigence. Their other principles, their curiosity, communicativeness, desire of action; their sense of honour, their compassion, benevolence, gaiety, and the moral faculty, could have little or no exercise in solitude, and therefore might lead them to haunt together, even without an immediate or ultimate impulse, or a sense of their indigence.[50]

---

47 'An Inquiry concerning Virtue and Merit', II, I, I, *Characteristicks*, II, p.78; and ibid., II, p.175.

48 'Misc.', IV, II, *Characteristicks*, III, p.223.

49 R. Cumberland, *A Treatise of the Laws of Nature*, translated, with Introduction and Appendix, by J. Maxwell (1727), ed. by J. Parkin, Liberty Fund, Indianapolis, 2005, p.653.

50 F. Hutcheson, *A System of Moral Philosophy*, Millar, London, 1755, vol.1, p.34.

It is not a sense of indigence – Locke's 'uneasiness' – that obliges individuals to associate, but rather it is an 'immediate principle, a natural impulse to society': and this would be sufficient apart from the present indigence, because the moral faculty, not being possible in solitude, is a well-founded motivation for individuals to choose to live together. It is worth noting once again that what is essential is not a vulgar naturalistic perspective, but rather the fact that human specificity is unthinkable outside society. In other words, only society can make valuable what is human – which, in turn, is natural. For this very reason, human beings feel disinterested affections *stricto sensu* not subordinated to their self-love.[51] These affections belong to all individuals, to their original and natural moral faculty. This latter has no relationship with other perceptive powers or perceivable qualities:[52] reason is only a 'subservient power':

> There is therefore, [...], a natural and immediate determination to approve certain affections and actions consequent upon them; or a natural sense of immediate excellence in them, not referred to any other quality perceivable by our other senses or by reasoning. When we call this determination a *sense* or *instinct*, we are not supposing it of that low kind dependent on bodily organs, such as even the brutes have. It may be a constant settled determination in the soul itself, as much as our powers of judging and reasoning. And this pretty plain that *reason* is only a subservient power to our ultimate determinations either of perception or will.[53]

The fact that the moral faculty is the original determinant of human nature implies that moral judgement can be expressed only within a society in which the succour of reason provides the most apt 'language' to express what the natural human being can or cannot do. To put it another way, what is specifically human is that foundation that only society can make true. Because such an original disposition is a social, benevolent instinct, innate to human nature, it moves directly towards public happiness as its supreme goal. It is not the natural hypothetical gratification, but rather the supreme social sense of public good that leads men towards the public interest. The impression of

51   Ibid., I, p.49.
52   Ibid., I, p.52.
53   Ibid., I, p.58.

a strong opposition between the individual's private interests and the indulgence towards the generous affections required by virtue can be easily removed by considering the enrichment produced in the natural human being when respecting the moral sense, which society improves:

> The most benign and wise constitution of a rational system is that in which the degree of selfish affection most useful to the individual is consistent with the interest of the system; and where the degree of generous affections most useful to the system is ordinarily consistent with or subservient to the greatest happiness of the individual.[54]

The constitution of a 'rational system' can only be conformed to the individual constitutions that, in turn, give to the former its shape and essence. The coincidence between individual selfish affections and social generous affections follows suit. Were this not the case, 'an irreconcilable variance' would occur, a blemish would dim the constitution of a rational system. Society not only guarantees what nature pushes to obtain, but also improves the value of the efforts of each of its members, leading them towards a result innate in the essence of each natural being: morality. Hutcheson's interpretation of the state of nature is based upon the belief that the immutable laws of nature simply express what from which and upon which they originate and are founded: the common good. 'Precepts of the law of nature [...] are deemed immutable and eternal, because some rules, or rather the dispositions which gave origin to them, and in which they are founded, must always tend to the general good [...]'.[55]

Certainly, because the role of the civil institutions cannot be disregarded, many exceptions are given and forecasted. In Hutcheson, not only is it possible to find Shaftesbury's echo, but also the deepening of both Grotius and Pufendorf's themes, mediated by Carmichael via Locke. And it cannot be forgotten how underneath this line of thought there is a careful reflection upon juridical and economic doctrines. As a result – Pietro Costa has noted –, it is in this way that laws become the fundamental instrument of a social mediation

---

54   Ibid., I, p.149.
55   Ibid., I, p.273.

between individual needs and the social whole. The distinction between perfect and imperfect rights gives rise to different interpretations of the notion of obligation, essentially underpinned by both the moral sense informing the 'publick interest' and by legal cogency. Besides a disinterested moral obligation and an obligation motivated by economic calculation, there is always the threat of coercion. However, it is certain that the different interpretations of the notion of obligation are interesting exactly because of their intertwining, more than as distinct 'forms'. That 'the sphere of right is an economic zone within which the ethical investment is prominent'[56] is made possible by the fact that the dialectic between benevolence and self-love is thought of and structured as the ethical government of the passions in view of a perfectly legitimized *inter-esse*. Put differently, although relevant, Hutcheson's attention towards Locke's juridisprudencial themes – his great but moderate innovation – would concentrate on a specific ethical approach, within which the economic ratio, putting aside the preoccupation related to Locke's tradition, would impose itself as an 'ethical government' of the human passions.

It is at this point that Hutcheson overturns Hobbes' political anthropology. That, in the state of nature, conflicts occur does not prove an alleged state of war. Otherwise, given that crime exists within civil society, it would be legitimate to conclude that civil society is dominated by a state of war. Undoubtedly, the fact that for Hobbes is this the *punctum saliens* shows the fragility of Hutcheson's critique of the selfish system; but, in spite of this fragility, what is here antithetical is the general anthropological perspective, not some of its questionable elements. To credit human beings with a sympathetic disinterested and benevolent disposition means not only to deny Hobbes' anthropological conception, but also to substitute it with another, a totally opposite one.[57] At the base of human industriousness,[58] rather than reciprocal fear, is a 'calm' disposition of affection,[59]

---

56   Costa, *Il progetto giuridico*, p.154.
57   L. Limentani, *La morale della simpatia*, Formiggini, Genova, 1914, p.15.
58   Hutcheson, *A System of Moral Philosophy*, vol.1, p.319.
59   Ibid, vol.1, pp.100 ff.

an acting 'with calculation and rationality', [60] which would find in Smith's notion of propriety, *mutatis mutandis*, a specific point of reference.

Such an optimistic anthropological vision becomes even more problematic in Joseph Butler. He argues that the link between society and nature is shaped by the relationship between benevolence and self-love, respectively connected to the social sense and to the natural sentiment. On these grounds, the difference between the natural condition of the single man and the social condition expressed by the union among individuals is sublimated in the coincidence between benevolence and self-love, a foundation upon which it is possible to observe the combining together of both public good and individual happiness:

> *First*, there is a natural principle of *benevolence* in man, which is in some degree to *society*, what *self-love* is to *individual*. [...] [T]hough benevolence and self-love are different; though the former tends most directly to public good, and the later to private: yet they are perfectly coincident, that the greatest satisfaction to ourselves depend upon our having benevolence in a due degree; and that self-love is one chief security of our right behaviour towards society. [61]

The difference between self-love and benevolence gives rise to a complementarity; in their differing, these terms are complementary, in the same way as are the individual and society. With an appropriate degree of self-love, the individual preserves himself. Preserving himself, he accomplishes his duty towards society. Human nature maintains an explicit social character, given that, rarely can incoherence be produced between an individual's interests and his duty, because '[t]here is a much more exact correspondence between the natural and moral world, than we are apt to take notice of'. However, in Butler, a

---

60   A.O. Hirschman, *The Passions and the Interests*, Princeton University Press, Princeton, 1977, p.65.

61   J. Butler, *Fifteen Sermons*, I, 6, 9 (*The Works of Bishop Butler*, ed. by J.H. Bernard, Macmillan, London, 1900, vol.1). On Butler see E. Garin, 'L'etica di Giuseppe Butler', *Giornale critico della filosofia italiana*, 1932, vol.32, pp.281–303; I. Cappiello, 'Amor di sé e benevolenza, virtù e interesse in Joseph Butler', in *Tra antichi e moderni*, Liguori, Napoli, 1990, pp.311–39, part. pp.326, 333.

finalism, a teleological dimension that overcomes the relationship between nature and society, is present. 'The several passions and affections in the heart of man' – he observes – 'compared with the circumstances of life in which he is placed, afford, to such as will attend to them, as certain instances of that final causes as any whatever which are more commonly alleged for such [...]'. This teleology – or, better, correspondence between 'principles of action in the heart of man' and the 'condition he is placed in' – shows 'what course of life we are made for, what is our duty, and in a peculiar manner enforce upon us the practice of it'.[62]

From Butler's point of view, the emphasis should inevitably be placed upon the distinction between morality and positive law, where one considers, above all, the possibility of understanding the notion of command, intended as government of the moral dimension. In this framework, morality is understood as essence-consciousness, always primary in the constitution of civil society.[63] Thus, there is an irreducible problem – God as *mysterium tremendum* –, which constantly pushes us to grasp the mystery that envelops reality; and this is true with reference to both Hobbes' pessimism and Shaftesbury's optimism. In brief, what it is here defined is a reasonable self-love, which explains both the innate human morality and the role of consciousness as restraint. Goodness and wickedness are therefore not subjugated by the tyranny of self-love. Rather, a reasonable self-love poses in relation to the *ego* the *alter*. Thus, it is necessary to assume human nature as it is and to consider that between the natural and the moral world there is a strict correspondence: stimulated by passions – which in turn affect self-love – and controlled by reason.

A further development in this direction can be found in Lord Kames' *Essay on the Principles of Morality and Natural Religion*, in which the author amplifies the moderate essence of that approach, attributing to self-love an essentially positive role, equal to that accomplished by other appetites and passions that develop according to different aims. During childhood – Lord Kames simplifies – appetites and passions are the sole impulse for action; but in the subsequent

62   Butler, *Fifteen Sermons*, III, 8; V, 1, 10; VI, 1; VIII, 1; XI, 2, 19; XII, 27.
63   Butler, *Six Sermons*, III, 7; and *The Analogy of Religion*, II, I, 21–5.

phases of life we learn to distinguish, around us, different passions and their varying degrees. Although it is true that self-love is 'a strong motive to search about for every thing that may contribute to happiness', anyhow, it not only operates 'by means of reflection and experience', but also in conjunction with other passions that, though not reducible to a hypothetical universal benevolence, are constitutive of that mutual sympathy 'which is the cement of human society'. In short, also in Kames' *Essay* the relationship between nature and society is inescapable.

> In a word, we are evidently formed by nature for society, and for indulging the social, as well as the selfish passions; and therefore to contend, that we ought to regard ourselves only, and to be influenced by no principles but what are selfish, is directly to fly in the face of nature, and to lay down a rule of conduct inconsistent with our nature.[64]

Hence, although Kames is mainly interested in establishing the difference between benevolence and justice – affirming, in doing so, the naturalness of the latter in explicit disagreement with Hume's artifice –, what is of interest is that, for him, it is not the human natural goodness that characterizes the essence of the optimistic anthropological paradigm, but rather the natural sociality of human beings that it entails. Here an alternative to Hobbes' selfish system is defined: for men, the sole state of nature is *society*. That is, human nature is social *tout court*. In this framework, what remains highly problematic is surely the absence of conflict, as well as the relevance attributed to the relationship between instinctiveness and morality. Nevertheless, what is at stake is the sharp contraposition between the moral sense and the rationalism, which characterizes the theoreticians of the selfish system.

These latter, and Mandeville above all, mark the point of maximum contrast in relation to the dispute concerning vice and virtue in the determination of what is the behaviour of man towards his fellows. The issue can be faced and, at the same time, made explicit, recalling the considerations provided by the advocates of the selfish system

---

64 H. Home, Lord Kames, *Essays on the Principles of Morality and Natural Religion* (17582), G. Olms, Hildesheim, 1976, p.64.

with regard pride. For Mandeville, what renders the natural being a sociable animal 'consists not in his desire of Company, Good-nature, Pity, Affability, and other Graces of a fair Outside; but that his vilest and most hateful Qualities are the most necessary Accomplishments to fit him for the largest, and, according to the World, the happiest and most flourishing Societies'.[65] Such meanness of spirit, only dissimulated by education, is not only natural, but also socially sound.

Mandeville's radicalism goes beyond the desecrating spirit characterizing the mechanistic materialism of the second half of the eighteenth century. Neither La Mettrie, nor Helvétius or d'Holbach would reach the same conclusions. For them, education is the final bastion without which the human meanness of spirit would find no obstacle. As noted by La Mettrie, snakes and mad dogs should be suppressed.[66] At any rate, such a preoccupation is not that of Mandeville; rather, meanness of spirit is for him the pure expression of the radical passion that is self-love. Without a doubt, the European culture already knew La Rochefoucauld's radicalism, according to which vices are a constituent part of the virtue as poisons are a constituent part of drugs. Wisdom mixes up and tempers vices, utilizing them usefully against the evil of life.[67] It is not unintentionally that Smith, from the first to the fifth edition of *TMS*, places Mandeville and La

65   Mandeville, *The Fable of the Bees: or Private Vices, Publick Benefits*, ed. by C.B. Kaye, Oxford University Press, Oxford, 1924, vol.1, p.4.
66   La Mettrie, *Traité de l'Ame*, and *Anti-Séneque ou Discours sur la Bonheur* (*Oeuvres philosophiques*, G. Olms, Hildesheim, 1970, vol.1, pp.174–5; vol.2, pp.83–166); Helvétius, *De l'esprit*, II, XXIV; IV, XVII (*Oeuvres*, éd. par I. Belaval, G. Olms, Hildesheim, 1969, vol.3, pp.113 ff.; vol.4, pp.181 ff.); D'Holbach, *Système de la nature*, I, XIV (éd. par I. Belaval, G. Olms, Hildesheim, 1966, vol.1, pp.343–70).
67   See La Rochefoucauld, *Maximes*, 81–5, 121, 143, 182, 187, 236, 246, 253, 298, 305 (éd. par J. Truchet, Garnier, Paris, 1967). The issue is internal to the eighteenth century debate concerning the definition of self-love: Voltaire, 'Amour-propre', in *Dictionnaire* (*Oeuvres*, éd par L. Moland, Garnier, Paris, 1878–1883, vol.22, pp.221–4); Pope, *Essay on Man*, II; Rousseau, *Discours sur l'inégalité parmi les hommes* (*Oeuvres*, éd. par B. Gagnebin, Gallimard, Paris, 1964, vol.3, pp.219–20); Helvétius, *De l'Esprit*, II, XV–XVI, XXIV (*Oeuvres*, vol.2, pp.236–60; vol.3, pp.113 ss).

Rochefoucauld side by side. In effect, the former seemingly repeats the latter by heart, for example when he wrote:

> The meanest Wretch puts an inestimable value upon himself, and the highest wish of the Ambitious Man is to have all the World, as to that particular, of his Opinion; so that the most insatiable Thirst after Fame that ever Heroes was inspired with, was never more than an ungovernable Greediness to engross the Esteem and Admiration of others in future Ages as well as his own [...].[68]

Pride is a natural faculty thanks to which any human being tends to overestimate himself. As noted by La Rochefoucauld, it seems that nature gives to us pride in order to let us forget our imperfections.[69] The dissimulation, in this context, has a double function: public, with respect to the humanity to which it is addressed; private, with respect to the dissimulating subject, who utilizes it when dealing with others and with himself.

It is possible to infer how relevant this premise is for Mandeville from the fact that, similarly to Hobbes, he considers self-preservation as an imperative for any being. With respect to the advocate of the moral sense, it is evident that Mandeville does not consider society as inessential; nevertheless, individuals should defend themselves from society, because within it only 'singular individuals' live. Both the fear of death and shame represent the higher incentive for self-love aimed at self-preservation:

> There is nothing so universally sincere upon Earth, as the Love which all Creatures, that are capable of any, bear to themselves [...], so there is nothing more sincere in any Creature than his Will, Wishes, and Endeavours to preserve himself. [...] The only useful Passion then that Man is possess'd of towards the Peace and Quiet of a Society, is his Fear [...].[70]

Certainly not sufficiently robust from a theoretical point of view, Mandeville's position cannot be equated to Hobbes' theory of the

68   Mandeville, *The Fable of the bees*, vol.1, pp.54.
69   La Rochefoucauld, *Maximes*, 36.
70   Mandeville, *The Fable of the bees*, *Rem. M*, vol.1, p.124; *Rem. R*, vol.1, pp.200, 206.

Political.[71] At any rate, for our purpose, it is sufficient to note what this position discloses: that is, the sharp contraposition between nature and morality, and the impossible connection between moral rationality and human nature. Mandeville can therefore be proud of having overturned the principle of natural law – the foundation of any form of sociality – attributing to human kind the worst vices belonging to the individual.

> After this I flatter my self to have demonstrated that, neither the Friendly Qualities and kind Affections that are natural to Man, nor the real Virtues he is capable of acquiring by Reason and Self-Denial, are the Foundation of Society; but that what we call Evil in this World, Moral as well Natural, in the grand Principle that makes us sociable Creatures [...].[72]

Although in nature there are friendly qualities, natural affections, and real virtues acquired via reason and self-denial, they do not support society. Rather, without evil, society would be impoverished, and perhaps would disappear. In this way, the divide between the anthropological optimism of the moral sense, in its different articulations, and those 'endeavours to preserve himself', exacerbated by Mandeville's doctrine, is defined.

Undoubtedly, Hutcheson's critique of Mandeville would show the weaknesses intrinsic to the moral sense, particularly with respect to Hobbes's political model. However, it would be sufficiently sound to face the economic transposition of that model via the invention of an ethical-practical sphere disjointed from the Lockean conception of moral power. In this way, Hutcheson overturns – *contra* Mandeville – Hobbes' same political anthropology. Nonetheless, the alternative remains weak in its foundations, because it is linked to an aprioristic emphasis of an innate moral sense related to individual self-love (as it is testified also by Berkeley's *Alciphron*).[73] Such an alternative re-

71 Cf. D. Taranto, *Abilità del politico e meccanismo economico*, Liguori, Napoli, 1982.
72 Mandeville, *A Search into the Nature of Society*, ed. by C.B. Kaye, in *The Fable of the bees*, vol.1, p.369.
73 We are referring to the *Discourses* II and III, where Berkeley discusses Mandeville and Shaftesbury's systems (*The Works of George Berkeley Bishop of Cloyne*, ed. by A.A. Luce, T.E. Jessop, Nelson, London, 1950, vol.3).

mains rather fragile until the advent of Hume, who would impose a drastic change of paradigm. He wrote:

> Self-love is a principle in human nature of such extensive energy, and the interest of each individual is, in general, so closely connected with that of the community, that those philosophers were excusable, who fancied, that all our concern for the public might be resolved into a concern for our happiness and preservation.[74]

Consequently, a fundamental shift occurs: from a mere contra-position between the optimistic and pessimistic anthropological approaches, to the consideration of the principles that, on the basis of experience, guide human action. The power of self-love is neither questioned, nor is there an attempt to provide an alternative to it via an aprioristic moral-sympathetic foundation. However, social utility appears to be a datum, unthinkable without a mutual dependency among individuals. And indeed such a utility is the spring of moral sentiment: *atque ipsa utilitas, justi prope mater et aequi.*[75]

If we consider the individual as a solitary being – Hume says –, what is left to him are only sensual and speculative pleasures, because without the stimulation of others his heart beats alone. For this reason, any individual participates in human misery or fortune. Sympathy, in fact, does not rest upon any other speculation if not the consideration of an honest utility connected to human action. Hence, one's judgement concerning the behaviour of others cannot leave out of consideration the implications of one's actions in relation to social happiness or unhappiness. The asserted impossibility according to which one would be totally indifferent to the well-being or malaise of one's fellow men – even if one's interest is stronger than one's natural benevolence towards society – might perhaps seem aprioristic; but such an approach is aprioristic only in appearance. For Hume it is a datum of pure experience, stemming from considering the conse-

---

74 D. Hume, *Enquiry concerning the Principles of Morals*, in *The Philosophical Works*, ed. by T.H. Green, T.H. Grose, Scientia Verlag, Aalen, 1964, vol.4, pp.206.
75 In a letter to Hutcheson dated 17 September 1739, Hume recalls Horatius' passage (*Satires*, I, III, 98). S. Buckle discusses of this at length in his *Natural Law and the Theory of Property*, Clarendon Press, Oxford, 1991, pp.263 ff.

quences of human action, because utility is only a factual issue. As Costa notes, only within society can individuals' satisfaction occur, because its conditions are simultaneously posited with them.[76]

Glenn R. Morrow[77] rightly noted the weakness of Shaftesbury and Hutcheson's opposition to Hobbes' ethical egoism in relation to an essential assumption of rationalism: the maintenance of the individualistic paradigm.[78] In fact, rather than questioning the fallacy of the individualistic conception of human nature, the moralists founded their refusal of the egoistic principle upon Hobbes' very same assumption. Consequently, only with Hume did a significant shift of paradigm occur, precisely when he argues that an objective judgement can be found not in the mere contraposition between moral sense and self-love, but rather in some inter-individual principles, thanks to which humanity becomes a whole. That is, Hume's critique of Hobbes and Descartes' rationalism, abandoning any aprioristic ethical individualism, reformulates the individualistic anthropological instance and therefore reshapes the relationship between reason and sentiment, the balance between self-love and benevolence. Hence, if Shaftesbury is far from having understood the artful antinomy constituted by self-love and benevolence; if Hutcheson is chained by this antinomy; if Butler overcomes it without understanding the balance existing among the elements that constitute it and, therefore, subordinating them to an authoritative principle: namely, the consciousness; it is only with Hume that occurs what Willey described as the great divide.

With Hume, the eighteenth century anthropological paradigm undergoes a significant 'twisting'. The criterion of experience shifts the dispute upon the original characters of human nature: from an aprioristic natural-sentimentalist dimension, that of moral sense, to an experiential dimension. In the famous letter dated 17 September 1739 addressed by Hume to Hutcheson, it is possible to find all the prin-

76   Costa, *Il progetto giuridico*, p.167.
77   G.R. Morrow, *The Ethical and Economic Theories of Adam Smith*, Kelley, New York, 1969, pp.22–6.
78   Cf. É. Durkheim, *Les règles de la méthode sociologique*, PUF, Paris, 1960, pp.120–3.

cipal motives of such a shift. In response to Hutcheson's observations upon the manuscript of the III Book of the *Treatise*, Hume wrote:

> What affected me most in your Remarks is your observing, that there wants a certain Warmth in the Cause of Virtue [...]. I must own, this has not happen'd by Chance, but it is the Effect of Reasoning either good or bad. There are different ways of examining the Mind as well as the Body. One may consider it either as an Anatomist or as a Painter; [...]. I imagine it impossible to conjoin these two Views.

And furthermore:

> I cannot agree to your Sense on *Natural*. This founded on final Causes; which is a Consideration, that appears to me pretty uncertain and unphilosophical. For pray, what is the End of Man? Is he created for Happiness or for Virtue? For this Life or for the next? For himself or for his Maker? Your Definition of *Natural* depends upon solving these Questions, which are endless, and quite wide of my Purpose.[79]

As we can see, moving from the basis of experience, Hume does not deny the importance of social affections; rather, he recognizes as useful the connection between self-love and public interest. As a result, his critique of the selfish system is not aprioristic. It is inferred from the analysis of the rationalist model and grounded in the denial of any form of contractualism, intended as the basis of social utility. As Eugenio Lecaldano notes, in relation to Shaftesbury and Hutcheson's naturalism and Hobbes' artificialism, Hume imposes a variety of instinctual natural virtues that cannot be reduced to the mere egoistic calculation, and makes them coexist with an ensemble of artificial but not arbitrary virtues. In brief, it is possible to claim that Hume's position concerning the opposite unilateralism – respectively represented by the moral sense and the selfish system – rests upon the criterion of experience, which provides 'real data' that should be reconstructed in their genesis. In doing so, he expels from them what is fictitious, if not distorted, in the traditional philosophical systems.[80]

---

79 *The Letters of David Hume*, ed. by J.Y.T. Greig, Oxford University Press, Oxford, 1932, vol.1, pp.32–3.

80 We follow the interpretation of E. Lecaldano, *Hume e la nascita dell'etica contemporanea*, Laterza, Roma-Bari, 1991, pp.33; 52 ff.; 198 ff.; Ibid., 'Para-

From this perspective, Hume gives sway to Smith's critique of moral sense; but such a critique, although owing much to Hume himself, would reveal significant differences. In his remarks concerning the Hutchesonian anthropological optimism, Smith observes that among those who equate virtue and benevolence, 'the late Dr. Hutcheson was undoubtedly, beyond all comparison, the most acute, the most distinct, the most philosophical'. Nevertheless, the traced path, its foundation in an innate moral sense, seems to explain only a perfect degree of benevolence, putting aside what is truly relevant for human nature: 'from whence arises our approbation of the inferior virtues'; so that, the propriety of the affections referring to the inferior virtues, '[t]heir suitableness and unsuitableness, to the cause which excites them, are disregarded altogether'. This represents, however, a major shortcoming, which Smith is able to stigmatize, because he abandons any aprioristic moral individualism. It is admirable, he says, that Hutcheson considers virtue absolutely insensible to self-love, to the point that he sees in the moral satisfaction of the well-founded consciousness of a wise man a mere egoistic motive. However, this perspective is unacceptable, because it moves from an aprioristic denial of the correct interaction between a measured self-love and public interest. For Hutcheson, the habits of economy, industry, and discretion – in a word, all those behaviours that constitute prudence and therefore affect our interests and private happiness – seem to be qualities cultivated for a purely egoistic interest. Vice versa, Smith argues, they are qualities worthy of our attention and to neglect them would expose the individual to public disapproval, in the same manner as he who would cultivate his own natural self-preservation only for the sake of his own relatives and not as a good worth to be pursued *per se*:

> The mixture of a selfish motive, it is true, seems often to sully the beauty of those actions which ought to arise from a benevolent affection. The cause of

digmi di analisi della filosofia morale scozzese', in Geuna, Pesante (a cura di), *Passioni, interessi, convenzioni*, pp.13–40; Buckle, *Natural Law*, pp.256 ff. For an overview on these themes see K. Haakonssen's seminal essay: *The Natural Jurisprudence of David Hume and Adam Smith*, Cambridge University Press, Cambridge, 1981, pp.12–26.

this, however, is not that self-love can never be the motive of a virtuous action, but that the benevolent principle appears in this particular case to want its due degree of strength, and to be altogether unsuitable to its object.[81]

The very same *a priori* of moral sense not only rejects what it is impossible to deny *a posteriori* – the existence of an interaction between self-love and public interest –, but also is silent with regard to the most important question: the criteria of approval and disapproval with respect to the degree of propriety of the inferior virtues, which are not as perfect as the highest benevolence. For Smith this is the pivotal point, because if is true that the approval of the impartial spectator – and his identification – is at its highest possible degree when he is faced with a totally disinterested virtuous behaviour, it is also true that his approval will not be lessened in the presence of a socially virtuous and therefore imperfect behaviour.

On the opposite side, Smith's critique to Mandeville is equally radical.[82] Mandeville's mistake is *de facto* specular to that made by Hutcheson. Smith wrote:

---

81 A. Smith, *The Theory of Moral Sentiments*, ed. by A.L. Macfie, D.D. Raphael, in *The Glasgow Edition*, vol.1, p.304. As it is well-known, Smith's interpretation of Hutcheson here proposed is incorrect: see Buckle, *Natural Law*, p.199; Teichgraeber, *'Free Trade'*, ch. II.

82 Despite this, Mandeville's influence upon Smith has been emphasized on many occasions and in different ways (K. Marx, *Das Kapital*, *MEW*, Dietz, Berlin, 1956 ff, Bd.23, pp.375, footnote 57; pp.642–5; E. Halévy, *La formation du radicalisme philosophique*, Alcan, Paris, 1901, vol.1, p.162; J.A. Schumpeter, *Epochen der Dogmen- und Methodengeschichte*, in *Grundrisse der Sozialökonomik*, I, Mohr, Tübingen, 1914, p.27; Id., *History of Economic Analisis*, Allen & Unwin, London, 1954, p.184; F.B. Kaye, 'Commentary', in Mandeville, *The Fable of the Bees*, vol.1, pp.CXVI–CXIX). An ambiguity of judgement has been seen concerning Smith's analysis of the so called Mandeville's paradox (L. Colletti, *Ideologia e società*, Laterza, Bari, 1969, pp.289–90). Such an ambiguity has been referred to the different influences exerted on Smith (Stephen, *History of English Thought*, vol.2, p.67), on the one hand, by Hobbes' rationalism, and on the other – via Shaftesbury and Hutcheson –, by Cambridge Platonism (E. Cassirer, *Die Platonische Renaissance in England und die Schule von Cambridge*, Studien der Bibliothek Warburg, Hft.24, Leipzig-Berlin, 1932). As a result, on the one side, it has been possible to claim a certain weakness of Smith's critique to Mandeville (in *TMS*), and on the other the inevitable

Whether the most generous and public-spirited actions may not, in some sense, be regarded as proceeding from self-love, I shall not at present examine. [...] I shall only endeavour to show that the desire of doing what is honourable and noble, of rendering ourselves the proper object of esteem and approbation, cannot with any propriety be called vanity.[83]

In other words, Smith is not interested in rejecting 'the system of Dr. Mandeville', moving from the overturn of his anthropological pessimism, and offering an opposite assumption, anyhow aprioristic with regard to experience. He is keen to concede that such a system would not have aroused so much interest if 'had it not in some respects bordered upon the truth'. This – he argues – is not the problem. Mandeville's anthropological pessimism is rejected because it renders absolute a baseless point of view. According to Smith, a measured self-love can be present in any human action: this does not imply that the sole motivation for human action is a boundless pride. A vain person is either one who pretends undeserved or exaggerated praise, or one who claims merits he does not deserve. He who is moved by true love for glory acts neither for pride, nor relates with society only in an instrumental way, as the search for glory 'is a just, reasonable, and equitable passion'. According to Cicero, 'quae quia recte factorum plerumque comes est, non est bonis viris repudianda'.[84] What then is Mandeville's error? It resides in representing 'every passion as wholly vicious, which is so in any degree and in any direction'.[85] In doing so, he portrays the human condition in an altered way, excluding the notion of propriety, which Smith considers fundamental in order to describe the behaviour of the middle social agent.

Earlier, we mentioned the specular character of Smith's critique to both Hutcheson and Mandeville. In it, a positive disposition with respect to Hutcheson and a correspondent aversion to Mandeville is taken for granted. The mistake of this latter is only more serious in the

acceptation of Mandeville's paradox (in *WN*). Cf. J. Robinson, *Economic Philosophy*, C.A. Watts & Co, London, 1962, p.18.

83   *TMS*, p.309.
84   Cicero, *Tusc. disp.*, III, 2, 3.
85   *TMS*, p.310–12.

consequences, but specular to that of Hutcheson with respect to the fundamental question: he is not able to recognize the proper degree of any passion, the sole criterion, that is, that *a posteriori*, in experience, allows the redefinition of an anthropological paradigm, moving from the 'ideal experiment' of a middle social agent, apart from an equally indefinable moral sense or wild pride. Thus, it is not the dispute upon the true human nature that is of interest to Smith, but rather what experience allows us to observe of it. Neither Hutcheson, nor Mandeville seem to be able to take into account such a paradigm. The innatism of the former and the scepticism of the latter are aprioristic forms unable to confront with the propriety that human nature discloses and that society requires. If we were allowed to express ourselves in 'anachronistic' terms, one might say that Smith is not interested in knowing what human nature truly 'is', but rather what it 'does'. The 'general rule' that he proposes is a 'product' and not a 'principle'. It is produced by considering approval and disapproval that, by experience, some kind of action may or may not receive.

When, in 1759, Smith published the first edition of *TMS*, half a century had elapsed since the publication of Shaftebury's *Charactheristick* and Mandeville's *Fable*: a time sufficient to allow thinkers of different kinds to provide comparison between nature, sentiment, and reason. Comparisons that were however blocked, so to speak, by their respective aprioristic attitude, incapable of telling us why human nature should be considered absolutely benevolent or wicked. From here, thanks to the fracture produced by Hume, arises Smith's double but specular critique: to Mandeville, for having privileged a merely egoistic definition of self-love, and to Hutcheson, for having excluded it from his benevolent system.[86] A critique that has been made possible not by advancing extreme hypotheses concerning human nature, but by assuming, according to the experience, the existence of a canon of 'means' in human behaviours, connected to both self-love and benevolence.

On these grounds, it is possible to say that with Hume and Smith the relationship between nature, reason, and sentiment reaches a sufficiently robust synthesis starting from the double critique to

86   A.L. Macfie, *The Individual in Society*, Allen & Unwin, London, 1967, p.56.

Hobbes and Descartes' rationalism and from a new epistemological dimension: the Newtonian moral inductivism. Obviously, this is a provisional synthesis, but it represents the point of arrival for the parable characterizing the eighteenth century anthropological paradigm. In particular, Smith's ethical reflection represents an essential part of such a parable, as it provides an original hermeneutic of the moral judgement, the political character of which is what structures the *imperfect genesis* of political economy. Any overcoming of ethics cannot be found; vice versa, what is fundamental here is the consideration of its problematic endurance *within* the political economy, apart from any projected paradigmatic foundation.

3. Imagination and morality

To fully comprehend the theoretical structure of Smith's ethical reflection it is indispensable to evaluate the epistemological premises that qualify the inductive nature of his thought. This further step requires that attention be given to the role played by imagination within the relationship between 'knowledge' and 'system of knowledge'.[87] Apropos, it is useful to briefly recall the modification of the concept of reason that occurred during the passage from the seven-

---

87   During the eighteenth century, the Scottish academia developed a strong interest in the results obtained by natural science and, in particular, by Physics. Consequently, the extension of its method to the field of moral Philosophy was noteworthy. The Scottish philosophers, noted R. Olson (*Scottish Philosophy and British Physics 1750–1880*, Princeton University Press, Princeton, 1975), believed that it was necessary to begin from the comprehension of human nature and, only later, upon the base of such comprehension, to move towards the understanding of the universe. This is the reason why Newton represented a moment of high and particular interest in Scotland. A case in point were MacLaurin's *Discoveries of Sir Isaac Newton* – published posthumously in 1748 –, which had a similar influence on natural philosophy to that exerted by Hutcheson in the field of moral philosophy.

teenth to the eighteenth century.[88] As it is well known, this passage was characterized by the juxtaposition between Descartes' deductive method and Newton's analytical-inductivism.[89] The dispute on the philosophical notion of 'system' occurred among Cartesians and Newtonians represents one of the peaks of modern European culture. Descartes believed that whilst experience could indeed be deceitful, only arithmetic and geometrical deductions were consequential, pure deduction from one thing to another, allowing even less acute intellect to understand them. Newton, on the contrary, was convinced that, given the experimental character of philosophy, the propositions obtained from observable phenomena by induction ought to be considered true as long as other phenomena would not prove them false. As Ernst Cassirer noted,[90] this epochal contrast established the gnoseological primacy of phenomena upon principles. Thus, the consequent affirmation of an 'acquisitive reason' entailed the acceptance of an inductive method that was derived from 'decomposing' and 'reassembling' physical phenomena.[91]

The theoretical references of such a confrontation cannot be traced back to the sole physical-mathematical revolution. To support

88 On the term 'passage' it is necessary to be very cautious: P. Rossi, 'Le tradizioni di ricerca nella storia della scienza', in *Il newtonianesimo nel Settecento*, pp.9–18; S. Moravia, *Filosofia e scienze umane nell'età dei lumi*, La Nuova Italia, Firenze, 1982, pp.4–5.

89 Descartes, *Regulae ad directionem ingenii*, Regula II (*Oeuvres*, éd. par C. Adam, P. Tannery, Vrin, Paris, 1974, vol.10, pp.366–70); Newton, *Principia*, III (*Opera*, ed. by S. Horsley, J. Nichols, Londini, 1779, vol.3, pp.2–4). Cf. L. Turco, *Dal sistema al senso comune*, Il Mulino, Bologna, 1974, pp.56 ff.

90 E. Cassirer, *Die Philosophie der Aufklärung*, Mohr, Tübingen, 1932; Id., *Das Erkenntnisproblem in der Philosophie und Wissenschaft der neueren Zeit*, W. Kohlhammer, Stuttgart, 1957.

91 We are referring to Voltaire's *Traité de métaphysique*, III, and to *Métaphysique de Newton*, VII (*Oeuvres*, vol.22, pp.202–6, 427–32). But see also Condillac, *Traité des systemes*; Mclaurin *Discoveries of Sir Isaac Newton*; D'Alembert's *Discours* (*Encyclopédie ou dictionnaire raisonné des sciences, des arts et des metiers*, vol.1, pp.XXII–XXVII) and entry 'Experimental' (ibid., vol.6, pp.276 ff.); Diderot's *De l'interpretation de la nature*, XXIII–XXVII, XLVII (*Oeuvres*, éd. par J. Assézat, M. Torneux, Kraus Reprint, Nendeln, 1966, vol.2, pp.20–2, 43) and entry 'Systèmes', *Enciclopédie*, vol.15, pp.745 ff.

this claim, it would be sufficient to consider Bayle's remarks on the Cartesian notion of doubt and to compare them, for example, with the theoretical architecture of Bousset's work. By analogy, in a different context, we might consider Buffon's critical argumentations concerning the systematic knowledge of nature. In short, during the time shift between the seventeenth and eighteenth century, a particular scientific conception of rationality, along with an entire systemic-deductive *Weltanschauung*, expired. The crisis of the Renaissance pathos[92] gave sway to a great epochal travail, of which the notion of 'knowledge' informing the Enlightenment and modern Scepticism represented the essential knot. In order to comprehend the inductive nature of Smith's ethical reflection, its articulating by comparison and imagination, one cannot avoid keeping the above context in mind.

In Smith's reflection, we can infer the epistemological relevance of induction and imagination – the 'imaginary machines'[93] – from the *History of Astronomy*, in which, from the outset, the analysis of the notions of *surprise* and *admiration* introduces the relationship between past experience and present knowledge:

> When one accustomed object appears after another, which it does not usually follow, it first excites, by its unexpectedness, the sentiment properly called Surprise, and afterwards, by the singularity of the succession, or order of its appearance, the sentiment properly called Wonder. [...] When two objects, however unlike, have often been observed to follow each other, and have constantly presented themselves to the senses in that order, they come to be so connected together in the fancy, that the idea of the one seems, of its own accord, to call up and introduce that of the other. [...] But if this customary connection be interrupted, [...], the contrary of all this happens. We are at first surprised by the unexpectedness of the new appearance, [...]. The imagination

---

92 Cf. A. Negri, 'Problemi di storia dello Stato moderno. Francia: 1610–1650', *Rivista critica di storia della filosofia*, 1967, vol.22, 2, pp.208 ff.; Id., *Descartes politico*, Feltrinelli, Milano, 1970, *passim*.

93 *EPS*, p.66; but cf. *TMS*, pp.19, 289, 316, 326. Regarding Smith's metaphorical figures, see O. Mayr, *Authority, Liberty and Automatic Machinery in Early Modern Europe*, Johns Hopkins University Press, Baltimore, 1986; S. Fiori, *Ordine, mano invisibile, mercato. Una rilettura di Adam Smith*, Utet, Torino, 2001.

no longer feels the usual facility of passing from the event which goes before to that which comes after.[94]

Imagination – a concept that Smith borrowed from the modern philosophical tradition – is central in authors such as Bacon, Descartes, Spinoza, and Hobbes. It is a concept whose importance is not merely epistemological, because it entirely pervades the ethical sphere.

According to Hume's 'science of human nature',[95] for example, imagination has a double role, logical and ethical, and for this reason it occupies a pivotal place in his philosophical system. In the *Treatise of Human Nature*, the prominent role given to perception suggests an immediate ethical transposition, implicit in the epistemic differentiation of perception in impression and ideas – in the 'difference betwixt feeling and thinking'. Indeed, impressions come to one's mind 'with most force and violence'; ideas, instead, are only 'the faint images of these'[96] – the simple presence in the spirit of impression. Through memory or imagination, they bring back to one's mind those very same impressions that are no longer perceivable. Regarding this, Hume said: 'When we remember any past event, the idea of it flows in upon the mind in a forcible manner; whereas in the imagination the perception is faint and languid, and cannot without difficulty be preserv'd by the mind steddy and uniform for any considerable time'.[97] But, if in the memory the colours are more vivid, in the imagination it is possible to associate ideas (and sentiments) by resemblance. In effect, 'the imagination is not restrain'd to the same

---

94 *EPS*, pp.40–1. In this regard, it is worth recalling Descartes' *Passion de l'âme*, II, 53, 70, 72, 73, 75 (*Oeuvres*, vol.11, pp.373, 380–4).
95 D. Hume, *A Treatise of Human Nature*, in *The Philosophical Works*, vol.1, pp.317–19; Id., *Philosophical Essays concerning Human Understanding*, in *The Philosophical Works*, vol.4, pp.13 ff.. Cf. M. Dal Prà, *Hume e la scienza della natura umana*, Laterza, Roma-Bari, 1973, pp.100–16; and, specifically, S. Cremaschi, *Il sistema della ricchezza*, F. Angeli, Milano, 1984, pp.65–7. A different analysis has been provided by Turco, *Dal sistema al senso comune*, pp.299–344.
96 Hume, *A Treatise of Human Nature*, in *The Philosophical Works*, vol.1, p.311.
97 Ibid., pp.317–18.

order and form with the original impressions'.[98] Thus, the imagination is the sphere of the manifold, of the epistemic association and of its possible *ethical transposition*. As Hume noted, sympathy is merely an idea transformed into impression.

If experience is the starting point, the 'idea of causation' is the only relationship 'that can be trac'd beyond our senses, and inform us of existences and objects, which we do not see or feel [...]'.[99] This is one of the seminal points of Hume's philosophical system; and beyond the enormous issues it raises – starting from those inherent to space and time –, what is worth investigating here is the epistemological and ethical relationship between the basis upon which a 'necessary connection' between cause and effect and imagination is possible. Hume says:

> When we infer effects from causes, we must establish the existence of these causes; which we have only two ways of doing, either by an immediate perception of our memory or sense, or by an inference from other causes; which causes again we must ascertain in the same manner [...].[100]

The sequence of experiences allows the discovery of a 'new relation betwixt cause and effect', defined as 'constant conjunction'; this latter, however, can only provide an explanation of the possible repetition of known events. To recall 'past experience decides nothing in the present case; and at the utmost can only prove, that that very object, which produc'd any other, was at that very instant endow'd with such a power; but can never prove, that the same power must continue in the same object [...]'.[101] In this context, the acquisitive ability of reason proves to be limited. Either when its basis is experience, or when experience invokes reason, there is no sufficient inference to establish an ultimate connection between past and future experience. Consequently, Hume concludes, '[t]he inference, therefore, depends solely on the union of ideas', it is determined 'by certain principles, which associate together the ideas [...] and unite them in

98   Ibid., p.318.
99   Ibid., p.377.
100   Ibid., p.384.
101   Ibid., p.392.

the imagination'. Imagination and association of ideas are mixed up; in the first instance, they connect logic and ethics, and then, they allow us even to establish the primacy of the latter upon the former. [102]

Imagination is a concept that Smith directly borrowed from Hume's philosophy. Although Smith owes much to Hume, nevertheless, his epistemology goes much further than accepting Hume's theory of imagination: he widens it, extending it from customs of ordinary human life to those contexts within which it is necessary to give an explanation of facts that break the objective regularity of the external world. [103] When Smith underlines the role played by imagination in the perception of things that normally come one after the other or, even better, when he emphasizes the relevance that a reasonable imagination has for the philosophical and scientific innovation – the very same with which the Copernican system should come to terms – the reference to Hume is explicit. Smith says:

> Nothing now embarrassed the system of Copernicus, but the difficulty which the imagination felt in conceiving bodies so immensely ponderous as the Earth, and the other Planets, revolving round the Sun with such incredible rapidity. It was in vain that Copernicus pretended, that, notwithstanding the prejudices of sense, this circular motion might be as natural to the Planets, as it is to a stone to fall to the ground. The imagination had been accustomed to conceive such objects as tending rather to rest than motion. This habitual idea of their natural inertness was incompatible with that of their natural motion. [104]

---

102 Ibid., p.393.
103 Lecaldano, 'Paradigmi di analisi della filosofia morale scozzese', pp.31–2. Many of the fundamental themes of Hume's philosophy that can be found in Smith can be referred to the Illuministic critiques of Descartes' system. In this sense, Condillac's theses are absolutely indicative. It is sufficient to look at his *Traité des sensations* on issues like memory (*Oeuvres*, de l'imprimerie de Ch. Houels, Paris, 1798, vol.3, pp.77–9, 227; but see also Helvétius, *De l'esprit*, I, 1; III, 3, *Oeuvres*, vol.1, pp.189 ff.; III, pp.183 ff.), its relationship with imagination (*Oeuvres*, vol.3, pp.245–6), habit (ibid., pp.221–2, 330–1), trust and uncertainty (ibid., pp.372–3).
104 *EPS*, p.91.

For Smith, similarly to Hume,[105] imagination is based upon a customary connection, whose eventual interruption produces a fracture, so that the individual is surprised, amazed, unable to connect, *prima facie*, bodies and events never previously associated. For this reason, as human imagination was used to conceive what is immense as motionless, the Copernican idea of movement appeared as totally unusual, and therefore incongruent. However, what is surprising and amazing provides the subject with an imaginative freedom. Being a *practical instance*, imagination contributes to the creation of an ethical 'freedom to act'. In spite of the apparent paradox that the conjugation of Newton's epistemology and Hume's philosophy seems to create,[106] there is no conflict, in effect, between the explicit trust accorded to the Newtonian system – trust which, for some interpreters,[107] represents a sort of renewed and insuppressible systematic exigency – and the acceptance of Hume's sepsis. This is even truer, if we think that in Smith the appreciation of Newton's philosophy does not imply the assumption of 'another' definable and unquestionable truth. Simply, Newton's system 'is everywhere the most precise and particular that can be imagined':

> Neither are the principles of union, which it employs, such as the imagination can find any difficulty in going along with. [...] And even we, while we have been endeavouring to represent all philosophical systems as mere inventions of the imagination [...] have insensibly been drawn in, to make use of language expressing the connecting principles of this one, as if they were the real chain which Nature make use to bind together her several operations.[108]

The recognition of these 'real chains' does not imply Smith's denial of the role of imagination; rather, such recognition represents

---

105 Cf. G. Streminger, 'Hume's Theory of Imagination', *Hume Studies*, 1980, vol.6, 2, pp.91–118.
106 Cf. S. Moscovici, 'A propos de quelques travaux d'Adam Smith sur l'histoire et la philosophie des sciences', *Revue d'histoire des Science et de leurs applications*, 1959, 9. On this issue see Cremaschi, *Il sistema della ricchezza*, pp.50–67; Id., 'L'illuminismo scozzese e il newtonianismo morale', p.59.
107 Turco, *Dal sistema al senso comune*, p.344.
108 *EPS*, pp.104–5. Cf. A. Smith, *Lectures on Rhetoric and Belles Lettres*, ed. by J.C. Bryce, in *The Glasgow Edition*, vol.4, p.146 – henceforth *LRBL*.

an attenuation of scepticism. Smith is not a critic of Descartes' system as such, but a moderate sceptic, aware of the precariousness of any absolute doubt.[109]

The explicit and constant influence of Hume's philosophy upon Smith's thought[110] is even more relevant if we consider that the assumption of associationism is not a mere epistemological hypothesis, but rather a prefiguration of those ethical mechanisms that regulate human nature and civil society. As Gilles Deleuze noted, if we interpret Hume's associationism as a psychology of knowledge, we risk misinterpreting its significance. Associationism is a theoretical explanation of what is practical, moral.[111] In this sense, it is inevitable to see in the 'belief' an anticipation of the role played by sympathy within the moral world.[112] An immediate similitude is the one that allows us to associate 'belief' and the primacy of sentiment in the constitution of civil society – and to identify the refusal of an abstract contractualistic naturalism: something that occurs both in Hume and Smith. By analogy, it is immediate to associate the role played by

109   For an overview of the themes here discussed, see H.J. Bitterman, 'Adam Smith's Empiricism and the Law of Nature', *Journal of Political Economy*, 1940, vol.48, 4; J.F. Becker, 'Adam Smith's Theory of Social Science', *Southern Economic Journal*, 1961, vol.28, July; H.F. Thompson, 'Adam Smith's Philosophy of Science', *Quarterly Journal of Economics*, 1965, vol.79, 2; J. Cropsey, *Polity and Economy*, Nijhoff, The Hague, 1957, p.44; Skinner, *A System of Social Philosophy*, pp.14–41; Campbell, *Adam Smith's Science of Morals*, pp.25 ff.; J.R. Lindgren, *The Social Philosophy of Adam Smith*, Nijhoff, The Hague, 1973, pp.6–7; A.D. Megill, 'Theory and Experience in Adam Smith', *Journal of the History of Ideas*, 1975, vol.36, 1; Brown, *Adam Smith's Economics*, pp.25 ff.

110   Cf. D.D. Raphael, '"The true old Humean Philosophy" and its Influence on Adam Smith', in *David Hume: Bicentenary Papers*, ed. by G.P. Morice, Edinburgh University Press, Edinburgh, 1977, pp.23–38; Id., *Adam Smith*, pp.10, 24, 102 ff.; Skinner, *A System of Social Science*, pp.14–15.

111   G. Deleuze, *Empirisme et subjectivité*, PUF, Paris, 1953. By the same author see also 'Hume', in F. Châtelet (ed. by), *Histoire de la philosophie*, Hachette, Paris, 1972, vol.4.

112   E. Ronchetti, 'Hume e il problema dell'identità personale', in A. Santucci (ed. by), *Scienza e filosofia scozzese nell'età di Hume*, Il Mulino, Bologna, 1976, p.130. See also Lecaldano, *Hume e la nascita dell' etica contemporanea*, pp.81 ff.

sympathy – intended as that faculty of knowing via imagination – with the check of reason. In fact, more than a similitude, we are here in the presence of the transposition of logical atomism in ethical associationism. This is the problem that characterizes empiricism, as well as the imperfect genesis of political economy: to transform, via the explicative power of imagination, pessimism and scepticism in associationism. After and beyond Shaftesbury and Hutcheson, the radical reconfiguration of the optimistic anthropological paradigm reaches its maturity with Hume and Smith. Such a reconfiguration give sway to a paradigm no longer based upon an innate human virtue, but upon a virtue acquired by experience, and conforming to the habits of a middle social agent. In this sense, imagination assumes a central role. In effect, what happens in epistemological terms – where the primacy of interpretation is nothing other than logical *Anfang*, because it is reflection that qualifies the mind as a subject –, also happens in ethical terms. Imagination allows the overcoming of naturalistic partiality.

Above all in Smith, imagination allows one's identification with other fellow men. It transforms natural epistemology both as a hermeneutic principle – according to which sympathy becomes a judgement either of approval or disapproval – and as an anthropological referent, which is never qualified by sympathy in normative terms. It follows that, also for Smith, the problem concerning the making of society is not a problem of 'limitation', but rather of 'association'. Through the judgement of an ideal middle social agent – the spectator – sympathetic imagination becomes the measure of the proper degree of social propriety. The very same imagination is the instrument measuring the social degree absent both in Hutcheson's moral sense and in Mandeville's anthropological pessimism. In brief, it represents the foundation of the logical and ethical structure of *TMS*, having as sole canon the judgement of an *ideal* middle social agent. Identification and comparison are possible only via imagination.

4. The prudent man's social means

The point of conjunction between the early writings and *TMS* is explicitly confirmed by the way in which, in this latter, experience and imagination are intended and utilized in the moral realm. Experience and imagination are the two notions around which *TMS* gravitates. Its main theme rests upon the comparison between the experience of an acting agent and the judgement of the impartial spectator who, sympathetically, tries to identify himself with the sentiments of the former. From the outset, the dialectics between these two realms is made explicit. Setting aside any moral sense and apriorism concerning the characters of human nature, Smith's notion of experience primarily refers to the description of human relationships as they occur within civil society. A situation ascertained, with no added adjectivation, with no presupposed value. In brief, a recalled experience that ought to be investigated as such.[113]

Concerning imagination, Smith introduced it as an unavoidable reference, assuming that the interest of the spectator towards the destiny of others cannot stem from an aprioristically defined moral sentiment, but rather from an identification, more or less possible, with them. Such an identification can be made possible via imagination, and, therefore, it does not require a declared 'value', but the simple existence of some principles, which, in turn, are not a prerogative of one who is 'virtuous and humane'. 'As we have not immediate experience of what other men feel' – Smith claims – 'we can form no idea of the manner in which they are affected, but by conceiving what we ourselves should feel in the like situation'. Our senses cannot convey to us the destiny of others; however, via the

---

113 'How selfish soever man may be supposed, there are evidently some principles in his nature, which interest him in the fortune of others, and render their happiness necessary to him, though he derives nothing from it except the pleasure of seeing it' (*TMS*, p.9). J.Z. Muller is right (*Adam Smith in his Time and ours*, Princeton University Press, Princeton, 1995, p.48) when he observes that Smith's attempt consists of describing the human being for what he is. Cf. also Griswold, jr., *Adam Smith and the Virtues of Enlightenment*, pp.78–83.

imagination, we can perceive another's feelings. 'By the imagination we place ourselves in his situation, we conceive ourselves enduring all the same torments, we enter as it were into his body, and become in some measure the same person with him [...]'.[114]

This can only happen through a process of identification occurring between the agent who experiences and the spectator who observes, imagines, and makes his own the agent's experience. The observation of the difficulties of others – Smith claims – generates in the spectator a sentiment analogous to the one who is effectively experiencing such difficulties. We imagine what our preoccupations would be if we were in the same circumstances; we identify ourselves with those who really face them. And it would be wrong to assume that this happens only in painful or difficult circumstances; sympathetic participation can be raised also by the joy of others: we can imagine ourselves in such circumstances, that is, as spectators *we could participate* in the passions of others, whatever they might be. However, as Smith reminds us, this is not universally true: the conditional is mandatory here, because of the existence of unsocial passions that do not inspire any particular sympathy.

It is worth noting that the two key terms, the 'spectator' and 'sympathy', had already been introduced. Both belonged to the Scottish tradition prior to Smith and were utilized by Hutcheson, Butler, Lord Kames, and, above all, by Hume. However, in *TMS* these terms assume a proper and distinct characteristic.[115] Let us consider how it is by means of imagination that the spectator might comprehend another's situation and, therefore, demonstrate a sympathetic disposition. *Stricto sensu*, the mutual interest that human beings share one for another should be traced back to this possibility. Only on these grounds can we imagine a possible comparison or articulation of the moral judgement within society; on this basis, sympathy, intended as participation in any passion, whatever it might be, may occur. So, it

---

114   *TMS*, p.9.
115   R.H. Campbell and A.S. Skinner (*Adam Smith*, Croom Helm, London, 1982, pp.101 and 106) synthesized the reasons that differentiate Smith both from Hume and from Hutcheson with regards to the formation of the moral judgement and, thereby, with regards also to the role of the spectator.

would be wrong to conceive of sympathy as motivation for moral action. Its role is simply that of making explicit the nature and the origin of moral judgements of approval or disapproval. As such, it is not the precondition for a theory of the nature of morality: whatever the context might be, the principle of sympathy makes possible only the process of moral approval or disapproval.[116] Conceived as a compassionate sentiment, moved by a benevolent disposition, sympathy would produce a radical mistake. *De facto*, more than any other, this has been the misunderstanding that has delayed the correct interpretation of *TMS*. Sympathy only refers to the possibility of identifying oneself with situations of others; and such identification is never an aim in itself, but rather represents a transitory task, as its sole purpose is that of making possible a judgement of approval or disapproval:

> Sympathy, therefore, does not arise so much from the view of the passion, as from that of the situation which excites it. We sometimes feel for another, a passion of which he himself seems to be altogether incapable; because, when we put ourselves in his case, that passion arises in our breast from the imagination, though it does not in his from reality. We blush for the impudence and rudeness of another, though he himself appears to have no sense of the impropriety of his own behaviour; because we cannot help feeling with what confusion we ourselves should be covered, had we behaved in so absurd a manner.[117]

116 'It is a mistake to suppose, [...], that Adam Smith's first book treats sympathy as the motive of moral action. The role of sympathy in his book is to explain the origin and the nature of moral judgment, of approval and disapproval' (Raphael, *Adam Smith*, p.29). As Morrow (*The Ethical and Economic Theories*, p.32) observed, the doctrine of sympathy does not presuppose 'any concrete theory of the nature of morality': 'whatever may be the content of morality, the basis of moral approbation and disapprobation is found in the principle of sympathy'. Cf. J. Cropsey, 'The Invisible Hand: Moral and Political Considerations', in G.P. O'Driscoll, jr. (ed. by), *Adam Smith and Modern Political Economy*, Iowa State University, Ames, 1979, p.174; Campbell, *Adam Smith's Science of Morals*, pp.98 ff. Thus, Stephen's interpretation is baseless (*History of English Thought*, vol.2, p.64). Vice versa, J. Rae's synthesis (*Life of Adam Smith*, Macmillan, London, 1895, p.141) is still acceptable.

117 *TMS*, p.12.

The fundamental aspect is that sympathy does not manifest itself in relation to a passion, but rather to the situation that provokes it, and in which, by consequence, it expresses itself. This happens because sympathy neither implies a shared participation, nor gives rise to a generic empathetic motion; rather it gives rise to a possible ident-ification, within which the spectator does not consider the passion *in se*, but the relationship between the expressed passion – type and degree – and the situation within which it occurs. This is the sole canon according to which one can express a judgement simply bound to a propriety *without* 'normative foundations'. Such a judgement, however, should come to terms with a fundamental problem that only imagination can overcome. Of human conduct, Smith says, we can only have a direct experience as long as it is our conduct; we cannot have, vice versa, an immediate experience of what others are feeling. What we can do is to attempt to imagine ourselves in the same situation, so as to understand 'what we ourselves should feel in the like situation'.[118] Nonetheless, as imagination allows the *ideal* middle social agent to identify himself with his fellow men – to the point of becoming, to a certain degree, 'the same person with him'[119] –, it is a fundamental 'ethical instrument'.[120] Epistemology and morality, in-evitably, overlap.

118 *TMS*, p.9. 'A man may sympathize with a woman in child-bed [...]' (*TMS*, p.317).
119 Once acknowledged the relevance of imagination, Macfie distinguishes be-tween 'immediate sympathy' and 'imaginative sympathy', noticing how only in the latter is it possible to identify oneself with the situations of others: 'to put ourselves in their situation' (*The Individual in Society*, p.50; on this aspect, relevant is 'Thomas Reid's Criticism of Adam Smith's *Theory of Moral Sentiments*', ed. by E.H. Duncan and R.M. Baird, *Journal of the History of Ideas*, 1977, vol.38, 3). Therefore, if one would interpret sympathy as 'a philosophical fiction', it could not be intended as 'moral fiction' – differently from what A. Macintyre argues in his *After Virtue. A Study in Moral Theory* (University of Notre Dame Press, Notre Dame Ill., 1981–1984).
120 This matter is correctly underlined by Skinner (*A System of Social Science*, pp.14–41), L. Bagolini (*La simpatia nella morale e nel diritto*, Giappichelli, Torino, 1975, pp.27–34; Id., *David Hume e Adam Smith*, Patron, Bologna, 1979, p.38) and Preti (*Alle origini dell'etica contemporanea*, pp.91 ff.).

Imagination, the pivotal notion around which *TMS* gravitates, is therefore the means that allows the spectator, the *ideal* social agent, to understand the condition of others, without expressing any generic *cum-passio*. According to Galvano della Volpe, this social agent is only *given*. However, as Morrow soundly noted, the figure of the impartial spectator introduces a regulating principle within the moral order: it personifies what in sympathy is permanent, universal, and rational; it is 'the guardian of social welfare'.[121] When the social agent is well informed about the cause that generates the pain or joy of others, he might feel sympathy, although of different degree, because he can understand, through imagination, the situation that generates them in other persons:

> When the original passions of the person principally concerned are in perfect concord with the sympathetic emotions of the spectator, they necessarily appear to this last just and proper, and suitable to their objects; and, on the contrary, when, upon bringing the case home to himself, he finds they do not coincide with what he feels, they necessarily appear to him unjust and improper, and unsuitable to the causes which excite them. To approve of the passions of another, therefore, as suitable to their objects, is the same thing as to observe that we entirely sympathize with them; and not to approve of them as such, is the same thing as to observe that we do not entirely sympathize with them.[122]

---

121 G. Della Volpe, *La filosofia dell'esperienza di Davide Hume*, II (*Opere*, ed. by I. Ambrogio, Editori riuniti, Roma, 1972, vol.2, p.327); Morrow, *The Ethical and Economic Theories*, p.37. This point of view has been thoroughly discussed by E.L. Khalil ('Beyond Self-Interest and Altruism', *Economics and Philosophy*, 1990, vol.6, 2, pp.255–73) who, with regards to the spectator, correctly distinguished, in Smith, the approval according propriety (self-command) and the judgement of merit (prudence, justice, beneficence). The author's intention seems to be to lessen the social interpretation of the spectator, stressing, above all, upon the role of the spectator within.

122 *TMS*, p.16. Important echoes are present in the *Lectures on Jurisprudence* (ed. by R.L. Meek, D.D. Raphael, P.G. Stein, in *The Glasgow Edition*, vol.5 [henceforth *LJ(A)*, *LJ(B)*)], in relation to the 'causes from whence property may have its occasion': *LJ(A)*, pp.17–19; *LJ(B)*, p.459 (Of Occupation), *LJ(B)*, p.461 (Prescription); in relation to the 'obligations which arise from contract or agreement': *LJ(A)*, p.87; in relation to the punishment: *LJ(A)*, p.104; *LJ(B)*, p.475.

From such an understanding, in fact, is derived the possibility that the spectator has to identify himself, via imagination, with the sentiments of others, without making any assumptions 'from which the principles of right and justice may be derived'.[123] Rawls' observation is here extremely pertinent, although it might seem to contrast with Smith's previous quotation. Indeed, a spectator considers specific passions to be right or wrong not in themselves, but rather in relation to the situation within which they are expressed. It follows that to judge the behaviour, which in turn is a relationship, on the basis of the adequacy between the situation and the induced passion, cannot lead to the expression of a judgement concerning passions in abstract. Undoubtedly, they are distinct – they are social, selfish, unsocial –, they are not grouped in a sort of limbo within which it is not possible to distinguish between malevolence and benevolence, justice and injustice. However, against the landscape represented by the common sense of natural justice, sympathy does not allow the expression of unappealing judgements, because it considers *only* the relationship between context and passions. On these aspects, it is fundamental to keep in mind the long note which closes the first Section of Part II of *TMS*. Apparently, although not renouncing the criterion according to which passions are just or unjust *per se*, it would be odd to judge with the same criterion of value a 'situation', that is a given 'relationship' between *context* and *passion*. Conceived of as an impartial judge who establishes the evaluative criteria, the spectator can only express the degree of social acceptance that he sympathetically feels or does not feel towards the original passions to which the acting agent is directly subjected in a given situation.[124] Such a criteria are expressed in relation to the propriety that the very same passions reveal towards their object or cause. In the degree of agreement or disagreement resides the possible identification between spectator and agent: 'To approve or disapprove, therefore, of the opinions of others is acknowledged, by everybody, to mean no more than to observe their agreement or disagreement with our own. But

---

123   J. Rawls, *A Theory of Justice*, Harvard University Press, Cambridge MA, 1980, p.185.
124   See Haakonssen's relevant remarks: *The Science of a Legislator*, p.66.

this is equally the case with regard to our approbation or disapprobation of the sentiments or passions of others'.[125] It is necessary to restate that epistemology and morality overlap here, exhibiting the propriety as a canon which assigns to imagination a prominently ethical, practical task.

One of the most complex issues inherent to *TMS* arises exactly at this point: when the degree of accordance and sympathetic identification of the spectator is posed, firstly, in relation to the adequacy or inadequacy existing between sentiments and what causes them and, secondly, in relation to merit or demerit of the action that these sentiments generate in terms of effects:

> In the suitableness or unsuitableness, in the proportion or disproportion which the affection seems to bear to the cause or object which excites it, consists the propriety or impropriety, the decency or ungracefulness of the consequent action. In the beneficial or hurtful nature of the effects which the affection aims at, or tends to produce, consists the merit or demerit of the action, the qualities by which it is entitled to reward, or is deserving of punishment.[126]

It is not by chance that on this basis it is possible to distinguish virtues and vices. Here the impartial spectator, the *ideal* middle social agent, fully exerts his functions. Smith says: 'When we judge in this manner of any affection, as proportioned or disproportioned to the cause which excites it, it is scarce possible that we should make use of any other rule or canon but the correspondent affection in ourselves'.[127] The spectator manifests a more immediate identification towards the joy, rather than the pain of the agent[128] – although sympathy, being a criterion of possible evaluation, can be moved either by joy or pain. As a result, the spectator could not only identify himself, to a varying degree, with those who express socially laudable passions, but also, within certain limits, with those who express not laudable social passions, such as resentment towards those who have

125   *TMS*, p.17.
126   *TMS*, pp.18; and pp.74–5.
127   *TMS*, p.18.
128   Cf. *TMS*, p.45; *Letter from D. Hume, London 28 July 1759*, in *Correspondence of Adam Smith*, ed. by E.C. Mossner, I.S. Ross, in *The Glasgow Edition*, vol.6, p.43, henceforth *C*; and *TMS*, p.46.

attempted to undermine their human dignity.[129] In effect, the problem resides in the adequacy of the passions *vis-à-vis* the causes that generate them and the effects that those passions induce. Via imagination, the spectator can identify himself in the situation of the agent, find a correspondence of sentiments, and understand the situations of others. Nevertheless, the original passion is always more intense than any sympathetic participation that the *ideal* middle social agent could reach. Thus, when the spectator places himself in the original situation from which the agent's passion originates, he can only express, via imagination, an evaluation of the propriety of the very same passion. It is evident that the degree of such propriety represents a 'social parameter'.[130] Noting the easiness with which human beings are predisposed to sympathize with the wealthy and powerful,[131] Smith claimed that the virtuous and laborious man is likely to feel different sentiments:

> He must be patient in labour, resolute in danger, and firm in distress. These talents he must bring into public view, by the difficulty, importance, and, at the same time, good judgment of his undertaking, and by the severe and unrelenting application with which he pursues them.[132]

Probity and prudence, generosity and frankness appear to be those middle degrees of virtue with which the spectator, intended as social expression, can easily sympathize and agree. Any man, in fact, is reciprocally bound to his fellows: human society constitutes the

---

129 Cf. *TMS*, p.48.
130 Morrow soundly insists upon the fact that Smith's theory of sympathy explicitly abandons the individualistic instance. In this resides the radical innovation in British ethics (*The Ethical and the Economic Theories*, pp.29–32; Id., 'Adam Smith: Moralist and Philosopher', *Journal of Political Economy*, 1927, vol.35, June). Cf. also Macfie, *The Individual in Society*, p.100 and *passim*; E.R. Gill, 'Justice in Adam Smith: The Right and The Good', *Review of Social Economy*, 1976, vol.34, December, pp.275–94; L. Calabi, 'Adam Smith e la costituzione dell'economia politica', *Critica Marxista*, 1976, 3–4, p.246; Id., 'L'"uomo mercante" di Adam Smith. Rapporti reali e rapporti personali alle origini dell'economia politica', *Angelus novus*, 1970, 19, pp.7–100.
131 Cf. *TMS*, pp.50 ff., 201.
132 *TMS*, p.55.

reciprocal bond that supports individuals. The social consortium does not exist only when a total reciprocity of affections occurs; however, the middle social agent 'can subsist only in society', he 'has a natural love for society', independent from his own self-interest: this latter 'is connected with the prosperity of society'.[133] The middle degree of virtue becomes a 'social parameter'. In this sense, not only does Smith describe the social relationships among human beings, but also defines the relationship between man and himself. In effect, in the same way in which we approve or disapprove of the behaviour of others – he claims –, 'we either approve or disapprove of our own conduct, according as we feel that, when we place ourselves in the situation of another man, and view it, as it were, with his eyes and from his station, we either can or cannot entirely enter into and sympathize with the sentiments and motives which influenced it'.[134] That is, man, grounding his judgement on what is, or might be, the judgement of others, should become his own impartial judge, accepting a possible judgement of an internal impartial spectator. Man becomes, at the same time, judge and judged, spectator and agent, expression of rationality and sentiment. Making human being social, nature provides him with an original desire for pleasure and a natural aversion to offend their fellows. 'Nature, accordingly, has endowed him, not only with a desire of being approved of, but with a desire of being what ought to be approved of [...]'.[135] In such a desire to be worthy of approval, even before being approved of, the approval of others substantiates the self-approval.

Thus, in describing the role of the impartial spectator, Smith establishes a clear distinction between *man without* and *man within*. He maintains that for the 'man within the breast' what is essential is not an immediate approval, but rather the desire of being worthy of it. As the final aim of a wise man is not the fulfilment of his immediate interest, he finds in 'the impartial and well informed spectator' the most convenient evaluative and comparative criterion 'between our

133 *TMS*, pp.85, 88.
134 *TMS*, pp.109–10.
135 *TMS*, p.117.

72

own interests and those of other people'.[136] As Luigi Bagolini noted, to the immediate reality of the *man without* corresponds an abstract mediation of the *man within*, which is social in kind. In brief, from an irrational sympathetic immediateness, through the examination of the process of practical deliberation and hence of the inquiry concerning the evaluation of the elements, the impartial spectator arrives, via reason, at a fair social judgement.

This explains what differentiates Smith's argumentation from the ethics of the moral sense. Nevertheless, an excessive emphasis should not be given to the role of *reason* with regard to *sentiment*, because this would lead to the impossible deduction of the rationality of human action from the sentiment itself. Here it is not Bagolini's interpretation that is inadequate but, perhaps, his connecting the adjective 'irrational' to the notion of sentiment, as this implies a stronger concept of critical rationality. No less strong is Brown's reference to a 'practical reason'. As a result, with regard to the immediate passion, more apt, *au fond*, is the emphasis that Preti placed upon a 'universalizing abstraction', from which on the part of the spectator is derived the 'interiorization of society'. In this way, in fact, the illusion of the so-called 'real spectator' is equally indicated, without referring to categories that ought to be 'critically' resolutive of the relationship between *reason* and *sentiments* – that which would become, in Kantian terms, 'unfoundedly'.

In this context, also Haakonssen's argumentation, according to which the man within has 'sufficient' autonomy in relation to the social morality, although relevant, runs the risk of being misplaced, as propriety is, in any case, a social expression.[137] As Eugenio Garin

---

136 *TMS*, p.134.
137 *TMS*, pp.130 ff.; but cf. pp.319–20. See Bagolini, *La simpatia nella morale e nel diritto*, p.36; Id., *David Hume e Adam Smith*, p.33; L. Schneider, 'Adam Smith on Human Nature and Social Circumstance', in O'Driscoll, jr. (ed. by), *Adam Smith and Modern Political Economy*, pp.58–60; Preti, *Alle origini dell'etica contemporanea*, pp.93, 105. Bearing in mind its limits, Cousin's *Philosophie écossaise* (pp.167, 205–6), is still relevant. Unacceptable, instead, are Bittermann, 'Adam Smith's Empiricism on the Law of Nature', and Cropsey, *Polity and Economy*, p.5 and *passim*. Cf. therefore Macfie, *The Individual in Society*, pp.64–7, 85–8; Morrow, *The Ethical and Economic*

observes, the spectator is the *alter*; he is not mine or your 'voice', but rather is the voice of humanity. It is neither from our point of view, nor from that of our fellow men that we might identify the right comparison, but rather 'from the point of view of a third person, who has no particular connection with both, and who judges with impartiality between us'. If this is so – according to Haakonssen's same argumentation –, it is possible to claim that it is the search for a third, completely impartial point of observation that defines the sociality of what is at stake – where the search appears more important than the reach of its aim.[138] Consequently, 'the wise and just man who has been thoroughly bred in the great school of self-command' 'does not merely affect the sentiments of the impartial spectator. He really adopts them'.[139] He identifies himself with them, so as to become 'himself that impartial spectator'. The highest degree of self-command, the calm, constant humanity allow him to understand the joy and pain of others, their social characters.[140]

Human beings do not have an innate moral sense. Differently from Shaftesbury and Hutcheson, Smith argues that because 'the violence and injustice of our own selfish passions are sometimes sufficient to induce the man within the breast to make a report very different from what the real circumstances of the case are capable of authorising',[141] man is destined to struggle within himself against the strongest iniquity. The point of view of the individual is in reality subjected to an extreme partiality: before acting, due to the strong passions that move the action; after having acted, so as justify the

    Theories, pp.39, 42; Brown, *Adam Smith's Economics*, pp.99, 179–80; Haakonssen, *The Science of a Legislator*, pp.57–8.

138   *TMS*, p.135. E. Garin, *L'illuminismo inglese. I Moralisti*, Bocca, Milano, 1942, p.229. Lindgren distinguishes between *aesthetic* and *moral* sympathy (*The Social Philosophy of Adam Smith*, p.25).

139   *TMS*, p.146.

140   It is important here the distinction between 'passive' and 'active disposition', underlined by Limentani, *La morale della simpatia*, pp.123, 125, 126, 165, 171, 177, 185.

141   *TMS*, p.157.

action. Such self-deceit,[142] 'this fatal weakness of mankind', is 'the source of half the disorder of human life'.[143] Anyhow, even if man has not been endowed with an innate moral sense, the general rules of behaviour and morality can be acquired via experience.[144] 'Our continual observations upon the conduct of others, insensibly lead us to form for ourselves certain general rules concerning what is fit and proper either to be done or to be avoided'.[145] Social experience – the sociality of the rules of which nature did not deprive us – indicates the proper degree of propriety and merit that is the constant reference for the judgements of approval. Thus, there are no original judgements concerning what is right or wrong. Only a habitual reflection induces us to correct 'the misrepresentations of self-love concerning what is fit and proper to be done in our particular situation'.[146]

---

142 Macfie (*The Individual in Society*, pp.61, 68, 79) has perfectly clarified how the explanation of the 'deception theory' should be found in the social dimension within which the individual appetites develop. The deception theory (of which Butler's *Fifteen Sermons*, VII, 10, provide a relevant precedent) and, in a more general sense, the theory of the individual pursuit of wealth as implicit part of the plan of nature (P. Salvucci, *La filosofia politica di Adam Smith*, Argalia, Urbino, 1966, p.107), has been underlined by Lukács (*Der junge Hegel und die Probleme der kapitalistischen Gesellschaft*, Europa Verlag, Zürich, 1948) and related to Kant's 'abstract' interpretation via the idea of *ungesellige Geselligkeit* (*Idee zu einer allgemeinen Geschichte in weltbürgerlicher Absicht, Werke*, hrsg. von W. Weischedel, Wissenschaftliche Buchgesellschaft, Frankfurt, 1968, XI, p.37). Very interesting is M. Shell's interpretation: *Money, Language and Thought*, University of California Press, Berkeley, 1982, ch.V.
143 *TMS*, p.158.
144 In this light, Smith's moral theory is neither absolute nor normative (A. Giuliani, 'Adamo Smith filosofo del diritto', *Rivista internazionale di filosofia del diritto*, 1954, vol.6, 4, p.531; see also: Macfie, *The Individual in Society*, p.117; Skinner, *A System of Social Science*, p.65). Nevertheless, Campbell's interpretation seems unacceptable (*Adam Smith's Science of Moral*, pp.115, 139, 170); hence, Lindgren's distinction between an analytical-relativistic disposition and moral relativity is more appropriate (*The Social Philosophy of Adam Smith*, p.37; cf. also Brown, *Adam Smith's Economics*, p.67). For a recent interpretation of this matter see Ch.T. Wolfe, 'Smith's Crypto-Normativity', *Fenomenologia e società*, 2000, vol.23, 2, pp.110–40.
145 *TMS*, p.159. Cf. Macfie, *The Individual in Society*, p.53.
146 *TMS*, p.160.

There is indeed a strong connection between sympathy and propriety: when the former is correctly understood as means that allows the impartial spectator to identify himself with the situations of others, the latter becomes the judgmental canon, conforming to a habitual reflection. And this is not only true for a 'third person', but also for ourselves, as the internal impartial spectator should deal with that fatal self-deceit that threatens each of us. The relevance of this process stems from the fact that it presides over the constitution of specific 'general rules', which are formed within and derived from experience. These rules are those 'positive principles' – which can be defined as ethical rules, differentiated from individualistic moral criteria –, that Smith distinguishes from the norms of justice.

This is an issue of fundamental importance and to which we shall soon return. However, before doing so, we should notice how this experience is related to one of the problems characterizing *TMS*: the discussion concerning utility that, in turn, cannot be addressed without making reference to the criterion of propriety. It is an inevitable bottle-neck, which the sympathetic principle cannot avoid. Smith does not deny that utility is one of the main sources of beauty; that is, he does not deny that the spectator could sympathize with the agent, the utility of whose object, 'this happy contrivance of any production of art', is adequate to its aim. Smith takes this for granted. What he believes should be considered is the instance that precedes the aim, 'the exact adjustment of the means for attaining any conveniency or pleasure',[147] irrespective of its end. Smith exemplifies in this manner: entering a room, one can be shocked by the disorder to the point of deciding to sort it out. Whoever thinks in this way, nonetheless, might sit comfortably on an empty chair. What would diminish his immediate comfort? Not the possibility of being seated, but rather 'that arrangement of things which promotes it'. By analogy, what is the end of a watch? To point out the time, but it can also be the object of other considerations; for example, apart from its immediate utility, it might be collected. Under these circumstances, we appreciate beauty independently from utility; that is, we place a specific propriety before utility. The reference is here to Hume, who claimed that 'it is a

147   *TMS*, p.179.

contradiction in terms, that anything pleases as means to an end, where the end itself no wise affects us'.[148] At any rate, one should not believe that Smith's hypothesis is, so to speak, 'enchanted'. It pursued a strategic objective: to tailor any criterion of convenience to the middle social agent:

> [I]f you would implant public virtue in the breast of him who seems heedless of the interest of his country, it will often be to no purpose to tell him, what superior advantages the subjects of a well-governed state enjoy; [...]. You will be more likely to persuade, if you describe the great system of public police which procures these advantages, if you explain the connexions and dependencies of its several parts, their mutual subordination to one another, and their general subserviency to the happiness of the society [...].[149]

In these terms, the sentiment of expected approval has within itself a sense of convenience, a 'measure', absolutely distinct from the perception of the immediate utility. Hence, '[t]he prudent, the equitable, the active, resolute, and sober character promises prosperity and satisfaction, both to the person himself and to every one connected with him'.[150] Without a doubt, when we place the most intense future pleasure before the present one, we conform it to a measure. If this is so, those scholars – as for example Campbell – who placed Smith in the utilitarian universe are on a wrong path.[151] It can be sufficient to recall that for Bentham,[152] the sentiment of sympathy among men, firstly, does not necessarily increase the happiness of all, and, secondly, is based upon individual interests. And although it is true that one's happiness cannot be abstracted from the happiness of all, it is

---

148 Hume, *An Enquiry concerning the Principles of Morals*, in *The Philosophical Works*, vol.4, p.207. Cf. D. Stewart, *Account of the Life and Writings of Adam Smith* (1794), in *EPS*, pp.279, 289; Stephen, *History of English Thought*, vol.2, pp.61–2; Morrow, *The Ethical and Economic Theories*, p.32; Macfie, *The Individual in Society*, pp.45 ff.; 59 ff.; Campbell, Skinner, *Adam Smith*, p.100.

149 *TMS*, p.186. This passage, clearly Stoic, seems to be inspired to Marcus Aurelius, *Meditations*, VI, 45.

150 *TMS*, p.187.

151 Campbell, *Adam Smith's Science of Morals*, pp.205, 218.

152 J. Bentham, *Déontologie ou science de la morale*, XI, *Oeuvres*, éd. par E. Dumont, Hauman, Bruxelles, 1840, vol.3, pp.393 ff. Cf. M.E.L. Guidi, *Il sovrano e l'imprenditore*, Laterza, Roma-Bari, 1991, pp.91 ff., part. p.106.

also true that the happiness of the former depends only marginally upon the happiness of others. As Bagolini cogently noted, because Smith excludes an immediate coincidence between utility and propriety, he integrates them according to the criteria and rules inherent to the social means of the prudent man.[153]

What is prudence? What are its foundations? The virtue of prudence is the most useful to the individual, as it allows the pursuit of his happiness and security; it calls for cautiousness rather than resourcefulness. The prudent man, Smith says, is a man who takes care of himself, of his life and reputation, relying upon the real knowledge of his task, labour, and effort; he only begins well thought out projects and enterprises and is able to forecast their possible outcome; he 'always studies seriously and earnestly to understand'. He considers 'any new projects or enterprises', because he 'has always time and leisure to deliberate soberly and coolly concerning what are likely to be their consequences'. Nevertheless, he only accepts those responsibilities imposed by his duty. Furthermore, although he is always sincere, he is not always open and frank, nor does he feel obliged to tell the complete truth, unless explicitly required. In fact, to be silent is not necessarily a disloyal behaviour, but rather it might be the attempt not to compromise his own utility for an excess of zeal. Thus, the prudent man limits himself 'to his own affairs', trying to act 'with the most perfect propriety in every possible circumstance and situation'. As a result, he also respects the 'political means': contrary to the 'man of system' who plans the future of humanity according to the prevailing ideas of his time, the prudent man 'will respect the established powers and privileges even of individuals, and still more those of the great orders and societies, into which the state is divided'.

Constantly, the theme of an adequate correspondence returns. The prudent man, through small but constant accumulations, increases his situation in society, mitigating 'the rigour of his parsimony' via the increase of exchange. So, 'every prudent man in every period of society [...] must naturally have endeavoured to manage his affairs in

---

153 Bagolini, *David Hume e Adam Smith*, p.59; Id., *La simpatia nella morale e nel diritto*, pp.79–83.

such a manner, as to have at all time by him, besides the peculiar produce of his own industry, a certain quantity of some one commodity or other, such as he imagined few people would be likely to refuse for the produce of their industry'.[154] Consequently, '[i]n the steadiness of his industry and frugality, in his steadily sacrificing the ease and enjoyment of the present moment for the probable expectation of the still greater ease and enjoyment of a more distant but more lasting period of time, the prudent man is always be supported and rewarded by the entire approbation of the impartial spectator [...]'.[155] The prudent man refuses uncertainty and indeterminacy. He is able to calculate the social adequacy of his choice – being other than the incarnation of that prudential virtue informing the *Hausvaterliteratur*.[156] He can do it because he acts with calm and constancy, and because, at the bottom of his heart, 'he would prefer the undisturbed enjoyment of secure tranquillity, [...] to the real and solid glory of performing the greatest and most magnanimous actions'.[157]

Rather than the plain man – whose behaviour does not respect the common forms of relation because he flaunts, with presumption, his own reasons, convinced that he can rely upon 'his own superior sense and judgement' – the prudent man resembles the simple man, although he is more reserved, less disenchanted, and a more

154 A. Smith, *An Inquiry into the Nature and Causes of the Wealth of Nations*, ed. by R.H. Campbell, A.S. Skinner, W.B. Todd, in *The Glasgow Edition*, vol.2, 1, pp.37–8 – henceforth *WN*.
155 *TMS*, p.215. Costa (*Il progetto giuridico*, pp.61 ff., part. 77, 91), analysing the theme of 'deferment', posed it in relation to the issue of accumulation. See also Pesciarelli, *La jurisprudence economica di Adam Smith*, pp.45–54; Id., 'Smith, Bentham and the Development of Contrasting Ideas on Entrepreneurship', *History of Political Economy*, 1989, vol.21, 3, pp.521–36.
156 See the classic work by O. Brunner, 'Das "ganze haus" und die altereuropäische "Ökonomik"', *Zeitschrift für Nationalökonomie*, 1958, vol.13; cf. D. Frigo, *Il padre di famiglia*, Bulzoni, Roma, 1985. Regarding the classical tradition concerning the concept of prudence, cf. G. Vivenza, *Adam Smith and the Classics: The Classical Heritage in Adam Smith's Thought*, Oxford University Press, Oxford, 2001; V. Dini, G. Stabile, *Saggezza e prudenza*, Liguori, Napoli, 1983, pp.13–123.
157 *TMS*, p.216.

calculating person.[158] As Richard Teichgraeber noted, it is true that in *WN* the notion of prudence informs the behaviour of the merchant; but this is so indeed because this is its aim from the very beginning, and not because prudence is 'morally neutral'. The rare and heroic virtue – from which can descend either fame or infamy –, although ineffable, cannot be said to be an attribute of the middle social agent. An essential prudence is instead the virtue entailing the systematic actions of a man who, with calm and constant determination, is able to identify the *eukairìa*, the occasion, the opportunity of an action at the right time; hence, the very same *eutassìa*, the right measure, becomes the degree of propriety corresponding to the social means: *mediocritas optima est.*[159]

These are the terms in which the notion of invisible hand can be adequately understood. The wealthy, Smith argues, in spite of their egoism and 'stomach', share the goods with the poor 'and thus without intending it, without knowing it, advance the interest of the society'.[160] Notoriously, in Book IV of *WN* Smith claims that there is nothing more damaging than profit deriving from a position of monopoly that increases more than its ordinary rate, because, 'if we may judge from experience', it destroys parsimony. Thus, even the wealthiest is subjected to a limit: in spite of his richness, he is a part of the whole. That is, efficiency, keeping a criterion of equity and justice, visible and invisible,[161] is constantly in relation to a measure, to a mediating criterion that can be inferred from social experience. The same applies to utility. This is the core of the issue concerning the integration between utility and propriety. As Smith puts it:

> We expect in each rank and profession, a degree of those manners, which, experience has taught us, belong to it. But as in each species of things, we are particularly pleased with the middle conformation, which, in every part and

158 *LRBL*, pp.36–8. On this topic see Seneca, *Ad Lucilium Epist.*, I, XI–XIII, 85.
159 Cicero, *De off.*, I, 40, 142–3.
160 *TMS*, p.185. In the very same terms, the metaphor of stomach is present in Seneca, *Ad Lucilium Epist.*, II, XIV, 89. But, above all, we should notice here the evident differences with respect to Rousseau's *Discours sur l'inégalité parmi les hommes*, II (*Oeuvres*, vol.3, pp.164 ff.).
161 Lindgren, *The Social Philosophy*, pp.82, 86.

feature, agrees most exactly with the general standard which nature seems to have established for things of that kind; so in each rank, or, if I may say so, in each species of men, we are particularly pleased, if they have neither too much, nor too little of the character which usually accompanies their particular condition and situation.[162]

This is the core of the matter, because what 'we expect' is what is consistent for all. The postponement of a present happiness for a future intense one, the accumulation for the future, the respect of the established powers, in short, the government of needs, is what assures to the middle social agent a peaceful life, away from the evanescent noise of glory; is what prudence guarantees to the 'simple man': the respect of a 'means' according to nature. The spectator can easily identify himself with this means and, for this reason, the prudent man appears as an acting subject, whose behaviour becomes a canon for the judgement expressed by an impartial spectator. Hence – taking back the argument earlier presented –, imagination is really what links Smith's ethical articulations together. The fact that imagination makes it possible to express a judgement concerning what one pleases because it is consistent with one's habitual reflection confirms the argument that Smith puts forward in the *History of Astronomy*. Although it contemplates amazement and surprise, ethics resembles *habitus*. Therefore, the spectator always clings to a prudent middle conformation. If sympathy is nothing but an approval criterion via identification, without possessing *in se* the value of such a criterion; if the very same spectator is impartial because he can imagine himself in someone else's situation, as if he were the same person; it becomes evident that the propriety cannot but be a middle custom, inferred from experience, within which specific general rules arise and are made available to an habitual reflection. Consequently, and without creating a paradox, in regard to the inferior virtues, the middle social agent's behaviour becomes the referential canon for the impartial spectator. In brief, we can think of a diagramatization within which the input is represented by the faculty of imagination and the output is

---

162   *TMS*, p.201. Cf. A. Zanini, 'The Individual and Society: On the Concept of "Middle Conformation" in Adam Smith's Theory of Moral Sentiments', *History of Economic Ideas*, vol.1, 2, 1993, pp.1–19.

represented by the constitution of general rules aimed at guiding a prudent man's behaviour. In this case, sympathy becomes the 'operator', whose rules are established according to propriety. In other words, imagination allows sympathy and discloses the role of propriety which is produced by social customs. Within this framework, although clearly introduced in Part V of *TMS*, the concept of *middle conformation* synthesizes Smith's ethical dimension.

Once again we face the problem mentioned earlier: when these general rules are construed as ethical rules, inferred from social experience, we can refer to them as 'standard of judgement, in debating concerning the degree of praise or blame that is due to certain actions'.[163] The observance of these rules constitutes the meaning of moral approval, the only positive principle 'by which the bulk of mankind are capable of directing their actions'.[164] However, this is only a positive principle, and therefore any society affiances it with a legal principle, negative in kind: justice.[165] The positiveness of propriety, in effect, possesses in itself an elasticity that justice should not and cannot admit.

5. The aporias of justice

It is not by chance that some of the most careful commentators of *TMS* have seen in the chapter concerning *universal benevolence* an inescapable dualism. The action of prudent men, in fact, is neither able to renounce a criterion that is 'extrinsic' if compared to ethical positiveness (justice is therefore a 'negative principle'), nor to pay attention to the superior interest of the Universe, as they do not have *an*

163   *TMS*, p.160.
164   *TMS*, p.162.
165   With regard to Smith's definition of justice see: *LJ(A)*, p.7; *LJ(B)*, p.399. Moreover, it should not be underestimated the emphasis posed upon the separation between juridical and executive power: *LJ(A)*, p.271; *WN*, II, pp.722–3; *Letter to Lord Hailes, Kirkcaldy, 5 March 1769* (*C*, pp.141–3).

sich the determination and wisdom that universal benevolence requires. On the basis of this unquestionable datum, justice, as a 'negative principle', would show, on the one hand, the distance between a prudent man and a just man, and on the other the difference between a wise man, totally devoted to an ideal of universal benevolence, and a middle social agent, who is surely sensible, but unable to conform to it. Such a twofold issue is certainly accountable to Smith, but for reasons that the critics have utterly overlooked.

In effect, the problem has two facets. Smith refers not only to the primacy of mundane criteria of justice, but also – when this 'negative' criteria is insufficient to guarantee the respect of justice – he invokes the supreme and just universal benevolence of God's will.[166] So, we can identify two distinct but related issues. Firstly, if it is thanks to the mediation of mundane justice that universal benevolence and divine justice *de facto* coincide, then it becomes difficult to sustain that Smith's reflection on justice would delineate a clear theoretical profile. Secondly, the coincidence between 'divine justice' and 'universal benevolence' does not exclude, *ex definitione*, the existence of different degrees of benevolence proper to the social passions. Accordingly, although defined as 'ornaments', when we consider the 'economic discourse', the same degrees cannot be disregarded. In fact – Smith says –, 'the condition of human nature were peculiarly hard', if social affections, which frequently influence our conduct, 'could upon no occasion appear virtuous'.

It is reasonable to say that Smith's theory of justice should be referred here to Lord Kames, rather than to Hume.[167] Kames saw in the lack of distinction among the terms *right, obligation, duty, ought,* and *should* the main flaw of Hutcheson's system. Following this train of thought, he traced back the missed distinction between morality and justice to the missed distinction between moral approval and obligation. The benevolent and generous actions, Lord Kames wrote:

---

166 Cf., for example, *LJ(A)*, p.5; *TMS*, p.131.
167 Hume, *A Treatise of Human Nature*, III, II; Lord Kames, *Essays on the Principles of Morality and Natural Religion*, pp.43–51. On this point, we disagree with Haakonssen's interpretation (*The Science of a Legislator*, p.2).

though considered as *fit* and *right* to be done, are not however considered to be our *duty*, but as virtuous actions beyond what is strictly our duty. Benevolence and generosity are more beautiful, and more attractive of love and esteem, than justice. Yet, not being so necessary to the support of society, they are left upon the general footing of approbatory pleasure; while justice, faith, truth, without which society could not at all subsist, are objects of the foregoing peculiar sense, to take away all shadow of liberty, and to put us under a necessity of performance.[168]

Consequently, '[a]s justice, and the other primary virtues, are more essential to society than generosity, benevolence, or any other secondary virtue, they are likewise more universal'.[169] Obviously, the distinction concerns 'social utility', over which the inferior virtues assert their primacy, and not 'dignity'.

As we shall see below, Smith shared Kames's point of view; nevertheless, apropos the degree of benevolence, his reasoning would lead him to a different conclusion. Smith's analogy and comparison are eloquent: there are no explicit rules 'of what is sublime and elegant in composition', however, rules do exist concerning grammar in the strict sense. If, intended as social experience, morality can be articulated according to different degrees proper to the nature of men, justice does not allow any degree or exception. More radically than Kames – for whom justice, although related to a possible punishment, is above all 'law within us' –, Smith qualifies the negative character of justice. Thus, facing the elasticity of general rules, of morality as experience of the middle social agent, it is the legal character of justice to embody the *extrema ratio* of coexistence. According to Montesquieu's model, as *créature sensible*, human being is subjected to a myriad of passions:

> Un tel être pouvait à tous les instants oublier son créateur; Dieu l'a rappelé à lui par les lois de la religion. Un tel être pouvait à tous les instants s'oublier lui-même ; les philosophes l'ont averti par le lois de la morale. Fait pour vivre dans

168 Lord Kames, *Essays on the Principles of Morality and Natural Religion*, p.43.
169 Ibid., pp.46–7.

la société, il y pouvait oublier les autres ; les législateurs l'ont rendu à ses devoirs par les lois politique et civiles.[170]

In *TMS* Smith explains what he intends when he refers to the rule of justice:

> The rules of justice are accurate in the highest degree, and admit of no exceptions or modifications, but such as may be ascertained as accurately as the rules themselves, and which generally, indeed, flow from the very same principles with them [...]. The rules of justice may be compared to the rules of grammar; the rules of the other virtues, to the rules which critics lay down for the attainment of what is sublime and elegant in composition. The one, are precise, accurate, and indispensable. The other, are loose, vague, and indeterminate [...].[171]

An abstract definition in many respects, but one that in the *Lectures* assumes a more concrete connotation:

> The first and chief design of all civil government, is, as I observed, to preserve justice amongst the members of the state and prevent all encroachments on the individuals in it, from others of the same society [...] A man merely as a man may be injured in three respects, either 1st, in his person; or 2dly, in his reputation; or 3dly in his estate.[172]

In both definitions it is possible to observe the already established negative character of justice: it *delimitates* as it *guarantees.* Smith's definition of justice, however, is strictly linked to that of benevolence, at least because he insists on the reasons for which they differ. More specifically, it seems that justice is defined by differentiation. Regarding this, one claim seems relevant: 'The man who barely abstain from violating either the person, or the estate, or the reputation of his neighbours, has surely very little positive merit. [...] We may often fulfil all the rules of justice by sitting still and doing

---

170   *De l'esprit des lois, Oeuvres,* éd. par A. Masson, Nagel, Paris, 1950, vol.1, p.4. Similarly to Montesquieu (*Lettres Persanes*, XCIV, *Oeuvres*, vol.1, pp.187–8), also for Smith the inquiry upon the genesis of an alleged 'original contract' is simply meaningless. See *infra.*
171   *TMS*, pp.175.
172   *LJ(A)*, pp.7–8; and *WN*, 2, pp.687–8.

nothing'[173] (once again it should be noted that the source here is Stoic).[174] In fact, if this were not the case, if Smith were not to restate the 'differential risk' between passivity and action, what would constitute the difference from Locke's normative concept derived from the *lex naturae*? His famous definition[175] would simply be re-proposed; vice versa, the breaking with its normative structure is possible because Smith's idea of justice is not only derived from, or intended as the result of the just and compulsory strength of the *lex naturae* translated into the juridical system, but rather it is established as historical assumption, according to a model of economic jurisprudence. We shall see below that it is not by chance that the issues concerning 'police' never reach the stage of grazing a model that is political *stricto sensu*.

Needless to say, this should be explained. In our opinion, however, the simple juxtaposition between justice and benevolence would be inadequate. The explanation should rather focus upon the analysis of the relationship between the degrees of benevolence and justice. Smith's approach to human nature does not follow either Hobbes or Locke's schemes, as they overlook the fact that the individual is 'habitually' characterized by choices related to a criterion of 'middle conformation', which, in turn, is nothing other than the expression – habitual as well – of a social propriety, defined, via a sympathetic imagination, by an 'impartial and well-informed spectator'. In other words, this latter is a sort of 'social mirror', the 'measure' against which any human behaviour is tested according to a proper degree of any passion, which, in turn, is defined, by propriety, as social means. Of such a means, Hobbes' artifice, Locke's compact, Hutcheson's moral sense are unable to give a satisfactory explanation. For the very same reason, any interpretation that understands egoism

173   *TMS*, p.82.
174   Marcus Aurelius, *Meditations*, IX, 16.
175   'This makes him willing to quit a Condition, which however free, is full of fears and continual dangers: And 'tis not without reason, that he seeks out, and is willing to join in Society with others who are already united, or have a mind to unite for the mutual *Preservation* of their Lives, Liberties and Estates, which I call by the general Name, *Property*': Locke, *Two Treatises of Government*, II, IX, §123, p.368.

and benevolence as antithetical sentiments – setting aside Smith's distinction between unsocial and selfish passions – becomes inadequate. Inadequacy that is even more evident when the antithesis is posed in order not to be resolved, but rather to be conformed to the superior *ratio* of justice as an inevitable, or anyhow consequential, alternative to benevolence. In effect, if this latter is considered only as a perfect and therefore universal divine virtue, it is unable to provide the necessary mundane guarantees.

Although it is very difficult to deny the complexity of this passage, it is possible to observe that the twofold dualism is due to the fact that there are two problems. The first is represented by the relationship between natural and divine law. As Preti noted, in Smith, the ethics of sentiments – as it is a social disposition, *lex naturae*, distinct, if not opposed to juridical norm – would disappear as soon as 'the harmonic circle of sentiment' is under check, being unable to resolve itself in positive justice, and being forced to appeal to an infallible Judge as a last resort. Here the 'theological hat' would become inevitable: after the attempt to establish an ethics without theology, Smith should surrender to the fact of 'being unable to achieve his aim'.[176]

---

176 Preti, *Alle origini dell'etica contemporanea*, pp.149–65. Cousin (*Philosophie écossaise*, p.174; but cf. Stephen, *History of English Thought*, vol.II, p.60) noted: 'Smith n'interrompt donc point, il continue et il fortifie la tradition de la théodicée écossaise'. A different point of view is expressed by Campbell (*Adam Smith's Science of Morals*, pp.60, 70, 230 ff.; Id., 'Adam Smith's Theory of Justice, Prudence, and Beneficence', *American Economic Review*, 1967, vol.57, 2, pp.571–7), Morrow (*The Ethical and Economic Theories*, pp.54, 58), Lindgren (*The Social Philosophy of Adam Smith*, pp.145–6), and J. Viner ('Adam Smith and Laissez Faire', *Journal of Political Economy*, 1927, vol.35, April, pp.198–232), according to whom the explicit reference to divine benevolence made in *TMS* would be excluded in *WN*. In such a way, Smith would be 'free to find defects in the order of the nature, without casting reflections on the workmanship of its Author'. Cf. Macfie, *The Individual in Society*, pp.103 ff., where the discussion is deepened minutely; Bagolini, *La simpatia nella morale e nel diritto*, pp.72–3; Id., 'Sulla "Teoria dei sentimenti morali" di Adam Smith', *Rivista internazionale di filosofia del diritto*, 1977, vol.64, pp.563–4; C.M.A. Clark, 'Adam Smith and Natural Law', *Quaderni di storia dell'econ-*

Regarding this, it is possible to say that universal benevolence indeed belongs to the Superior Entity, which is, in its perfection, always divinely just. Hence, between universal benevolence and divine justice there is no difference; in its benevolence, the Superior Entity is only and always just. The inferior degrees of benevolence, instead, belong to the socially wise and prudent man. Whilst the difference between universal benevolence and divine justice is evasive, the one between human benevolence and mundane justice is fundamental; but with respect to the 'form', rather than the diverse 'intensity' of virtue – in spite of the ambiguity that we shall address later. Concerning the action of the prudent man, whilst human benevolence and mundane justice relate to him directly, universal benevolence and divine justice do so only implicitly. Preti's dualism, therefore, is acceptable only to the extent that either we juxtapose interrelated terms or we confound the two problems. By contrast, if we accept that for Smith benevolence can also be ascribed to the prudent man – according to a proper degree –, the issue changes. First of all, when Smith claims that 'the care of the universal happiness of all rational and sensible beings, is the business of God and not of man',[177] he does not limit himself to the simple acknowledgement of the difference. Rather, he underlines that men should take care of the interest of society, relying upon a mundane criteria, without omitting an essential truth: that is, benevolence finds only in God its perfect and universal expression, but humanly, it also belongs to the more humble department of the prudent man. Benevolence can also be ascribed to human beings because they are able to express its social means. Accordingly, we do not believe that in Smith it could be possible to find a twofold level of analysis, concerning a double reality; rather, two are the problems. Equally, we do not believe that there is an irreducible conflict between an ideal of perfection of life (wise man) and an ideal of preservation of life (prudent man) – as pointed out by Joseph Cropsey. The consistent problem is to define

omia politica, 1988, vol.6, 3, pp.59–86; E.G. West, *Adam Smith. The Man and his Works*, Liberty Fund, Indianapolis, 1976, pp.120 ff.
177 *TMS*, p.237.

the proper degree of the middle social agent, the middle degree of propriety. Benevolence does not escape such a logic.

Benevolence can escape this logic only if we assume an indistinct identity between benevolence and divine justice, and when, in the attempt to assign a primary role to mundane justice, we pose an undue *aut aut* between human benevolence and prudence. Not only does it escape, but it also creates a short circuit, in which what is human and divine can no longer be discerned. As a result, the prudent man would not be able to aspire to any degree of benevolence, since he is unable to aspire to the perfection of divine justice. Vice versa, if we admit that the reference to the Supreme Entity – and therefore to the divine justice – is in Smith a Lockean 'appeal to heaven', then the issue assumes a different aspect. Because it is obvious, the identity between divine justice and universal benevolence becomes secondary; but the very same benevolence is not only universal, is not only the higher expression of a perfect virtue: it admits some degrees, which cannot be absent in the propriety – which is not merit, of course – of the different passions, social and egoistic in kind.

Concerning this, Smith is unequivocal: benevolence is only an 'ornament', a perfect virtue to which nothing can be asked. Blame and punishment, therefore, are not coincidental. But it is unthinkable that the propriety of passions (also the selfish ones, which are not unsocial) can set aside an 'ordinary degree of proper beneficence', that appears to be neither blameworthy nor laudable. 'Pernicious actions are often punishable for no other reason than because they shew a want of sufficient attention to the happiness of our neighbour'. If it is true that '[b]enevolence may, perhaps, be the sole principle of action in the Deity' and, therefore, that 'so imperfect a creature as man, the support of whose existence requires so many things external to him, must often act from many other motives'; anyway, '[t]he condition of human nature were peculiarly hard, if those affections, which, by the very nature of our being, ought frequently to influence our conduct, could upon no occasion appear virtuous [...]'.[178] For this reason, we stated that it would be difficult to deny that benevolence admits some degrees; beneath which – beneath a middle custom, an appropriate

178   *TMS*, pp.301–2; 305.

degree –, blame ceases to be sufficient and there is only one remedy that is offered by a negative principle, a different 'form': mundane justice. In fact, this last does not measure the gulf between an effective social behaviour and its distance from an ideal of divine benevolence and justice; rather, it measures the manifestations, in the very same behaviour, of those predictable mundane violations, whose effects are intolerable for a social means ethically constituted in the problematic relationship among interests.

The second and more important problem, represented by the relationship between benevolence and justice, has recently been studied with more determination, ascertaining that this relationship is devoid of any extrinsic theological connotation. The declared objective is that of verifying the articulations of Smith's allegedly dominant preoccupation concerning justice, directly linking it, via politics, to the themes of *WN*, making any theoretical reference to benevolence as secondary. *De facto*, this is Haakonssen's central thesis, according to which, what specifically links the general theory of moral sentiments and jurisprudence is the concept of rights. Such a concept is certainly central to jurisprudential tradition; but the distinction between perfect rights (commutative justice) and imperfect rights (distributive justice) is, in Smith, the specific result of the distinction between positive and negative virtues. It follows that what he defines as right, as well as just, derives from the concept of injury. If this is so, the objects of natural jurisprudence are those rules establishing what we have to abstain from in order not to damage others: justice. This allows Haakonssen to claim that '[t]he concept of *"injury"* is understood in pure spectator-terms' and that what the spectator recognizes as *injury* is decisive in order to define both *absolute rights* and *justice*.[179] Consequently, it is possible to infer that there is no 'formal difference' between justice and benevolence, as both are governed by the laws established by the impartial spectator. Therefore, in spite of the philosophical relevance of Hobbes and Locke's jurisprudential models, according to which the primacy of civil law with respect to natural law was grounded upon a normative model, it is not within the categories of juridical positivism that it is possible to

179   Haakonssen, *The Science of a Legislator*, pp.99–100.

understand Smith's natural jurisprudence. Rightly, Haakonssen's argument takes up Smith's critique to Hobbes' juridical positivism, which 'presupposes that there are not moral distinctions between right and wrong'.[180]

As Haakonssen's argument emphasizes Smith's theoretical relevance of a natural jurisprudence, it sounds agreeable. There is no impediment to the idea that from a moral obligation derives a theory of justice. In the *Lectures*, the spectator has a similar role: he 'would readily go along with...', 'would justify...', 'can enter into the expectations of...', 'would conceive...'. Nevertheless, Haakonssen's interpretation gives rise to a doubt: is it possible that Smith's insistence upon justice and its link with politics could be conformed to a universal natural jurisprudence? That is, the unaccomplished project promised in the closure of *TMS* ought not to be related to a complete theory of justice, the very same that Smith was never able to fully articulate? But if this had been Smith's approach, would it not have forced him to refer to a codified system of norms that would jeopardize the impartial spectator, and therefore, the paradigmatic centrality of civil society? And if this is admissible, should it not follow that what is fundamental for Smith is the degree of the inferior virtues, rather than the primacy of natural justice, that forcibly has no relevant place in *WN*, if not in a translated form, as legal theory? And, for what reason should an essential concept like propriety be suddenly abandoned? Finally, and above all, if it is to a universal natural jurisprudence that he wishes to refer, why is there such an insistence upon a mundane justice? Is it possible to argue that, indeed because he did not reach a proper level of analytical formulation able to address all the issues that the problem presented, rather than central, the theory of justice is Smith's unaccomplished project? In the absence of this 'formal' analytical completeness, and not being allowed to count upon a historical-thematic reconstruction *à la* Montesquieu, would we not be faced with a mere jusnaturalistic approach? But then, would not its normative transposition inevitably have to weigh up much more deeply the contractualistic tradition, putting aside the generic assertion of the primacy of natural right, and confronting the problem of the

---

180   Ibid., p.148.

foundation of the concept of sovereignty? That is, given the premises of *TMS* and in sight of *WN*, would it not have been consequential to privilege an approach such as the one made possible by the analysis of the inferior virtues, in spite of the well known difficulty?

Obviously, these questions are debatable. However, an example can be explicative. In the *Lectures*, there is a passage in which, speaking about crime, Smith says that 'in all cases the measure of the punishment to be inflicted on the delinquent is the concurrence of the impartial spectator with the resentment of the injured';[181] that is, the victim delegates the revenge to the magistrate, as embodiment of the spectator. What does this mean? To appeal to a magistrate, whose action establishes the existence of a singular criterion of the norm. It is society that authorizes the victim to ask for revenge and to delegate it to the magistrate. Thus, Smith does not invoke any criterion of obligation that is not the duty (and the utility) of abstaining from damaging others; it is not mere coincidence that the peculiarity of his political paradigm is that of being part of the overlapping of the Ethical and Economical. At any rate, when the middle degree concerning the ethical relation is *singularly* violated, justice has only a suppletive role: it allows the judgement of single individuals, not human kind. As Lord Kames already noted, 'the object of human law is man, considered singly in the quality of a citizen'.[182] But if this is true, what is partially missed is exactly the *universality* of a natural jurisprudence (not as a value but as a criterion) and what arises instead is a clear intentionality. This is what creates the ambiguity: when justice is not only a value for the spectator, but empirical criterion in the hands of a spectator-magistrate, any formal difference between benevolence and justice is simultaneously required and excluded.

In *TMS*, at least two passages explain the relationship between justice and natural jurisprudence. In the first one, after having claimed that it resides in the wisdom of any state to utilize the strength of society to impede reciprocal damage, Smith concludes that:

181   *LJ(A)*, p.104.
182   Lord Kames, *Essays on the Principles of Morality and Natural Religion*, p.100.

92

The rules which it (*the wisdom of every state*) established for this purpose, constitute the civil and criminal law of each particular state or country. The principles upon which those rules either are, or ought to be founded, are the subject of a particular science, of all sciences by far the most important, but hitherto, perhaps, the least cultivated, that of natural jurisprudence; concerning which it belongs not to our present subject to enter into any detail.[183]

In the second passage, after having stated that any system of positive rights is only an attempt, more or less successful, to get close to a system of natural jurisprudence, he claimed that:

To prevent the confusion which would attend upon every man's doing justice to himself, the magistrate, in all governments that have acquired any considerable authority, undertakes to do justice to all, and promises to hear and to redress every complaint of injury. In all well-governed states too, not only judges are appointed for determining the controversies of individuals, but rules are prescribed for regulating the decisions of those judges; and these rules are, in general, intended to coincide with those of natural justice. [...] Systems of positive laws, therefore, though they deserve the greatest authority, as the records of the sentiments of mankind in different ages and nations, yet can never be regarded as accurate systems of the rules of natural justice.[184]

Hence, the relevance of justice resides both in its ability to express itself as natural jurisprudence, and in its efficacy as a system of positive justice. As testified by the insistence upon the role of the impartial spectator, if interpreted as the manifestation of the universal natural jurisprudence, justice runs the risk of being indistinguishable both from the moral doctrine and from the ethical system. But, as justice does not renounce its status as a doctrine of punishment, it cannot avoid the determination of a positive system of law. Thus, if on the one side it is improper to assume the existence of a 'formal difference' between positive and negative virtues, on the other it is impossible not to do so. In this light, we believe that Haakonssen's interpretation undervalues this aspect, and in doing so legitimates a circular self-referentiality between justice and politics. Furthermore, to put aside benevolence, rather than establishing the primacy of justice, entails some contradictions: firstly, because the way in which

183 *TMS*, p.218.
184 *TMS*, p.340.

this self-referentiality is articulated in the *Lectures of Jurisprudence* does not allow a dismissal of the positivist hypothesis; secondly, because in *WN* the primacy of justice is diluted into a legal theory. Indeed for this reason the presence of benevolence is irreducible to and not residual *vis-à-vis* justice. There would be no problem if we could advance an unequivocal 'formal difference' between justice and benevolence. Instead, a serious problem arises if, in order to maintain the centrality of a universal natural justice, we want to claim the role of 'social ethics': this is almost a contradiction in terms. Nevertheless, a fundamental aspect remains: the presence of the themes of justice as confutation of any liberalistic economic apology – an aspect for which Winch and Haakonssen's analyses are seminal. However, it is not Smith's 'analytical depth' that allows this, but rather the implicit richness of his economic jurisprudence, which never solves the overlapping between ethics, economics, and politics.

6. Middle social agent, exchange and labour

Smith's moral hermeneutic rests upon an ethical conception according to which the possible perfection of human action is not concerned with the 'means' of the human *negotium*. It rests upon a hypothesis according to which, although any human being can err, human kind as a whole cannot. In *TMS*, this is explicit and not contradicted by the suppletive role of justice, which sanctions only those individual violations whose effects would be intolerable for an ethical 'middle means' constituted by the problematic relationship between individual interests. Although not being God, in fact, man can be, on average, wise and socially just. Obviously, this might not be the case, but only as a singular individual. This is what Smith's 'science of human nature' reveals. In Weber's terms, we might perhaps distinguish between the sphere of convention (*Konvention*), legitimized by possible disapproval (*Mißbilligung*), and the sphere of right (*Recht*), legitimized by possible coercion (*Zwang*).[185] On the other hand, according to Émile Durkheim, for example, one might observe that it is not possible to find a society where individuals do not depart from the collective type, that is, from a middle social agent *typus*. From here the functions of mundane justice are derived. As negative criteria, however, they regard only individual actions, rather than the social nature of humankind. This latter, in fact, is supposed to be on average respectful and timorous of the precepts of justice.

If we reject the idea that Smith's problem resides in the definition of the proper degree of a middle social agent's affections – the middle degree of propriety that governs all the passions –, then, in spite of what Smith claims when he criticizes Mandeville and Hutcheson, there is no other option but to utterly ignore the proper degree that characterizes all the passions. Consequently, given the underlined interaction of the different analytical planes, this would imply, at least in principle, turning to the *extrema ratio* of justice, whose absolute relevance and centrality, however, do not permit to distinguish, with due clarity, Smith's 'science of human nature' from 'natural theology'. Some authoritative interpreters have argued that exactly in the tensions that such a complex passage presents, an appeal to an 'ultimate instance' cannot be disregarded. At any rate, it seems plausible to assert that this 'appeal to heaven' is simply an important but problematic residual, which has a place within the complex and contradictory configuration of justice. At this stage, in fact, the ethical realm can no longer be distinguished from the economic one.

Accordingly, it is at this point insufficient to conceive of the sympathetic principle only as a hermeneutical criterion of evaluation, and not as a criterion of action. In fact, consideration should also be given as to what precedes that principle: that is, the ethical landscape *towards* and *from* which the moral evaluation moves. This is the reason why it is almost impossible to distinguish the mechanisms that allow the translation of the 'micro moral' instance into the 'macro ethical' one. The reason is that the 'moral' hermeneutic is included in an 'ethical' vision, towards to and from which it moves. In this light, it

185   M. Weber, *Wirtschaft und Gesellschaft*, hrsg. von J. Winckelmann, J.C.B. Mohr (P. Siebeck), Tübingen, 1956, vol.1, p.17.

is also feasible to interpret the reservations expressed by Smith in Part VII of *TMS* about those systems that understand virtue as propriety:

> Deliberate actions, of a pernicious tendency to those we live with, have, besides their impropriety, a peculiar quality of their own by which they appear to deserve, not only disapprobation, but punishment; and the objects, not of dislike merely, but of resentment and revenge [...].[186]

Although it might seem to confute the interpretation proposed here, such a conclusion asserts that in a judgement concerning propriety, the same presence of reward or punishment (which is not a legal sanction inflicted by justice, but resentment and revenge) proves the *practical character* of morality, as it is ethics, rather than casuistry. Smith, certainly, goes far beyond this: after having claimed that in the common degree of moral qualities there is no virtue, he refers explicitly to the distinction between virtue and propriety. In other words, in order to act with propriety, in most cases only a common and ordinary degree of self-control is required; and for this reason, there is a significant difference between respectable and amiable virtues, as previously shown by Hume. More specifically, in the opening of Part II of *TMS* Smith maintains that there is a distinct propriety and impropriety concerning merit or demerit. However, this does not alter the matter. In effect, in the long footnote at the end of Section I of Part II, he clarifies that the distinction stems from the fact that whilst the approbation of propriety requires not only that we should entirely sympathize with the person who acts, but also that we should perceive the perfect concordance between his sentiments and our own, in the case of approbation of the merit or demerit, no actual correspondence of sentiments is required. Hence, it is indifferent what is felt by the man who is benefited from or is damaged by an action worthy of merit or demerit. Therefore, if in some exceptional cases the criterion of means can be left aside, the social criterion of judgement can never be ignored, because, as Smith observes, it is not only a mundane judgement, but also a judgement based on experience.

Thus, there is a difference between mere propriety and an ethically conformed propriety. The latter is open to the scrutiny of the

---

186   *TMS*, p.294.

impartial spectator, for whom, anyhow, not only the inferior virtues, but also benevolence has its proper degree – although, *in se*, benevolence could aspire not only to social propriety but also, and above all, to merit. As a result, albeit benevolence is only an 'ornament', yet it is unthinkable that the propriety of the different passions (also the egoistic ones, which are not unsocial) could be separated from an 'ordinary degree of proper beneficence', which is neither blameworthy nor laudable. Not only because the damaging actions are often due to insufficient attention to the happiness of others; not only because the human condition would be particularly hard if the affections present in our behaviour were not, under any circumstances, worthy of appraisal; but also because, if this were not the case, Smith's critique to Mandeville and Hutcheson would be both incongruent and useless. For this, the ethical realm cannot be distinguished from the economical one.

This seems to be a legitimate conclusion. What is at stake is not the evaluation of the relationship between *TMS* and *WN*, but rather, and even before, the evaluation of the same *TMS*. Here, as Costa noted, the difficulty resides in understanding that, because there is no distinction between ethical and economic order, there is no necessary relationship between the middle degree of benevolence and philanthropy, which is the reciprocal of subjection. Better still, it seems that there is no reason to support the idea that a twofold biunique relationship between *benevolence* and *ethics* and between *egoism* and *the economic sphere* do exists. In reality, many authors have underlined the relationship between ethics and the economic sphere, but privileging, always and anyhow, the primacy of egoistic passion over the social passions. Nevertheless, it is one thing to claim that the anthropological complexity of the prudent man is such that it is never possible to separate the ethical and the economic spheres, exactly because egoism and altruism always interact; it is quite another to claim apparently the same thing, but to argue that, although the prudent man cannot be represented as a Hobbesian wolf – being socially prompt to exchange – he is entirely subjected to egoistic passions, that exclude any possible benevolence. The substantial difference is this: in the first train of thought, the twofold and biunique relationship is entirely unjustified, because if any passion exists, *simultaneously*, in the political, ethical and economical spheres, the problem resides in the determination of the propriety and therefore in the 'degree' of those passions. In the second interpretative line, the biunique relationships is foundational and therefore indispensable, as it is assumed that, although the 'degree' is pertinent to different passions, these latter are *previously* considered as inherent to such a twofold biunique relationship, according to which benevolence pertains *only* to the realm of ethics and egoism *only* to the economic realm. Thus, there is no reason why we have to accept the second line of interpretation, which, at best, can be amended by an appeal to justice. This, at least, can confirm – and it will do so – that, in the interaction between ethics and economics, politics cannot surface as a proper 'canon'.

Thus, to argue – as Cropsey[187] does – that the paradigm of the commercial society requires that benevolence should be set aside, is tantamount to relying upon a perspective that denies Smith's reflection upon the middle degree of passions. Similarly, to claim, as William D. Grampp,[188] that in *TMS homo oeconomicus* is 'a disembodied creature', unable to explain the main characteristics of the economic processes, leads to the exclusion of any possible interaction between ethical and economical action. At any rate, it is worth noting that these approaches have not been entirely abandoned. For example, in spite of the different theoretical context, Jerry Evensky's reflection[189] is no different in its outcome, as he assumes a gap between an *ideal* and a *real* society, which finds support neither in *TMS* nor in *WN*. The same could be said of those scholars who explicitly argue that Smith's genius resides not in the refusal of the Empiricist approach, but rather in the fact that he brought it to its extreme logical consequence, eliminating the arbitrary hypothesis of benevolence.[190] It is not by chance that a seminal author such as Hirschman, after having

---

187 Cropsey, *Polity and Economy*, p.33.
188 W.D. Grampp, 'Adam Smith and the Economic Man', *Journal of Political Economy*, 1948, vol.56, 4, pp.315–36.
189 J. Evensky, 'The Evolution of Adam Smith's Views on Political Economy', *History of Political Economy*, 1989, vol.21, 1, pp.123–45.
190 E. Screpanti, S. Zamagni, *Profilo di storia del pensiero economico*, NIS, Roma, 1991, pp.69–70.

argued for 'the Smithian farewell to benevolence', reminds us that 'the economy is in fact liable to perform poorly without a minimum of benevolence'.[191] Hence, in spite of his critical intentions, Campell is therefore more convincing when he claims that in *TMS* there is no moral justification for the economic system presented in *WN*. In effect, it is not of justification that we should speak, but rather of a possible continuity in the same theoretical approach.[192]

As Skinner noted, the alleged contrast between sympathy and self-interest is the result of a mistaken interpretation of the two terms. In fact, if it could be said that Smith simply describes a general tendency of human nature and of some of its main economic consequences, it should be acknowledged that the pursuit of 'self-regarding goals' is always worthy of moral approval.[193] This means that moral approval is not bound to a supreme ideal of benevolence from which it moves. Moral approval is implicit in economic behaviour that, pursuing a *measured interest* in the perspective given by an *inevitable interlacing* of interests, shows their balanced integration in a middle social degree, rather than the possible *coincidentia* between benevolence and self-interest. It would be very odd to interpret Smith as a utopian philanthropic thinker; actually, the problem resides somewhere else. The middle social degree, rather than being an estimate of well-being due to everybody, reveals what is socially indispensable. In this perspective – as Hirschman observed –, 'an activity such as the rationally conducted acquisition of wealth could be categorized and implicitly endorsed as a calm passion that would at the same time be strong and able to triumph over a variety of turbulent (yet weak) passions'.[194]

Thus, the emphasis placed by Smith upon the prudent man is entirely intentional. He is a man who acts with rationality after having

191   A.O. Hirschman, *Essays in Trespassing. Economics to Politics and beyond*, Cambridge University Press, Cambridge, 1981, p.299. More in general, R. Anspach, 'The Implications of the Theory of Moral Sentiments for Adam Smith's Economic Thought', *History of Political Economy*, 1972, vol.4, Spring, pp.176– 206; M.L. Pesante, *Economia e politica*, F. Angeli, Milano, 1986, pp.16, 25–6.
192   Campbell, *Adam Smith's Science of Morals*, p.52.
193   Skinner, *A System of Social Science*, p.107.
194   Hirschman, *The Passions and the Interests*, p.66.

evaluated the situation; he does not put at risk his standard of living, but he prefers to postpone immediate pleasure for a future and more intense one. In short, he is a middle social agent aware that to the degree of the 'inferior virtue of prudence' is connected both the maintenance and the development of human *negotium*. Or, better still, the prudent man is a middle social agent in whose acting the realization of the proper degree of the relationship between benevolence and self-interest is expressed. At this point it is once again worth reflecting upon the first lines of *TMS*:

> How selfish soever man may be supposed, there are evidently some principles in his nature, which interest him in the fortune of others, and render their happiness necessary to him [...].[195]

In this passage, even before a 'moral hermeneutic' (this is only the prologue), it is possible to grasp the ethical landscape upon which it will be drawn. In the sentence 'and render their happiness necessary to him' an entire dialectic of needs, a social articulation of the economic relations proper to the action of the prudent man is prefigured. In reality, Smith is rather less optimistic than how his commentators portrayed him. For example, in the concluding part of Book I of *WN*, he says that the three classes constituting society do not have sufficient awareness of the fact that their own interest is indissolubly linked to general interest. The landlords, independently 'of any plan or project of their own', are indolent and incapable of understanding 'the consequences of any publick regulation'. Those who depend upon wages, by contrast, are less informed and well educated. Hence, in the government of the *res publica*, they will have no voice. Finally, those who live by profit, although better informed, will always be more interested in widening the market and narrowing the competition. Nevertheless, the invisible hand[196] governs the interests of each class,

---

195   *TMS*, p.9.
196   Smith utilized this locution for the first time in a completely different setting, in the *History of Astronomy* (*EPS*, p.49): A.L. Macfie, 'The Invisible Hand of Jupiter', *Journal of the History of Ideas*, 1971, vol.32, October–December, pp.595–9. We shall find it, in the very same terms, in *WN*. Cf. A.M. Iacono, 'Adam Smith e la metafora della "mano invisibile"', *Teoria*, 1985, vol.5,

so that, even under the worst possible administration, the effort of each man to better his own condition and that of others 'is every where much greater than that of injudicious and unsuccessful ones'.[197]

Although it is extremely different from the nineteenth century apology of *laissez-faire*, the image representing such an effort is the Market. From this perspective, one cannot question the intention underlying Smith's metaphor of the invisible hand. He certainly believed that the pursuit of self-interest was an unintentional part of, and contributed to the pursuit of the general interest. However, in order to avoid the mistake of transforming Smith into a banal utilitarian, from the outset, it is necessary to notice the indeterminacy and interchangeableness of individual aims, because such a non-subjective perspective is incompatible with the liberalistic contextualization. The issue of the market, its role, its explication via the metaphor of the invisible hand, do not have an immediate ideological connotation; they are given data, confirmed by the proceedings of human *negotium*. The ideological value is consequent to the naturalization of a social datum, re-elaborated via the analysis of the division of labour. It would be a mistake to think that the difference is of secondary importance: to naturalize the market and assuming and exhibiting it as a 'value' *sans phrase* are two very different ideological operations.

pp.77–94; J. Persky, 'Adam Smith's Invisible Hand', *Journal of Economic Perspectives*, 1989, vol.3, 4, pp.195–201; S. Ahmad, 'Adam Smith's Four Invisible Hands', *History of Political Economy*, 1990, vol.22, 1, pp.137–44; J.R. Davis, 'Adam Smith on the Providential Reconciliation of Individual and Social Interests: Is Man Led by an Invisible Hand or Misled by a Sleight of Hand?', *History of Political Economy*, 1990, vol.22, 2, pp.341–52; H. Defalvard, 'La main invisible: mythe et réalité du marché comme ordre spontané', *Revue d'économique Politique*, 1990, vol.100, 6, pp.870–83; D.A. Martin, 'Economics as Ideology: On Making "The Invisible Hand" Invisible', *Review of Social Economy*, 1990, vol.48, 3, pp.272–87; E. Rothschild, 'Adam Smith and the Invisible Hand', *American Economic Review*, 1994, vol.84, 2, pp.319–22; J.D. Bishop, 'Adam Smith's Invisible Hand Argument', *Journal of Business Ethics*, 1995, vol.14, 3, pp.165–80.

197   *WN*, 1, p.342. It is also important to consider here the relationship between 'invisible hand' and 'unintended consequences' underlined by Brown (*Adam Smith's Economics*, pp.135–43).

In *WN*, after having recognized the distinction between labour and property (accumulation), Smith is not at all interested in defining an ideological foundation for the market. This latter is only the landscape against which the analysis of the division of labour is articulated – as Marx, Schumpeter, and more recently Maurice Brown, have noted. This confirms the relevance and the centrality of the market, but excludes any ideological liberalistic value. No *Harmonielehre*, no argumentation *à la* Bastiat is in place here. Smith says:

> A puppy fawns upon its dam, and a spaniel endeavours by a thousand attractions to engage the attention of its master who is at dinner, when it wants to be fed by him. Man sometimes uses the same arts with his brethren [...]. He has not time, however, to do this upon every occasion. In civilized society he stands at all times in need of the cooperation and assistance of great multitudes, while his whole life is scarce sufficient to gain the friendship of a few persons.[198]

If we compare the above passage with the earlier mentioned opening of *TMS*, the principle of nature that induces man to be interested 'in the fortune of others, and render their happiness necessary to him' becomes evident: it is a reciprocal dependence, the constant need 'of the cooperation and assistance of great multitudes'. In this anthropological *datum*, the dialectic between exchange and the evolution of the division of labour is 'revealed'. A social process confirms such an anthropological datum, making a leap forward, which may appear, in effect, an 'ideological leap'. Such advancement, however, is rather different from the one that the liberalistic tradition pretends to ascribe to Smith's *homo oeconomicus*. Certainly, following on from the above passage, we find the famous *adagio* in which Smith affirms that it is not from the benevolence of the butcher, but from his interest that we can expect the satisfaction of our needs. However, if what we have said until now is correct, then to halt at that sentence would make no sense at all.

---

198 *WN*, 1, p.26. It is necessary here to recall Simmel's statement, according to which, as man is the animal who exchanges (*tauschende Tier*), he can be said to be an objective animal (*das objektive Tier*) (*Philosophie des Geldes, Gesammelte Werke*, Duncker & Humblot, Berlin, 1958, vol.1, p.306).

At this stage, we need to look back a little. Another passage from *WN* should be quoted in full. In the second Chapter of Book I, Smith wrote:

> Whether this propensity [to truck, barter, and exchange one thing for another] be one of those principles in human nature, of which no further account can be given; or whether, as seems more probable, it be the necessary consequence of the faculties of reason and speech, it belongs not to our present subject to enquiry.[199]

This passage is not the result of a rhetorical rambling. What Smith has in mind here is another passage from the *Lectures in Jurisprudence*, where we can read: 'If we should enquire into the principle in the human mind on which this disposition of trucking is founded, it is clearly the natural inclination every one has to persuade'. And more:

> Thus we have shewn that different genius is not the foundation of this disposition to barter, which is the cause of the division of labour. The real foundation of it is that principle to perwade which so much prevail in human nature. When any arguments are offered to perswade, it is always expected that they should have their proper effect [...]. We ought then mainly to cultivate the power of persuasion, and indeed we do so without intending it. Since a whole life is spent in the exercise of it, a ready method of bargaining with each other must undoubtedly be attained.[200]

Undoubtedly, such a power of persuasion – to which it is easy to attribute an incorrect weight, either by ignoring it or by giving to it too much relevance – is in many ways enigmatic as, although touched upon in Smith's previous reflection upon language, it has not been elaborated. If a sort of proximity to the ethical neo-empiricism and therefore a sharp 'anachronism' were admissible, one might recall Charles L. Stevenson,[201] according to whom the persuasive methods, although not rational, cannot be said to be irrational, as they make no less use of the rational medium of language and, therefore, become an

---

199   *WN*, I, p.25.
200   *LJ(A)*, p.352; *LJ(B)*, p.493–4.
201   L. Stevenson, *Ethics and Language*, Yale University Press, New Haven, 1944, ch. 6.

integral part of ordinary discourse. Pure 'anachronism', indeed. That Smith may have had a 'similar' idea concerning exchange is partially proved by the fact that in *WN* he poses the problem in the same terms. At any rate, it is certainly more correct to ask why he also claims that the issue 'belongs not to our present subject to enquiry'.

The obvious answer seems to be that Smith had changed his mind, but this reply is too simplistic. It is of a certain relevance here to keep in mind the difference between unsocial and selfish passions as it is presented in *TMS*, although the confutation of the 'dogmatic' of egoism cannot be derived from the simple consideration according to which egoism would be a 'fictitious proposition' that relies upon an axiom from which one can deductively proceed in order to demonstrate the baselessness of the selfish system. This idea – proposed, among others, by Hans Vaihinger, in the wake of Henry T. Buckle's interpretation and, above all, of Friedrich A. Lange's *Geschichte des Materialismus* – is construed upon the usual misunderstanding concerning the relationship between *TMS* and *WN*.[202] It is rather possible to hypothesize, as Claudio Napoleoni did, that in *WN* Smith did not consider essential to clarify what he intended with the locution 'power of persuasion'; however, it would be incorrect to assert that Smith might have been interested in writing about something else. As Winch noted, in the opening of Book IV, Smith stated that the system of political economy is a 'branch of the science of a statesman or legislator'.

At this point it is useful to return back to the notion of prudence. If persuasion has not a Sophistic value, can it be interpreted as a reciprocal *take-into-consideration* – something similar to the Ciceronian 'quae virtus ex providendo est appelata prudentia'[203] –, as a means through which, being alien to deceit as a usual course of action, the exchange between prudent men would be simultaneously useful and conformed to reciprocal interest? We believe that the answer is positive. Although, in fact, it is true that in Smith there is a preponderant Stoic influence, nonetheless, a weak Epicurean vein can be noted.

202 H. Vaihinger, *Des Philosophie des Als Ob*, Meiner, Leipzig, 1922.
203 Cicero, *De leg.*, I, 60.

Notoriously, in Part VII of *TMS*, Smith criticizes the Epicurean system, to the point of claiming that it totally conflicts with what he maintains. However, in admitting its plausibility, he leaves an important door open. As it is known, in the *Letter to Meneceus*, Epicurus not only claims that, since it teaches us that one's life cannot be happy if it is not conducted wisely, prudence should be considered the highest good (something that is not sufficient for Smith), but also that it is 'a wise calculation inquiring the cause of any choice and refusal'. Now, Smith's affirmation, according to which '[i]t is that which is most apt to occur to those who are endeavouring to persuade others to regularity of conduct',[204] seems to comment upon this sentence.

Possibly, our 'philology' is here rather hazardous, but we believe that the power of persuasion cannot but lead to the recognition that, in the commercial society, each *alter* is potentially an *ego*. As Dupuy noted, here is given a sort of *autoréference indirecte*, according to which it is evident that Smith was interested in the behaviour of human kind, rather than in those of the single individuals and, consequently, the *suppletive role* of justice facing prudence is clear – if, at least, the underlined ambiguity between an ethical universalistic fundament and the mundane exigency of normative effectiveness is true.

In this light, the famous *adagio* becomes indeed more problematic. In effect, although Smith writes that '[i]t is not from the benevolence of the butcher, the brewer, or the baker, that we expect our dinner, but from their regard to their own interest', in a long premise he describes the sociality of human beings and their interest toward reciprocal cooperation, and so he concludes:

> In civilized society he [the man] stands at all times in need of the cooperation and assistance of great multitudes, while his whole life is scarce sufficient to gain the friendship of a few persons.[205]

It is true that, shortly after, he claims that it is in vain that an individual might expect aid from the pure benevolence of others; however, it is worth giving consideration to precisely what he affirms:

204   Epicurus, *Lett. to Men.*, 132; cf. *TMS*, p.299.
205   *WN*, 1, p.26–7.

> But man has almost constant occasion for the help of his brethren, and it is in vain for him to expect it from their benevolence only. He will be more likely to prevail if he can interest their *self-love* in his favour, and shew them that it is for their own advantage to do for him what he requires of them.[206]

We believe that two nuances are of great relevance here: firstly, the word 'only' indicates that Smith does not exclude benevolence; and secondly, on the basis of the following argumentation, the sentence 'if he can interest their self-love' might imply the idea of arousing, of persuading and mediating between benevolence and interest, rather than simply turning the egoism of others in our favour. In effect, although Smith claims that exchange is not the result of benevolence, he does not deny the interaction between benevolence and self-interest. Fundamentally, he does not state that it is pure interest that makes the market function. More exactly, he affirms that only the beggars can partially live upon the benevolence of others and not, by contrast, that the prudent man could and should live solely according to his own self-interest. Hence, the words 'by treaty' 'by barter', 'by purchase' refer explicitly to the power of persuasion of which he discussed in the *Lectures*. As Simmel observed, exchange presupposes an objective evaluation, a reflection, a reciprocal recognition, derived from the tensions present in the market.

In short, the unconscious conjugation of benevolence and interest within a universe that is never singular, is an act of persuasion that the prudent man carries out in the marketplace. As Haakonssen noted, a fully developed philosophy of unintended consequences, derived from Mandeville and mediated by Hume, is clear here. In fact, it is not necessary to deny that the logic of the persuasive action is instrumental. As Smith said in his *Lectures on Rhetoric*, persuasion is a rhetorical form 'that magnifies all the arguments of the one side and diminishes or conceals those that might be brought on the side

---

206 *WN*, 1, p.26. The Maussian anthropological approach fails to understand this passage: J.T. Godbout, *L'Esprit du don*, Editions de la découverte, Paris-Montréal, 1992.

contrary to that which it is designed that we should favour'.[207] However, as Talcoltt Parsons argued, even within an instrumental action, the relational problem arises when 'alter becomes significant not only passively as a means or condition of the attainment of ego's goal, but his reactions become a constitutive part of the system which includes ego's own goal striving'.[208] Again, the needs of the individual bring us back to mankind, where prudence is determinant, although only justice can provide for the individual (and therefore to mankind) the negative guarantees necessary for a common life. In short, Smith's sharp departure from Mandeville occurs when he maintains that an unintended consequence is not necessarily instrumental or morally blameworthy.

As it is well-known, twentieth-century European culture has insistently dwelled upon this aspect, either directly or indirectly. Besides Parsons, the most obvious reference is Weber's analysis of the relationship between 'scruples' and 'interest' in relation to the specific degree of the bourgeois-capitalistic development. No less pertinent is to recall once again Simmel's *Philosophie des Geldes*, where exchange is described as the most noble, pure, and elevated interaction (*Wechselwirkung*) characterizing human life. Furthermore, it is not possible to ignore Durkheim's *De la division du travail social*, in which, by saying that exchange implies two parties who re-ciprocally depend one upon the other (as they are both incomplete), such a mutual dependence is emphasized.[209]

---

207 *LRBL*, p.62. In these terms, the argumentation has a Stoic ascendant: Epictetus, *Ench.*, I, 8, 7; Seneca, *Ad Lucilium Epist.*, I, x, 81; Marcus Aurelius, *Meditations*, VI, 50.

208 T. Parsons, *The Social System*, Free Press, Glencoe (Ill.), 1959, p.70.

209 M. Weber, *Der protestantische Ethik und der Geist des Kapitalismus*, *Gesammelte Aufsätze zur Religionssoziologie*, J.C.B. Mohr (P. Siebeck), Tübingen, 1978, vol.1, p.42; Simmel, *Philosophie des Geldes*, *Gesammelte Werke*, vol.1, p.33; È. Durkheim, *De la division du travail social*, Alcan, Paris, 1960, p.125; but cf. S. Moscovici, *La machine à faire des dieux. Sociologie et psychologie*, Fayard, Paris, 1988. As problematic reference, we can also recall Veblen's distinction between financial and economic behaviour, above all, when he underlines the impersonality entailed by the modern industrial system: T. Veblen, *The Theory of the Leisure Class*, Kelley, New York, 1965.

In short, we believe that the above arguments help to define a realm within which the primacy of social ethics upon individual morality is clearly expressed. In other words, we believe that the action of the prudent man is directly distinct from any individualistic morality. If this is so, there is no contradiction – either implicit or explicit – between *TMS* and *WN*. Smith's economic project cannot be said 'other' when compared with his moral system: firstly, because – if Haakonssen's distinction between 'contextual knowledge' and 'system knowledge' is correct – it is not possible to speak of a moral system in normative and therefore individualistic terms; secondly, as benevolence is a kind of practical behaviour, proper to social ethics, rather than a moral virtue belonging to a just man's good conscience, distinct from *homo oeconomicus*. The impartial spectator does not judge human actions normatively, according to a *summum bonum*; rather, he considers the degree of human passions according to a practice that appears, socially, to be the most convenient and appropriate for the specific situation or experience. Hence, the eventual condemnation is not only mundane, human blame, but clearly social. Again, exchange, the 'naturalised' social relationship, represents the place of decantation of such a logic of action.

In this synthetic image, both the middle degree of human passions, and the consequent acting of the prudent man are presented via the dialectic occurring between benevolence and self-interest. This is an elementary dialectic of needs, based upon experience. Accordingly, we do not understand the sense of the old but never entirely neglected observation according to which a 'conflit logique entre deux tendances, l'une rationaliste, qui dérive de Newton, l'autre presque sceptique, ou, plus précisément, naturaliste, qui dérive de Hume', is here expressed.[210] Rather, we believe that Smith reaches the highest elaboration of an ethical inductive paradigm, in which there is no longer a privileged place for the spectator, and where the pure 'impersonal market'[211] is impersonal because it has become a completely socialized and transparent instance. It is not by chance that the inductive nature of the ethical paradigm makes the disjunction be-

---

210 Halévy, *La formation du radicalisme philosophique*, vol.1, p.192.
211 Macfie, *The Individual in Society*, pp.103–4.

tween the contradictory characters of the market impossible. This can happen thanks to the relationship between epistemological and moral instances, synthesized by the role played by sympathy. Not for this reason should sympathy be interpreted in a way that is incompatible with *TMS*. More simply, facing the above mentioned ethical landscape, sympathy, from being a criterion of possible approval by identification, is transformed into a social criterion of possible comparison by association. In this, any affinity between sympathy and benevolence is neither implicit, nor necessary: it is not due to sympathy that the prudent man acts, comparatively, within society. Sympathy is 'logically' inherent to the *ratio* of exchange, given the real intermingling of interests that exists in the market, and that requires comparison. An intermingling that, totally alien to any philanthropic criterion, cannot be intended as separated from a 'measured' integration between benevolence and self-love. In this sense, there is no contradiction: not because of an alleged philanthropic character, but because of the comparison among human interests – resulting from the abandonment of 'that early and rude state of society which precedes both the accumulation of stock and the appropriation of land [...]'[212] – sympathy becomes inherent to the logic of exchange. A comparison in which the individual is not sympathetic to the interests of others; however, because he is socially induced to think of his own interest as being related to others, he will compare it to that of others. As Peter L. Danner noted, what, in the first place, expresses this harmony, is the 'notion of sympathy' and then, via an economic actualization, the concept of economic good as an 'exchangeable value' that, in order to be produced, necessitates both the support and cooperation of others.[213] The ethical becomes the expression of the mediation inherent to the economic logic of the market. According to Morrow, sympathy is the necessary presupposition for the economic logic underpinning *WN*: as the individual is 'social by nature', when he compares his interest with that of others, he acts in the most

---

212   *WN*, 1, p.65.
213   P.L. Danner, 'Sympathy and Exchangeable Value: Keys to Adam Smith's Social Philosophy', *Review of Social Economy*, 1976, vol.34, December, pp.317–31; Brown, *Adam Smith's Economics*, p.98.

advantageous way for the achievement of 'common welfare'.[214] Once again, it should be said that the criterion of sympathy should not be intended as an aim, but as a *neutral means*, although it refers to an explicit ethical landscape.

In this light, an overlapping between ethics and economics is established via the paradigm of commercial society. On the basis of this overlapping, Smith elaborated the fundamental mediation – both anthropological and ethical-economic – involved in labour. Smith wrote:

> Each animal is still obliged to support and defend itself, separately and independently, and derives no sort of advantages from that variety of talents with which nature has distinguishes its fellows.[215]

As Hegel would later claim, differently from animals, man 'in his dependence proves his universality and his ability to become independent, firstly, by multiplying his wants [*Vervielfältigung der Bedürfnisse*]'.[216] In the exchange, in fact, the universal character of human activity is shown in the complementarity of the social division of labour, that produces that common stock 'where every man may purchase whatever part of the produce of other men's talents he has occasion for'.[217] Certainly, before Smith, many authors had reflected upon the specificity of human labour.[218] Among others, Hume, for example, explicitly argued that labour is a specific anthropological

214 Morrow, *The Ethical and Economic Theories*, pp.43–4. Cf. S. Hollander, 'Adam Smith and the Self-Interest Axiom', *Journal of Law and Economics*, 1977, vol.20, April, pp.133–52.

215 *WN*, 1, p.30.

216 W.G.F. Hegel, *Die 'Rechtsphilosophie' von 1820. Mit Hegels Vorlesungsnotizen 1821–1825*, in *Vorlesungen über Rechtsphilosophie 1818–1831*, hrsg. von K.-H. Ilting, Frommann-Holzboog, Stuttgart-Bad Cannstatt, 1974, Bd.2, p.634; *Philosophy of Right*, trans. by S.W Dyde, Batoche Books Limited, Kitchener, 2001, p.160.

217 *WN*, 1, p.30.

218 E.A.J. Johnson, *Predecessors of Adam Smith*, King & Son, New York, 1937, pp.243–56. Relevant are the etymological observations upon *Art* and *Ingenious Labour* (pp.259–77).

mediator.[219] For Smith, however, labour assumes a systematic rather than episodic relevance. It is the source of all values: their cause and measure.

We believe that it is unnecessary to stress such a well-known aspect – although it presents some disputable issues.[220] At any rate, what is relevant to our endeavour is the fact that the mediation of labour confirms the 'inevitable' relationship between benevolence and self-love. The mediation of labour is so because it solidifies the 'means' of the social agent, the role of sympathy as 'comparison by association'. In this way, the paradigm of the commercial society is projected towards a model within which property and accumulation reorganize social relationships between individuals that are social by definition. A new criterion of measure, adequate to a new dialectic of needs, arises. It is not by accident that there is a *social division* of labour: not only can its technical aspects be distinguished, but also its duration can be subdivided. Labour and time, tendentially, become a unique element: Marx's interpretation is unescapable here. As in Newtonian terms a unique temporal scansion exists, so there exists a sole measure, a 'crucial experiment', able to combine, in exchange, different labours. This 'experiment' is represented by social labour. In the marketplace, money establishes what labour measures in terms of time; social time of production and reproduction of a model within which the middle social agent, the prudent man, expresses, *in primis*, the middle degree of the ethical relationship; hence, the 'impossible' alternative between ethical and economic order; and finally, the

219 D. Deleule, *Hume et la naissance du libéralisme économique*, Aubier Montaigne, Paris, 1979.
220 With regard to the twofold criteria of 'contained' and 'commanded' labour in Smith's determination of the theory of value [*WN*, 1, pp.47–71, but also *LJ(A)*, pp.353 ff., *LJ(B)*, pp.494 ff.], see Ricardo, *On the Principles of Political Economy and Taxation*, in *The Works and Correspondence of David Ricardo*, ed. by P. Sraffa, Cambridge University Press, Cambridge, 1951–1973, vol.1, pp.13–14; Malthus, *Principles of Political Economy*, Kelley, New York, 1964, pp.83 ff.; and Marx, *Theorien über den Mehrwert*, *MEW*, Bd.26, 1, pp.41 ff. But cf. also R.L. Meek, *Studies in the Labour Theory Value*, Lawrence & Wishart, London, 1973; S. Hollander, *The Economics of Adam Smith*, University of Toronto Press, Toronto, 1973; C. Napoleoni, *Smith Ricardo Marx. Observations on the History of Economic Thought*, Blackwell, Oxford, 1975.

interlacing of interests, which does not shows the possible *coincidentia* between benevolence and self-love, but rather their 'measured' integration in a middle social order. In short, the proper degree of propriety is established by the 'calm and calculating' actions of the prudent man, who is the only *artificem* of the 'impossible' separation between ethics and economics. Not only, as John G.A. Pocock argued, does Smith determine a theory of *homo faber* according to which human labour represents the force that creates values, but also, as Deleuze noted, in Smith, labour alters the order of wealth.[221] Labour is the paradigm around which is established what Michel Foucault has defined as *mathesis*, intended as the general science of all the possible orders, as a 'casualité circulaire',[222] within which labour is simultaneously the object of the analysis and its representative instrument, limit and fulfilment of an expansive anthropology that, even though based on an experience detached from an incautious naturalism, cannot contemplate the 'finitude' as a specific modern perspective – which would be typical of Ricardo's pessimism.

Besides this, the relationship between labour and time is of great relevance with regard to another fundamental aspect: because it expresses a duration, labour overcomes the mere anthropomorphic instrumentality, becoming social labour as such, and therefore subject to comparison and measure. Commenting upon Hobbes' famous passage according to which wealth is power – 'Riches joined with liberality, is power' –, Smith observes that those who inherit a reasonable fortune do not acquire, *per se*, such a power. Although Smith's intention is quite different, here, it seems that a Machiavellian influence is at work. In effect, he believes that wealth can generate power only when it implies the ability to command the time of labour of others, otherwise it is inert money.[223]

To this passage should be accredited a high relevance. Because labour no longer represents a mere anthropological mediation, it

221   G. Deleuze, *Foucault*, Minuit, Paris, 1986, p.135.
222   M. Foucault, *Les mots et les choses*, PUF, Paris, 1966, pp.267–9.
223   As Pesante observes: 'Su questa contrapposizione nell'uso della ricchezza è fondata tutta la storia del rapporto tra commercio e libertà in Europa [...]' (*Economia e politica*, p.17).

becomes the link connecting the already occurring overlapping between ethics and economics, and the political sphere. The same passage expresses the clearest contraposition between Smith and Hobbes, because, thanks to labour, it excludes both the possibility and the necessity of measuring oneself with the limit constituted by the *finitude of the Political* as pure domination, detached both from the ethical and the political *ratio*: something that for Smith is simply indissoluble. In the contraposition between the definition of a market ideology based upon a possessive individualism, on the 'fear of death',[224] and the one based upon an inevitable but 'measured' integration between benevolence and self-love, at this stage shaped by labour, an entire and efficacious alternative to the Hobbesian image of the Political becomes fully developed: an alternative embedded entirely in modern 'social thought'. Labour is the means in a society now released not from the reality, but from the ideology of *bellum omnium contra omnes*, and in which the 'fear of death' is no longer exorcised by a vague naturalistic optimism *à la* Shaftesbury, or by a moral power *à la* Locke, but rather by the peculiarity of a new mediation created by labour as producer of wealth and, therefore, of the basis on which political power can be exerted. Human activity has become the generator of a new order: ethical, economical, and therefore political.

From *TMS* to *WN*, the profound revision of the paradigm characterizing the eighteenth century consists above all of this new order, efficaciously represented by the overlapping that Smith's theory articulates via the propriety that governs the different social and egoistic passions. Without any discontinuity, the overlapping between ethics and economics is extended to the Political; via labour, it defines

---

224 Hobbes, *Elements*, I, 1, 6–7, I, 2, 13 (*The English Works*, ed. by W. Molesworth, Scientia Verlag, Aalen, 1962, vol.4, pp.83, 92), *De cive*, I, 3, 7 (*Opera philosophica, quae latine scripsit, omnia*, ed. by W. Molesworth, Scientia Verlag, Aalen, 1961, vol.2, pp.162–3), *De homine*, XI, 6 (*Opera*, vol.2, p.98); *Leviathan*, I, XI, XIII; II, XX (*The English Works*, vol.3, pp.85 ss, 113, 188–9). See L. Strauss, *The Political Philosophy of Hobbes*, Clarendon, Oxford, 1936; more specifically, Borkenau, *Der Übergang vom feudalen zum bürgerlichen Weltbild*; Macpherson, *The Political Theory of Possessive Individualism: Hobbes to Locke*.

an anthropological *mathesis* and a social order that surpass both any naturalistic apriorism and any characterization of the Political as pure domination. It is not by accident that 'death' and 'labour' – the simple domination and the mediation operated by needs – would become the two prongs of that radical and conflictual relationship, which in Hegel's reflection would be destined to be assumed as the fundament of Modernity. With the exchange, the reciprocal human recognition [*Anerkennen*] becomes progressively unlinked 'from a singularity that is predisposed to accept the risk to die', from 'harming one another'. To define the realm of political economy – 'die einfachen Prinzipien der Sache', as Hegel claims – is now 'the labour of all for all'.[225] The new link between the Ethical and Economical established by labour erases the Classical and the Renaissance image of the Political. Within the modern public sphere, political experience no longer refers to the effort of a citizen-warrior or to a prince free from needs satisfied by others, but to a *bourgeois* who, in order to participate in the public (economic) sphere, has delegated to others his *sûreté*.

Yet in Smith, to whom Hegel would be obliged to pay attention, this is the role played by the prudent man *contra* Hobbes' ideology. Prudence is a private virtue according to which the middle social agent 'works' in the new public (economic) sphere of civil society. A virtue thanks to which he recognizes the 'value' of the political spirit as public utility, of which he does not believe himself to be the main creator. Thus, although it is for the overlapping between ethics and economics that it is impossible to delineate either a theory of the State or a political categorization, however, the Political does not remain

---

225 Hegel's interests in Smith is a strategic passage in the relationship between philosophy and political economy. Smith's presence in the German culture is documented in M.E. Vopelius, *Die altliberalen Oekonomen und die Reformzeit*, Fisher, Stuttgart, 1968. What is interesting in Hegel's reading of Smith concerns the themes of needs, labour, plebs and, therefore, the relationship between *bürgerliche Gesellschaft* and State (G.W.F. Hegel, *Gesammelte Werke*, Bd. 8, pp.223–7; Bd.9, pp.193 ff.; Id. *Die 'Rechtsphilosophie' von 1820. Mit Hegels Vorlesungsnotizen 1821–1825*, in *Vorlesungen über Rechtsphilosophie 1818–1831*, Bd.2, pp.633 ff.). This relationship has been analysed by an extremely wide body of literature. Cf. M. Riedel, *Studien zu Hegels Rechtsphilosophie*, Suhrkamp Verlag, Frankfurt am Main, 1969.

extraneous to the same overlapping. In effect, if it is true that *WN* condenses the previous philosophical and historical-juridical analysis developed both in *TMS* and in the *Lectures on Jurisprudence*, it would be in this last posthumous work – during those years that represent a theoretical foundry – that Smith would provide a major contribution to the reflection on politics. Essentially, he shapes and structures a framework for a stadial development, within which the ways of subsistence and the historical-political forms are related and resolved in an 'exchange economy', within which labour is socially divided. In this framework, the absence of the categorial dimension of the Political – and in this case we might refer to the categories of Machiavelli and Hobbes, where the Economical is intended only as an implicit structure – is not a lack, a void, but rather a specificity, built, as in Montesquieu, apart from any compact, state of nature, Leviathan or other normative systems; but, beyond Montesquieu himself, with a specific attention to the economic categorization, to which the government of passions is traced back.

In this sense it is possible to say that in the *Lectures*, thanks to the mediation of labour, a constant and reciprocal overlapping between the Ethical, Economical, and Political does exist. In fact, it is for this overlapping that a clear 'resolution' in favour of an impositive autonomy of one of these spheres upon the others (a 'resolution' so clear, vice versa, in sixteenth and seventeenth century political thought) becomes unfeasible. Certainly, there is not a 'resolution', but there is a specific historical-juridical result, in which causes and effects of the division of labour are prominent in the face of conquering violence, the death as a categorial paradigm of the Political. This is the meaning of Smith's critique to Hobbes, and from here Hegel's reflections upon needs would begin to move. The science of a statement or legislator synthesizes an analytical movement that represents the progressive defining of the 'space' of political economy, distinct from any alleged paradigmatic foundations. Indeed, Smith is not the father of political economy, but *one* of its creators.

7. Smith, the impolitical?

In order to understand the articulations of such a crucial passage, we should refer to the *Lectures*, where Smith developed his economic jurisprudence starting from the identification of the first form of a 'political order' in the age of shepherds. It was at that time that primitive expressions of wealth began to establish sharp differences between rich and poor and, consequently, the dependency between men:

> The age of shepherds is that where government properly first commences. And it is at this time too that men become in any considerable degree dependent on others. [...] The distinctions of rich and poor then arise. [...] And in this manner every wealthy man comes to have a considerable number of the poorer sort depending and attending upon him. And in this period of society the inequality of fortune makes a greater odd in the power and influence of the rich over the poor than in any other.[226]

Dependency, distinctions, disparity, and inequality are the 'key words' that, *de facto*, introduce the origin of 'political power' as the expression of an obedience due to census and, therefore, as the exercise of strength that, in a variety of ways, it grants and legitimizes. Inequality generates power, clan power, usually inheritable. 'In this stage, as property is introduced, one can be eminent not only for his superior abilities and renowned exploits, but also on account of his wealth and the estate he has derived from his forefathers'.[227]

Subsequently to this first rough 'political order', the establishment of the agricultural subsistence model, where 'political power' would be equated to the ability to acquire land and housing, would represent a radical innovation. Regarding the institution of govern-

---

226 *LJ(A)*, p.202. It is worth recalling here the work of Smith's disciple J. Millar: *Observations Concerning the Distinctions of Ranks in Society*, printed for John Murray, London, 1771. For an overview on the stadial theory, R.L. Meek, *Social Science and the Ignoble Savage*, Cambridge University Press, Cambridge, 1976.
227 *LJ(A)*, p.216.

ments similar to those of the Tartar in many parts of Ancient Greece, Italy, and Gaul, Smith observes:

> We may easily conceive that a people of this sort, settled in a country where they lived in pretty great ease and security and in a soil capable of yielding them good returns for cultivation, would not only improve the earth but also make considerable advances in the several arts and sciences and manufactures, providing they had an opportunity of exporting their sumptuous produce and fruits of their labour.[228]

It should be noted that the shift from the age of shepherds to the age of agriculture was characterized by the change in the 'key words' that legitimized 'political power'. Starting from the new permanent character of the farming civilization, these 'words' can be identified by terms such as 'abundance', 'security' and 'export'. Abundance and security reshaped the division of labour, from which the development of manufacturing arts and the increase of exchanges, due to the surplus then obtained, derived. Consequently, the new 'key words' explain why the exercise of 'political power' became more impersonal and widespread.

However, the 'political order' established after the diffusion of the agricultural subsistence model remained precarious or, at least, fluctuating. Essentially, because it was weak inside: 'The authority of the chief would not be at all agreeable to them [the great men of the country] if it came to be any way excessive [...]'. Therefore, '[t]hree or four of them combining would be able to wrest the authority and management of the state [...]'. Hence, 'the nobles, the chief men of the state, would endeavour to reduce the state into their power'.[229] It is easy to observe that, if the increase of production presupposed and generated the social division of labour, likewise the increase of the available social wealth required a new form of 'political order'.

In brief, in the first *tranche* of his historical-political research – which gravitates around the relationship between 'modes of sub-sistence' and types of 'political order' –, what Smith delineates is exactly what we want to underline: the 'constant' transformation of

228 *LJ(A)*, p.223.
229 *LJ(A)*, p.225.

the political organization as a result of the development 'of arts and commerce'. In effect, the very same approach would also be utilized in order to explain the crisis of the Greek *poleis* and the later Roman 'military government'. Concerning the former, Smith argues that the development of arts and the expansion of demand for refined manufacturing, whilst produced an increase of population, decreased the military power of the *poleis*. Differently from the age of shepherds – where, in case of war, all had to participate – in Ancient Greece only citizens were warriors. However, with the development of arts and manufactures that occurred through the centuries, the Greek citizen-warriors became even less available to abandon the city during war time. Taking as an historical example the case of Athens, Smith concludes that to the dramatic development in the fields of art and commerce corresponded a considerable decay in the ability of defence. At a later point in time, the aggressive Roman State had to face the same problem, represented by the decay of the civic and military soul as a result of a considerable economic development. The increase of trafficking, commerce, and manufactures determined the abandonment of the military art on the part 'of the better sort of people of fashion and honour', fully engaged in the exploitation of the long periods of peace and prosperity at home. As a result, in order to satisfy its desire for conquest, Rome had to resort to freedmen 'and all others of the lower class'.

Hence, what constitutes Smith's analytical point of reference is the relationship between the 'political order' and the 'degree of development' of arts and commerce. And we do not find a different explicative framework if we consider the analysis of the allodial and feudal economic systems, European absolutism and, finally, the commercial society. Carefully explaining the constitution of the allodial system, for example, Smith describes it as a period during which 'all commercial and productive activities of previous population' were destroyed. Having to seek the help of the allodial lords, those lived under this social system attributed considerable power to them. This is what led to the feudal system, the constitution of the feudal right, and the conflict between powerful lords and regal power.

In conclusion, independently from the ways in which one analyses the different analytical passages, the idea remains the same:

'The power of the nobles however declined in the feudal governments from the same causes as everywhere else, viz, from the introduction of arts, commerce, and luxury'.[230] That is, we can find always the same 'analytical constants' that, rather than producing a 'categorization' of the Political, constitute a historical-juridical paradigm connected to the specific dimension of the economic jurisprudence.[231] And it is for the same reason that, not being interested in defining a clear 'categorization' of the Political, Smith's historical-political approach remains tethered to the Illuministic philosophical frame – for instance, when compared to Ricardo's pessimism.[232]

On the other hand, it cannot be a mere coincidence that from the said reflections follow those concerning the social contract, the relationship between sovereignty and the legitimacy of rebellion, and, especially with reference to the English case, the analysis of the relations between monarchy and the *principle of authority*, on the one side, and between democracy and the *principle of utility*, on the other. This is because Smith's political reflection is not confined to a stadial economic theory and to the analysis of the different 'political forms' – from the insurgence of the crisis of the republic to the consequent establishment of monarchical absolutism. In effect, he is even interested in providing a theory of obedience, but such a theory is clearly not linked to the idea of 'original contract', towards which he addresses a radical critique.

---

230 *LJ(A)*, p.261.
231 It is true – as Hirschman observed (*Shifting Involvements. Private Interest and Public Action*, Robertson, Oxford, 1982) – that Smith's position towards the contemporary materialistic culture was significantly ambivalent, in particular when he dealt with themes like the acquisition of well-being and luxury: a central issue in the eighteenth century philosophical debate – from Mandeville to Butler's *Six Sermons* and Rousseau's famous Note IX of the *Discours*. However, what is more significant is that the intelligibility of this ambivalence is related not to the possibility of being resolved in one sense or another, but rather to its contradictory existence as such, typical of the Illuministic approach to material progress. On the topic, Ferguson's *An Essay on the History of Civil Society* (VI, 2) is paradigmatic. Cf. P. Salvucci, *Adam Ferguson*, Argalia, Urbino, 1972, pp.474 ff.
232 Foucault, *Les mots et les choses*, p.269; Brown, *Adam Smith's Economics*, p.182; Pesante, *Economia e politica*, p.10.

Similarly to Hume, for whom nearly all governments 'have been founded originally, either on usurpation or conquest, or both, without any pretence of a fair consent, or voluntary subjection of the people',[233] Smith observes that the vast majority of people seem to have a blurred idea of what an original contract is, and that, at best, it may result binding only for those who have established it. The social compact cannot provide the basis for the obedience of people, and, consequently, the underpinning of the concept of obedience must be found somewhere else: namely, in the 'principle of authority' and in the 'principle of utility'. If the former is a clear admission of a natural authority exerted by those to whom is attributed a superior rank – Smith recalls the image of a father and a child –, the latter indicates that 'every one sees that the magistrates not only support the government in general both the security and independency of each individual, and their see that this security can not be attained without a regular government'.[234]

Smith traces the principle of authority back to the monarchical government and that of utility to the republican one. If, in the former, obedience stems from sentiments expressing a deference *vis-à-vis* a natural superiority of the established power (although there is some residual of a sentiment of utility), in the latter, obedience is entirely due to utility. With due caution, it might perhaps be said that what constitutes the basis for a theory of obligation is utility in relation to the required obedience: if an act of obedience were useless, why should it be due? Apropos, it is worth noting that, with specific reference to the English case, Smith recognizes, firstly, that the principle of authority can be attributed not only to the individual but also to the public role and, secondly, that in a constitutional monarchy, *de facto*, the two principles cohabit. And because the singularity of the English case is explicitly related to the peculiar existence of the Whig and Tory political parties, with particular regard to the theory of the original contract, without referring to the well-known but worn-out

233   D. Hume, 'Of the Original Contract', in *Essays, Moral, Political, and Literary*, ed. by E.F. Miller, Liberty Fund, Indianapolis, 1987, p.471.
234   *LJ(A)*, p.318.

historiographical liberalistic tradition, it seems pertinent to refer here to Carl Schmitt's interpretation of such a singularity.

Although the reference may appear rather strange, it is worth recalling that in the *Verfassungslehre* Schmitt assumes that the primary rule for any political constitution or compact is that of embodying the political will of those who pose and grant the *Verfassung*. In the English case – he affirms – the formal contractual stipulation was given and the political unity prefigured. Nevertheless, the alliance between the Parliament and the King did not constitute, but rather presupposes the unity.[235] A peculiarity clear to Tocqueville who observed: 'des classes qui se pénètrent, une noblesse effacée, une aristocratie ouverte, la richesse devenue la puissance, l'égalité devant la loi [...]; tous principes nouveaux [...] qui, introduites peu à peu et avec art dans ce vieux corps, l'ont ranimé, sans risquer de la dissoudre, et l'on rempli d'une fraîche vigueur en lui laissant des formes antiques'.[236] In social terms – we could perhaps say – the mediation between land-owners and *bourgeoisie* gives sway to a compromise between authority and utility, in which the basis of the obligation does not stem from the stipulation of, but rather from the very same presupposed compact

Now, besides the specific, but indicative, interpretation of the English case provided by Schmitt, we might ask: is it possible to relate the principle of obedience to a compromise between authority and utility? Is it possible to limit Smith's political form to *this* compromise? Finally, is it correct to relate the action of the prudent man to it? We believe that the answer can only be positive. In effect, in spite of the alleged radicalism of some passages in which Smith, *à la* Locke, is mostly preoccupied with drawing a line to indicate the point at which the sovereign power can legitimately arrive – that which would require the articulation of a much more complex juridical architecture –, it is clear that it is to the prudent men, to their respect

235 C. Schmitt, *Verfassungslehre*, Duncker & Humblot, Berlin, 1928, pp.22, 46–7, 54.
236 A. De Tocqueville, *L'Ancien régime et la Révolution*, I, IV (*Oeuvres complètes*, M. Levy, Paris, 1952, vol.2, 1).

for upper ranks or communities into which the State is subdivided, that he alludes when he says:

> It is the sense of public utility, more than of private, which influences men to obedience. It may sometimes be for my interest to disobey, and to wish government overturned. But I am sensible that other men are of a different opinion from me and would not assist me in the enterprise. I therefore submit to its decision for the good of the whole.[237]

The principle of obedience cannot be thought of in abstract terms; not only should it be addressed to a 'tangible' subject, but also, if we could say, to an 'observable' subject in the common ethos; a subject that cannot be other than the middle social agent, the prudent men who constitute a vast sector of society; a subject well aware of the relevance of what for Smith represents an essential component of the principle of obligation: the public utility. This is what we have meant when we have said that it would have been impossible to establish a theory of obligation unless it refers to the middle social agent's ethos. In effect, it would be limiting to maintain that this is true only in order to distinguish between an acting and a judging middle social agent. Smith's knowledge of jurisprudence – influenced as it was by the European culture – was relevant. What fascinated him most was its historical, rather than normative aspect. He was not interested in those institutions that ought to be put into place, but rather in those already in place. If Smith's analysis of justice shows how vague and generic the bases for his theory of obligation were, in turn, this 'vagueness' characterizes the path that leads to its peculiar 'political form'.

The emphasis placed upon the ethical and historical-juridical paradigm – *this* 'political form' that Smith utilizes in order to discuss the principle of political obedience –, becomes inevitable, for, if the referent of the principle of public utility is the prudent man, it is for him that the establishment of common moral standards presented in *TMS* becomes essential. Thus, in order to understand how Smith alludes to the Political without producing a political theory, creating, instead, an unsolvable overlapping between economics (development

237   *LJ(B)*, p.402.

122

of arts and commerce), ethics (sense of public utility), and politics (principle of obedience), it is indispensable to note the extent to which his paradigm is indissolubly forged within an ethical and historical-juridical dimension. Political economy is the peculiar expression of such an overlapping. The ethical, economical, and political 'orders' become historically determinable thanks to the same character of the Smithian jurisprudence. Nevertheless, their unresolved relationship, which is not synthesized by 'egoism', constitutes the real problem with regard to the *political form* of economic jurisprudence.

For Smith, the Political is relevant not as a category, but only in its adjectival form. As such, it implies the 'mediation' between different interests, rather than 'decisions' taken in the name of *imperium*. This represents the difference between Smith and authors such as Machiavelli or Hobbes. In this light, leaving aside Schumpeter's severe judgement,[238] *WN* can really be seen as a 'container' rather than as a final synthesis. Therefore, the fact that in *WN* Smith adopts the historical-juridical language utilized in the *Lectures on Jurisprudence*, rather than utilizing the ethical language of *TMS*, does not imply that the relationship between ethics and economics finds its solution in politics. Indeed, it is in his ability to produce 'innovation' in spite of his 'conservatism' that resides the relevance and singularity of Smith's political economy: a 'branch of the science of a statesman or legislator'.

In this light, Edward Thompson's critique, expressed in his seminal *The Moral Economy of the English Crowd in the XVIIth Century*, seems improper. As it implies an economic system freed from the subjection to moral imperatives – Thompson argued –, Smith's economic doctrine is accountable for a general de-moralization, embodied by the crisis of the moral basis of exchange and consumption.[239] However, as Smith's political economy *cannot solve* what Thompson considers resolved – the overlapping between the Ethical and the Economical –, Thompson's argumentation is too simplistic. No less convincing is the thesis of those such as Gerard

---

238 Schumpeter, *History of Economic Analysis*, p.184.
239 E. Thompson, 'The Moral Economy of the English Crowd in the XVIIth Century', *Past and Present*, 1971, vol.50.

Mairet who, on the basis of the distinction between the 'wealth of the nation' and the mere 'market mechanism', considers Smith more as a philosopher of the State rather than as an economist.[240] This is simply paradoxical. It is certain that the limits of Smith's political philosophy – that can be attributed to its weak acknowledgement of the 'logic of the Political' – become evident after Hegel and Marx; however, even before them, it is impossible to ignore Hobbes' 'awkward' presence.

In short, what complicates the analytical comprehension of Smith's overlapping is the fact that the ethical, economic and political planes are not static. It is one thing to evaluate what in a social phenomenon relates to ethics, and what in another phenomenon relates to economics – in doing so, establishing the reciprocal irreducibility within the same problematic sphere; it is something else to evaluate what, in the same phenomena, relates to ethics, economics and politics, without eliminating the respective differences, and without solving the stratified overlapping via a fusion of different, although complementary, perspectives. In Smith's political economy the three planes, being interwoven, exist in their movement. In other words, Smith's politics, although historically understood, leads to an aporiae, based upon the modern 'dialectic of crisis' that Reinhart Koselleck traced back to the dualism between ethics and politics, and that characterized the Illuministic thought – a dualism developed and diversified by the presence of the Economical.

As it allows the understanding of its non-categorial nature, Koselleck's interpretation of the political proposed in his *Kritik und Krise* might indeed represent the starting point for a pertinent discussion of Smith's conception of politics. It is not a coincidence that the Illuministic dualism between ethics and politics became manifest exactly at the time when the epochal crisis of values, ideologies, and social models imposed the transformation of that dualism into a 'political instrument'.[241] As in the case concerning later liberal economic constitutionalism, also in Smith this would not lead to a cat-

---

240 We are referring here to the essay included in F. Châtelet, *Histoire des idéologies*, Hachette, Paris, 1978.

241 R. Koselleck, *Kritik und Krise. Ein Beitrag zur Pathogenese der bürgerlichen Welt*, Alber, Freiburg-München, 1959.

egorization of the Political, but rather to the transformation of the dualism between ethics and politics into an overlapping, where the presence of the Economical, far from offering a satisfactory solution to the problems raised by that dualism, makes the issue more complex. For this reason, Smith's political foundations – not by chance defined by Lionel Robbins as economic policy[242] – rest upon the notion of prudence intended as the *problematic interaction* between benevolence and egoism: an interaction often denied from time to time, either in order to sustain the thesis of Smith as a cynical Mandevillian, or to underpin an alleged theoretical ambiguity never proven, and resolved, at best, in the presence of a 'non'-normative justice. However, this is not an ambiguity, but a specificity. Within that interactive relationship, prudence, rather than justice, is able to forge the 'political space' of Modernity. The prudent man is a sort of practical 'problem solver' of what appears to be a duplicity in human nature; a duplicity, until this moment considered as the very same problem for which the exercise of an *imperium* was judged as legitimate. The prudent man is a practical 'problem solver', whose role is the same that Hegel would attribute to the modern *bourgeois*.

In this regard, also Winch's fundamental analysis concerning the shaping of Smith's politics in relation to justice and within the evolution of the different modes of subsistence and their respective juridical model, seem quite disputable. Winch declares from the outset that he is not interested in a 'categorization' of the problem. However, the said categorization represents a crucial node, given that Winch's 'hermeneutic' reconstruction of Smith's works is 'only' a precious piece of economic and institutional history. The Winchean reconsideration of Smith's main political options – the public debt, the army, and its relation to the civic sense – confirms their distance from the liberal doctrine, but without indicating a place upon which politics might be founded – even though independently from any normative categorization. Or, better still, although this place is indicated, its being indissolubly linked with the themes of economic policy exposed it to the doubts already expressed by the anti-liberalistic critiques –

---

242 L. Robbins, *The Theory of Economic Policy in English Classical Political Economy*, Macmillan, London, 1952.

and they require responses. It is worth noting that in Teichgraeber's analysis, which owes much to Winch, this aspect is explicitly present.[243] Winch's thesis is sharp: as Smith pays great attention to the economic-institutional aspects of a simple mercantile society, it becomes rather difficult to interpret his analysis as an apology of the capitalistic market. A position whose consequences are both reasonable and clear: Smith is neither the father of political economy, nor his politics a mere episode 'that occurred some way along a road which runs from Locke to Marx'.[244] If this is so, it becomes apparent that the relationship between ethics, economics and politics, cannot constitute the basis for political economy, in its modern specificity, but rather the achievement of a reflection, which in Smith's politics finds its completion. This implies that politics represents the achievement of the civic tradition[245] (via justice), within a simple mercantile society, and not a category inscribed in the philosophical ideology of Modernity (via prudence).

This appears not to be an adequate conclusion. It seems – as Joyce Appleby noted – that England was not the country in which the development of a capitalistic economy, the first constitutional monarchy, the first example of the modern society, occurred.[246] The problematic relationship between benevolence and egoism, its prudential transposition, shows, vice versa, that the fundamental problem posed by Smith – the overlapping between ethics, economics, and politics – is ideologically unthinkable setting aside the philosophical thought of Modernity. Teichgraeber is therefore convincing when he

243 Teichgraeber, 'Free Trade', p.151. As the exigency to assume 'political economy' as a new 'discoursive order' has not a *sequitur*, J. Robertson does not trespass such a limit: 'The Legacy of Adam Smith: Government and Economic Development in the *Wealth of Nations*', in R. Bellamy (ed. by), *Victorian Liberalism*, Routledge, London, 1990, pp.15–41.
244 Winch, *Adam Smth's Politics*, p.180.
245 But see Winch's remarks: 'Adam Smith and the Liberal Tradition', in K. Haakonsen (ed. by), *Tradition of Liberalism. Essays on J. Locke, A. Smith and J. Stuart Mill*, The Centre for Independent Studies, Sidney, 1988.
246 For a 'measured critique' to the civic paradigm, see J. Appleby, *Liberalism and Republicanism in the Historical Imagination*, Harvard University Press, Cambridge MA, 1992, pp.132–4.

points out that in the Scottish philosophical thought it is rather difficult to establish the priority according to which the confinement of the political activity or the rise of the economic realm occurred.[247] In this lost priority, so to speak, nothing can function as before. Doctrines, ideologies, concepts, social practices, the whole config-uration of an epoch are pushed forward, rather than being the accomplishment of what preceded it. Certainly, what Smith's political thought reveals is not the awareness of a fracture upon which to build a new science or representation of civil society. However, it reveals also the clear perception that a continuity, a pure consequentiality with the eighteenth century anthropological paradigms, can no longer be sustained. In this sense, it might be correct to say that Smith was an 'observer by choice' and an 'innovator by condition': closing one epoch, he opened another one – Modernity. A condition synthesized by setting aside any priority between the ethical, economic and political sphere: a 'setting aside' that is not an *impasse*, but rather an internal passage of the *imperfect genesis* of the political economy. Smith describes his time, but it is for that missed priority that we, the moderns, are so much concerned with Smith's inheritance.

8. Imperfect genesis

Today, there is a general agreement among historians of ideas upon the evolution of Smith's body of thought, at least in indicating its complexity and priorities. However, in order to address the problem concerning Smith's politics, there is 'another' fundamental approach, 'another historiography' to be taken into consideration. This historio-graphical line addresses Smith from a 'conceptual' perspective, rather than from a philological point of view and, in doing so, enables us to understand more clearly the 'doctrinal roots' of Smith's political economy. We are not referring to the most trivial and old historicist generalizations, but rather to those 'conceptual approaches' that, al-

247   Teichgraeber, *'Free Trade'*, p.18.

though one might say to be inadequate and sometimes misleading, cannot be ignored. At a certain point in time, they claim attention for the interrogations that they pose.

Given the variety of sharply distinct approaches and the theoretical and historical distances that separate the authors here considered, the plural is necessary. Nevertheless, despite this, they pose the same interrogation: what is the possible role of the political sphere after the 'outcomes' of Smith's reflection? This question characterizes both Schmitt's authoritarian reflection and Arendt's drastic critique to Modernity – not to mention Karl Polany's anthropology and Wolin's anomalous liberalistic pessimism. These authors argue that in Modernity the establishment of an economic realm has obliterated the *political space*, the imaginary space of the *polis*, imposing an exercise of the *private sphere of needs* detached from public virtue, and becoming the *science of civil society*. In short, the answers, though radically different in their articulation, tend to be similar. *Au fond*, the main assumption is in fact the same: the *science of civil society* is intended as the 'Smithian' political economy.

As Hegel had previously noted, *bourgeois* and *citoyen* become reciprocally distinct, as the former, in exchange for a 'politische Nullität',[248] enjoys the gains derived from economic activity, peace, and security. According to such an understanding, the economic sphere of civil society represents therefore the disappearance of the political experience – which, according to Plato, was tantamount to living totally immersed in the public sphere, away from the finitude of needs. This line of argument is not far from our specific question: *mutatis mutandis*, in the twentieth century, Arendt would raise *these* problems, moving from the recognition of what Smith underlined analysing the political crisis of the *poleis* in relation to the development 'of arts and commerce'.

Franz Neumann noted that in Smith we observe the 'elimination of politics', an exclusion that, in turn, bears fundamental conse-

---

248 Hegel, *Über die wissenschaftlichen Behandlungsarten des Naturrechts*, in *Gesammelte Werke*, hrsg. von H. Buchner, O. Pöggeler, Bd.4, p.458.

quences.[249] In our understanding, however, the issue ought to be posed moving from the evaluation of these consequences, rather than from the alleged elimination of politics. In this sense, Smith's *terminus ad quem* explains why he fully belongs to Modernity. A belonging that is certainly exasperated by the tradition associated with the economic liberalism, but not adequately understood in the most recent 'historiographical revision'. In fact, the difference with respect to Locke's normative model (clearly expressed in the *Lectures*), thoughcorrect and able to restrain the liberal interpretation – namely, the historiographical discrepancy between liberty and democratic freedom –, is unable to provide satisfactory answers to the questions posed by the twentieth century radical critics of the liberalistic tradition. As we shall see below, posing the theme of politics in a 'categorial' form, they included Smith in the sphere of the modern conception of the impolitical, exactly because of the paradoxical peculiarity of the Political intended in its adjectival form: as political economy.

It is worth observing that Louis Dumont's *Homo aequalis*[250] was published only one year before the first edition of Winch's famous book. As it is known, in his work Dumont re-proposed the traditional distinction between *TMS* and *WN*. Thus, the temptation to interpret this work as a banal re-formulation of the 'Adam Smith problem' might be legitimate. Nevertheless, although legitimate, it would be too simplistic. In effect, even if Dumont refers to a manifestly erroneous interpretation of Smith's thought, he attempts to walk a different theoretical path, for showing that in Western civilization the triumph of economic ideology has been possible only at the price of sacrificing

---

249 F. Neumann, *The Democratic and the Authoritarian State*, Macmillan, London, 1964. For the traditional economic reading of Smith's politics, see N. Rosenberg, 'Adam Smith and Laissez-faire Revisited'; E. Ginzberg, 'An Economy Formed by Men' – both in O'Driscoll, jr. (ed. by), *Adam Smith and Modern Political Economy*, pp.26–7, 37. For an ample discussion, see E.G. West, 'Adam Smith's Economics of Politics', ibid., pp.132 ff.; Skinner, *A System of Social Science*, pp.209 ff. Besides Winch's fundamental *Adam Smith's Politics*, see P.L. Porta, 'I fondamenti dell'ordine economico: "policy", "police", "politeness" nel pensiero scozzese', *Filosofia politica*, 1988, vol.1, 1, pp.37–68.

250 E. Dumont, *Homo aequalis*, Gallimard, Paris, 1977. See also Dupuy's critical observations made in 'De l'émancipation de l'économie'.

the sphere of the Political. In other words, although Dumont's work does not present any novelty, credit should be given to its attempt, as it re-proposes an issue ignored by most historiographical accounts: namely, the thematic re-contextualization of Smith's work within a fundamental articulation of the European political thought concerning the genesis of Modernity, via a rethinking of the relationship between ethics, economics, and politics. Dumont does not confine his reflection to the claim that the naturalistic primacy of the Economical would have overshadowed the relevance of the Political. Pushing the argument further, he maintains that it was exactly because of this primacy that the modern philosophical perspective could be constituted. Such a perspective was able to prevail thanks to the shift from holistic to individualistic social relationships, from relations involving a lively interconnection among fellow men, to those within which the exchange of goods became the medium that regulated their interactions. As a result, according to Dumont's thesis, Smith is not only the responsible for an individualistic perspective that transcends his intentions, but also its main maker.

Certainly, Dumont's idea according to which the subsumption of the Political to the Economical is what provides the basis of the synthesis operated by political economy is not particularly original and it entails an excess of discontinuity that overlooks the historical continuity of social processes. Thus, in order to achieve his purpose, Dumont re-states the interpretative misunderstanding for which, in Smith, the figures of the moralist and that of the economist are disjointed. It is certain that within the broader range of human actions Smith differentiates economic actions as the particular type that escapes morality without being opposed to it – Dumont argues. But the main assumption upon which this differentiation rests – he concludes – is that, in contrast to the general sphere of the moral sense based upon sympathy, economic activity is the sole human action that necessitates only egoistic motions. Dumont's approach is indeed baseless. However, as his conscious misunderstanding is not aimed at underpinning the eighteenth century liberal interpretation, his conclusions are stimulating.

Significantly, egoism is not interpreted as the fuel of competition, positive spirit of the market but, philosophically and anthropologically, as the Classic and Hegelian private sphere of individual security, guaranteed by the simple activity of the *bourgeois* who has accepted – or has been obliged to accept – the undifferentiated praxis characterizing modern societies, with its primacy of things upon men; a civil society *without* politics, without space for political relationships, unless they do not represent economic needs. Under these circumstances, the separation between the Economical and the Political entails the absorption of all human action in the former. Although his approach is clearly debatable, Dumont has therefore reproposed an old but nonetheless relevant problem that even the most accurate historiography tends to forget, reopening the discussion upon a nodal passage of the ideological formation of Modernity, in which he identifies Smith's fundamental role.

As the contextual element tends to be disregarded, it is legitimate to be suspicious of such a diachronic approach; anyhow, we agree with Cropsey when he accuses Winch's synchronism of being able to give only a backwards account of Smith.[251] In short, to place Smith in the pre-modern intellectual landscape seems to be misleading. This said, we do not underestimate the possible objections: first of all that concerning the impossibility of providing a sufficiently clear, temporal-philosophical definition of Modernity. But what we would like to underline is that the diachronic process emphasized by the liberal historiographical model advances a totally different approach. Certainly, it acknowledges Smith's modernity, but in order to render him the 'solver' of an *unsolvable problem*: the relationship between ethics, economics and politics. By contrast, we believe that what places Smith's theoretical 'outcomes' (and not his 'supposed' intention) within 'modern thought' is indeed the impossibility of solving the overlapping that, borrowing Arendt's words, is that *incipit* indicating role, space, and sense of political economy within the modern social landscape.

In the first half of the last century, around these themes, notable authors developed reflections that the following history of political philosophy would consider as seminal. In these analyses, Smith's

251 See J. Cropsey's review of Winch's work, in *Political Theory*, 1979, vol.7, pp.424–8.

presence was often forcibly related to the liberalistic paradigm that, at that time, was the only 'legitimate' interpreter of Smith's thought. But, with the due distinction, although different and expressed by authors whose paths were differently affected by the dramatic European experiences, it is thanks to such analysis that we can understand the depth of the problem that *unintentionally* Smith posed for Modernity.

During the 1920s, the most heretical interpretation of the relationship between the Ethical, Economical, and Political was that provided by Schmitt, who argued that the liberal tradition, in assuming the 'typical always recurring polarity' between the Ethical and Economical, was unable to solve the overlapping we have indicated, because it had explicitly overlooked the problem posed by the Political.[252] The liberal tradition 'has attempted only to tie the political to the ethical and to subjugate it to economics'.[253] Schmitt's thesis is radical: whilst any conception of the Political must 'presuppose man to be evil', the liberalistic anthropological optimism has negated 'the possibility of enemy and, thereby, every specific political consequences':[254] in the marketplace men cannot be enemies, but only competitors. This is not because the Economical is unattainable or unreachable, but simply because the economic categorization has depoliticized the whole society, becoming 'destiny'. Better still, the de-politicization produced by liberalism bears a political significance, from which, however, any political idea cannot be carved out. The liberalistic depoliticizing categorizations move from the Ethical to the Economical and, fluctuating between these two poles, try to get rid of the political sphere, the *contrasts*, now substituted, in the economic

252 C. Schmitt, *Der Begriff des Politischen*, Duncker & Humblot, Berlin, 1963, p.69; *The Concept of the Political*, trans. by G. Schwab, Rutgers University, Rahway (NJ), 1976, p.70.
253 Ibid., p.61; *The Concept of the Political*, p.61. In this way, Smith's distance from Hobbes' paradigm would be confirmed. Concerning the irreducibility of Smith's hypothesis to Hobbes' one, see C. Benetti, *Smith*, Etas, Milano, 1979, p.25.
254 Schmitt, *Der Begriff des Politischen*, p.64; *The Concept of the Political*, p.64. See also Schmitt, *Der Hüter der Verfassung*, Duncker & Humblot, Berlin, 1931; Id., *Politische Romantik*, Duncker & Humblot, Berlin, 1968².

sphere, by *contracts*. In this way, political concepts are misrepresented: the 'fight' is turned into 'competition', the 'State' into a 'society' based upon a system of production and exchange; the 'will' into rational economic 'calculation'; 'domination' and 'power' into mere tools of 'economic control'. In brief, the Political intended as an autonomous sphere retreats into an individualistic morality.

As it is simple to note, Schmitt refers to liberalism *en général*, but what is under scrutiny here is its alleged Smithian (and Lockean) connotation, the naturalistic optimism, the mixing of ethical and economic arguments with a pure political calculation, the submission of political power to a mere rational economic calculation, intended as a mirror of the coming civil society. In much more aseptic terms, an anomalous liberal like Wolin has argued that the primacy of society over politics has established the decline of the meaning of political philosophy. If economics becomes 'the knowledge of society', nothing can impede the reduction of all social relationships into a mere economic categorization. The decline of interest in the political action, the belief that the analysis of the economic relation constitutes 'the proper study of mankind' and the economic activity 'the proper end', are all causes that accelerated the decline of political philosophy.[255]

If this is the issue – and Schmitt's argument is relevant here –, being unable to solve the above mentioned overlapping, liberalism depoliticizes society. It does not resolve, but enacts the relationship between ethics, economics and politics. However, as, '[p]olitically, the rule of morality, law, and economics always assumes a concrete political meaning [*einen konkreten politischen Sinn*]',[256] liberalism assumes anyhow a *political form*. In a system that assumes to be non-political and that is apparently anti-political, the overlapping is functional to the hostility towards different social groupings. This, in turn, generates new hostility, as it cannot escape the consequentiality of the Political. According to Strauss,[257] Schmitt does not claim that

255 S.S. Wolin, *Politics and Vision*, Little, Brown & Co., Boston, 1960, pp.300–2.
256 Schmitt, *Der Begriff des Politischen*, p.72; *The Concept of the Political*, p.73. See also N. Luhmann, *Politische Planung*, Westdt. Verl., Opladen, 1971.
257 L. Strauss, 'Anmerkungen zu C. Schmitt, Der Begriff des Politischen', *Archiv für Sozialwissenschaft und Sozialpolitik*, 1932, vol.67.

during the nineteenth and twentieth century the Political becomes an unessential 'form'. More simply, as the dominant tendency in human behaviour is now towards the 'neutralization', the bargain at all costs, the Political loses its role with regard to the new 'central fields'. With respect to the social sphere – the centrality of a society now intended as main loci of the covenant, rather than as the loci of the ultimate conflict –, the Political loses the role previously held, and it is subjected to Economical mediation.

In the centrality of society – Arendt would subsequently note – the transformation of what was previously conceived of as private sphere into public sphere occurs; and this process involves the fading out of 'political virtue' as a peculiar category. It is not that in the classical and pre-modern societies economy was irrelevant; simply, it was an 'activity' to be pursued in the private sphere of the *oikos*. The major transformation consisted of the fact that in the age of Modernity, individuals would act publicly according to private needs, rather than according to public ends conforming to political virtue; a transformation whose origin coincided with the rise of civil society and its science *par excellence*: namely, political economy. Until the advent of Modernity, the Economical represented a relatively tiny part of ethics and politics. For this reason, a specific 'economic discourse' would have become possible 'only when men had become social beings and unanimously followed certain patterns of behaviour'[258] – what we have defined as the ethos of the middle social agent.

These, in synthesis, are the terms in which the great season of contemporary political historiography measured Smith's heredity. Dumont's analysis makes them resurface. Now, putting aside the totally debatable articulations of the above philosophical approaches to Modernity, in which Smith appears implicitly chained to a generic liberalism, for us it is sufficient to look at the 'conceptual', rather than historiographical terms. In effect, they can be traced back to the problems 'unintentionally' posed by Smith with respect to the con-stitution of the paradigm of political economy; particularly, when it is possible to observe that the establishment of modern primacy of

258 H. Arendt, *The Human Condition*, The University of Chicago Press, Chicago, 1958, p.42.

society is unable to unravel the relationship between the Ethical, Economical, and Political, delineating, as such, a de-politicization, which is, in reality, only alleged. It is obvious to observe that this does not lead to the idea of Smith *politicus*, however, the political peculiarity of the Economical allows us to assume, rather than to exclude, the terms of the problems posed by Smith's political economy.

In the modern age, the peculiarity of Smith's position resides in the definition of those relationships that would present themselves as 'inconceivable' for the following philosophical generation. When ethics is correctly understood as an expression that connects, via persuasion, benevolence and self-love in the action of the prudent man in the marketplace, its relationship with economics becomes un-solvable. Also unsolvable is the relationship between ethics and politics, because the former pervades the latter, subtracting its 'value', without subtracting itself from the reality and dynamics of political interests. Both relationships are unsolvable, as their nature belongs to a clearly expansive social model, and to that expansibility to which the crisis generated by the unbalanced dynamic that characterizes the overlapping of the ethical, economical, and political planes, is inherent. This insolvability is the peculiar characteristic of Smith's political economy, but only an anomalous historiography seems able to understand it. To say this does not mean overlooking the difference between one approach that respects rules and conditions inherent to the historiographical analysis, and another highly diachronic by statute, and sometimes clearly misleading. It simply means that it would be wrong to surrender to those concepts that transcend an environment and a biography, if they are indispensable to the comprehension of both. In our case, they are indispensable to what we have defined as *imperfect genesis* of one of the key paradigms of Modernity: political economy.

Smith's reflection is not characterized by a shift of paradigm that provides the basis for the foundation of a 'new science': political economy. Thus, despite the intrinsic differentiation characterizing the Illuministic anthropological paradigm, political economy can be articulated as a result of a 'discrete' continuity of thought. However, Smith's reflection does not simply generate a more complex science of human nature, which fails to meet the modern age. Apart from the intentions of its maker, such a more complex science of human nature gives rise to a *novum*, a 'slow paradigm', which does not impose itself via a revolution. In other words, if it is correct to speak of an overlapping, then we are simultaneously faced with a continuity and a fracture: there is continuity in the overlapping of ethics, economics, and politics; there is a fracture when it appears clear that such an overlapping does not give rise to a fusion of the three planes and, for this reason, it is destined to become 'inconceivable'. Smith's political economy – it should be said that the locution classical political economy, though heuristically correct, seems too vague in this case – is both the keeper of an 'inheritance' and the maker of an unintended 'innovation'. The intricate relationship between inheritance and innovation gives rise to an *imperfect genesis*, despite any following historiography, more or less apologetic.

There can be many explanations for this: perhaps, the most convincing is also the most obvious. There is another way to deal with the issue concerning the genesis of civil society and, next and within it, of political economy as its scientific paradigm. We should pose the following questions. What happened to the 'political concept' 'when, in the modern age and not before, men began to doubt that poverty is inherent in the human condition'; when it was proclaimed 'that labour and toil, far from being the appanage of poverty, [...], were, on the contrary, the source of all wealth'?[259] What happened when the Political had to deal not only with the determinacy of that historical shift, but also with the overthrowing of any representation of the political categories implied in such a shift? In other words, what has the Political become when it has been understood and interpreted moving only from the adjectival form of political economy? The answer that one may provide should face a preliminary choice. Much depends upon the way in which we mean the genesis of political economy itself. It is one thing to hypothesize that it provokes a radical innovation, able to destroy the rationality of any previous political model; but it is something else to hypothesize that the very same process, although prefiguring a radical change, presents itself as

259   H. Arendt, *On Revolution*, Penguin Books, Harmondsworth, 1986, pp.22–3.

unable to produce a sharp fracture, giving sway to a slow process of detachment, within which the specificity of the modern 'political form' rests. This is a historiographical and conceptual problem that, introduced by Smith's economic philosophy, stretched far beyond him.

The idea defended here is that Smith is the last author able to conjugate ethics, economics, and politics, giving them a unitary representation, although the manifest impossibility of solving their overlapping confirms that the problem posed by the paradigmatic specificity of political economy is finally a mature fruit. In brief, *after* Smith, what appeared as 'unsolvable' would become 'inconceivable'. Schematically, if the crisis of the eighteenth century, on the one hand, establishes and, on the other, reopens the controversy concerning anthropological optimism and pessimism, it would be exactly in Hegel's analysis of Smith that the tension between ethics, economics, and politics – its political conclusion – would be definable as 'highly indeterminate'.[260] The pressure of the low rank of society – 'der Ansicht des Pöbels, dem Standpunkte des Negativen überhaupt gehört' –, whose point of view belongs to the suspicion that State is not a guarantor, constantly brings to the surface the individualistic point of view, *das System der Bedürfnisse*, the economic interest as a new political sphere.

Concerning this, Arendt has written seminal pages. She has indicated how the social sphere and, within it, the genesis of the paradigm of political economy liberated 'an unnatural growth' of the natural, a constant acceleration of the submission of human action to the new public sphere: the economic one. Having lost its original meaning, against the economic sphere, the Political has become unrecognizably, defenceless. The equality introduced by the advent of the social sphere – of the middle social agent – has replaced the differentiating action with an anonymous kinds of behaviour, the only one relevant on a statistical basis, as it is part of 'one interest of society as a whole, which, with "an invisible hand", guides the behaviour of men and produces the harmony of their conflicting in-

260   M. Cacciari, *Dialettica e critica del Politico*, Feltrinelli, Milano, 1978, p.52.

137

terest'.[261] Obviously, it is Smith that Arendt referred to – and it is (ir)-relevant that this is Ashley's Smith. Apropos, it is rather of interest to note the assumed simultaneity between the birth of the 'social sphere' and the development of the 'Smithian' economic science, which would be the 'main technical instrument' of the former, and a final explication of the alleged disappearance of the Political.

In our opinion, however, such an explication is not the result of the 'Smithian' *Harmonielehre*, but rather the indication that, *after* Smith, 'the concept of the Political' can only express its 'impossible autonomy' and its consequent inclusion in the political economy.[262] The overlapping between ethics, economics and politics – overlapping that implied the reciprocal autonomy of the three spheres – becomes 'inconceivable'. Thus, *after* Smith, its dissolution would manifest the irreducibility of the 'social realm' to the Political. Only at that point in time, the 'form' of pure decision-making – Hobbes's political theology –, the Political as autonomous category, would appear simply as ineffectual.

261 Arendt, *The Human Condition*, pp.44; Ead., *On Revolution*, pp.22–3.
262 See the critique provided by A. Negri, *Il potere costituente*, SugarCo, Milano, 1992, part. p.305.

Chapter II
Critique
Karl Marx: surplus-value and difference

1. Introduction

The philosophical *concept of difference* informs the entire work of Karl Marx. It concerns two sets of relationships: namely, those existing between the political economy 'discursive order' and Marx's *Kritik*, and those existing between profit and surplus-value, respectively intended as an economic 'measure' and as a social 'relationship'. The notion underpinning these relations is represented by the potential character of the *living labour*, which implies the specific capacity to generate an *Überschuß*, a surplus-value. Within this theoretical framework, the subsumption of abstract labour constitutes the specific difference of the capitalistic mode of production and is the peculiar expression of a monetary economy.[1] This coagulates into a 'discursive strategy' that, in turn, is represented by the categorial approach underpinning Marx's critique of political economy[2] and by what is definable in it as rational

---

1   Although our analysis of the theory of labour-value reaches different conclusions (see sect. 6), it is necessary to recall those authors who insisted on tracing back Marx's analysis of value within the so called monetary theory of production (A. Graziani, 'The Theory of the Monetary Circuit', *Thames Papers in Political Economy*, 1989, Spring; Id., *The Monetary Theory of Production*, Cambridge University Press, Cambridge, 2003). See in particular, R. Bellofiore, 'A Monetary Labour Theory of Value', *Review of Radical Political Economy*, 1989, vol.21, 1–2, pp.1–25; R. Bellofiore, R. Realfonzo, 'Finance and the Labour Theory of Value. Towards a Macroeconomic Theory of Distribution in a Monetary Perspective', *International Journal of Political Economy*, 1997, vol.27, 2, pp.97–118.

2   On the relevance of Marx's *Kritik*, see R. Rosdolsky, *Zur Entstehungsgeschichte des Marxschen 'Kapital'*, Europäische Verlagsanstalt-Europa Verlag, Frankfurt-Wien, 1968; *The Making of Marx's 'Capital'*, trans. by P. Burgess, Pluto Press, London, 1977.

abstraction [*verständige Abstraktion*]. The role of this latter consists of the generation of abstract determinations [*die abstrakten Bestimmungen*]: 'It consists of the methodical assertion that one cannot find the categories beginning naively with the "real" or the "concrete", but only on the basis of the development of a "process of synthesis" of the givens of intuition and of representation'.[3] Hence, Marx's critique defines the distance that exists between a 'positive paradigm', aimed at investigating *given* economic relations, and a 'de-structuring instance', aimed at subverting those relationships on the basis of a political assumption, scientifically grounded upon its *critical* character.[4]

Because in Marx the relationship between economic doctrine and political categories is absolutely clear, what we shall try to reconsider is something that for a long time has been taken for granted: namely, the alleged inefficacy of a political doctrine whose categorial apparatus is undistinguishable from the one informing the critique of

3   A. Negri, *Marx beyond Marx. Lessons on the Grundrisse*, trans. by H. Cleaver, M. Ryan and M. Viano, ed. by J. Fleming, Bergin & Garvey Publishers, New York, 1984, p.47. On this issue the contributions of L. Althusser are to be considered: *Pour Marx*, Maspero, Paris, 1965; (with E. Balibar) *Lire Le Capital*, Maspero, Paris, 1965. But see also E.V. Il'enkov, *Dialektika abstraktnogo i konkretnogo v 'Kapitale' Marksa*, Izdatel'stvo Akademii Nauk SSSR, Moskva, 1960; G. Della Volpe, *Chiave della dialettica storica*, in *Opere*, ed. by I. Ambrogio, Editori riuniti, Roma, 1973, vol.6, part. p.291; G. Pietranera, *Capitalismo ed economia*, Einaudi, Torino, 1972, pp.179–211.

4   Particularly relevant was the Italian theoretical analysis developed between the 1960s and 1970s. Once slashed the historicist *Kultur*, the change on Marxian studies provided by the so-called 'workerist school' was decisive. It gave rise to a radical change whose importance was unanimously recognized also by those who did not accept it: from France to the US, from Great Britain to Germany. Fundamental analyses are those of R. Panzieri, 'Sull'uso capitalistico delle macchine', *Quaderni rossi*, 1961, 1, pp.53–72; Id., 'Plusvalore e pianificazione', *Quaderni rossi*, 1964, 4, pp.257–88 (followed, in the same number of the journal, by the translation of the *Fragment on Machinery* from *Grundrisse*; but cf. R. Panzieri, *La ripresa del marxismo leninismo in Italia*, Sapere Edizioni, Milano-Roma, 1973; and the special issue of *aut aut*, 1975, 149–50); M. Tronti, *Operai e capitale*, Einaudi, Torino, 1966; A. Negri, 'Marx sul ciclo e la crisi', *Contropiano*, 1968, 2, pp.247–95 (after in in AA. Vv., *Operai e stato*, Feltrinelli, Milano, 1972, pp.191–233); Id., *Marx beyond Marx*.

political economy.[5] Thus, we are not particularly interested in the re-consideration of the heterodoxy of Marx's critique;[6] rather, we will try to make explicit the paradigmatic subversion of the political criteria that it entails. A subversion that has been declared ineffectual exactly because of its political intent is declined in economic terms. Providing the fact that we are not interested in proposing, once again, the 'actuality' of Marx (and even less a Marx *politicus*), the questions we shall pose are the following: in Marx's analytical apparatus, is it possible to find a 'truth effect', not exhaustible in a noble economic sociology of social inequality? Is this effect devoid of a *political analyticity*?

2. An abstract determination

The first step of our analysis will be devoted to the reconsideration of Marx's 'discursive strategy'. As Jacques Rancière[7] pointed out in an essay published in 1965, in Marx the role of the *Kritik* is extremely relevant, as it pervades any single phase of the development of his work, designating the specificity of its approach. What constitutes this

5   Different interpretations have been given by N. Bobbio, 'Esiste una dottrina marxista dello Stato?', *Mondo Operaio*, 1975, September–October, pp.24–31; A. Negri, 'Esiste una dottrina marxista dello Stato?', *aut aut*, 1976, 152–3, pp.35–50; and M. Tronti, *Sull'autonomia del politico*, Feltrinelli, Milano, 1977, p.15.

6   The emergence of the question of Marx's heterodoxy is widely present in Anglo-Saxon economic literature, characterized by issues such as 'alienation' and 'fetishism', the problem of 'transformation', the relationship between Marx and other heterodox authors, particularly Keynes and Schumpeter. Cf. J. Cunningham Wood (ed. by), *Karl Marx's Economics: Critical Assessments*, Croom Helm, London, 1988, vol.4; M. Blaug, *Karl Marx (1818–1883)*, Elgar, Aldershot, 1991; M. Howard, J.E. King, *Marxian Economics*, Elgar, Aldershot, 1990, vol.3.

7   J. Rancière, *Le concept de critique et la critique de l'économie politique*, Maspero, Paris, 1965. Although 'scholastic', see also E. Renault, *Marx et l'idée de critique*, PUF, Paris, 1995.

141

specificity and what is its object? It is worth noting that, though Marx's subject matter is the classical political economy, he neither carried out nor provided the foundations for an 'alternative' political economy. Hence, it would be mistaken to limit his endeavour within the problematic horizon of the classical school.[8] The attempt to identify a macroeconomic framework within which it would be possible to define the genesis of both the surplus and the income distribution associated with it cannot exhaust Marx's effort. Such identification, in fact, qualifies the *object* of the critique, but not the *critique* itself. Although this latter assumes the very same object as the classical political economy, it intends to identify within it not only its interpretative mistakes, but also its *ideological artifices*. Through them, the object is scientifically transfigured, portraying historically determined social relationships as 'natural'. This allows the claim that Marx's critique of the ideology is a qualifying aspect of his critique of political economy. The aim of the former is to show the theoretical insufficiency of the classical political economy and its ideological function. A function that is based upon a scientific idea which is satisfied by 'what is true of all forms of appearance and their hidden background'. To these forms are related the 'current and usual modes of thought', which reproduce themselves with an immediate spontaneity, without understanding the 'essential relation' [*wesentlichen Verhältnis*] that 'must first be discovered by science'.[9]

In these terms, however, the key distinction between the classical and the vulgar political economy is not yet clearly crystallized. In

8   According to Marx's definition: 'Let me point out once and for all that by classical political economy I mean all the economists who, since the time of W. Petty, have investigated the real internal framework [*innern Zusammenhang*] of bourgeois relations of production, as opposed to the vulgar economists who only flounder around within the apparent framework [*des scheinbaren Zusammenhangs*] of those relations, ceaselessly ruminating on the materials long since provided by scientific political economy [...]' (K. Marx, *Capital. A Critique of Political Economy*, trans. by B. Fowkes, Penguin Books, London, 1990, vol.1, pp.174–5, footnote 34; *MEW*, Dietz, Berlin, 1956 ff., Bd.23, p.95, footnote 32).

9   K. Marx, *Capital*, vol.1, p.682 (*MEW*, Bd.23, p.564). Cf. H. Reichelt, *Zur logischen Struktur des Kapitalsbegriffs bei Karl Marx*, Europäische Verlagsanstalt GmbH, Frankfurt am Main, 1970.

effect, Marx's argumentation is in these pages particularly concise, because it refers to the crucial distinction between value and price of labour power. The differences between classical and vulgar political economy are better understood in other and more explicit places. For example, where he distinguishes between the 'vulgar economists' and the 'economic investigators' – these latter being 'critical economists'.[10] 'Classical political economy seeks to reduce the various fixed and mutually alien forms of wealth to their inner unity by means of analysis and to strip away the form in which they exist independently alongside one another. It seeks to grasp the inner connection in contrast to the multiplicity of outward forms'[11] – although it has no interest in developing those different forms genetically, because it considers them as *given* assumptions. Differently, the vulgar economy imposes itself when political economy 'has, as a result of its analysis, undermined and impaired its own premises'. 'Only when political economy has reached a certain stage of development and has assumed well-established forms – that is, after Adam Smith – does the separation of the element whose notion of the phenomena consists of a mere reflection of them taking place, i.e., its vulgar element becomes a special aspect of political economy'.[12] Say, Bastiat, and Roscher define the different degrees of an apologetics that moves from the problem towards its harmonicistic or professorial dissolution:

> The more the vulgar economists in fact content themselves with translating common notions into doctrinaire language, the more they imagine that their writings are plain, *in accordance with nature* and the public interest, and free from all theoretical hair-splitting. Therefore, the more alienated the form in which they conceive the manifestations of capitalist production, the closer they approach the nature of common notions, and the more they are, as a consequence, in their natural element.[13]

---

10 K. Marx, *Theories of Surplus-value*, trans. by E. Burns, Progress Publishers, Moscow, 1969, vol.3, pp.453, 499 (*MEW*, Bd.26.3, pp.445, 490).
11 Ibid., p.500 (*MEW*, Bd.26.3, p.490).
12 Ibid., p.501 (*MEW*, Bd.26.3, p.491).
13 Ibid., p.503 (*MEW*, Bd.26.3, p.493).

Therefore, according to the scientific economy, the apologetic element, defined by its scientific nature, is an outcome which derives from a reasoning in which the *natural order* is confirmed by a rational argumentation that considers it a solid basis for the *social order*. The vulgar economy, instead, skips the problem of the scientific legitimization. In other words, although it is true that classic economy 'does not conceive the *basic form of capital*, i.e., production designed to appropriate other people's labour, as a *historical* form but as a *natural form* of social production', it is nonetheless true that it 'paves the way for the refutation of this conception'.[14] Obviously, the critique of the political economy is the critique of the scientific economy, not of its apologetic degeneration. The critique deals with the specific ideological function of the political economy, but because of its *scientific nature*.

Regarding this, the original fault of the classical political economy is enlightening. Classical economists – Marx observes – base production upon eternal natural laws, detached from history, attributing then to the distribution a variety of arbitrary acts. In doing so, they preclude themselves the possibility of understanding both production and distribution – and their relationship. 'The production, distribution, exchange and consumption form a regular syllogism; production is the generality, distribution and exchange the particularity, and consumption the singularity in which the whole is joined together. This admittedly a coherence, but a shallow one'.[15] Furthermore, and consequently: when we refer to production, we are referring to a specific degree of social development, that is, to a production generated by social individuals [*gesellschaftlicher Individuen*]. All stages of production have common characteristics and determinations. In general terms, production is therefore an *ab-*

14   Ibid., p.501 (*MEW*, Bd.26.3, p.491).
15   K. Marx, *Grundrisse. Foundations of the Critique of Political Economy*, trans. by M. Nicolaus, Penguin Books, London, 1993, p.89 (*Grundrisse der Kritik der Politischen Ökonomie*, Dietz, Berlin, 1953, p.11).

straction,[16] which is rational 'in so far as it really brings out and fixes the common elements':

> Still, this *general* category, this common element sifted out by comparison, is itself segmented many times over and splits into different determinations. Some determinations belong to all epochs, other only to a few. Some determinations will be shared by the most modern epoch and the most ancient. No production will be thinkable without them; however, even though the most developed languages have laws and characteristics in common with the least developed, nevertheless, just those things which determine their development, i.e. the element which are not general and common [*den Unterschied von diesem Allgemeinem und Gemeinsamen*], must be separated out from the determinations valid for production as such, so that in their unity – which arise already from the identity of the subject, humanity, and of the object, nature – their essential difference [*wesentliche Verschiedenheit*] is not forgotten. The whole profundity of those modern economists who demonstrate the eternity and harmoniousness of the existing social relations lies in this forgetting.[17]

In Marx's critique of the classical economists, the establishment of the diversity represents a turning point defined by an *essential difference*, that is, by what is historically determined. Nevertheless, although wrapped by a comparatistic aura, it is not by means of such a comparative methodology that such an establishment represents and qualifies the *wesentliche Verschiedenheit*. The difference arises not only from the comparison between what *seems* common, but also from the incommensurability of different discursive strategies. That in reality a subject and an object of production do exist, is by no means obvious. Radically different instead are the outcomes when subject and object are traced back not to a natural order, but to a socially determined order, within which it is possible to identify a *specific* subsumption relationship: no longer between the subject and the object of production, but rather between capital and labour power.

We should not be deceived by the fact that Marx attributes to Smith the merit of having rejected any determinate character of the

---

16   Although only partially acceptable, on this specific issue, it is worth recalling the stimulating analysis proposed by H.J. Krahl, *Konstitution und Klassenkampf*, Verlag Neue Kritik, Frankfurt am Main, 1971.
17   Marx, *Grundrisse*, p.85 (*GKPÖ*, p.7).

process of wealth creation, considering it as 'labour in general'.[18] In effect, the general character of the common element does not correspond to the general character of what for Marx is an *abstract determination*. Whilst in the former case we have a simple comparison, in the latter, we have the individuation of a difference between what is common – the general, transformative activity of subject *vis-à-vis* the object – and what is radically different compared to the 'generic common'. 'Indifference towards any specific kind of labour presupposes a very developed totality of real kinds of labour, of which no single one is any longer predominant'.[19] The difference characterizes the 'labour in general', as it is abstract labour that qualifies a general transformative capacity:

> As a rule, the most general abstractions arise only in the midst of the richest possible concrete development, where on thing appears as common to many, to all. Then it ceases to be thinkable in a particular form alone. On the other side, this abstraction of labour as such is not merely the mental product of a concrete totality of labour. Indifference towards specific labours corresponds to a form of society in which individuals can with ease transfer from one labour to another, and where the specific kind is a matter of chance for them, hence of indifference.[20]

Hence, what is here *indifferent* is the result of a *specific difference*, which arises precisely when a common characteristic ceases to be thought of merely in its particular form. That is, what is common in the form of determined labour is fixed as specific difference, abandoning its particular form. 'Not only the category, labour, but labour in reality has become the means of creating wealth in general, and has ceased to be organically linked with particular individuals in any specific form'.[21] Labour is no longer 'labour *sans phrase*' as it is general transformative activity, but rather because this latter is abstract labour, with no particular relation with the individual.[22] 'Such a state

18   Ibid., p.104 (*GKPÖ*, p.24).
19   Ibid. (*GKPÖ*, p.25).
20   Ibid.
21   Ibid.
22   Tronti's comment is particularly relevant: 'Il lavoro "in generale" segna la raggiunta indifferenza verso un genere di lavoro determinato e al tempo stesso

146

of affaire is at most developed in the most modern form of existence of bourgeois society – in the United States. Here, then, for the first time, is the point of departure of modern economics, namely the abstraction of the category 'labour', 'labour as such' [*Arbeit über-haupt*], labour pure and simple, become true in practice'.[23]

An abstract determination prefigures a tendency that is 'true in practice', insisting upon what in the comparison differs.[24] What differs, differs primarily in historical terms. 'This example of labour shows strikingly how even the most abstract categories, despite their validity – precisely because of their abstractness – for all epochs, are nevertheless, in the specific character of this abstraction, themselves likewise a product of historic relations, and possess their full validity only for and within these relations'.[25] The comparative aura, however, soon tends to dissolve:

> Bourgeois society is the most developed and the most complex historic organisation of production. The categories which express its relations, the comprehension of its structure, thereby also allows insights into the structure and the relations of production of all the vanished social formations out of whose ruins and elements it built itself up, whose partly still unconquered remnants are carried along with it, whose mere nuances have developed explicit significance within it, etc.[26]

The comparative aura dissolves, because the categories express modes of being and determinations of existence of a specific form of society that, from a scientific point of view, does not begin 'only at the point where one can speak of it *as such*'. The temporal lag insinuates a difference that should be considered. But such a difference, stemming from the pure comparison, warns us against a mere 'anachronism'. Vice versa, when the abstract general category be-

presuppone una totalità molto sviluppata di generi reali di lavoro. I due processi sono strettamente uniti. Quanto più si fa concreto il lavoro particolare, tanto più si può astrarre da questo lavoro in generale' (*Operai e capitale*, Einaudi, Torino, 1971[2], p.79).

23 Marx, *Grundrisse*, pp.104–5 (*GKPÖ*, p.25).
24 Negri, *Marx beyond Marx*, pp.41–58.
25 Marx, *Grundrisse*, p.105 (*GKPÖ*, p.25).
26 Ibid. (*GKPÖ*, pp.25–6).

comes an instrument of anticipation that allows us to understand what is 'true in practice', the advancement is something else. What is 'true in practice', in fact, represents capital as 'the all-dominating economic power of bourgeois society'. This means that it would be mistaken to display the economic categories in the order in which they were historically determinant. Furthermore, this allows us to affirm that their sequence is determined by the relations in which they find themselves in modern bourgeois society. Certainly, 'human anatomy contains a key to the anatomy of the ape'. But, again, it is not here that the argumentation makes the most significant advance. Here the difference is *aufgehoben*. The most significant advance is induced by the re-qualification that the categories have undergone as a result of the insertion of a subjective, abstract but defined determination: the *living labour*. What does it mean that where the capital dominates, 'the social, historically created element' prevails? And, how should the claim according to which the capital 'must form the starting-point as well as the finishing-point' be interpreted?

It is clear that the search for a Marxian methodology aimed at founding a materialistic philosophy is out of place and time. And it is also certain that in the 1857 *Einleitung* Marx expresses above all the *critique* of what he considers to be the method of political economy. An advance is nevertheless defined, as – besides any comparativism – it comes to outline what goes beyond the critique itself: namely, the anticipatory dimension of an *abstract determination*, which moves analytically from the apex of the capitalistic development. This dimension uprooted any comparativism indeed, because in it the difference is not *aufgehoben*. What differs expresses the very essence of the capitalistic mode of production, within which labour has become the means that creates wealth in general and, as determination, it has ceased to grow together with the individuals in a particular dimension. It is 'labour in general' because it is *abstract labour*, without any particular relation with the individual. And it is worth noting that labour is abstract not because it is alienated; rather, it is alienated because is abstract. Its alleged universality is, in real terms, the *differentia specifica* that makes it possible to identify in an abstract determination what is 'true in practice', because it is tendentially delineated as such in the apex of the capitalistic development:

> It would therefore be unfeasible and wrong to let the economic categories follow one another in the same sequence as that in which they were historically decisive. Their sequence is determined, rather, by their relation to one another in modern bourgeois society, which is precisely the opposite of that which seems to be their natural order or which corresponds to historical development.[27]

Apart from Marx's method, it is evident that what is historically determined, and thereby what differs, only approximately is the result of comparison. That is, the critique has its own *pars construens*, which is based entirely upon what can be intended as the higher moment of abstraction. Both the critique of political economy and *verständige Abstraktion* become homogeneous: analysis of the socially determined production according to a political perspective, which is, in turn, both historical interpretation and revolutionary foresight, at the same time. *Critique* and *crisis* constitute a hendiadys, already foretold in the analysis devoted to the concept of political revolution. A hendiadys that, after the autumn of 1850, would be radicalized, when, withdrawn from the public struggles and from the party life 'into my study',[28] Marx claimed his disinterest towards any unrealistic minority ambition. A revolution would have been possible 'only as a result of a new crisis' but 'as certain as this'[29] His exile in London provided Marx with the most adequate milieu for his inquiry into political economy:

27 Ibid., p.107 (*GKPÖ*, p.28).
28 'I have given up associations – *organised* ones. [...] and since the Cologne trial, I have withdrawn completely into my study. My time was too precious to be wasted in fruitless endeavour and petty squabbles' (*Marx to Weydemeyer, 1 February 1859*, in Marx-Engels, *Collected Works*, Progress Publishers – Lawrence & Wishart, Moscow and London, 1975 and ff., vol.40, p.374; *MEW*, Bd.29, p.572).
29 'Eine neue Revolution ist nur möglich im Gefolge einer neuen Krisis. Sie ist aber auch ebenso sicher wie diese' (K. Marx, F. Engels, *Revue, Mai bis Oktober 1850*; *MEW*, Bd.7, p.440), quoted in F. Mehring, *Karl Marx, Geschichte seines Lebens*, in *Gesammelte Schriften*, Dietz, Berlin, 1964, Bd.3, p.259.

I am working enormously, as a rule until 4 o'clock in the morning. I am engaged on a twofold task: 1. Elaborating the outlines of political economy. For the benefit of the public it is absolutely essential to go into the matter *au fond* [thoroughly], as it is for my own, *individually, to get rid of this nightmare*. 2. The *present crisis*. Apart from the articles for the *Tribune*, all I do is keep records of it, which, however, takes up a considerable amount of time. I think that, somewhere about the spring, we ought to do a pamphlet *together* about the affair as a reminder to the German public that we are still there as always, and *always the same*.[30]

In his post 1848 exile,[31] whilst anxiously awaiting news from the industrial district of Manchester, what Marx aimed at was a political *rentrée*. Concerned both with Bonaparte's *general rottenness* and the events occurring in the United States, he carried out only an apparent 'twofold task', because his true and paramount aim was to rearrange his economic studies, 'so that I at least get the outlines clear before the *déluge*'.[32] He believed that 'Boustrapa will hardly be able to extricate himself in 1858 unless he holds out for a bit longer with the help of martial law and *assignats*'.[33] Hence, the outstanding crisis might have provided the grounds for his return to politics, mediated, and this is the seminal point, by the theoretical analysis that was condensing in *Grundrisse*.[34] Marx's articulation of the critique of economy, ideology, and politics, therefore, is what the hendiadys 'critique and crisis' imposes and the *rational abstraction*, concretely, radicalizes, moving from the money-form.

30 *Marx to Engels, 18 December 1857*, in Marx-Engels, *Collected Works*, vol.40, p.224 (*MEW*, Bd.29, p.232).
31 Cf. B. Nikolaevskij, O. Maenchen-Helfen, *Karl Marx. Eine Biographie*, J.H.W. Dietz, Hannover, 1963; D. McLellan, *Karl Marx his Life and Thought*, Macmillan, London, 1973; G. Mayer, *Friederich Engels. A Biography*, Chapman & Hall, London, 1936.
32 *Marx to Engels, 8 December 1857*, in Marx-Engels, *Collected Works*, vol.40, p.214 (*MEW*, Bd.29, p.225).
33 *Marx to Engels, 25 December 1857*, in Marx-Engels, *Collected Works*, vol.40, p.228 (*MEW*, Bd.29, p.239).
34 V.S. Vygodskij, *Geschichte einer großen Entdeckung*, Verlag Die Wirtschaft, Berlin, 1967, p.18.

3. The sudden changes of 1856

A 'revolution from above'.[35] In this way it is possible to measure the incredibly ponderous task condensed in *Grundrisse*, present in Marx's activity as correspondent for the *New York Daily Tribune*, and documented in the daily exchange of letters during the period between 1856–1858. From this point of view – as observed by Roman Rosdolsky –, the same interruption of the preparatory work for *Zur Kritik* due to Marx's activity as publicist should not be considered as a parenthesis in his research, because it constituted a sort of fundamental apprenticeship.[36] As Marx himself wrote in the 'Preface' of the book published in 1859: 'Since a considerable part of my con-

35 Sergio Bologna clarified the meaning of 'the revolution from above' ('Money and Crisis: Marx as Correspondent of the New York Daily Tribune, 1856–57', trans. by Ed Emery, *Common Sense*, 1993, 13, p.52). He considered *The Economic Crisis in Europe* published in the *New York Daily Tribune* the 15th October 1856. In it Marx ridiculed Mazzini and his henchmens, that did not know 'the life conditions of the people and the real conditions of the historical development' (cf. *MEW*, Bd.12, p.55). And, above all, Marx underlined that 'today it is accepted as obvious a social revolution even before the political one has been declared; and in particular, a kind of social revolution that is not stirred up by clandestine conspiracies of secret societies among workers, but rather by the public artifices of the ruling classes' *Crédits Mobiliers*' (*MEW*, Bd.12, p.54). As Bologna noted, this was the thesis of the 'revolution from above': the new capitalistic powers appeared as instruments of a revolution whose outcome was much more significant than that forecasted by the revolutionaries of 1848.

36 Rosdolsky, *The Making of Marx's 'Capital'*, p.7. It is interesting to consider the titles of the most important articles that Marx wrote for the *New York Daily Tribune* between 1856 and 1858: 'The French Credit Mobilier, I, II, III' (21 and 24 June; 11 July 1856); 'The Economic Crisis in Europe' (9 and 15 October 1856); 'The Causes of the Monetary Crisis in Europe' (27 October 1856); 'The Economic Crisis in France' (22 November 1856); 'The European Crisis' (6 December 1856); 'Credit Mobilier' (30 May 1857); 'Credit Mobilier' (20 June 1857); 'The French Credit Mobilier' (26 September 1857); 'The Financial Crisis in Europe' (22 Deember 1857); 'The Crisis in Europe' (5 January 1858); 'The French Crisis' (12 January 1958); 'The Economic Crisis in France' (12 March 1858); 'The Financial State of France' (30 March 1858). The German version of the above articles can be found in *MEW*, Bde.11 and 12.

tributions consisted of articles dealing with important economic events in Britain and on the continent, I was compelled to become conversant with practical details which, strictly speaking, lie outside the sphere of political economy'.[37] It is very much indicative – as Rosdolsky again observes – the fact that the immediate decision to put in writing the material constituting *Grundrisse* were mainly due to the economic crisis that occurred in 1857. However, how is it possible to interpret the more than forty pages, in the opening of the manuscript, addressed to confute the so called labour-money theory?[38] – a theory briefly summarized in *Zur Kritik*, and just mentioned in a footnote of the final version of Book I of *Das Kapital*.

Compared with Book I of *Capital*, the opening of *Grundrisse* – a marvellous laboratory inserted into the middle of the *déluge* recalled in the already mentioned letter dated 8 December 1857 – presents a fundamental difference. Marx moves from money, rather than from the notion of commodity fetish, which is skipped, and then briefly retrieved below, and finally poured into that 'didactic' effort represented by the 1859 *Zur Kritik*.[39] It is a choice that belongs to the sphere of what for long time has remained a private and impenetrable

---

37   K. Marx, *A Contribution to the Critique of Political Economy*, Marx-Engels, *Collected Works*, vol.29, p.265 (*MEW*, Bd.13, p.11).

38   Rosdolsky, *The Making of Marx's 'Capital'*, p.109.

39   On 13th January 1859 Marx wrote to Engels: 'The manuscript amounts to *about* 12 sheets of print (3 instalments) and — don't be bowled over by this — although entitled *Capital in General*, these instalments contain *nothing* as yet on the subject of capital, but only the two chapters: 1. *The Commodity*, 2. *Money or Simple Circulation*. As you can see, the part that was worked out in detail (in May, when I was staying with you) is not to appear at all yet. This is good on two counts. If the thing is a success, the third chapter on capital can follow very soon. Secondly, since the matter in the published part will, by its very nature, prevent the curs from confining their criticism solely to tendentious vituperation, and since the whole thing has an *exceedingly* serious and scientific air, the canaille will later on be compelled to take my views on capital *rather seriously*. Besides, I believe that, all practical considerations apart, the chapter on money will be of interest to experts' (Marx-Engels, *Collected Works*, vol.40, p.384; *MEW*, Bd.29, p.383).

stenography,[40] as shown by the numeration of the chapters, for example.[41] But besides this – and the genesis itself of Marx's theory of money –, is it possible to attribute a specific meaning to the urge that obliged Marx to move directly from the money-form, establishing an undoubted change of paradigm?

If what we have said about the *verständige Abstraktion* is true, the answer to the above question can only be positive: the meaning resides in the fact that the 'revolution from the above' – between a Bonapartist Sansimonianism and a helpless Proudhnianism[42] – should be understood in the sudden transformation of the world market and in the role of the banking system within the economic crisis of 1857.[43] In Marx's opinion, nothing better than the money-form seemed to explain the very essence of the capitalistic mode of production and, therefore, the nexus development/crisis within the world market. As Sergio Bologna noted, the pace of the monetary system expansion was faster than that concerning the diffusion of the industrial system, and the monetary system appeared to Marx's eyes the embodiment of the world market in its concrete materiality.[44] To come quickly to the point, in the nexus crisis/monetary form, the law of value could be

40   Cf. E.J. Hobsbawm 'Introduction' to K. Marx, *Pre-capitalist Economic Formations*, Lawrence & Wishart, London, 1964.

41   Regarding the genesis of Marx's text and its relationship with *Das Kapital*, see Rosdolsky, *The Making of Marx's 'Capital'*; Vygodskij, *Geschichte einer großen Entdeckung*.

42   Cf. F. Perroux, P.-M. Schuhl (sous la direction de), 'Saint-simonisme et pari pour l'industrie. XIXe–XXe siècles', *Economies et Sociétés*, vol.IV, 4, 6, 10; V, 7; VII, 1, Droz, Genève, 1970–1973.

43   As it is well-known, Marx emphasized the innovative financial role of the *Crédit Mobilier*. Regarding its pioneering action, cf. A. Gerschenkron, *Economic Backwardness in Historical Perspective*, University of California Press, Berkeley, 1943; R. Cameron, *Banking in the Early Stages of Industrialization*, Oxford University Press, New York, 1967; Id., *Banking and Economic Development*, Oxford University Press, New York, 1972; C.P. Kindleberger, *A Financial History of Western Europe*, Allen & Unwin, London, 1984; and, above all, B. Gille, *La banque en France au XIXe siècle: recherches historiques*, Droz, Genève, 1970; A. Plessis, *La politique de la Banque de France de 1851 a 1870*, Droz, Genève, 1985.

44   Bologna, 'Money and Crisis: Marx as Correspondent of the New York Daily Tribune, 1856–57', *Common Sense*, 1993, 14, p.64.

interpreted 'from the viewpoint of a stage of capitalist development now in its maturity'.[45]

This hypothesis explains the insistence with which Marx 'dissects' the modest work of the Proudhonian Alfred Darimon. In spite of the difficulties represented by the complicacy of Marx's reasoning, it is sufficiently easy to identify its *terminus a quo* and *terminus ad quem*. Both express a specific and contingent historic-economic judgement, which already includes, however, a fundamental theoretical assumption. Referring to Darimon's analysis, Marx claims from the outset that:

> In order to reach any conclusions about circulation at all, Darimon would above all have had to present a column showing the amount of notes in circulation next to the column on bullion assets and the column on discounted bills. In order to discuss the requirements of circulation, it did not require a very great mental leap to look first of all at the fluctuations in circulation proper. The omission of this necessary link in the equation immediately betrays the bungling of the dilettante, and the intentional muddling together of the requirements of credit with those of monetary circulation [das absichtliche Zusammenwerfen der Bedürfnisse des Kredits mit denen des Geldumlaufs] – a confusion on which rests in fact the whole secret of Proudhonist wisdom.[46]

Therefore, the perspective through which Marx criticized the Proudhonian utopia entails a judgement that goes far beyond the issues posed by Darimon, according to whom all evils relative to the present social organization (unequal exchange between capital and labour, usury, economic crisis, etc.) would be derived from the privileges arising from money and from the predominance enjoyed by the circulation of noble metals. The distinction between the 'requirements of credit' and the 'requirement of monetary circulation' is however possible if one acknowledge, simultaneously, not only the utopian nature of labour-money and the variety of socialist hypotheses concerning the time-chits, but also their incapacity to understand the

45   Bologna, 'Money and Crisis: Marx as Correspondent of the New York Daily Tribune, 1856–57', *Common Sense*, 1993, 13, p.31. Concerning the nexus money-form/law of value, see also Negri, *Marx beyond Marx*, pp.23–5; 35–40.
46   Marx, *Grundrisse*, p.115–16 (*GKPÖ*, pp.35–6).

first complete form of modern State, of a modern monetary system characterized by the government of liquidity.[47]

The question that Marx poses consists of asking whether it is possible to alter the relations of production characterizing modern society, as well as the relations of distribution associated with them, via a transformation of the means of circulation, namely, transforming the organization of circulation. In Marx's words: 'Can such a transformation of circulation be undertaken without touching the existing relations of production and the social relations which rest on them?'.[48] This is evidently a rhetorical question. Hence, Marx underlines how the lack of a distinction between the 'requirements of credit' and the 'requirements of monetary circulation' involves a misunderstanding concerning the 'inner connections between the relations of production, of distribution and of circulation'. In other words, the assumption 'to get around essential determinations of a relation by means of formal modifications' is untenable. Different forms of money could be better ascribed to social production; a form of money can eliminate the inconvenience that another is unable to resolve; 'but none of them, as long as they remain forms of money, and as long as money remain an essential relation of production, is capable of overcoming the contradiction inherent in the money relation, and can instead only hope to reproduce these contradictions in one or another form'.[49]

It is here that we find the *terminus ad quem*, which restates the starting point: 'This much is evident right at the beginning of Darimon, namely that he completely identifies *monetary turnover* with *credit*, which is economically wrong'.[50] Darimon's misrepresentation of the capitalistic character of credit implies his misrepresentation of the capitalistic mode of production. It is here that the 'revolution from the above' becomes apparent and the Proudhonism appears to be merely a passive instrument. It is not accidental that in the critique to John Gray's time-chits we can find the decisive theme

47   Bologna, 'Money and Crisis: Marx as Correspondent of the New York Daily Tribune, 1856–57', *Common Sense*, 1993, 13, p.37.
48   Marx, *Grundrisse*, p.122 (*GKPÖ*, p.42).
49   Ibid., p.123 (*GKPÖ*, pp.42–3).
50   Ibid. (*GKPÖ*, p.43).

of the world market. To hypothesize an equivalence between the price of commodities and their exchange value – Marx observes – would be tantamount to assuming a *'Proportionate Production'*, so as to render the problem of money of secondary importance. In other words, to make such an assumption would mean to ignore that '[t]he dissolution of all products and activities into exchange values presupposes the dissolution of all fixed personal (historic) relations of dependence in production, as well as the all-sided dependence of the producers on one another'.[51] The social bond among individuals is represented by a mutual and generalized dependency, within which the social character of the activity and the social form of what is produced appear something extraneous and objective to the individual, 'not as their relation to one another, but as their subordination to relationships which subsist independently of them'. 'The general exchange of activities and products, which has become a vital condition for each individual – their mutual interconnection – here appears as something alien to them, autonomous, as a thing. In exchange value, the social connection between persons is transformed into social relation between things; personal capacity into objective wealth'.[52]

For the above reasons, nothing is 'more erroneous and absurd than to postulate the control by the united individuals of their total production, on the basis of *exchange value*, of *money*' – according to the hypothesis underpinning the time-chits. Thus, 'a bank which directly creates the mirror image of the commodity in the form of labour-money is a utopia'. In effect, much more complex are the terms that the 'revolution from the above' presents. The division of labour creates agglomeration, combination, co-operation, the antithesis of private interests, class interest, concentration of capital, etc. – 'so many antithetical forms of the unity which itself brings the antithesis to the fore [...]'. In the same way that the exchange allows the global commerce, the private independence generates a complete dependency upon the world market, within which 'the *connection of the individual with all*, but at the same time also the *independence of this connection from the individual*, have developed to such a high level that the

51   Ibid., p.156 (*GKPÖ*, pp.73–4).
52   Ibid., p.157 (*GKPÖ*, p.75).

156

formation of the world market already at the same time contains the conditions for going beyond it'.[53]

Potential conditions, expressed in a real 'revolution from the above', politically identified in the economic crisis of 1857 and in the *theory of crisis* as an explicative paradigm. In spite of its explicit limit – linked to the contemporary international golden standard – in this paradigm the category of *Weltmarkt* is central, exactly because the money form is analysed as a monetary instrument *tout court*.[54] On the other hand, such a limit is pushed beyond itself, if it is true that in these pages we can find all those elements that define, via the very same *Welmarkt*, the 'revolution from the above' analysed in *Grundrisse*. The internal articulation of production, its crystallization in the State, and the world market: these are the borders within which production is understood as totality and as contradictory totality of its moments. 'The world market then, again, forms the presupposition of the whole as well as its substratum. Crises are then the general intimation which points beyond the presupposition, and the urge which drives towards the adoption of a new historic form'.[55]

Grundrisse as *Rough Draft*? Certainly, it is. It is sufficient here to recall the importance of the fifth Section of Book III of *Das Kapital*, because it is there that Marx analyses in depth the argument concerning the money capital and credit: 'The fetish character of capital and the representation of this capital fetish is now complete'. It is at this point that 'the capital mystification in its most flagrant form'[56] occurs:

---

53   Ibid., p.161 (*GKPÖ*, p.79).
54   The most evident limit is synthesized in the statement according to which 'the fragmented acts of exchange create a banking and credit system whose books, at least keep a record of the balance between debit and credit in private exchange' [Ibid., p.159 (*GKPÖ*, p.77)]. See A. Graziani, 'La teoria marxiana della moneta', in C. Mancina (a cura di), *Marx e il mondo contemporaneo*, Editori riuniti, Roma, 1986, pp.207–29; Bellofiore, 'Per una teoria monetaria del valore-lavoro. Problemi aperti nella teoria marxiana, tra radici ricardiane e nuove vie di ricerca', in G. Lunghini (a cura di), *Valori e prezzi*, Utet, Torino, 1993, pp.94–5.
55   Marx, *Grundrisse*, pp.227–8 (*GKPÖ*, p.139).
56   Marx, *Capital*, vol.3, p.516 (*MEW*, Bd.25, p.405).

In interest-bearing capital, the capital relationship reaches its most superficial and fetishised form. [...] The form of commercial capital still exhibits a process, the unity of opposing phases, a movement that breaks down into two opposite procedures, the purchase and sale of commodities. This is obliterated in M–M', the form of interest–bearing capital.[57]

The valorization of money by means of money hides the processual character of commercial capital and of industrial capital; it hides, moreover, the mediation enacted by commodities: the relationship M–C–M' – 'the general formula for capital'[58] –, as it manifests itself in the circulation, is simply extinguished:

M–M'. Here we have the original starting-point of capital, money in the formula M–C–M', reduced to the two extremes M–M', where M' = M + ΔD, money that creates more money. This is the original and general formula for capital reduced to a meaningless abbreviation. It is capital in its finished form, the unity of the production and circulation processes, and hence capital yielding a definite surplus-value in a specific period of time. In the form of interest-bearing capital, capital appears immediately in this form, unmediated by the production and circulation processes.[59]

'It is capital in its finished form'. The 'fragment on credit' is its most mature representation, because – as Suzanne De Brunhoff noted[60] – the monetary analysis of monetary financing develops via the study of credit. In effect, it is here where Marx notes, among other things, that capital 'now receives the form of social capital [*Gesellschaftskapital*] (capital of directly associated individuals) in contrast to private capital [...]. This is the abolition of capital as private property within the confines of the capitalist mode of production itself'.[61]

At any rate, in *Grundrisse*, although within the treatment of *capital en général*, the issue is posed, indicating how credit is 'a form in which capital tries to posit itself as distinct from the individual

57   Ibid., p.515 (*MEW*, Bd.25, p.404).
58   Ibid., vol.1, p.257 (*MEW*, Bd.23, p.170).
59   Ibid., vol.3, pp.515–16 (*MEW*, Bd.25, pp.404–5). See also Marx, *Theories of Surplus-value*, vol.3, pp.466–8 (*MEW*, Bd.26.3, pp.458–9).
60   S. De Brunhoff, *Le monnaie chez Marx*, Ed. Sociales, Paris, 1973.
61   Marx, *Capital*, vol.3, p.567 (*MEW*, Bd.25, p.452).

capitals', as 'new element of *concentration*, of the destruction of capitals by individual, centralising capitals'.[62] No less clear is the reference present in *Urtext*, where Marx establishes – not without some uncertainties – an explicit nexus between the modern mode of production that characterizes developed countries, and the credit system, within which the exclusive relevance that money has on the basis of the simple metallic circulation is vanishing.[63] Rosdolsky is right when he underlines that most of the results stemming from Marx's later analysis of the credit system are already present in *Grundrisse*.[64] But if this is true, it is also legitimate to interpret the confutation of the so-called labour-money theory in the wider and general relationship between money form and the theory of crisis – a relationship characterized by the new liquidity forms. Darimon's shabbiness and his intentional muddling between the 'requirements of credit' and the 'requirements of money circulation' are here evident. As Marx would observe later in *Zur Kritik*, '[a]ll the illusions of the Monetary System arise from the failure to perceive that money, though a physical object with distinct properties, represents a social relation of production [*gesellschaftliches Produktionsverhältnis*] [...]'.[65]

Critique and *crisis*: the hendiadys expresses the monetary essence of the capitalist mode of production. Hence, the 'revolution from the above' induces us to grasp, exactly in the illusions relative to the monetary system, the explanation of the *real foundation* of social relationships. Nevertheless, this can only happen when, and not before, the monetary character of the capitalistic economy is identified. Marx comes to an easy closure with the Proudhonian, shabby dilettantism and its intentional confusion noting that the product of labour in the form of exchange labour, although expressing itself for and in society, is not immediately social. Individuals are subsumed to

---

62   Marx, *Grundrisse*, p.659 (*GKPÖ*, p.552). Cf. Rosdolsky, *The Making of Marx's 'Capital'*, pp.383 ff.
63   Marx, *GKPÖ*, p.876.
64   Rosdolsky, *The Making of Marx's 'Capital'*, p.397.
65   Marx, *A Contribution to the Critique of Political Economy*, Marx-Engels, *Collected Works*, vol.29, p.276 (*MEW*, Bd.13, p.22).

the social production, which 'exists outside them as their fate; but social production is not subsumed under individual, manageable by them as their common wealth'.[66] As a result, nothing appears to be more trivial than the supposed realization of the control of the associate producers global production on the basis of the exchange value and of a different form of money, according to the idea lying beneath the proposal of a bank of time-chits.

More articulated, however, is the set of issues that the same confutation raises moving from the absent distinction between the requirements of the credit and those of monetary circulation – absence that should be considered as the real crucial point. Here the nexus critique/crisis, which is political by definition, finds its foundations. A nexus of which it is relevant to understand the autonomy (expressed in terms of money and credit acting at the level of *Weltmarkt*), and that certainly informs the issues dealt in Book II of *Das Kapital*.[67] As Bologna has noted, development and crisis are indissolubly linked and unified in the very same institutions. 'Without a disproportionate expansion of money supply and credit there could be no expansion of industrial capacity; without a disproportionate growth in the organic composition of capital there could be no increase in the mass of profit; without a disproportionate growth of the sphere of exchange, no world market; without a disproportionate increase of surplus-labour no control over necessary labour. The causes of crisis are the causes of development; they are intrinsically necessary to capitalist development'.[68] Thus, it is the emphasis placed upon the monetary and credit character of the 1857 crisis that allows the understanding of the anomalous opening of *Grundrisse*.

---

66   Marx, *Grundrisse*, p.158 (*GKPÖ*, p.76).
67   It is worth noticing that, starting from the critique developed by R. Hilferding and R. Luxemburg (see Rosdolsky, *The Making of Marx's 'Capital'*, pp.445 ff.), the interpretation of Book II of *Das Kapital* would concern first of all the problems related to the concept of crisis. Regarding this, particularly important is the posthumous work of H. Grossmann, *Das Akkumulation und das Zusammenbruchsgesetz des kapitalistischen Systems*, Verlag Neue Kritik, Frankfurt, 1967.
68   Bologna, 'Money and Crisis: Marx as Correspondent of the New York Daily Tribune, 1856–57', *Common Sense*, 1993, 13, p.39.

And it is at this point that the relationship between capital and labour power, only seemingly secondary,[69] become understandable moving from the abstract nature of money. In fact, the need for exchange, division of labour, and power of money go hand in hand, as 'the exchange relation establishes itself as a power external to an independent of the producers'.

> The product becomes a commodity; the commodity becomes exchange value; the exchange value of the commodity is its immanent money-property; this, its money-property, separates itself from it in the form of money, and achieves a general social existence separated from all particular commodities and their natural mode of existence; the relation of the product to itself as exchange value becomes its relation to money, existing alongside it; or, becomes the relation of all products to money, external to them all. Just as the real exchange of products creates their exchange value, so does their exchange value create money.[70]

Money immediately appears as 'real common substance [*Gemeinwesen*], since it is the general substance of survival of all, and at the same time the social product of all'.[71] However, for the isolated individual, this 'common substance' is 'a mere abstraction', even if it is the means of his satisfaction. Any production is an objectification of the individual, but in the money 'the individual is not objectified in his natural quality, but in social quality (relation), which is, at the same time, external to him'.[72]

The dissolution of all fixed personal relations of dependence [*Abhängigkeitsverhältnisse*] in production, as well as the all-sided dependence [*allseitige Abhängigkeit*] of the producers, indicate 'that private interest is itself already a socially determined interest'. It is certainly made up of interests of private persons, 'but its content, as well as the form and means of its realisation, is given by social conditions independent of all'.[73] In the determination of the money relation, 'all inherent contradictions of bourgeois society appear extinguished', as, 'in so far as the commodity or labour is conceived of

69   Ibid., pp.33–4.
70   Marx, *Grundrisse*, pp.146–7 (*GKPÖ*, p.65).
71   Ibid., p.225 (*GKPÖ*, p.137).
72   Ibid., p.226 (*GKPÖ*, p.137).
73   Ibid., p.156 (*GKPÖ*, p.74).

only as exchange value', between formal character and economic character there is no difference: the sole evident relationship is that concerning equality. What is invisible is 'that already the simple forms of exchange value and of money latently contain the opposition between labour and capital etc'.[74] It is therefore correct to affirm that the theory of value and surplus-value should be thought of as a whole.[75] At this stage, the analysis of the commodities presupposed in *Grundrisse* loses its propedeutic character, as the political essence of the law of value is fully revealed via the hendiadys critique/crisis. It is to capital *en général* that Marx returns, but in the form of a direct opposition between abstract labour and capital. In this light, the starting point is now M–C–M': '*Money as capital* is an aspect of money which goes beyond its simple character as money'.[76]

4. Labour as subjectivity

This 'going beyond' involved in *Grundrisse* presupposes the transformation enacted by the use-value of labour power as living labour, compared to dead and objectified labour. This presupposition sends back to Marx's analysis of the law of value, according to which the social form of the labour power and the commodities it produces are central. Is it a step back regarding the opening of the *Grundrisse*?[77] Certainly it is, but it is a brief step and it is necessary to explain because, already in the simple determination of the exchange value and of money, it is contained, in a latent form, the antithesis between labour power and capital. This explanation involves what Marx has

74   Ibid., p.248 (*GKPÖ*, p.159).
75   Vygodskij, *Geschichte einer großen Entdeckung*, p.71.
76   Marx, *Grundrisse*, p.250 (*GKPÖ*, p.162).
77   It might be useful to recall Althusser's opinion, who, not fascinated by *Grundrisse*, maintained that in order to adequately understand *Das Kapital*, it would have been necessary to provisionally put aside Section I and to start from Section II ('Avertissement aux lecteur du Livre I du Capital', in K. Marx, *Le Capital*, Garnier-Flammarion, Paris, 1969).

already established: the *monetary character* of the capitalistic mode of production.

In Marx's analysis, the value-form is notoriously related to the commodity-form.[78] Commodities are simultaneously objects of use and depositary of value. They manifest themselves as such 'in so far as they possess a double form, i.e. the natural form and the value form'.[79] This latter is determined within them by the twofold character [*Doppelcharakter*] of the capitalistic labour – at the same time, concrete and abstract – that, in turn, renders possible the determination of the quality as a function of quantity, the use-value as a function of the exchange value.[80] Accordingly, commodity is socially distinguished from the simple product of human activity. The objective character it expresses is in fact purely social and 'can only appear in the social relation between commodity and commodity'.[81] Hence, annulling and incorporating the existence of the product as separated existence – whose use-value is the direct aim of the producer –, the commodity becomes *social synthesis*.

In the Marxian analysis, the exchange value is a relationship that obliterates any natural and subjective residual of the exchange. This relationship is, in the first instance, the specific result of a merely quantitative comparison among commodities having different qualities. Thanks to this comparison, it is possible to establish the proportion in which use-values of a certain kind are exchanged with other use-values, a quantity of objectified labour in a commodity with

78 Concerning the issues posed by *Wertfornanalyse* and inherent to the difference between the Ist and IVth edition of *Das Kapital*, cf. C. Pennavaja, 'Introduzione' in K. Marx, *L'analisi della forma valore*, Laterza, Roma-Bari, 1977, pp.V–LII. For an extensive overview, cf. I.I. Rubin, *Essays on Marx's Theory of Value*, Black Rose, Detroit, 1972; R.L. Meek, *Studies in the Labour Theory of Value*, Lawrence & Wishart, London, 19732; C. Napoleoni, *Smith Ricardo Marx. Observations on the History of Economic Thought*, Blackwell, Oxford, 1975; Ibid., *Valore*, Isedi, Milano, 1976.
79 Marx, *Capital*, vol.1, p.138 (*MEW*, Bd.23, p.62).
80 'Che la merce fosse qualcosa di duplice, insieme valore d'uso e valore di scambio, era cosa ovvia ai tempi di Marx. Ma che il lavoro espresso nel valore avesse caratteristiche diverse dal lavoro produttore di valore d'uso, era ignoto al pensiero del tempo' (Tronti, *Operai e capitale*, p.123).
81 Marx, *Capital*, vol.1, p.139 (*MEW*, Bd.23, p.62).

a quantity of objectified labour in another commodity. This implies the simultaneous extension of the sphere of exchange and circulation. The social character of the division of labour and the consequent loss of the subjective and teleological character of the labour process imply the progressive increase of unsatisfied needs and the increased reciprocity of the labour processes. When labour *per se* no longer represents the immediate product as its aim, the producer, any producer is obliged to engage in a series of exchanges, 'not only in order to take part in the general productive capacity, but also in order to transform his own subsistence'.[82] The relationship between commodities – expressed in the exchange value as a social nexus – is based upon the historical process of abstract determination of labour, which renders the concrete and useful labours *indifferent* to the social relations among *different* individuals. It follows that a use-value refers to another only as an exchange value, and both refer to a commodity as 'the converted form of all other commodities', as 'the direct *reification of universal labour-time*, i.e., the product of universal alienation and of the suppression of all individual labour'.[83] Consequently, the social widening of this specific relationship imposes money as means of exchange, as a *general equivalent*.[84]

---

82   Marx, *Grundrisse*, p.158 (*GKPÖ*, p.76).
83   Marx, *A Contribution to the Critique of Political Economy*, Marx-Engels, *Collected Works*, vol.29, p.288 (*MEW*, Bd.13, p.33).
84   Only apparently plain, this passage implies relevant issues inherent to the fact that, for Marx, money, intended as 'general equivalent', is a commodity, and this contradicts its credit function. See M. Messori's interpretation ('Teoria del valore senza merce-moneta? Considerazioni preliminari sull'analisi monetaria di Marx', *Quaderni di storia dell'economia politica*, 1984, vol.2, 1–2, pp.185–232) of the relationship between 'theory of value' and 'commodity-money', in juxtaposition to the so-called school of abstract social labour (M. Aglietta, A. Orlean, *La violence de la monnaie*, PUF, Paris, 1982; C. Benetti, J. Cartelier, *Marchands, salariat et capitalistes*, Maspero, Paris, 1980; M. De Vroey, 'La théorie marxiste de la valeur, version travail abstrait. Un bilan critique', in B. Chavance (éd par), *Marx en perspective*, Éd de l'École des Hautes Études en Sciences Sociales, Paris, 1985). The authors belonging to this school move from the critique of the commodity-money, questioning, at least in its quantitative aspect, Marx's theory of value. See also Graziani, 'La teoria della

It is only via money, in fact, that the circulation assumes the character of a realized process, simultaneously as presupposition and effect of the production of commodities. As a general equivalent, money becomes a need stemming from the very same process of exchange. Only in the money is it possible to resolve the contradiction concerning commodities as such. 'Thus the contradiction inherent in the commodity as such, namely that of being a particular use-value and simultaneously universal equivalent, and hence a use-value for everybody or a universal use-value, has been solved in the case of this one commodity'.[85] The social function of what is produced – as an expression of the interpersonal relationships – is now *formally mediated* by a general and abstract figure: the money-form.

As distinct from the 'form-function' of the product of human activity, the commodity-form operates only apparently as a relation among things; in reality, it hides what constitutes the social relation among human beings, who 'do not therefore bring the products of their labour into relation with each other as values because they see these objects merely as the material integuments of homogeneous human labour'. 'Value, therefore, does not have its description branded on its forehead; it rather transforms every product of labour into a social hieroglyphic'.[86] The transaction of commodities loses its eminently physical character, as it expresses a socially and historically determined relation. Hence, the value-form is not separable from the twofold character of the capitalistic labour, as the duplicity of the commodity form is undetachable from the abstract character of the labour that creates wealth.

It is in this sense that the already mentioned change of paradigm occurs: abstract labour and value are mirrored in the money form; from here descends the magic of money.

> Men are henceforth related to each other in their social process of production in a purely atomistic way. Their own relations of production therefore assume a

moneta in Marx', in Mancina (a cura di), *Marx e il mondo contemporaneo*, pp.207–29; Bellofiore, 'Per una teoria monetaria del valore-lavoro', pp.79–80.

85   Marx, *A Contribution to the Critique of Political Economy*, Marx-Engels, *Collected Works*, vol.29, p.288 (*MEW*, Bd.13, p.34).

86   Marx, *Capitale*, vol.1, pp.166–7 (*MEW*, Bd.23, p.88).

material shape which is independent of their control and their conscious individual action. This situation is manifested first by the fact that the products of men's labour universally take on the form of commodities. The riddle of the money fetish is therefore the riddle of the commodity fetish, now become visible and dazzling to our eyes.[87]

In its specificity, the existence of the value presupposes a relation of production within which the single product has ceased to be as such for the producers and it is nothing if it does not realize itself via the circulation. In this kind of production, the established social relationships are the expression of the loss of the originary, social character proper of human labour. Value manifests itself in a separated existence *vis-à-vis* the nature of the product and, even more, the subjectivity of the producer. Here, in the capitalistic mode of production, the social production is not subsumed to individuals and controlled by them; it exists as a factor extraneous to them. The determination of value implies in fact the subsumption of use-value in the exchange value. All the specific proprieties of commodity present themselves as an object different from it, as a form of a social existence expressed in terms of money, detached from its natural existence. Consequently, stemming from the capitalistic process of abstraction of concrete labour, such a subsumption/separation explicates itself in the money form, pure commodity, general use-value. 'The entire contradiction of commodity – observes Vitaly S. Vigodskij – finds its external solution in the exchange process, in the division of the commodity in commodity and money, in the fact that the value of the commodity reaches its autonomous existence in a specific commodity, namely money'. [88]

The scenario is therefore the following:

Exchange, [...], produces a differentiation [*Verdopplung*] of the commodity in two elements, commodity and money, an external opposition which express the opposition between use-value and value which is inherent in it. In this opposition, commodities as use-value confront money as exchange value. On

---

87   Ibid., p.187 (*MEW*, Bd.23, pp.107–8). On fetishism, cf. Rubin, *Essays on Marx's Theory of Value*; F. Petry, *Der soziale Gehalt der Marxschen Werttheorie*, Fischer, Jena, 1916.

88   Vygodskij, *Geschichte einer großen Entdeckung*, p.59.

the other hand, both sides of this opposition are commodities, hence themselves unities of use-value and value. But this unity of differences is expressed at two opposite poles, and at each pole in an opposite way.[89]

In this relationship, whilst commodity as use-value appears only ideally as value, money, apart from its material form, is directly a materialization of value. In the existence of commodity as money, 'commodities acquire a definite *measure* of their value [...]; they all become manifestations of social, abstract, general labour [*als Dasein der gesellschaftlichen, abstrakt allgemeinen Arbeit*] and as such they all act as social labour, that is to say, they can be *directly exchanged*'.[90]

Indeed, it is *this* relationship that characterizes the capitalistic society, within which 'the aim of labour is not a particular product standing in a particular relation to the particular needs of the individual'.[91] The use-value, the same organic replacement among different useful works, is subordinated to that specific 'general industriousness' for which 'every act of labour produces general wealth, not a particular form of it'. Commodities should find their realization as values before being able to realizes themselves as use-value, because the exchange-value 'as direct product of labour is money as direct product of labour'.[92] It is only via this specific subordination that it comes to a delineation the complex structure represented by circulation, within which 'commodities and money confront each other in the same way; the seller represents the commodity, the buyer the money'.[93]

It is obvious that the development of both circulation and capital intended as social relationship go hand in hand. Marx explains such a relationship in the *Formen*, where he notes that the development of exchange value 'dissolves production which is more oriented towards direct use value and its corresponding forms of property [...] and thus

89   Marx, *Capital*, vol.1, p.199 (*MEW*, Bd.23, p.119).
90   Marx, *Theories of Surplus-value*, vol.3, p.136 (*MEW*, Bd.26.3, pp.133–4).
91   Marx, *Grundrisse*, p.225 (*GKPÖ* p.135).
92   Ibid., (*G*, pp.135–6).
93   Marx, *A Contribution to the Critique of Political Economy*, Marx-Engels, *Collected Works*, vol.29, p.334 (*MEW*, Bd.13, p.79).

pushes towards the making of the *labour market*'. Therefore, because 'the domination of exchange value itself, and of exchange-value-producing production, presupposes alien labour capacity itself as an exchanging value',[94] the development of the exchange value is the result of and the presupposition of the abstract determination of labour. Thus, Marx assumes that the labour capacity becomes commodity and that the private labour is immediately represented as its contrary: as social labour.

Exchange and formation of capital proceed in parallel. However, it cannot be said 'that exchange value as such is realised in simple circulation'.[95] If the movement is C–M–C (commodity–money–commodity), value disappears when it is no longer within circulation aimed at satisfying a specific need. If the movement is M–C–M (money–commodity–money), there are two phases: in M–C, 'the disappearance of the form of exchange is posited; the form is posited as a merely formal mediation for the purpose of gaining possession of the natural material of the commodity';[96] in C–M, the money-form persists 'only as long as it stays outside exchange'. Finally, if the form is M–M, 'not even a formal difference appears between the things distinguished; [...]; not only does exchange value disappear, but also the formal movement of its disappearance'.[97] In all these metamorphoses, either 'the form of exchange value is extinguished', or its substance is extinguished. The realization is evanescent. Hence, in the money as such, 'exchange value has already obtained a form independent of circulation, but only a negative, transitory or, when fixated, an illusory form'.[98] In effect, money exists only in relation to circulation. When it is realized, it loses its determination of 'money as money' becoming the measure of the value and means of exchange.

The presuppositions that explain the exchange do not explicate the formation of capital. Within it, the exchange value stemming from circulation 'preserves itself within it and by means of it'; it aims at 'its

94   Marx, *Grundrisse*, p.508–10 (*GKPÖ* pp.407–9).
95   Ibid., p.260 (*GKPÖ*, p.171).
96   Ibid.
97   Ibid.
98   Ibid., p.259 (*GKPÖ* p.170).

real self-positing as exchange value, its self-realisation as exchange value'.[99] In other words, capital as exchange value presupposes circulation and, in it, it multiplies itself. It is not only simultaneously commodity and money, 'but alternatively takes the form of the one and of the other, though no longer merely by passing out of the one into the other, as in simple circulation, but rather by being in each of these roles at the same time a relation to its opposite, i.e. containing it ideally within itself'.[100] Consequently, only in the capital the exchange value realizes itself as such, as only within the capitalistic process it 'neither becomes substanceless, [...] nor loses its specific form [...]. It therefore always remains money and always commodity'.[101] But as commodity, the exchange value does not embody a determinate use-value, as it represents the totality of commodities. Capital 'is not indifferent to the substance, but to the particular form; [...] in so far as it is then posited as a particular content of exchange value, this particularity itself is a totality of particularity; hence indifferent not to particularity as such, but to the single or individuated particularity'.[102]

Thus, within the sphere of circulation, Marx distinguishes two specific characters: one defined as simply negative [*das einfach Negative*], according to which the value exchanged becomes 'inorganic ashes'; and one defined as positively negative [*das positiv Negative*], in which 'money is negated not as objectified, independent exchange value', but as 'the *antithetical* independence [*die gegensätzliche Selbständigkeit*], the mere abstract generality [*die bloß abstrakte Allgemeinheit*] in which it has firmly settled [...]'.[103] An exchange is a simply negative process when it implies pure consumption; on the contrary, it becomes a positively negative process when, in the sphere of circulation, the value, intended as abstract richness, money, does not disappear, but rather confirms itself, simultaneously, as a presupposition and as a result. This implies a valorization process and, therefore, a subject able to multiply a determinate exchange value, an

99   Ibid., p.260 (*GKPÖ* p.170).
100   Ibid., p.261 (*GKPÖ*, pp.172–3).
101   Ibid., pp.260–1 (*GKPÖ*, p.172).
102   Ibid., p.262 (*GKPÖ*, p.173).
103   Ibid., pp.262–3 (*GKPÖ*, p.174).

objectified quantity of working time, while he is reproducing the condition of his subsistence. The pace of this passage is articulated starting from the 'particular exchange' between capital and labour power:

> Differently expressed: Exchange value, as regards its content, was originally an objectified amount of labour time; as such it passed through circulation, in its objectification, until it became money, tangible money. It must now again posit the point of departure of circulation [...]; this point was labour; but [it must do so] now no longer as a simple equivalent or a simple objectification of labour, but rather as objectified exchange value, now become independent, which yields itself to labour, becomes its material, only so as to renew itself and to begin circulating again by itself. And with that it is no longer a simple positing of equivalents [*einfaches Äquivalent*], a preservation of its identity, as in circulation; but rather *multiplication* of itself [*Vervielfältigen seiner selbst*]. [...] *Money* (as returned to itself from circulation), *as capital, has lost its rigidity, and from a tangible thing has become a process.*[104]

What pushes beyond the equalization, beyond the commodity-money, is therefore a *multiplication*, as a result of a valorization process, which concerns labour's relation with itself: better still, between the 'forms' that it assumes. In fact, 'labour has changed its relation to its objectivity; it, too, has returned to itself. But the nature of the return is this, that the labour objectified in the exchange value posits living labour [*die lebendige Arbeit*] as a means of reproducing it, whereas, originally, exchange value appeared merely as a product of labour'.[105] What changes are not the terms of the exchange, but rather the relationships of one of them with itself (objectivation of itself), with the living labour. For this reason, the passage from *simply negative* to *positively negative*, the negation of the antithetical independence [*gegensätzliche Selbständigkeit*] and the transformation of money in capital (M–C–M′), manifest themselves not only as a result of labour, but also as a result of a specific transformative action that the use-value of the living labour – an ensemble of physical and intellectual attitudes – exerts upon the objectified labour.

104   Ibid., p.263 (*GKPÖ*, p.174).
105   Ibid. (*GKPÖ*, pp.174–5).

Such a specific action triggers a particular process, whose nature rests upon the specific ability to transform *in actu* what is only *in potentia*. If we analyse the exchange capital/labour power, what emerges is that the worker's use-value is not materialized in a product, 'does not exist apart from him at all, thus exists not really, but only in potentiality, as his capacity [*Fähigkeit*]'.[106] What is common to all commodities is the objectified labour and their common denominator is represented by their being exchange values. In this sense, the only thing distinct [*der einzige Unterschied*] from objectified labour 'is *non-objectified* labour, labour which is still objectifying itself, *labour as subjectivity*', 'as the *living subject*, in which it exists as capacity, as possibility; hence as worker'.[107] However, the fact that the non-objectified labour – *der einzige Unterschied* – is one of the components of the exchange generates a specificity that exchange cannot explain. The exchange cannot explain the anomaly according to which, as a result of the specific transaction occurring between capital and labour power, the use-value of the latter, its potential *Fähigkeit*, creates a difference that cannot be recognized before its manifestation as multiplication, produced by labour as subjectivity [*Arbeit als Subjektivität*]. Therefore, between an exchange in general and the specific exchange capital/labour power there is an *Unterschied*, a difference, which does not arise from a simple comparison:

> In the exchange between capital and labour, the first act is an exchange, falls entirely within the ordinary circulation; the second is a process qualitatively different from exchange, and only by misuse could it have been called any sort of exchange at all. It stands directly opposite exchange; essentially different category.[108]

What renders the exchange capital/labour power a category qualitatively different, a non-exchange, only apparent,[109] is a sort of indispensable oxymoron. It is assumed that the proprietor of the labour power 'be the free proprietor [*freier Eigentümer*] of his own

106   Ibid., p.267 (*GKPÖ*, p.178).
107   Ibid., p.272 (*GKPÖ*, p.183).
108   Ibid., p.275 (*GKPÖ*, p.186).
109   Ibid., p.322 (*GKPÖ*, p.228).

labour-capacity', that he will always sell 'for a limited period only'. Hence, it is assumed that the proprietor of the labour power and the proprietor of the money are 'equal in the eyes of the law'. At the same time, however, we should admit that the former is 'compelled to offer for sale as a commodity that very labour power which exists only in his living body'.[110] The separation [*Trennung*] of property from labour appears as the necessary law of the exchange between capital and labour power. Labour 'is not-raw-material, not-instrument of labour, not-raw-product'; rather, it is 'the not-objective itself in objective form', that is, 'only an objectivity coinciding with his immediate bodily existence [*unmittelbaren Leiblichkeit*]':

> Labour not as an object [*Gegenstand*], but as activity [*Tätigkeit*]; not as itself *value*, but as a *living source* of value. [Namely, it is] general wealth (in contrast to capital in which it exists objectively, as reality) as the *general possibility* of the same, which proves itself as such in action. Thus, it is not at all contradictory, or, rather, the in-every-way mutually contradictory statements that labour is *absolute poverty as object*, on one side, and is, on the other side, the *general possibility* of wealth as subject and as activity [*als Subjekt und als Tätigkeit*] [...].[111]

Indubitably, there is an evident contrast inherent in the fact that a 'free proprietor' is subjected to a constraint on the part of others. This renders baseless the formal assumption according to which the proprietor of his own labour power and the proprietor of money would be 'equal in the eyes of the law'.[112] However, what is more interesting is to underline the fact that, as it is the expression of a living body [*lebendige Leiblichkeit*], the labour power exists as commodity. That is, not in spite of, but because it is *Arbeit als Subjektivität*. Thus, a

110   Marx, *Capital*, vol.1, pp.271–272 (*MEW*, Bd.23, pp.182–183).
111   Ibid., I, p.296 (*GKPÖ*, p.203).
112   Pertinent here are the observations that can be derived from the theory of monetary circuit, from which it can be inferred not only the difference between those who have access to credit and those who are excluded from it (historically excluded), but also, and above all, the impossibility for workers to bargain their real wage (A. Graziani, 'L'analisi marxista e la struttura del capitalismo moderno', in *Storia del marxismo*, Einaudi, Torino, 1982, vol.4, p.720; Id., *The Monetary Theory of Production*, pp.25–31).

process qualitatively different implies the natural capacity [*Fähigkeit*] inherent to the living labour, that transforms *in actu* what is only *in potentia*. Such an ability expresses a difference [*Unterschied*], upon which a historically determined multiplication [*Vervielfältigen*] is founded; it expresses a valorization process that stems from *Arbeit als Subjektivität*. In short, the relation money/capital is mediated by the living labour. For this reason in the nexus crisis/money-form it is possible to enucleate the law of value moving from a mature stage of the capitalistic development. What would be posed 'dialectically' as a problem in *Das Kapital*[113] – the exchange of equivalents as starting point –, in *Grundrisse* is (*already*) overcome.

The mediation enacted by the living labour is expressed in the relationship of subsumption between the labour process [*Arbeitsprozeß*] and valorization process [*Verwertungsprozeß*]. The labour process, *prima facie* independent from any determined form, as a result of the exchange between capital and labour power becomes 'a process between things the capitalist has purchased, things which belong to him'.[114] Among these 'things' is included the labour power, whose peculiarity is to be living labour. In other words, the monetary exchange (wage) refers to the past labour [*vergangne*] that is latent in it, and not to the living labour [*lebendige*] given by the specific use-value of labour power. It follows that 'the value of labour power, and the value which that labour power valorises [*verwertet*] in the labour-process, are two entirely different magnitudes'.[115] The labour process is transformed in a valorization process.

Within the capitalist process of production,[116] the 'process between things' manifests itself for what it is: a relation of exploitation of the living labour on the part of the dead labour – the capitalistic

---

113 Marx, *Capital*, vol.1, pp.258 and ff.
114 Ibid., p.292 (*MEW*, Bd.23, p.200).
115 Ibid., p.300 (*MEW*, Bd.23, p.208).
116 'The production process, considered as the unity of the labour process and the process of creating value, is the process of production of commodities; considered as the unity of the labour process and the process of valorisation, it is the capitalist process of production, or the capitalist form of the production of commodities' (Ibid., p.304; *MEW*, Bd.23, p.211).

form of commodity production.[117] The labour process is no longer distinguishable from the valorization process, as the labour socially necessary to pay the wage is fused, from the beginning, to an additional quantum. The capacity [*Fähigkeit*] of the labour power makes possible what in the interaction between objective and subjective conditions is only *in potentia*. The potential capacity of the labour power generates a valorization process historically determined, as a result of the subjectivity of the living labour. This is a 'multiplication' [*Vervielfältigen*] constituted by 'one single, indivisible labour process. Work is not done twice, once to produce a useful product, a use value, to *convert* the means of production into products, and the second time to produce *value* and *surplus-value*, to *valorise value*'.[118] Here, two different results are simultaneously reached, through a singular labour. Obviously, the 'twofold nature of the result' [*Doppelseitigkeit*] can be only explained by the twofold character [*Doppelcharakter*] of labour:[119]

> There is, however, the following specific distinction [*spezifischer Unterschied*] to be pointed out here: Real labour is what the worker really gives to the capitalist as equivalent for the part of the capital that has been converted into wages, for the purchasing price of labour. It is the expenditure of his life force [*Lebenskraft*], the realisation of *his* productive capacities, his movement, not the capitalist's. Viewed as a personal function [*persönliche Funktion*], in its reality, labour is the function of the worker and not of the capitalist. Viewed from the point of view of exchange, the worker is what the capitalist receives from him in the labour process, not what the capitalist represents towards him in the same process. This therefore stands in contrast to the way the objective conditions of labour, as capital, and to that extent as the existence of the capitalist, confront the subjective condition of labour, labour itself, or rather the *worker* who works, within the labour process itself.[120]

117 Cf. Tronti, *Operai e capitale*, pp.162–8.
118 K. Marx, *The Process of Production of Capital, Draft Chapter 6 of Capital. Results of the Direct Production Process*, in Marx-Engels, *Collected Works*, vol.34, p.400 [*Resultate Des Unmittelbaren Produktionsprozesses: (6. Kap. d. 1 Bd.d. 'Kapitals'. Entwurf 1863/1864)*, Dietz Verlag, Berlin, 1988, p.87].
119 Marx, *Capital*, vol.1, p.307 (*MEW*, Bd.23, p.214).
120 Marx, *The Process of Production of Capital*, p.391 (*Resultate*, p.75).

The explication of vital energy, its movement, its being personal function, are so because the living labour 'is a *fluid magnitude*, in the process of becoming – and therefore contained within different limits – instead of *having become*'.[121] The juxtaposition between objective and subjective conditions subsequent to the exchange generates the subsumption of a fluid magnitude, which is the manifestation of the vital function [*Lebensäußerung*] of the labour power. What in the labour process is a means to a determined aim, in the valorization process it becomes a means that subsumes the vital manifestation of the labour power:

> It is not a matter of living labour being realised in objective labour as its objective organ, but of objective labour being preserved and increased by the absorption of living labour, thereby becoming *self-valorising value*, capital, and functioning as such. The means of production now appear only as *absorbers* of the largest possible quantity of living labour. Living labour now appears only as a means for the valorisation and therefore capitalisation of existing values.[122]

The objective conditions are not mere passive *instrumenta*, but rather the means that command the living labour. They make possible its involvement in the process of its objectivation; but to the extent that past labour valorizes itself, it becomes a process in itself. 'To the extent that past labour sets living labour to work, it becomes a process in itself, *it valorises itself*, it becomes a *fluens* that creates a fluxion. This absorption of additional living labour is past labour's *process of self-valorisation*, its real *conversion into capital*, into self-valorising value, its conversion from a *constant magnitude of value* into a variable magnitude of value, value *in process*'.[123] In this process, the manifestation of the vital energy of the living labour, its movement, manifest themselves as capital. 'Only through the conversion of labour into capital during the production process is the pre-posited quantity of value, which was only δυνάμει capital, realised as *actual capital*'.[124] The transformation of money in capital (M–C–M') is

121   Ibid., p.393 (*Resultate*, p.77).
122   Ibid., p.397 (*Resultate*, p.83).
123   Ibid., p.402 (*Resultate*, p.90).
124   Ibid., p.423 (*Resultate*, p.118). For an overview concerning Marx's many references to Aristotle's δύναμις, cf. M. Vadée, *Marx penseur du possible*,

175

therefore possible as s result of a specific transformative action that the use-value of the living labour – an ensemble of physical and intellectual attitudes – exerts upon the dead labour that, in turn, from thing becomes process, a *fluxio* within the sphere of the valorization process, as it is the result of the manifestation of the vital function of the living labour.

A decisive issue remains however unresolved, and should be at least touched upon before proceeding. Is this *money as capital* (M–M′) the very same to which Marx refers to in the opening of the *Grundrisse*? Although according to Marx's intention the answer is certainly positive, in his analysis only partially. In other words, it could be said that whilst the 'money-form' always implies money as 'means of payment', this latter does not necessarily imply the former. The problem, in short, is represented by the necessity to make Marx's analysis of capital compatible with a definition of the credit money able to incorporate what Marx himself observes with regard the nexus money/crisis, bearing in mind that his analysis of credit is only a sketch, whilst many are the problems inherent to the developed notion of commodity-money.

As Augusto Graziani observed, from this point of view, the emphasis cannot be placed but upon the initial exchange between money-form and labour power, as it is here that money manifests itself as social relationship (not as a mere general equivalent) and, for this reason, it 'assumes necessarily the nature of credit money'.[125] In fact, in order to produce commodity, the capitalist acquires labour power, and 'if money would have been a commodity, the process should be turned upside down'. Not only this: 'it should be the result of a previous productive process, which, in turn, would necessitate money in order to be realised.'[126] It is possible to assume that in the sphere of circulation money can manifest itself also as a commodity-money, but

L'Harmattan, Paris, 1998, pp.276–82, who underlines, in particular, that the potential character of labour power cannot be understood as a 'force mécanique', but rather as 'l'être-en-puissance aristotélicien', which becomes other from itself thanks to its activity.

125   Graziani, 'La teoria marxiana della moneta', p.210.
126   Ibid., p.212.

'when production starts, a typical and exclusive moment of the capitalistic economy, money cannot be intended but as credit money.'[127] As a result of this analysis, we can infer a conclusion, according to which whilst in Book I of *Capital* the money-form appears to be the wealth in general, in Book III and in other works on finance, it results in a connection to the problem inherent to the fluxes of payment as such. Hence, 'from these works nothing can be inferred in a definitive way concerning the general theory of money.'[128]

Among these works, should we also have to take into consideration the long passages of the Notebook I of *Grundrisse* earlier mentioned? It would be difficult to give a negative answer. However, Graziani's analysis, surely indispensable to discern the problems, here could run the risk of simplifying their multiplicity. In Marx's intention, these issues ought to keep together the baselessness of Proudhon's utopia and the theory of crisis within a *political critique* that focuses its attention upon the 'money-form'. This latter is therefore intended not only as general wealth, but also as historical presupposition for the valorization process, which, in turn, is cause and effect of the world market [*Weltmarkt*]. Within this latter – and this is the essential aspect – the presence of credit money is explicit, although contradictory.

Discussing Darimon, upon what does Marx insist? He insists upon the confusion of 'the requirements of credit with those of monetary circulation'. This allows him to pose a key question: is it possible to transform the sphere of circulation without altering the actual relationships and the social relations resting upon them? The answer is well-known; less expected is the possibility of resolving the problems generated by passing from one argument to another. On the other hand, to define the money-form as 'general wealth' seems to be reductive, perfectly apt to satisfy the exigencies posed by a rigorous critical economic theory (or, more exactly, in order to avoid the problems that

---

127 Ibid., p.213.
128 Ibid., p.217.

arises from it), but not suitable to understand the *political ambitions* of Marx's *Kritik*. Obviously, contradictions included.[129]

5. Surplus-value and difference

On the 16th of January 1858, Marx wrote to Engels: 'I am, by the way, discovering some nice arguments. E.g. I have completely demolished the theory of profit as hitherto propounded'.[130] Vygodskij has no doubt: if we compare this letter with the chapter of *Grundrisse* that Marx was preparing at that time, it is possible to conclude that what he wanted to communicate to his friend was to have posed the basis of the theory of surplus-value.[131] If we carefully consider the pages in question, we cannot but agree with Vygodskij.[132] Furthermore, it could also be said that there is no discontinuity amid the difference between dead and living labour and the theory of surplus-value. The *difference*, at any rate, expresses a relationship. What is fundamental, however, is the conceptual deepening that such a relationship requires and that only the theory of surplus-value as 'a measure of difference' allows to be spelled out. Obviously, to measure means calculating the spread between profit and surplus-value; but, even before, it means to evaluate the 'subjective difference' that the increase M–M′ includes. Hence, a correct evaluation is possible only on the grounds of the reproduction on an increasing scale, which involves the de-realization process of labour [*der Entwirklichungsprozeß der Arbeit*]. It is here where the living labour 'posits itself objectively, as its own not-being

---

129　It is emblematic what Marx claims concerning money 'κατ' ἐξοχήν as medium of international payments': *Grundrisse*, p.873 (*GKPÖ* p.756).
130　*Marx to Engels, 16 January 1858*, in Marx-Engels, *Collected Works*, vol.40, p.248 (*MEW*, Bd.29, p.260).
131　Vygodskij, *Geschichte einer großen Entdeckung*, p.65. Cf. also Rosdolsky, *The Making of Marx's 'Capital'*, vol.1, pp.220 ff.
132　But see Negri's critical remarks: *Marx beyond Marx*, pp.8–9.

[*als ihr eignes Nichtsein*] or as the being of its not-being [*oder als das Sein ihres Nichtseins*] – of capital'.[133]

It has already been said that the distinctive trait of the valorization process involves two aspects. The objective conditions of production 'transfer value to the new product only when during the labour process they lose value in the shape of their old use-value'. The subjective conditions, on the contrary, cannot add new labour, create new value, without conserving old values. 'The property therefore which labour power in action, living labour, possesses of preserving value, at the same time that it adds it, is a gift of nature which costs the worker nothing, but is very advantageous to the capitalist [...]'.[134] This 'gift of nature' is the result of the twofold nature of labour, that, at any time of the working day, creates an added value, a surplus-labour that exceeds the labour necessary to pay the worker's wage. Now, if it is true that the labour process would not make any sense if it merely reproduced a *mere equivalent* of the value of the labour power, it follows that in the commodity-form – the social synthesis by definition – the respective contribution provided by both objective and subjective conditions appears indistinguishable. What appears indistinguishable is the origin of that *Überschuß* constituting the surplus-value, exactly because the valorization process is present at any given time of the labour process. Briefly: 'Work is not done twice'.

This issue become fundamental when we have to define the *difference as a relationship*: namely, when we have to 'measure' not ΔM incorporated into M′, but their relationship. To this aim, as it is well known, Marx proposed the distinction between 'constant capital' (the fraction of anticipated money constituted by the means of production, which, in the valorization process, does not change its value) and 'variable capital' (the fraction of anticipated money that instead changes its value). Such a distinction, fundamental in order to define the *Überschuß* as a relationship, has an immediate aim: the definition of the rate of surplus-value as 'the degree of exploitation of labour power'. Having subdivided capital into two parts – one constant and one variable –, Marx can argue, by means of a sequence of algebric

133   Marx, *Grundrisse*, p.454 (*GKPÖ* p.358).
134   Marx, *Capital*, vol.1, p.315 (*MEW*, Bd.23, pp.220–1).

179

operations, that the rate of surplus-value should be calculated as the relationship between the surplus-value and the *sole* variable capital. In effect, the constant capital is simply transferred to the end product and, therefore, algebraically, can be said to be equal to zero. We are facing a debatable theoretical achievement, but nonetheless fundamental.

It should be noted, anyhow, that the relevance of such an achievement is not yet disclosed, as the *difference* really manifests itself only when the shift from what is an *absolute relation* to what becomes a *relative relation* occurs. This passage calls into question the analysis of the capitalistic mode of production in its historical development. To come quickly to the point, it refers to the shift from the formal subsumption [*Formelle Subsumtion*] to the real subsumption [*Reelle Subsumtion*], and therefore, from the absolute to the relative surplus-value. For the explication of this passage the de-realization process of labour within the reproduction on an increasing scale is decisive. In this process, in fact, the surplus-value becomes capital and the labour power becomes a collective subjectivity *stricto sensu*.

To understand what is in our interest, it is not necessary to go along the path from cooperation to large-scale industry;[135] it is sufficient here to say that by formal subsumption Marx intends the subsumption of a modality of labour already developed before the rise of capitalism and, at the same time, the specific form that the said subsumption assumes at the very point in which the process occurs under the capitalistic direction and as a result of the imposition of purely monetary relationships between buyers and sellers of labour power. Hence, on the basis of a given labour process – which is a result of tradition – the formal subsumption of the labour power is characterized by the progressive imposition of the *Trennung* between property and labour. This separation is established by a formally unexceptionable exchange, but characterized by a 'relation of compulsion' [*Zwangsverhältnis*]. Its aim is the extraction of surplus-labour, obtained by extending the working day further than the time

135 We shall return later to this issue. Besides Panzieri's already quoted analysis, see J. Fallot, *Marx et le machinisme*, Éditions Cujas, Paris, 1966.

necessary to the reproduction of the labour power. This is however only a *nominally* capitalistic relation.[136] In fact, the extension of the working day is subjected to physical limits and, at any rate, the scale of production is not such that it can determine the increase and to require the utilization of 'the productive powers of directly *social, socialised* (common) labour'; powers developed 'through cooperation, through the division of labour within the workshop, the employment of *machinery* [...]'.[137]

The employment of machinery, instead, characterizes the real subsumption, whose aim is the 'production for production's sake', with no constraints towards a predetermined limitation of needs. Here the technological development is decisive. It modifies the nature of the labour process and its real conditions, making the exploitation of the fundamental contribution embodied by the standardization of the labour process possible. Hence, 'with the development of the *real subsumption of labour under capital* or the *specifically capitalist mode of production* it is not the individual worker but rather a *socially combined labour capacity* that is more and more the *real executor* of the labour process as a whole [...]'.[138] The real subsumption is in fact based upon a collective labour power [*Gesamtarbeiter*], whose productivity is increased by its ability to cooperate as *Gesamtarbeitsvermögen* and by the technological development embodied in fixed capital.[139] The nexus between 'necessary labour' and 'surplus-labour' is radically subverted:

---

136 It should be noted that although Marx's judgement [*The Process of Production of Capital*, p.427 (*Resultate*, p.123)] implies certainly an historically determined passage, the same judgement does not exclude – as he elsewhere underlines – the simultaneous existence of formal subsumption and real subsumption and, therefore, the dialectic between absolute and relative surplus-value.

137 Ibid., p.428 (*Resultate*, p.125).

138 Ibid., p.443 (*Resultate*, p.146).

139 Marx wrote: 'He [the capitalist] pays the value of 100 independent labour powers, but he does not pay for the combined labour power of the 100. [...] Hence the productive power developed by the worker socially [*gesellschaftlicher Arbeiter*] is the productive power of capital. [...] Because this power costs capital nothing, while on the other hand it is not developed by the worker until his labour itself belongs to capital, it appears as a power which capital possesses by its nature – a productive power inherent in capital'

In order to prolong the surplus-labour, the necessary labour is shortened by methods for producing the equivalent of the wage of labour in a shorter time. The production of absolute surplus-value turns exclusively on the length of the working day, whereas the production of relative surplus-value completely revolutionizes the technical processes of labour and the groupings into which society is divided.[140]

In the calculation of the absolute surplus-value it is assumed that the quantity of labour contained in the means of subsistence is given and, therefore, also given is the technological situation of the whole economic system. It follows that the extension of the working day automatically increases the surplus-value. In the calculation of the relative surplus-value, instead, the technological situation is subjected to mutation, to a progress that, bringing about the reduction of the value of commodities, also reduces the value of the variable capital utilized. Hence, even if the working day is always the same, the rate of surplus-value increases. It should be noted that although the real subsumption implies the increase of the rate of the surplus-value as a result of the increase of the relative surplus-value, the absolute surplus-value can also increase in the sphere of the real subsumption, as the extension of the working day can be combined with an increase of technological development:[141]

(*Capital*, vol.1, p.451 (*MEW*, Bd.23, pp.352–3)). In the last section of this chapter we shall analyze the 'context' within which it is possible to exactly understand Marx's judgement. At this stage, it is sufficient to recall that Marx's passage is repeatedly mentioned by Panzieri, both in 'Sull'uso capitalistico delle macchine nel neocapitalismo', and in 'Plusvalore e pianificazione'. Cf. also Tronti, *Operai e capitale*, pp.162–8.

140   Marx, *Capital*, vol.1, p.645 (*MEW*, Bd.23, pp.532–3).
141   'The tendency of capital is, of course, to link up absolute with relative surplus-value; hence *greatest stretching of the working day with the greatest number of simultaneous working days, together with reduction of necessary labour time to the minimum, on one side, and of the number of necessary workers to the minimum, on the other*'. A necessary consequence 'is the *greatest possible diversification of the use value of labour – or of the branches of production –* so that the production of capital constantly and necessarily creates, on one side, the *development of the intensity of the productive power of labour*, on the other side, the *unlimited diversity of the branches of labour*, i.e. thus the most universal wealth, in form and content, of production, bringing all sides of nature

182

From one standpoint the distinction between absolute and relative surplus-value appears to be illusory. Relative surplus-value is absolute, because it requires the absolute prolongation of the working day beyond the labour-time necessary to the existence of the worker himself. Absolute surplus-value is relative, because it requires a development of the productivity of labour which will allow the necessary labour-time to be restricted to a portion of the working day. But if we keep in mind the movement of surplus-value, this semblance of identity vanishes. Once the capital mode of production has become the established and universal mode of production, the difference between absolute and relative surplus-value makes itself felt whenever there is a question of raising the rate of surplus-value.[142]

As the relationship between living labour and capital is a relative relation, to the diminishing of the necessary labour due to the increase of productivity will follow, *coeteris paribus*, the increase of the rate of surplus-value. But beyond this aspect, for many reasons a scholastic one, the *relative character* of the relation expresses something even more important; namely, the dissolution of the physical limits implicit in the duration of the working day. As a result, it follows the subsumption of the specific difference [*spezifischer Unterschied*] of the use-value of the labour power within the reproduction on an increasing scale. The *Überschuß* generated by the living labour, no longer subjected, in abstract, to any limitation of the productivity, is now established by the present and transient conditions of science embodied in fixed capital.

We shall return to this issue in the next section, to evaluate its many consequences. At the moment, we have to look at the nexus between 'reproduction on an increasing scale' and 'the de-realization process of labour'.[143] The point from which we move is the general cyclical form of the accumulation process, which reveals how, already in the sphere of 'simple reproduction', any process of production should be, simultaneously, a reproductive process. In fact, it involves both the dissolution of those apparent characters that might make us think that we are facing an isolated process, and the manifestation of

        under its domination' [Marx, *Grundrisse*, p.770 (*GKPÖ* p.656); but funda-
        mental is also *Capital*, vol.1, pp.455 and ff. (*MEW*, Bd.23, sect. 5, ch. 14)].
142   Marx, *Capital*, vol.1, p.646 (*MEW*, Bd.23, pp.533–4).
143   Cf. Rosdolsky, *The Making of Marx's 'Capital'*, pp.256–67.

new characters. In this sense, the cyclical form reproduces, in time and continuatively, both the objective and subjective conditions inherent to the productive process, plus a surplus-value – as 'a periodic increment of the value of the capital' – in the form 'of a revenue arising out of capital'.[144] The basis upon which this cyclical form is founded is the division [*Scheidung*] 'between the objective conditions of labour and subjective labour power', because 'the worker's product is not only constantly converted into commodities, but also into capital',[145] under the same conditions that require and perpetuate the commodified labour. Hence, the capitalistic productive process reproduces, via its development, the *Scheidung* between labour power and labour condition, the capitalistic relation itself.[146]

However, this separation assumes much more relevance when the surplus-value is no longer considered as simple revenue, but as new capital *stricto sensu*, within which the former is only a fraction of the latter. In such a case, in fact, the productive process not only reproduces the capitalistic relation, but dilates it to the point where the surplus-value reinvested as money generates other surplus-value. The surplus produces new surplus, and transforms capital into a surplus-capital. It is the labour that poses the conditions of its de-realization, via the surplus that it generates and that is now accumulated in order to be reinvested. 'From this moment on, the capital-value and the surplus-value are both sums of money, and their re-conversion into capital takes place in precisely the same way'.[147]

Setting aside the consequence generated by the foreseeable variation of the organic composition of capital [*die organische Zusammensetzung des Kapitals*] and assuming that the technical composition of capital [*technische Zusammensetzung des Kapitals*] within the whole economic system remains the same,[148] what is worth noting is

144 Marx, *Capital*, vol.1, p.712 (*MEW*, Bd.23, p.592). Schumpeter's *Kreislauf* – which admits within it 'growth' but not 'development' – re-proposes a similar scenario (see the following chapter). Cf. Negri's remarks, included in 'Marx sul ciclo e la crisi'.
145 Marx, *Capital*, vol.1, p.716 (*MEW*, Bd.23, pp.595–6).
146 Ibid., p.723 (*MEW*, Bd.23, pp.603–4).
147 Ibid., p.726 (*MEW*, Bd.23, p.606).
148 Ibid., p.762 and ff.

that the *general wealth* is now reproduced and increased by what in the system constitutes a 'difference'. In short, there is a strict interconnection between *Unterschied* and *Überschuß*; and this linkage is established by a *Trennung*, a *Scheidung* inherent to a specific social relation of production. This explains why Marx insisted upon the fact that 'the laws of appropriation or of private property, laws based on the production and circulation of commodity, become changed into their direct opposite [...]'. In effect, the semblance of exchange between capital and labour power – its being mere form [*bloße Form*], non-exchange [*Nicht-Austausch*] – not only is confirmed, but confirms, in turn, that the fundamental assumption of the social relation of production can only be represented by the separation between property and labour.[149] This stems from an exchange within which the living labour was exchanged with a quantity of dead labour:

> except that this objectified labour – these external condition of his being, and the independent externality [*das selbständige Außerihmsein*] to him of these objective conditions – now appears as posited by himself, as *his own product*, as his own self-objectivation as well as the objectivation of himself as a power independent of himself, which moreover rules over him, rules over him through his own actions.[150]

This depends on the fact that '[a]ll moments which confronted living labour capacity, and employed it as *alien, external* powers, and which consumed it under *certain conditions independent of itself*, are now posited as *its own product and result*'.[151] The valorization process that creates what Marx defines as *surplus-value I* was generated by a transaction based upon the law of exchange among equivalents. Although 'illusory', such equivalence, in juridical terms, 'presupposed nothing other than everyone's right to property over his own products'. In the process of reproduction on an increasing scale, in which a *surplus-capital II* is generated by a *surplus-capital I*, what happens is that the right to property is turned upside down, 'so that on

149   Ibid., p.729 (*MEW*, Bd.23, pp.609–10).
150   Marx, *Grundrisse*, p.453 (*GKPÖ*, p.357).
151   Ibid., p.451 (*GKPÖ*, p.355).

the side of capital it becomes the right to an alien product, or the right of property over alien labour'. The exchange of equivalent:

> which appeared as the original operation, an operation to which the right of property gave legal expression, has become turned round in such a way that the exchange by one side is now only illusory, since the part of capital which is exchanged for living labour capacity, firstly, is itself *alien labour*, appropriated without equivalent, and, secondly, *has to be replaced with a surplus by living labour capacity*, is thus in fact not consigned away, but merely changed from one form into another.[152]

It should be noted that the exchange 'without equivalent', if compared to the semblance of the 'original operation', that appeared as 'exchange of equivalent', 'to which the right of property gave legal expression', involves a leap. The surplus-value becomes the presupposition from which the process of valorization now moves. Marx places great emphasis upon this passage. 'The independent, for-itself existence of value [*das selbständige Fürsichsein des Wertes*]', its *Dasein*, its 'existence as capital' – all that manifests itself as produced by labour, as its objectivation –, reveals the alien quality of the objective conditions of labour *vis-à-vis* living labour capacity, the 'divorce' between objective and subjective conditions, the 'separation' between property and living labour power. *Fremdheit, Scheidung, absolute Trennung*: these are the terms through which Marx introduces what he defines the de-realization process of labour, in which labour 'posits itself objectively, but it posits this, its objectivity, as its own not-being or as the being of its not-being'.[153] In other words, the presupposition of the reproduction on an increasing scale consists of the fact that the previous appropriation of alien labour is now '*the simple precondition for the new appropriation of alien labour*'.[154]

The de-realization process of living labour power is posed at the very centre of the shift from absolute to relative surplus-value. As a result of this shift, the physical constraint constituted by the temporal duration of the working day disappears: the increase of value

152   Ibid., p.458 (*GKPÖ*, p.362).
153   Ibid., p.454 (*G*, p.358).
154   Ibid., p.457 (*G*, p.361).

expressed as relative surplus-value is no longer subjected, in abstract terms, to any productive limit. In historical terms, the reproduction on an increasing scale involves not only the reproduction of the objective conditions on the basis of the living labour accumulated 'without equivalent', but also their qualitative transformation, above all due to the science embodied in fixed capital. At any rate, if the relative surplus-value assumes its meaning because of the strict interconnection between *Unterschied* e *Überschuß*, it becomes easy to understand why the comparison between the rate of surplus-value and the rate of profit loses its merely quantitative feature. Such a comparison, in fact, entails a radically different representation of the money relation:

> In actual fact, the rate of profit is the historical starting-point. Surplus-value and the rate of surplus-value are, relative to this, the invisible essence to be investigated, whereas the rate of profit and hence the form of surplus-value as profit are visible surface phenomena.[155]

It is not accidental that the *vexata quaestio* of the transformation of commodities values into prices of production has always been stranded at this point.[156] It is well known that the surplus-value intended as profit has generated a series of well-founded critiques, aimed at confuting such an idea (alleged uniformity of the rate of surplus-value, non homogeneity of the organic composition of capital, inequality of the rates of profit, etc.[157]) that have always and anyhow led to the *famosissima quaestio* of the 'transformation'. Following this path, once the well-known radical correctives are accepted, it is anyway possible to demonstrate the reality of exploitation,[158] but in

155 Marx, *Capital*, vol.3, p.134 (*MEW*, Bd.25, p.53).
156 For a new approach, see A. Freeman, G. Carchedi, *Marx and non-equilibrium Economics*, Elgar, Cheltenham, 1996. More in general, see R. Bellofiore (ed. by), *Marxian Economics: a Reappraisal. Essays on Volume III of Capital*, Macmillan, London, 1998.
157 Cf. F. Vianello, 'Plusvalore e profitto in Marx', in P. Sylos Labini (a cura di), *Prezzi relativi e distribuzione del reddito*, Boringhieri, Torino, 1973, pp.75–117.
158 The position of P. Garegnani (*Marx e gli economisti classici*, Einaudi, Torino, 1981, pp.55 ff.) is emblematic; but, with the due differences, it is worth

this way the theory of surplus-value results useless.[159] So, putting aside the recurring temptation to separate qualitative and quantitative aspects[160] – philosophy and economy –, what remains is the alternative from which we moved: to bring the comparison between profit and surplus value within the sphere of a macroeconomic theory of exploitation, qualified from the relationship between abstract labour and money, and within which the antagonistic relation between *social classes*, not a distributive asymmetry, is expressed. The difference between surplus-value and profit is relating to this antagonistic class relation. If amid capital and labour power the sole possible relation is the one expressed in the valorization process, then, in the 'calculation' of this *Verwertungsprozeß*, it is correct to set aside what is not living labour – namely, what the capitalistic class *already* possesses: *realiter*, but also *potentialiter*, in the form of money capital. This is even truer if, as it occurs in the reproduction on an increasing scale, the de-realization process of labour is already *in actu*.

remembering also M. Morishima (*Marx's Economics: A Dual Theory of Value and Growth*, Cambridge University Press, Cambridge, 1973, pp.179 ff.), and I. Steedman (*Marx after Sraffa*, New Left Books, London, 1977, pp.34–6). On this issue, cf. C. Napoleoni, 'La teoria del valore dopo Sraffa', in L. Pasinetti (a cura di), *Aspetti controversi della teoria del valore*, Il Mulino, Bologna, 1989, pp.35 ff.; A. Salanti, 'La teoria del valore dopo Sraffa: una nota', *Rivista internazionale di scienze economiche e commerciali*, 1990, vol.37, 8, pp.685–9; S. Perri, 'La "significatività" del saggio di plusvalore dopo Sraffa', *Rivista internazionale di scienze economiche e commerciali*, 1991, vol.38, 6–7, pp.573–84; R. Marchionatti, 'Sulla significatività del saggio di plusvalore dopo Sraffa', *Economia politica*, 1993, vol.10, 2, pp.203–21; S. Perri, 'Neovalore e plusvalore', *Economia politica*, 1997, vol.14, 2, pp.209–33. For an overview see D. Cavalieri, 'Plusvalore e sfruttamento dopo Sraffa: lo stato del problema', *Economia politica*, 1995, vol.12, 1, pp.23–56.

159 S. Biasco, 'Sfruttamento e profitto in Sraffa', in Sylos Labini (ed. by), *Prezzi relativi e distribuzione del reddito*, pp.127–8.

160 Here reference is not made to the old Sweezy's thesis (*The Theory of Capitalistic Development*, Monthly Review Press, New York, 1942), but rather to the similar interpretations advanced some decades later, re-proposing, although in a different and refined form, the same argument. In particular, we are referring to the 'anello' between abstract labour, fetishism and distribution of income, upon which insisted Vianello, 'Plusvalore e profitto in Marx', p.115.

Now, apart from the indicative function that the rate of profit has in relation to the growth velocity of employed social capital, for Marx the character of the rate of profit is from the outset deceiving: 'Since all sections of capital equally appear as sources of the excess value (profit), the capital relation is mystified':[161]

> In surplus-value, the relationship between capital and labour is laid bare. In the relationship between capital and profit, i.e. between capital and surplus-value as it appears on the one hand as an excess over cost price of commodities realized in the circulation process and on the other hand as an excess determined more precisely by its relationship to the total capital, capital appears as a relationship to itself [*als Verhältnis zu sich selbst*], a relationship in which it is distinguished, as an original sum of value, from another new value that it posits.[162]

The essence of the mystification, however, is not due to the mutation of the numerical result, but rather to what renders such mutation legitimate; it is due to the fact that capital can now manifest itself as a relationship to itself, *als Verhältnis zu sich selbst*. From the 'rational' point of view involved by profit, in fact, all the constituent parts of capital appear equally as sources of a surplus, which is generated, *realiter*, only by living labour. If in the surplus-value the nexus between objective and subjective conditions of production is laid bare, in the nexus capital-profit, the former manifests itself as a relationship to itself, so that the process of valorization appears to concern the *whole capital*: any distinction between constant and variable capital vanishes. The ability of dead labour to command the living labour not only appears to be as inherent property *in se* and *per se* to the means of production, but also as a property that is due to these latter as 'things'. The link between *Unterschied* e *Überschuß* disappears, as surplus-value and rate of surplus-value are 'the invisible essence [*das Unsichtbare*] to be investigated', whilst the profit and the rate of profit 'are visible surface phenomena [*Oberfläche der Erscheinungen*]'.[163]

The difference that distinguishes 'the invisible essence' from 'visible surface phenomena' goes far beyond the numerical relation,

---

161 Marx, *Capital*, vol.3, p.136 (*MEW*, Bd.25, p.55).
162 Ibid., p.139 (*MEW*, Bd.25, p.58).
163 Ibid., p.134 (*MEW*, Bd.25, p.53).

and aimed at what Claudio Napoleoni once defined as 'a substantial relationship of generation, of cause and effect'.[164] Dialectical miracles, *Hegelian stuff and nonsense?*[165] It could be, but there is much more to it than this. The mystification – beyond any calculation – is based upon what for Marx is *already* a concrete de-realization process of labour, for which also the objective conditions are reproduced by living labour. Although – as already mentioned – the substantial assumption upon which the social relations of production are based can only be the separation between property and labour, it is not the juridical aspect, but rather the historical and cyclical feature of the process of capitalistic accumulation that is decisive. Such a character is unthinkable apart from the subsumption of the difference of the living labour – not only of the surplus that it produces, but exactly of the *living labour*: 'the real *not-capital* is *labour* [*Nicht-Kapital*]'.[166] Hence, from a certain point onward, the surplus-value seems to be transformed into an ontological category.[167]

Certainly, the 'being of difference' comes up against a further obstacle represented by the most celebrated characterization of the meaning of the rate of profit, namely its presumed 'tendential fall'. But, at this stage, we believe that such an *impasse* – relativized by the action of the well-known 'counteracting factors' –,[168] even if considered literally, cannot question what is historically incontestable: namely, the fluctuations and the sharp breaks that present themselves as 'crisis' and that as such characterize capitalism. Marx addressed this issue 'correctly'; with regard to the rest, it is easier to agree with those who have shown the rigidities and the analytical fallacies inherent to 'The Law Itself', also in order to discharge the idea of

---

164 C. Napoleoni, *Lezioni sul capitolo VI inedito*, Boringhieri, Torino, 1972, p.139.
165 This definition is advanced by J. Robinson (*On Re-Reading Marx*, Students' Bookshops Ltd, Cambridge, 1953, p.20; afterwards in Ibid., *Collected Economic Papers*, Basil Blackwell, Oxford, 1980, vol.4, p.265; see also Ead., *An Essay on Marxian Economics*, Macmillan, London, 1949) and recalled by R. Rosdolsky, *The Making of Marx's 'Capital'*, p.530.
166 Marx, *Grundrisse*, p.274 (*GKPÖ*, p.185).
167 See *infra*, par. 7.
168 Cf. M. Dobb, *Political Economy and Capitalism*, Routledge, London, 1940².

katastrophé – that is not the most significant aspect of Marx's analysis inherent to the relationship between fixed capital and living labour.

6. A controversial fragment

More than the increase as such of fixed capital, in fact, it is its 'powerful effectiveness' to be significant – something that does not necessarily require the increase of the organic composition of capital, with the well-known analytical rigidities that follow. Historio-graphically, the issue is linked in particular to the interpretation of the so called *Fragment on Machinery* included in *Grundrisse*. Its 'steno-graphical character' is of rare efficacy, but if compared, for example, with the chapter 13 of *Das Kapital*, it complicates the matter to the point of rendering difficult to understand the same *difference* at-tributed to living labour.

In chapter 13 of *Das Kapital*, such a difference is explicit and unequivocal. Marx pays great attention to the historical development of the so-called machinism, moving from the fundamental assumption according to which machinery, with a few exceptions, 'operates only by means of associated labour, or labour in common'.[169] From here, he carries on analysing the effects upon labour power, underlining the paradox stemming from the fact that 'the most powerful instrument for reducing labour-time suffers a dialectical inversion and becomes the most unfailing means for turning the whole lifetime of the worker and his family into labour-time at capital's disposal for its own valorisation'.[170] Apparent paradox, as the dialectic occurring between formal and real subsumption is always at work. Accordingly, the presumed 'tendential fall in the rate of profit' is effectively counter-balanced by the 'counteracting factors', which represent, *de facto*, a barrier, upheld by the changing technical class composition inherent to

---

169   Marx, *Capital*, vol.1, p.508 (*MEW*, Bd.23, p.407).
170   Ibid., p.532 (*MEW*, Bd.23, p.430).

the world labour market. But, apart from this, it is interesting to note the conclusion reached in *Das Kapital*:

> Every kind of capitalist production, in so far as it is not only a labour process but also capital's process of valorisation, has this in common, but it is not the worker who employs the conditions of his work, but rather the reverse, the conditions of work employ the worker. However, it is only with the coming of machinery that this inversion first acquires a technical and palpable reality. Owing to its conversion into an automaton, the instrument of labour confronts the worker during the labour process in the shape of capital, dead labour, which dominates and soaks up living labour power. The separation [*die Scheidung*] of the intellectual faculties [*der geistigen Potenzen*] of the production process from manual labour, and the transformation of those faculties into powers exercised by capital over labour, is [...], finally completed by large-scale industry erected on the foundation of machinery. The special skill of each individual machine-operator, who has now been deprived of all significance, vanishes as an infinitesimal quantity in the face of the science, the gigantic natural forces, and the mass of social labour embodied in the system of machinery, which, together with those three forces, constitutes the power of the 'master'.[171]

Two indirect references are here made to both the *Draft Chapter 6 of Capital* and to *Grundrisse*. However, beyond the mere philology, it is opportune to focus our attention upon the way in which the juxtaposition between dead labour and living labour is now explicitly qualified by the *separation* between *intellectual faculties* inherent to the productive process and manual labour; that is, by their transformation into powers exercised by capital over labour. The 'special skill of each worker' intended as a mere accessory disappears when faced with science that makes mass social labour possible. Certainly, this passage can be understood according to the more or less traditional interpretation: from the Frankfurt School to authors such as Alfred Sohn-Rethel and Harry Braverman.[172] However, these *geistige*

171 Ibid., p.549 (*MEW*, Bd.23, p.446).
172 See among others F. Pollock, *Automation. Materialien zur Beurteilung der ökonomischen und sozialen Folgen*, Europäische Verlagsanstalt, Frankfurt am Main, 1956; A. Sohn-Rethel, *Geistige und körperliche Arbeit. Zur Theorie der gesellschaftlichen Synthesis*, Suhrkamp Verlag, Frankfurt am Main, 1970; and H. Braverman, *Labor and Monopoly Capital. The Degradation of Work in the Twentieth Century*, Monthly Review Press, New York and London, 1974.

Potenzen contain something more. Their identification with what Marx in the *Grundrisse* defined as 'general intellect' would certainly be wrong, as they rather refer to the definition of a 'social brain' [*gesellschaftliches Hirn*], provided in the same work. Nevertheless, the *intellectual faculties* allow the establishment of an explicit and specific link between the two texts, although only in *Grundrisse* an explanation of the acceleration that leads to questioning the labour-value as a measure is provided.[173]

First of all, we have to indicate the explicit convergences. At the end of Notebook VI of *Grundrisse*, Marx underlines that the point from which it is necessary to move in order to understand the social nature of the fixed capital as machinery is 'an automatic system of machinery', set in motion by an automaton, of which the worker is only a 'conscious linkage' [*bewußte Glieder*]. In this system, the virtuousness of the worker is no longer required, as it is the machinery 'itself the virtuoso'.[174] Labour is only a 'conscious linkage' of a 'mighty organism': 'a mere living accessory of this machinery'. The increase of productivity of labour and the highest negation of the necessary labour render the transformation of the means of labour in machinery effective. In this way, the activity of labour power is reduced to a 'mere abstraction of activity'.[175] 'The science which compels the inanimate limbs of the machinery, by their construction, to act purposefully, as an automaton, does not exist in the worker's consciousness, but rather acts upon him through the machine as an alien power, as the power of the machine itself'.[176] In brief, this extraneity is nothing else but the *separation* between the *intellectual faculties* of the process of production and the *manual labour* – of which Marx would discuss in *Das Kapital*:

> The accumulation of knowledge and of skill, of the general productive forces of the social brain [*des gesellschaftlichen Hirns*], is thus absorbed into capital, as

173 Tronti, *Operai e capitale*, pp.210 ff.; Negri, *Marx beyond Marx*, pp.139 ff.; Napoleoni, *Discorso sull'economia politica*, Boringhieri, Torino, 1985, pp.75–83.
174 Marx, *Grundrisse*, pp.692–3 (*GKPÖ*, p.584).
175 Ibid., p.693 (*G*, p.584).
176 Ibid.

opposed to labour, and hence appears as an attribute of capital, and more specifically of *fixed capital*, in so far as it enter into the production process as a means of production proper. *Machinery* appears, then, as the most adequate form of *fixed capital*, and fixed capital, in so far as capital's relations with itself are concerned, appears as *the most adequate form of capital* as such [*des Kapitals überhaupt*].[177]

Up to here, the overlapping between chapter 13 of *Capital* and the *Fragment on Machinery* is explicit. But from then onwards, the convergences become even more problematic: the homogeneity of meaning between the *geistige Potenzen* and *gesellschaftliches Hirn* gives rise to what might appear to be a true and proper paradox. When we say paradox, we refer, obviously, to what emerges as regards the difference characterizing the living labour, because only partially can this paradox be paralleled to the inauspicious forecast involved in the alleged 'tendential fall in the rate of profit'.

The problem can be identified at the end of Notebook VI of *Grundrisse*, in two short passages where we can read:

Further, in so far as machinery develops with the accumulation of society's science [*der gesellschaftlichen Wissenschaft*], of productive force generally, general social labour presents itself not in labour but in capital. The productive force of society is measured in *fixed capital*, exists there in its objective form; and, inversely, the productive force of capital grows with this general progress, which capital appropriates free of charge.

And further on:

In machinery, knowledge appears as alien, external to him [the worker]; and living labour [as] subsumed under self-activating objectified labour. The worker appears as superfluous to the extent that his action is not determined by [capital's] requirements.[178]

According to a legitimate, but perhaps superficial approach, one could read in these passages only a mere emphasizing of what it has already been said: when the means of labour is transformed into an automatic system of machinery, the living labour, subsumed by dead

177   Ibid., p.694 (*G*, p.586).
178   Ibid., pp.694–5 (*G*, p.586).

labour as fixed capital, is subjected to a further and more explicit alienation. This is already said, certainly, and it restates the homogeneity of meaning between the *gesellschaftliches Hirn* and the *geistige Potenzen*. Nevertheless, in the above quotations there is something else: namely, the 'superfluity' of labour is not simply the result of the fact that the development of fixed labour implies technological unemployment and produces an industrial reserve army. In addition to this (and not alternatively), it is said that this can occur because the activity of labour is not conditioned by the needs of capital, because, now, the objectified labour acts in an autonomous way, and the living labour, *die lebendige Arbeit*, is subsumed under self-activating objectified labour [*subsumiert unter die selbständig wirkende vergegenständlichte*].[179]

How can we explain this autonomy? – established that in it, it is not possible to grasp only the stronger domination exerted by the intensification of the extraction of relative surplus value. Is this autonomy contradictory and paradoxical in Marx's analysis? What happens to the difference characterizing the living labour within the valorization process? The answer can be found in the *Fragment* itself:

> To the degree that labour time – the mere quantity of labour – is posited by capital as the sole determinant element, to that degree does direct labour [*die unmittelbare Arbeit*] and its quantity disappear as the determinant principle of production – of the creation of use value – and is reduced both quantitatively, to a smaller proportion, and qualitatively, as an, of course, indispensable but subordinate moment [*aber subalternes Moment*], compared to general scientific labour [*gegen die allgemeine wissenschaftliche Arbeit*], technological application of natural science, on one side, and to the general productive force arising from social combination in total production on the other side – a combination which appears as a natural fruit of social labour (although it is a historic product). Capital thus works towards its own dissolution as the form dominating production.[180]

In Marx's terms, it is clear that the paradox can only have one long term historical outcome – the dissolution of capitalism itself. But even for Marx himself this answer cannot be satisfactory. Certainly,

179   Ibid.
180   Ibid., p.700 (*G*, p.587–588).

the few pages of the *Fragment* allude to the most simplistic of solutions; but it is in these same pages, more than in any other place, that Marx indicates with absolute clarity how complex the relationship is between living and dead labour – apart, therefore, from the 'mechanics' inherent to the tendential fall in the rate of profit. The problem is given by the fact that the relation between dead and living labour is, already in Marx's epoch, relativized, as, given 'the basis on which large industry rests, the appropriation of alien labour time, ceases, with its development, to make up or to create wealth, so does *direct labour* as such cease to be the basis of production [...]'.[181]

At this stage, the question can only be posed in the following terms: what substitutes 'direct labour'? And, how can we characterize what substitutes it: the 'general scientific labour'? Although we face the same context delineated by the separation between intellectual faculties inherent to the productive process and manual labour, by their transformation in powers exercised by capital over labour – transformation that occurs in large-scale industry –, we have to make a mental leap if we want to fully understand the terms of the problem posed in the *Fragment*. In other words, if we only refer to the higher exploitation made possible by the science embodied in fixed capital, it is difficult to understand what Marx tries to say with... 'the living labour [as] subsumed under self-activating objectified labour':

> The exchange of living labour for objectified labour – i.e. the positing of social labour in the form of the contradiction of capital and wage labour – is the ultimate development of the *value-relation* and of production resting on value. Its presupposition is – and remains – the mass of direct labour time, the quantity of labour employed, as the determinant factor in the production of wealth. But to the degree that large industry develops, the creation of real wealth comes to depend less on labour time and on the amount of labour employed than on the power of the agencies set in motion during labour time, whose 'powerful effectiveness' is itself in turn out of all proportion to the direct labour time spent on their production, but depends rather on the general state of science and on the progress of technology, or the application of this science to production.[182]

---

181   Ibid., p.709 (*G*, pp.596–597).
182   Ibid., p.704–5 (*G*, p.592).

The decisive point, evidently, does not consist only of the assertion according to which 'the creation of real wealth comes to depend less on labour time and on the amount of labour employed than on the power of the agencies set in motion during labour time'; but rather in the acknowledgement that the 'powerful effectiveness' of those agencies is not related 'to the direct labour time spent on their production'. In other words, this 'powerful effectiveness' neither limits itself to register the transformation of the living labour in objectified labour, fixed capital, nor to generate a even more complex labour, as a result of the utilization of *that* fixed capital. Rather, the powerful effectiveness expresses, first of all, the autonomy that, already in Marx's epoch, characterized the 'general scientific labour' as social knowledge, as such irreducible to fractions of direct labour. It is *knowledge* which transforms the means of labour in machinery, and it is to the same knowledge that it is possible to ascribe a specific ability of valorization: to knowledge, not to the automaton as such. In this transformative process, labour is even more constricted and exploited. The same process does not set aside labour; however, being an *innovative process*, it is no longer, and not necessarily, commensurate to direct labour.[183] Being even less concerned with the

---

183   The undoubted difficulty to grasp exactly the meaning of direct labour [*unmittelbare Arbeit*] explains the incorrect way in which Napoleoni posed the problem in an article dated 1970 ('La questione delle macchine in Marx', *La rivista trimestrale*, 1970, 31–2, pp.625–33). Napoleoni, who was a careful reader of Marx, perfectly understood the intricacy raised by Marx's text. However, entangled between two inadequate interpretative extremes – theory of alienation, on the one side, and transformation of value in prices, on the other – failed to see the true character of immediate labour. This latter is not mainly determined by its being natural activity, stemming from the relationship between human beings and nature, mediated by the instrument (a relationship that would be upset by the machinery, as it would transform humans in means), but rather from its being *already* the expression of '[t]he special skill of each individual machine-operator, who has now been deprived of all significance [...]' [Marx, *Capital*, vol.1, p.549 (*MEW*, Bd.23, p.446)]. From this perspective, the machinery 'operates only by means of associated labour, or labour in common' [Ibid., p.508 (*MEW*, Bd.23, p.407)]. Also M. Vadée (*Marx penseur du possibile*, pp.400–6) provided an interesting analysis concerning the specific valorization capacity entailed by machinery, above all in relation to the con-

197

quantum of labour and even more with the social organization of labour that produces such a development, 'the product ceases to be the product of isolated direct labour, and the *combination* of social activity appears, rather, as the producer'.[184]

It is superfluous to restate that the combination of social activity is primarily characterized by its being 'general social knowledge'. At any rate, the enormous disproportion between employed working time and its product evokes but does not justify a simple solution. In fact, although Marx prefigured the fall of production based upon the exchange value, he nonetheless re-stated that the tendency of production is 'on the one side, *to create disposable time, on the other, to convert it into surplus-labour*'.[185] Once again, we face the compensative dialectic between absolute and relative surplus-value. That 'the growth of the forces of production can no longer be bound up with the appropriation of alien labour'[186] appears, first of all, as a factual judgement and, secondly, as a political judgement able to reveal the explicit dismeasure that underpins the hendiadys earlier mentioned: *critique* of the scientific assumptions of the political economy and prefiguration of the *crisis* of the capitalistic social model.

It is this dismeasure that shows 'to what degree general social knowledge has become a *direct force of production*';[187] and it is on the basis of such a dismeasure that it appears clear how '[l]abour no longer appears so much to be included within the production process; rather, the human being comes to relate more as watchman and regulator to the production itself'. Clearly, labour manifests itself as an accessory, because capital, being science embodied in fixed capital, *knowledge*, generates processes of labour that tend to become autonomous from the immediate labour; but exactly for this reason, the

cepts of 'force' and 'machinery'. Nevertheless, totally ignoring the *Fragment*, he concluded in the most obvious way, avoiding the problem, when he said that: 'Mais la machine ne crée pas plus de valeur ou de plus-value que n'importe quel autre instrument. La plus-value provient toujours du surtravail ou travail effectué au-delà du temps de travail nécessaire'.

184 Marx, *Grundrisse*, p.709 (*GKPÖ*, pp.596–7).
185 Ibid., p.708 (*G*, p.596).
186 Ibid.
187 Ibid., p.706 (*G*, p.594).

labour process arrives to subsume the living labour as *lebendige Leiblichkeit*: 'it is, in a word, the development of the social individual which appears as the great foundation-stone of production and of wealth':[188]

> The development of fixed capital indicates to what degree general social knowledge has become a *direct force of production*, and to what degree, hence, the conditions of the process of the social life itself have come under the control of the general intellect and been transformed in accordance with it.[189]

Hence, the 'general intellect' essentially represents the inclusion – in Foucaultian terms – of the social individual: not only of the surplus that he produces, but also of the living labour as non-capital. This inclusion is possible only as a result of the transformation of the general social knowledge into an immediate productive force. Asking whether this social individual is more or less 'free' is a baseless question, as the problem is represented by something else. Whatever his conditions are, what is clear is that he is no longer only the holder of direct labour, of a living labour able to generate a simple surplus. In other words, the difference that he expresses is certainly re-qualified by the relative autonomy characterizing the 'general scientific labour'. But this re-qualification, *de facto*, deepens the dismeasure manifested by the enormous disproportion between the employed social working time and what is produced. Taking a further step forward, the logic subtended by the de-realization process of labour becomes, at this stage, pure dismeasure. Above, we have underlined how the exchange 'without equivalent' entails a leap if compared to the 'semblance of exchange', to the 'original operation' (M–C), which appeared as 'exchange of equivalent'. Hence, the fall of production based upon the exchange value of which Marx speaks in the *Fragment* represents a step forward.

From difference to dismeasure, from the principle of labour value to the crisis of the law of value, Marx's path is one and only one. It is a path that, although it does not allow to expel what is logically contradictory (the transformation of commodities values into prices of

---

188   Ibid., p.705 (*G*, p.593).
189   Ibid., p.706 (*G*, p.594).

production), put it aside. It is a path that qualifies in macroeconomic, rather than in merely distributive terms the argumentation, within which the dismeasure appears as exploitation inherent to the relationships, expressed in monetary terms, among social classes. From the assumption of the omitted distinction between labour content and labour-commanded to the omitted distinction between labour and labour power; from the 'semblance of exchange' to the exchange 'without equivalent'; from the principle of labour-value as measure to dismeasure pure and simple; the law of value becomes progressively relevant in consequences of the real contradictions to which it is subjected and to which it leads.[190] Contradictions stemming directly from the nexus value/valorization and, therefore, from the *Trennung* between labour and labour power, from the *differentia specifica* that generates the *Überschuß*.

7. An absolute separation

In Marx's analytical intention, this *specific difference* is qualified from the outset as a *political category*. The transformation of the labour power in the working class – produced by cooperation and of which the capitalistic development necessitates – implies *de facto* the radicalization of the critique of those political and representative institutions with which Marx had dealt with before 1850s.[191] At any rate, such a transformation implies, above all, both the refinement of the categories already experimented and the identification of new ones, forged within the critique of political economy and intended to render

---

190 C. Napoleoni, 'Sulla teoria della produzione come processo circolare', *Giornale degli economisti e Annali di economia*, 1960, vol.20, n.s., 1–2, pp.101–17.

191 Also from a chronological point of view, the claim made in *Lohnarbeit und Kapital* (1849) is relevant: '*Increase of capital, therefore, is increase of the proletariat, i.e., of the working class. [Arbeiterklasse]*' [*Wage Labour and Capital*, Marx-Engels, *Collected Works*, vol.9, p.214 (*MEW*, Bd.6, p.410). On this 'transformation', see Tronti, *Operai e capitale*, pp.123 ff.

thinkable a scientific – and therefore political in kind, just to be close to Marx's intentions – overturning of the *Trennung*. Among those categories, the one concerning relative wage, already defined before the end of 1850s, has a significant explicative role.[192]

Marx was not the first author who underlined the difference between nominal, real and relative wage. He himself acknowledged that '[t]he concept of *relative* wages is one of Ricardo's greatest contributions'.[193] However, as Rosdolsky noted following Luxemburg's line of thought, for Marx the category of relative wage transforms, from the outset, an economic relationship into a political one,[194] rendering the former an essential indicator of the 'position of the classes' [*Stellung der Klassen*].[195] Marx, in fact, assumes that our wants and pleasures 'have their origin in society; we therefore measure them in relation to society; we do not measure them in relation to the objects which serve for their gratification. Since they are of a social nature, they are of a relative nature'.[196] In other words, the relative wage contains 'many relations': not only because it can decrease when an increase of the real wage occurs, but also because 'the most favourable situation for the working class, namely, the most rapid growth of capital', would certainly lead the working class 'to forge for itself the golden chains by which the bourgeoisie drags it in its train'.[197]

Although picturesque and very much distant from our present sensibility, the image is adequate to clarify what it means to understand the relative wage as a political category. It means to see in it not

---

192   On the evolution of the theory of wage in Marx cf. Rosdolsky (*The Making of Marx's 'Capital'*, pp.57–62) and Negri (*Marx beyond Marx*, pp.128 ff.).

193   Marx, *Theories of Surplus-value*, vol.3, p.33 (*MEW*, Bd.26.3, p.27); and cf. Marx, *Grundrisse*, pp.595–6 (*G*, p.489–90).

194   Rosdolsky, *The Making of Marx's 'Capital'*, pp.294–5. On the same subject, Negri (*Marx beyond Marx*, pp.133–4) wrote, possibly even more radically: 'It is at this stage that we can fully understand what the book on waged labour is for Marx. It is the theoretical reasoning of the political in the economic and vice versa'.

195   Marx, *Theories of Surplus-value*, vol.2, p.419 (*MEW*, Bd.26.2, p.421).

196   *Wage Labour and Capital*, Marx-Engels, *Collected Works*, vol.9, p.216 (*MEW*, Bd.6, p.412).

197   Ibid., p.221 (*MEW*, Bd.6, p.416).

a variable degree of well-being, but a 'position of the classes'. And, in order to reduce misunderstandings to a minimum, it should be noted that the legitimacy of this claim does not rest upon the validity of the hypothesis concerning the increasing impoverishment of the working class – *in se* untrue. The relative wage expresses a *proportion*, apart from what is the entity of the difference. This is said with more clarity and less emphasis in the Notebook VI of *Grundrisse*, where Marx claims that classical economists – except Ricardo – 'want to have absolutely nothing to do with the proportional (and hence contradictory) nature of wage'. In effect, if on the one side it is so possible to hide the 'contradiction', on the other, it is possible to keep intact the 'semblance of exchange' between labour power and capital. In this way, from an economic point of view, the exchange is concerned 'only with *quantity*, the quantity of use value'. In short, it is a sort of barter, which shows all its limits when the living labour claims its pretences upon the profit that it has generated, 'so that the *proportion* itself becomes a real moment of economic life itself':

> Further, in the struggle between the two classes – which necessarily arises with the development of the working class – the measurement of the distance between them, which, precisely, is expressed by wages itself as a proportion, becomes decisively important. The *semblance of exchange* [*der Schein des Austauschs*] vanishes in the course of the mode of production founded on capital.[198]

Again: 'the semblance of exchange'; but, even before, it should be noted Marx's warning that the proportion should be correctly understood, so as to avoid the 'triviality' according to which when we divide a given value into two, the size of one part is necessarily inversely proportional to the other.[199] If this is so, it is not enough to identify the inverse relation between wage and profit. Before this operation, it is necessary to explicate what renders profit different from the surplus-value. And if it is true that classical economists render the value of labour 'an absurd tautology', as they do not make

198 Marx, *Grundrisse*, p.597 (*GKPÖ* p.491).
199 Ibid., p.596 (*G*, 490).

202

any distinction between labour and labour power,[200] it is also true that for Ricardo the proportion does not go beyond an inverse relation between wage and profit, because he 'wrongly identifies surplus-value with profit'.[201] Ricardo's proportion obliterates that *einziger Unterschied*, 'the only thing distinct', for which the proportion assumes a political meaning, as he presupposes the division [*Teilung*] between labour and capital 'as self-evident'.[202]

As we already said, to the relative wage we can attribute an exemplificative role in the representation of the relationship between the concept of the Economical and the concept of the Political. In effect, what is the proportion if not the index of a constitutive difference, for which the inverse variation of the economic datum *in se* is really a little thing? What is the proportion if not the index of the possibility to think of a turning upside down of the *Trennung*, of that category 'that underpins Marx's entire theoretical architecture'?[203] What is the proportion if not the direct attempt to unveil the mystification according to which the 'capital appears as a relationship to itself', because, in the profit, the valorization process is exhibited as an operation of capital as a whole? And, consequently, what is the proportion, if not a direct manifestation of the nexus *totus politicus* between *Unterschied* e *Überschuß*? A nexus intended to put in a correct light – beyond the juridical aspect – the political essence, historically grounded, of the exchange 'without equivalent', and to illuminate what, in relative terms, is 'the invisible essence to be investigated': that is, the surplus-value and the rate of surplus-value. The critique of the scientific project of political economy is, simultaneously, a critique of economy, ideology and politics. Here we find the apex of Marx's *political thought*, in the de-realization process of labour, of what is posed as not-capital but it is able to generate capital,

200 Marx, *Capital*, vol.1, pp.675–82 (*MEW*, Bd.23, pp.557–64).
201 Marx, *Theories of Surplus-value*, vol.2, p.426 (*MEW*, Bd.26.2, p.428).
202 Marx, *Grundrisse*, p.596 (*GKPÖ*, p.490).
203 On this specific issue, the last Napoleoni (*Discorso sull'economia politica*, p.41) is absolutely right. See also Id., 'Value and Exploitation. Marx's Economic Theory and Beyond', in G. Caravale (ed. by), *Marx and Modern Economic Analysis*, Elgar, Aldershot, 1991.

of what 'is absolute poverty as object, on one side, and is, on the other side, the general possibility of wealth as subject and as activity'.

At this point, we return back to the passage around which this chapter has grown: 'The only thing distinct [*der einzige Unterschied*] from *objectified* labour is *non-objectified* labour, labour which is still objectifying itself, *labour* as subjectivity'.[204] But besides this brief passage, it is necessary to quote at length another passage:

> Labour posited as *not-capital* as such is: (1) *not-objectified labour, conceived negatively* (itself still objective; the not-objective itself in objective form) As such it is not-raw-material, not-instrument of labour, not-raw-product: labour separated from all means and objects of labour, from its entire objectivity. This living labour, existing as an *abstraction* from these moments of its actual reality (also, not-value); [...]. Labour as *absolute poverty*: poverty not as shortage, but as total exclusion of objective wealth. Or also as the existing *not-value*, and hence purely objective use value, existing without mediation, this objectivity can only be an objectivity not separated from the person: only an objectivity coinciding with his immediate bodily existence [*mit ihrer unmittelbaren Leiblichkeit*]. Since the objectivity is purely immediate, it is just as much direct not-objectivity. In other words, not an objectivity which falls outside the immediate presence [*Dasein*] of the individual himself. (2) *Not-objectified labour, not value*, conceived *positively*, or as negativity in relation to itself, is the not-*objectified*, hence non-objective, i.e. subjective existence of labour itself. Labour not as an object, but as activity; not as itself *value*, but as the *living source* of value [*als die lebendige Quelle des Werts*]. [Namely, it is] general wealth (in contrast to capital in which it exists objectively, as reality) as the *general possibility* of the same, which proves itself as such in action.[205]

As Mario Tronti observed,[206] it is here that we can see the transformation of what labour is, as economic activity, into what it becomes politically as socialized subject, working class. Any short-cut and emphasis would be out of place. However, it remains historically true that the not-objectified existence of living labour has rendered labour something to be objectified. But such a process of objectification cannot be distinguished from the *Arbeit als Subjektivität*, from the existence, historically inconfutable, of a subject able to subvert

---

204 Marx, *Grundrisse*, p.272 (*GKPÖ*, p.183).
205 Ibid., pp.295–6 (*GKPÖ*, p.203).
206 Tronti, *Operai e capitale*, p.218 ff.

rules and concepts of the Political. The question about what this subject has become, today, is not of interest to us. It is not our intention to define Marx's actuality. Certainly, the living labour 'as the *living source* of value' has not ceased to be something to be objectivated. This explains the problem represented by the 'general intellect', its two-headed character. Where it seems that the difference is no longer present – within an innovative process not necessarily commisurated upon direct labour –, in reality such a difference is evoked. It is expressed as immediate bodily existence, as a general possibility of creating wealth, as *gesellschaftliche Produktivkraft der Arbeit*: 'it is, in a word, the development of the social individual which appears as the great foundation-stone of production and of wealth'.[207] But what at first sight might appear as a new Eden, is really the point of coagulation of the *einziger Unterschied*, an unfading image of the modern idea of conflict.

Therefore, the surplus-value seems to transform itself into an ontological difference that, it might be said, is a metaphysical category just as much as it is a political one. Marx's issue *par excellence*, the living labour, can be considered at least in two different ways. The first essentially focuses upon the implication inherent to the present constitution – historically changing, but *given* – of the living labour; the second focuses upon the ability of the living labour to *constitute* and *re-constitute* itself as potential capacity. Only the second approach, however, seems to be able to understand that changing *einziger Unterschied* that cannot be adequately recognized before its changing manifestation as subjective valorization, as a multiplication [*Vervielfältigen*], as the result of the labour of a subject.[208] Certainly, here, a hermeneutic circularity should not be invoked as such. What, however, seems possible is a synthesis, an onto-hermeneutical instance, able to keep in itself what in the 'critical economic theory', for example, is an insuperable limit. That is, what we are talking about is not a generic emergence of the social being as such, but rather the production of an *Überschuß*, only possible as a result of the historical

207   Marx, *Grundrisse*, p.705 (*GKPÖ*, p.593).
208   Cf. P. Virno, *Il ricordo del presente. Saggio sul tempo storico*, Bollati Boringhieri, Torino, 1999, pp.121–30.

separation between property and labour. This is the fundamental presupposition that allows the de-realization process of labour, so that an exchange without equivalent could be ratified and perpetrated. This, in the neo-Ricardian surplus approach, remains irremediably unspoken, as it cannot contemplate what for Marx is the real qualifying political aspect: the exchange *ohne Äquivalent*:

> He [the capitalist] pays the value of 100 independent labour powers, but he does not pay for the combined labour power of the 100. [...] Hence the productive power developed by the worker socially [*gesellschaftlicher Arbeiter*] is the productive power of capital. [...] Because this power costs capital nothing, while on the other hand it is not developed by the worker until his labour itself belongs to capital, it appears as a power which capital possesses by its nature – a productive power inherent in capital.[209]

When Marx thinks in terms of values, prices, and profit – all categories that can be *re*-written according to the *recta grammatica* of Sraffa's surplus – he should be considered as a 'classical author'; however, he ceases to be a 'classics' when he identifies in the *einziger Unterschied* the ability to produce *not* a simple spread, *but* a systematic surplus, able to forge the Modern Idea of World: a *political idea*. It is not by mere accident that when the last Napoleoni renounced this idea, in order to recuperate another idea, closer (perhaps only in his intention) to Heidegger's, he feels obliged to bring the Political into the Economical. But, at that point, and after having taken that path, the Political has become only an ecumenical *Prinzip Verantwortung*.

Therefore, our insisting from the outset upon the role of the *verständige Abstraktion* within Marx's critique had the ambition to identify, in the specific *neue Darstellung* that follows, not a new systemization of the world, but an ensemble of contradictory tendencies inherent to it, as the aim of the critique 'is to develop them fully'. It is, certainly, a specific representation, whose character – sometimes undoubtedly deterministic – aims to understand and emphasize *die Unterschiede* 'which express the *social relation*'.[210]

---

209   Marx, *Capital*, vol.1, p.451 (*MEW*, Bd.23, pp.352–3).
210   Marx, *Grundrisse*, p.265 (*GKPÖ*, p.176).

Marx's critique of economy, ideology and politics go hand in hand, giving rise to what can be defined a phenomenology of the political unveiling of the capitalistic economic relationships.

Hence, these *Unterschiede* underpin the critique with which Marx establishes the osmotic relations between the Economical and the Political. This is a fulfilment, in which the concept of political sovereignty as autonomous sphere is destined to be swept away. It is dragged beyond what Marx, in his critique of Hegel's *Rechtsphilosophie*, defined as the opposition of the universal as *form*, in the form of universality, and the universal as *content*.[211] In fact, it is the *difference as subject* that renders the economic sphere something untenable within the realm of the *bürgerliche Gesellschaft*. This latter is pushed beyond the formal and substantial aporias of the representation of interests, of the Hegelian *allgemeine Angelegenheit*, upon which Marx would exercise his irony.[212] Not for this reason it is a state and political mediation thinkable; nor it is thinkable an *illusorische Gemeinschaftlichkeit*[213] able to keep together what escapes the relationship between the Economical and the Political, starting from what the young Marx defined 'the political illusion of civil society'.[214] What remains is neither the result of an overlapping, nor a synthesis of heterogeneous elements and complementary rationalities. Rather, it is constituted by a true and proper fusion of the Economical and the Political, characterized by the instability intrinsic to the *difference as subject*, primary feature of the *Kritik der politischen Ökonomie*. This is the real divide between the scientific intent of Marx's critique and the classical political economy, to which any subsequent 'economic discourse' concerning the surplus would remain indissolubly linked.

211 K. Marx, *Kritik des Hegelschen Staatsrechts*, *MEW*, Bd.1, p.267.
212 W.G.F. Hegel, *Die 'Rechtsphilosophie' von 1820. Mit Hegels Vorlesungsnotizen 1821–1825*, in *Vorlesungen über Rechtsphilosophie 1818–1831*, hrsg. von K.-H. Ilting, Frommann-Holzboog, Stuttgart-Bad Cannstatt, 1974, Bd.2, p.766. Marx's critique of the 'affair of the people' (*allgemeine Angelegenheit*) can be found in the *Kritik des Hegelschen Staatsrechts*, § 301 (*MEW*, Bd.1, pp.263–5).
213 K. Marx, F. Engels, *Der Deutsche Ideologie*, *MEW*, Bd.3, p.33.
214 Marx, *Kritik des Hegelschen Staatsrechts*, § 301, *MEW*, Bd.1, p.265.

Chapter III
Disjunction
Joseph A. Schumpeter: the logos of
economic theory

1. Introduction

Surrounded simultaneously by Walras' inheritance and the progressive imposition of Keynes' paradigm, Schumpeter shared the same destiny reserved for any other *stummer Prophet*. In the eyes of his contemporaries his *opus* was always perceived as a great anomaly. Particularly for the advocates of Economics, it appeared to be too socially attentive to be also scientifically credible. Obviously, unpopularity was not the only reaction generated by its heterodoxy. It also managed to raise quite an interest in those scholars who stretched their reflections well-beyond the tradition – the neo-Marxist School is a clear case in point. This said, as speculation, the Schumpeterian *opus* always remained an *exemplum in margine*. In short, Schumpeter 'as a social scientist' was not a foregone epitaph.

Nevertheless, to accept *d'emblée* the correctness of this epitaph is problematic. Although raising such a doubt may appear paradoxical, it is the outcome of a legitimate perplexity. That Schumpeter's *opus* could be interpreted according to an historical-social paradigm is a correct and well-founded hypothesis. The presence of concepts such as 'development', 'innovation' and 'credit' – all that establish the prevalence of dynamics upon statics – suggests, *per se*, a social explanation of economic phenomena. However, far from all the neo-classical traditions, our interpretation will try to show that, in spite of the above concepts, a conspicuous number of elements calls into question the interpretation of Schumpeter 'as a social scientist' – at least, in its most obvious form. Although these elements pertain first of all to the methodological sphere, they are, *de facto* and without interruption, connected to Schumpeter's 'theoretical systematic', in which the reasoning of an entire life would be expressed, *in extremo spiritu*, by the aporetical nexus between economic science and ideology.

Essentially developed in an environment whose confines span heterodoxy to tradition, from Marx to Walras,[1] Schumpeter's methodological contribution comes to a clear definition a long time before his more mature theory of economic development. Based upon the so-called 'method of variation' (*Variationsmethode*), it took shape in a time that spans from the early writings to his first major work published in 1912. The method of variation provides the grounds for Schumpeter's seminal distinction between theoretical economics and economic theory. Both the relevance and the consequences that stem from this methodological approach are apparent: they enable the Austrian economist to determine the sense and set the limits of the applications of the neoclassical modelling, differentiating, at the same

---

1   Regarding the complexity of Schumpeter's biography, which had a relevant influence on the theoretical approach of the Austrian economist, cf. G. Haberler, 'J.A. Schumpeter: 1883–1950', *Quarterly Journal of Economics*, 1950, vol.64, 3; A. Smithies, 'Memorial: J.A. Schumpeter, 1883–1950', *American Economic Review*, 1950, vol.40, 4; E. Schneider, *J.A. Schumpeter: Leben und Werk einen großen Sozialökonomen*, J.C.B. Mohr (P. Siebeck), Tübingen, 1970; E. März, *J.A. Schumpeter: Forscher, Lehrer und Politiker*, Oldenbourg, München, 1983; R.L. Allen, *Opening Doors: The Life and Work of Joseph Schumpeter*, Transaction Publisher, New Brunswick and London, 1991; R. Swedberg, *Schumpeter. A Biography*, Princeton University Press, Princeton, 1993; W.F. Stolper, *Joseph Alois Schumpeter: The Public Life of a Private Man*, Princeton University Press, Princeton, 1994. For the specific Austrian context, fundamental for the formation of Schumpeter's *forma mentis*, see A. Fuchs, *Geistige Strömungen in Österreich 1867–1918*, Löcker, Wien, 1949; O. Jàszi, *The Dissolution of the Habsburg Monarchy*, Chicago University Press, Chicago and London, 1961; O. Breicha, G. Fritsch, *Finale und Auftakt: Wien, 1898–1914*, Müller, Salzburg, 1964; A.J. May, *Vienna in the Age of Franz Josef*, University of Oklahoma, Norman, 1966; W.M. Johnson, *The Austrian Mind: An Intellectual and Social History, 1848–1938*, University of California Press, Berkeley, 1972; C.E. Schorske, *Fin-de-siècle Vienna*, Weidenfeld and Nicolson, London, 1980; C. Magris, *Il mito absburgico*, Einaudi, Torino, 1997; A. Janik, S. Toulmin, *Wittgenstein's Vienna*, Weidenfeld and Nicolson, London, 1973; and M. Cacciari, *Dallo Steinhof*, Adelphi, Milano, 1980.

time, the static model from the dynamic model. This methodological analysis is neither a sterile nor a futile exercise. In effect, it allows the explanation of some of the most significant aporias, which pervade Schumpeter's theory of economic development, with respect to and apart from the comparison with the limits imposed by the Walrasian model.[2] The problematic relationship between the Economical and the Political that Schumpeter unfolds in his mature works, his disjunctive character, can be explained only within such a framework. As we shall see, only within this framework does it become possible to comprehend why this problematic relationship is imposed as an exogenous *datum*. Such an exogeneity informs Schumpeter's notion of *impoliticus*.

2. A functional gnoseology

Schumpeter's distance from an alleged 'natural' foundation of the method of economic science is sharp and it does not concede any residual doubt. Not interested in the disputes of those critics inclined to philosophy,[3] his aim was systematic rather than exegetic. It is noteworthy that in his *Epochen der Dogmen und Methodengeschichte* (1914) he did not linger over philosophical issues, not even when the comparison with the German Historical School – and thereby with the themes concerning the *Methodenstreit* – became particularly pressing. As it is possible to evince from his early works, Schumpeter's formation occurred in an extremely particular environment, from which he drew important stimulations. However, both his strong personality and

2   Cf. R. Arena, 'Schumpeter after Walras: "Economie pure" or "stylized Facts"?', in T. Lowry (ed. by), *Perspective on the History of Economic Thought*, Elgar, Aldershot, 1992, vol.8; Id., 'Schumpeter on Walras', in R. Arena and C. Dangel-Hagnauer (ed. by), *The Contribution of Joseph Schumpeter to Economics*, Routledge, London, 2002, pp.40–64.
3   For a preliminary discussion on these themes see A.F. Chalk, 'Schumpeter's Views on the Relationship of Philosophy and Economics', *Southern Economic Journal*, 1958, vol.24, 1, pp.271–82.

the originality of his analysis make it impossible to house him within the Austrian School.[4]

The most notable representative of the School was Carl Menger, one of the two main protagonists of the *Methodenstreit*. As it is well-known, in this 'battle', he played the role of a 'pure' scientist, taking the side of the deductive method, based upon the abstract notion of *homo oeconomicus*. This point of view was held in opposition to the representatives of the so-called young German Historical School, Gustav von Schmoller *in primis*. When Menger was working on his *Grundsätze* – published before the seminal works of Eugen von Böhm-Bawerk and Friedrich von Wieser, and before the same Austrian School came to life[5] – he was quite an isolated scholar, unaware 'of all the tactics employed in small circles in order to gain acceptance for new ideas'.[6] His reflection was substantially ignored by the German economists.[7] Schmoller, instead, enjoyed a considerable aca-

---

4   From the marginalist revolution to the 1930's, the Austrian School enjoyed notable and increasing scientific credit: S. Zamagni, 'Sui fondamenti metodologici della scuola austriaca', *Materiali filosofici*, 1983, vol.7. Cf. also N. Leser (hrsg. von), *Die Wiener Schule der Nationalökonomie*, H. Böhlau, Wien, 1986; W. Grassl, B. Smith (ed. by), *Austrian Economics: Historical and Philosophical Background*, Croom Helm, London, 1986; N. De Vecchi, 'La scuola viennese di economia', in G. Becattini (ed. by), *Il pensiero economico. Temi, problemi e scuole*, Utet, Torino, 1990, pp.311–47; Id., 'Da Menger ai Viennesi. Il rapporto tra individuo e istituzioni nella spiegazione del processo capitalistico', *Quaderni di storia dell'economia politica*, 1986, vol.4, 3; S. Gloria-Palermo, 'Schumpeter and the old Austrian School', in Arena and Dangel-Hagnauer (ed. by), *The Contribution of Joseph Schumpeter to Economics*, pp.21–39.

5   Within the Austrian School, there were competitive if not alternative views. However, beyond these differences, it appears clear that the critiques addressed by Wieser, Böhm-Bawerk, Mises and Hayek to *Historismus* directly descend from Menger's traditions. Cf. R. Cubeddu, *The Philosophy of the Austrian School*, Routledge, London, 1993.

6   J.A. Schumpeter, 'Carl Menger', *Zeitschrift für Volkswirtschaft und Sozial-politik*, 1921, vol.1 (afterwards in *Ten Great Economists. From Marx to Keynes*, Allen & Unwin, London, 1952, p.88).

7   'Theoretical economics had never become firmly entrenched in Germany [...], it was an alien plant which, moreover, had been transplanted by hands which were by no means especially skilful. [...] In the historical circle hardly any

212

demic influence, that allowed him to create 'a "school"', which became a force in our science'.[8] When Menger published his *Untersuchungen*,[9] Schmoller reviewed them in the *Jahrbuch*.[10] Deeply irritated by Schmoller's critique, Menger provided a fierce reply.[11] The 'battle of method' was triggered. The *querelle* referred not only to the different methodological perspectives of the social sciences, but also to the different concepts informing their realms.

attempts were made to penetrate into or to reform it but it was laid aside and condemned to death in general terms' [J.A. Schumpeter, *Economic Doctrine and Method*, trans. by R. Aris, George Allen & Unwin Ltd, London, 1954, pp.161–2; *Epochen der Dogmen- und Methodengeschichte*, in *Grundriss der Sozialökonomik*, I Abteilung, *Wirtschaft und Wirtschaftswissenschaft*, Mohr (Paul Siebeck), Tübingen, 1914, p.103]. For an overview of the German economic tradition, cf. J.G. Backhaus, 'The German Economic Tradition: from Cameralism to the Verein für Sozialpolitik', in M. Albertone, A. Masoero (ed. by), *Political Economy and National Realities*, Fondazione L. Einaudi, Torino, 1994, pp.329 ff.; K. Häuser, 'Historical School and Methodenstreit', P. Schiera, F. Tenbruck (ed. by), *Gustav Schmoller e il suo tempo: la nascita delle scienze sociali in Germania e in Italia / Gustav Schmoller in seiner Zeit: die Entstehung der Sozialwissenschaften in Deutschland und Italien*, Il Mulino-Duncker & Humblot, Bologna-Berlin, 1989, pp.307 ff.; E. Streissler, K. Milford, 'Theoretical and Methodological Positions of German Economics in the Middle of the Nineteenth Century', *History of Economic Ideas*, 1993–1994, vol.1–2, 3–1.

8   Schumpeter, *Economic Doctrine and Method*, p.156; *Epochen der Dogmen-und Methodengeschichte*, p.100.

9   C. Menger, *Untersuchungen über die Methode der Sozialwissenschaften, und der Politischen Ökonomie insbesondere*, Duncker & Humblot, Leipzig, 1883; *Investigations into the Method of the Social Sciences*, translated by F.J. Nock, New York University Press, New York and London, 1985. Cf. R. Cubeddu, 'Fonti filosofiche delle *Untersuchungen über die Methode der Sozialwissenschaften* di Carl Menger', *Quaderni di storia dell'economia politica*, 1985, vol.3, 3.

10   G. Schmoller, 'Die Schriften von C. Menger und W. Dilthey zur Methodologie des Staat- und Sozialwissenschaften', *Jahrbuch für Gesetzgebung, Verwaltung und Volkswirtschaft im Deutschen Reich*, 1883, vol.7; afterwards in *Zur Litteraturgeschichte der Staat- und Sozialwissenschaften*, Burt Franklin, New York, 1968, p.278.

11   C. Menger, *Die Irrtümer des Historismus in der deutschen Nationalökonomie*, Hölder, Wien, 1884.

The consequences were noteworthy. Thus, although we are not interested in dwelling upon the historical and theoretical complexity of this *querelle* – particularly with regard to the relationship between economics and politics informing Schmoller's approach[12] –, as it is repeatedly evoked in the works of the young Schumpeter,[13] we shall try to synthetically sketch its development, because – as Max Weber's reflection would show – it concerned the disciplinary statutes of all social sciences. In *Untersuchungen*, Menger's aim was to determine 'the nature of political economy, its subdivisions, and its truths'. On these grounds – he asks himself – what, at a theoretical level, can the reflection on method serve? Not very much indeed, if it is true that '[t]he most important scientific results have come from men who were far removed from methodological investigations'. The matter, however, dramatically changes when '[e]rroneous methodological principles supported by powerful schools prevail completely [...]'. In these circumstances, only the 'clarification of methodological problems' can create the conditions for the establishment – and the progress – of an *exact theory*,[14] whose sole rule of cognition is grounded in the idea that '*whatever is observed, even if in one case only, must always put*

12   G. Gozzi, *Modelli politici e questione sociale in Italia e in Germania fra Otto e Novecento*, Il Mulino, Bologna, 1988, p.172. Regarding this, also the role and the program of *Verein für Sozialpolitik* ought to be evaluated (A. Roversi, *Il magistero della scienza. Storia del Verein für Sozialpolitik dal 1872 al 1888*, F. Angeli, Milano, 1984). On Schmoller and Menger, cf. V. Gioia, *Gustav Schmoller: la scienza economica e la storia*, Congedo, Galatina, 1990; Schiera, Tenbruck (ed. by), *Gustav Schmoller e il suo tempo: la nascita delle scienze sociali in Germania e in Italia*. See also the monographic issue of *History of Economic Ideas*, 1993–1994, vol.1–2, 3/1; J.R. Hicks, W. Weber (ed. by), *Carl Menger and the Austrian School of Economics*, Clarendon, Oxford, 1972; E. Streissler, W. Weber (ed. by), *Carl Menger and the Austrian Economics*, Clarendon, Oxford, 1973; B.J. Caldwell (ed. by), *Carl Menger and his Legacy in Economics*, Duke University Press, Durham and London, 1990; R. Cubeddu, *Il liberalismo della Scuola Austriaca. Menger, Mises, Hayek*, Morano, Napoli, 1992.
13   R. Swedberg argued: 'The parameters of the discourse of his book [*Das Wesen*], in other words, were set by the *Methodenstreit*' (*Joseph A. Schumpeter*, p.25).
14   Menger, *Investigations into the Method of the Social Sciences*, pp.26–7.

in appearance again under exactly the same actual conditions [...]'.[15]
The knowledge informing the economic field is of a twofold kind: the individual and the general one. Whilst economic history and statistics deal with the former, theoretical economics deals with the latter. In effect, if economic history and statistics provide an enquiry of singular phenomena, theoretical economics aims at the investigation of 'the empirical forms and laws (the general nature and general connection) of economic phenomena'.[16] Hence – Menger concludes – whilst economic history and statistics are historical sciences, economics is a theoretical science. This is what the Historical School fails to understand.

To the above arguments, Schmoller replied that science aimed at describing phenomena is indispensable for the achievement of a 'general theory'. In his own words, descriptive science 'provides the background for the general theory. This preparatory work reaches is completeness when it is able to provide an account of all characters, variations, causes and essential effects'. Obviously, this presupposes an entire conceptual frame, a synoptic vision of all possible causes. 'Any exhaustive description is a contribution to the definition of the general essence of Science we are analyzing [*des generellen Wesens der betreffenden Wissenschaft*]'.[17] Differently from Menger's approach, according to which theoretical economics should be intended as confined merely to the analysis of the theories of value, prices, income distribution, and money, the historical approach – Schmoller affirms – not denying the importance of the theory, allows to avoid the risk that the isolation and the abstraction of the observer determine the impossibility of understanding the spatial and temporal dimension of the analysed phenomenon. On these grounds, he concludes, although abstraction is the basis of any knowledge, the researcher should abstract correctly.

15   Ibid., p.60.
16   Ibid., p.37.
17   G. Schmoller, 'Die Schriften von C. Menger und W. Dilthey zur Methodologie des Staat- und Sozialwissenschaften', p.278.

As the point in question was relevant, Menger's reply was equally sharp. 'Des generellen Wesens der betreffenden Wissenschaft': 'What does this mean?' – he asked:

What is the 'general essence' of science? Schmoller perhaps intends the knowledge of the general (of the phenomenal forms) in a given research field? [...] Between the theoretical political economy [*der theoretischen Nationalökonomie*] and the history of political economy [*der Geschichte der Volkswirtshaft*], and among the sciences in general [...] there is a well delineated border, the one which exists among sciences.[18]

As it is easy to evince, the question underlying the *querelle* between Menger and Schmoller was much more complex than the methodological one. As Schmoller vividly synthesized: 'How is it possible to outline the fundamental principles informing economics without explaining the relationship between the State and the economy?'[19] In short, the relationships between science and politics, and between the individualistic and social approaches, were the essential elements around which the radical transformation of the disciplinary statutes of modern social sciences gravitated; statutes certainly underpinned by different research traditions,[20] culminating in the Weberian *summa*.[21]

In this regard, Schumpeter's position was balanced and well-thought out. In his eyes, the strength of the German historical tradition and, thereby, the marginality of the pure theoretical approach, was absolutely clear. Nevertheless, in his opinion, the *Methodenstreit* failed to obtain substantial results because of its 'endless repetition of arguments', 'invincible dislike', and 'tendency of the parties to re-

18   Menger, *Die Irrtümer des Historismus*, pp.21 and 24.
19   G. Schmoller, 'Die Schriften von C. Menger und W. Dilthey zur Methodologie des Staat- und Sozialwissenschaften', p.282.
20   Cf. P. Schiera, *Il laboratorio borghese. Scienza e politica nella Germania dell'Ottocento*, Il Mulino, Bologna, 1987, pp.198 ff.
21   Cf. Y. Shionoya, 'Schumpeter on Schmoller and Weber: A Methodology of Economic Sociology', *History of Political Economy*, 1991, vol.23, 2; R. Faucci, V. Rodezno, 'Did Schumpeter change His Mind? Notes on Max Weber's Influence on Schumpeter', *History of Economic Ideas*, 1998, vol.6, 1.

proach each other with being unscientific [*Unwissenschaftlichkeit*]'.[22] For a science concerned with historical processes, he maintains, both the relevance of the historical research and the necessity to develop within it precise analytical instruments is undisputable. Later in time, in his posthumous *History of Economic Analysis*, he would define the *Methodenstreit* in the same way: 'a history of wasted energies'.[23]

It is apparent how wide the gulf was that separated Schumpeter from both the methodological contrapositions inherent to the *Methodenstreit* and from the same Austrian School *stricto sensu*. Such a gulf was the results of the combination of different elements: the refusal of Menger's and Wieser's dogmatism, the opposition to the psychological method, clearly explicated in *Das Wesen*, and the belief that mathematics ought to have a central role in economic analysis.[24] When, later in time, Schumpeter returned to these same arguments, he would consider the polemic between the advocates of induction and those of deduction as absurd, observing that 'any objectionable piece of methodology is immaterial whenever it can be dropped without forcing us to drop the result of the analysis that is associated with it'.[25]

Evidently, the Schumpeterian approach emphasized the direct observation of facts already presented in *Das Wesen* (1908), where he argued that 'we want, and can, contribute to the explanation of the

22 Schumpeter, *Economic Doctrine and Method*, pp.167–8; *Epochen der Dogmen- und Methodengeschichte*, p.106.
23 J.A. Schumpeter, *History of Economic Analysis*, Allen & Unwin, London, 1955, p.814 (henceforth *HEA*). Cf. also J.N. Keynes, *The Scope and Method of Political Economy*, Macmillan, London, 1891.
24 In this regard, D. Simpson ('Joseph Schumpeter and the Austrian School of Economics', *Journal of Economic Studies*, 1983, vol.10, 4, pp.15–28) wrote: 'Of the Austrian School, Menger, Mises and Hayek regarded as inappropriate the use of mathematical methods in economics. Their attitude ranged from skepticism on the part of Hayek to outright hostility on the part of Mises'. On Schumpeter's well-known difficulties with mathematics (Swedberg, *J.A. Schumpeter*, pp.117–18), see P.A. Samuelson, 'Schumpeter as a Teacher and Economic Theorist', in S.E. Harris (ed. by), *Schumpeter Social Scientist*, Harvard University Press, Cambridge MA, 1951, p.49.
25 *HEA*, p.537, footnote 9. On Schumpeter's methodology, see F. Machlup, 'Schumpeter's Economic Methodology', in Harris (ed. by), *Schumpeter Social Scientist*, pp.95–101.

economic phenomena merely describing them'.[26] Thus, the terms *Erklärung* and *Beschreibung* are synonymous. In this context – as the same Schumpeter notes – the claim according to which 'a theoretician is willing to describe reality' might appear to be paradoxical. However – he carries on –, on closer investigation, 'we may be persuaded that the heart of any theory, what it truly says [*was sie wirklich sagt*], is always and only a claim about the functional relations [*über funktionelle Beziehungen*] that exist among some quantities; all the rest should be considered as an accessory and unessential'.[27] Hence, for Schumpeter, the *Methodenstreit* was indeed something unessential.

The soundness of Schumpeter's statement can be easily derived from a transversal reading of his *Das Wesen und der Hauptinhalt der theoretischen Nationalökonomie*, where the reflection on the gnoseology of economic science plays a pivotal role, which can be fully appreciated only by bearing in mind the whole structure of the work. It is here, in fact, where, for the first time, Schumpeter addresses the fundamental distinction between statics and dynamics – a distinction that would characterize, *mutatis mutandis*, his entire reflection.[28] Of course, a correct appreciation of the 'sense' attributed by Schumpeter to the neoclassical theory is the precondition for understanding such a distinction, from which the boundary line between *theoretische Ökonomie* and *ökonomische Theorie* originated.

As it has been authoritatively observed, this work oscillates between orthodoxy and heterodoxy.[29] Significantly, the text – which,

---

26   J.A. Schumpeter, *Das Wesen und der Hauptinhalt der theoretischen National-ökonomie*, Duncker & Humblot, München-Leipzig, 1908, Dritte Auflage Berlin, 1998, p.37, henceforth *DW*.
27   Ibid.
28   See the classic P.A. Samuelson, 'Dynamics, Statics and the Stationary State', *The Review of Economics and Statistics*, 1943, vol.25, 1. On the twofold juxtaposition between 'statics-dynamics' and 'invariant-evolutive' process (*HEA*, pp.963 ss), M. Egidi, *Schumpeter. Lo sviluppo come trasformazione morfologica*, Etas, Milano, 1981, pp.152–61.
29   A. Graziani, 'Introduzione' in J.A. Schumpeter, *Il processo capitalistico. Cicli economici*, Ital. trans. by G. Ricoveri, Boringhieri, Torino, 1977. See also G. Calzoni, 'Alle origini della teoria dello sviluppo economico di Schumpeter: *L'essenza e i principi dell'theoretical economics*', in C. Filippini, P. Porta (ed.

from time to time, is difficult to read[30] – scrutinizes the static model for hundreds of pages, exposing its limits. The author does not aspire to reach 'a systematic completeness'; rather, he intends to deal with 'a smaller number of fundamental propositions', at the heart of which rests the issue of equilibrium, 'whose importance, although not so relevant for its practical applications, results nonetheless fundamental for economic science'. Following this train of thought, as his intention is to focus only upon the static model, 'few hints and occasional observations will be made concerning dynamics'.[31] Undoubtedly, one of Schumpeter's objectives was to indicate to German readers the scientific relevance of 'pure' economic theory. Nevertheless, it is difficult to escape the idea that, already at that point, he was utilizing the analysis of the conditions of static equilibrium as an antithetic point of reference for his theory of development.[32] Certainly, the relevance credited to statics reaffirms his specificity – *an sich* and *für sich* – in respect of the dynamics: 'we shall show – Schumpeter says – how unsatisfactory is the representation of reality given by statics, but, in the end, and in spite of this, its scientific importance is great and requires extreme careful elaboration'.[33] Notwithstanding its scientific importance, however, statics shows its weakness exactly where Schumpeter's *pars construens* – which would not bring about a methodological revolution on its own, but would consist of the idea (already utilized by both Marx and Arthur Spiethoff) that the economic cycle is the engine of capitalism – begins. Obviously, in

by), *Società, sviluppo, impresa. Saggi su Schumpeter*, Ipsoa, Milano, 1985, pp.173 ff.

30   A. Roncaglia (*Schumpeter. È possibile una teoria dello sviluppo economico?*, Banca Popolare dell'Etruria – Studi e Ricerche, Arezzo, 1987, pp.39 ff.) has pointed out how the young Schumpeter was unable to master the different analytical details of the theory of economic equilibrium.

31   *DW*, pp.XXI–XXII.

32   Roncaglia, *Schumpeter*, p.34. Similarly, N. De Vecchi, 'Introduzione' in E. v. Böhm-Bawerk, J. B. Clark, C. Menger, J.A. Schumpeter, *La teoria austriaca del capitale e dell'interesse. Fondamenti e discussione*, Ital. trans. by K. Röllin, Istituto dell'Enciclopedia Italiana, Roma, 1983, p.25.

33   *DW*, p.186.

order to make intelligible this *pars construens* it is necessary to provide a clear exposition of 'the gnoseology of economic science'.[34]

According to Schumpeter, the primary concern of statics is the analysis of the exchange relations occurring in a given economic system. 'In an exchange economy, any good, at a given time, is in a determinate relation of exchange with all other goods; it can, in other words, be bought or sold at a certain price'.[35] Hence, economic activity can only be framed as 'a change in the economic quantities'. Discarding *das Kostenprinzip*, in order to explain these relations of exchange and therefore 'what is the price so as to derive from it determinate formal laws of movement', Schumpeter assumes the 'principle of value', according to which the value of any economic good is given by its demand in relation to its scarcity. Such a principle is thereby 'a hypothetical function [*hypothetische Funktion*], unreal and, in principle, arbitrary, towards which we are driven by the observation of facts [*Tatsachenbeobachtung*]'.[36] Thus, the principle of value is only 'a basic assumption that allows us to generalize determinate scientific facts'.

Clearly, the argumentation is intrinsic to the neoclassical tradition, of which, however, Schumpeter refuses one of its essential aspects: namely, introspective psychologism, from which Marginalism derived its analysis of needs:

> From the relative intensity of the impulses of need of those who exchange, we can derive the relations of exchange and for this aim the laws of evaluation [*die Gesetze der Wertung*] are founded upon psychological observations. For example, it is said that with the rise in satisfaction, any further need of

34   If the methodological character of *Das Wesen* is entirely recognized, it should also be mentioned that the easy parallels with authors like Kuhn and Lakatos advanced by some scholars would require an adequate historiographical caution. Besides F. Machlup's essay (above mentioned), it should be remembered W.F. Stolper's balanced judgement: 'It [*DW*] is essentially a methodological study. Its main function in the Schumpeterian system is to clear the ground for the contributions to come. Its purpose is to determine the content and the explanatory limits of static-equilibrium theory' ('The Schumperiam System', *Journal of Economic History*, 1951, vol.9, 3, pp.272–7).

35   *DW*, p.49.

36   *DW*, p.73.

nourishment decreases and that therefore a satisfied individual will be ready to pay a lower price for any additional quantity. We can object to this reasoning: why is such an explanation given? What we see is only that the individual is ready to pay a lower price; why he does this is, at the moment, of no interest from an economic point of view and, furthermore, we infer from the fact that he so behaves is that he is satisfied. We are then facing the following alternative: either we admit that the only circumstance that allows us to infer the sensibility of the individual is his behaviour, or we have to recur to the result of introspection.[37]

At any rate, from a methodological point of view, the principle of value, setting aside its 'psychological foundation', rests a valid formal hypothesis. It allows the description of 'economic laws', which refer to the theory of price, in terms of a 'pure science'. In this theoretical context, 'the most important application of the theory of price' is the analysis of the processes of distribution: wages, rents, interests and profits. Nevertheless, although Schumpeter's theory of income is consistent with the marginalist approach, we shall see shortly that it contains a seminal difference regarding the theory of capital and, therefore, of interest and profit.

On the other hand, also with regard to the analysis of the general economic equilibrium, Schumpeter's argumentation manifests its specificity. It is carried out via the peculiar 'method of variation'. In a nutshell, its essential feature is this: in a static equilibrium model in which the resources are given, the method allows us to observe the possible changing of the economic quantity in the short term:

> The method of variation consists of the following: our system is initially in a state of equilibrium; a position in which, as we have seen, all its elements are univocally determined; increase or decrease now by a small quantity one of these elements and observe what happens. [...] Hence, if, as we have seen, all elements are univocally determined, it is neither possible that after one is changed the same condition of maximum utility occurs, and by consequence nor the state of equilibrium [....] The observation of these changes provides us with the laws of movement that we are looking for [...] The variations are produced as a result of the reactions against the modification of the equilibrium and bring about a new situation of equilibrium [...].[38]

37   *DW*, p.64.
38   *DW*, pp.451–2.

Thus, the method of variation can be utilized if, and only if, assuming the value functions relative to all the market actors as given, minimal quantitative variations occur in the short term. On the contrary, when quantitatively tangible variations occur in the long term, this method loses its heuristic character, as the considered model becomes dynamic:

> Metaphorically, our method might be described in the following way: we take, so to speak, an instantaneous picture of the economy. The image shows all the processes in a determinate moment and in a condition of apparent calm. But we are aware that the real word is characterized by a lively movement of which we would like to describe some aspects. Such a description should enable us – as this is its aim – to derive from this first image the representation of the economy that the reality would offer to us in a subsequent moment without taking another picture [...]. However, our instantaneous picture should confine itself only to the representation of the changes occurring in the quantity of the goods possessed by the single economic subjects.[39]

Therefore, the method of variation is not concerned with the long term, as 'in these circumstances [...], what becomes interesting are completely different factors'. Consequently, to consider only minimal changes 'merely means the necessity of confining ourselves to statics, as beyond it our method would fail'.[40] We can only look at changes occurring in the short term, between the initial and the new economic equilibrium, in a comparative perspective. This theoretical framework 'represents the abstraction of the instantaneous conditions of the reality', and 'can be utilized only for a moment'.[41] From a logical point of view, the path comes to an end. The method of variation serves to establish the 'laws' according to which the general economic equilibrium can subsist and modify itself without exceeding into the dynamic implications of development.

Apropos Schumpeter's interpretation of the static equilibrium, it has been observed that whilst his criticism to the models of stationary

---

39 *DW*, p.142.
40 *DW*, pp.461 and 460.
41 'Nicht nur ist unser theoretisches Bild der Wirklichkeit vom dem Zustande derselben in einem Momente abstrahiert, es ist auch nur brauchbar für einem Moment' (*DW*, p.461).

economic equilibrium is consistent, when it addresses the models of temporary equilibrium, it is not fully justified, as these models can analytically treat all the phenomena relating to the temporal structure of the economic activity, without incurring in any logical mistakes.[42] Even if this is true, however, it is also important to underline how the same limit explains what the method of variation *de facto* outlines: namely, the shift from a static to a comparative static model.[43] In this latter, in fact, to any variation of one of the quantities that determine its static equilibrium, there should follow firstly an analysis of the configuration of the newly realized equilibrium, and then a comparison of this latter with the previous one.

As it is known, in *Das Wesen* the argument is not fully developed. Schumpeter only concedes that the method of variation can uniquely reveals minimal, 'infinitesimal', variations in the short term. For this reason, at first glance, these variations might legitimately be interpreted as continuous variations, tending, in an infinitely short time, towards an infinitely small in mathematical terms. Nevertheless, in the attempt to shed light upon such an obscurity, Schumpeter briefly claims: 'Concerning [...] the quantity of variations – [...] we are not obliged to be bound, [...] to an order of quantities infinitely small in mathematical terms'.[44]

Thus, it seems reasonable to attribute a role to the method of variation within the models of comparative statics; a role that in 1908 Schumpeter did not take into consideration, although he hermetically admitted that between the static and the dynamic analysis 'it would be preferable to utilize another method'. To insist upon this point would lead us beyond the aim of our analysis. Anyhow, it should be noted that in Schumpeter's *opus* the models of comparative statics play a specific role. As Terenzio Cozzi noted, if we consider the difference between the concept of growth and that of development, it can be observed that whilst for Schumpeter the methods of comparative statics are suitable for analysing the consequences concerning the

42   F. Donzelli, 'Schumpeter e la teoria economica neoclassica', *Ricerche Economiche*, 1983, vol.37, 4, p.686.
43   Shionoya, 'Schumpeter and the Idea of Social Science', p.146.
44   *DW*, p.464.

variation in exogenous data, they are unsuitable to explain why the variations occur for endogenous reasons.[45]

Therefore, although for Schumpeter the issue of equilibrium is scarcely relevant with regard to 'the practical application of the theory', it should play a fundamental role in the economic science. It should hold a place at the heart of *theoretische Ökonomie*, but apart from any normative concept which is not *werfrei*. In effect, that in a given situation of equilibrium the distribution of goods appears 'normal', or even 'natural', says nothing about the potential ethical value of that distribution. As Weber observed in his seminal essay published in 1904, it is wrong to claim that political economy produces or should produce *Werturteile* deriving them from a specific *wirtschaftlichen Weltanschauung*.[46] Thus, following this train of thought, Schumpeter's claim for which the aim of the theoretician is to 'describe reality' loses its paradoxical feature. For him, in fact, at the heart of any theory, 'what it really says' is always and solely a claim concerning the functional relations existing between some given economic quantities. It is on these grounds that his interpretation of the theory of economic equilibrium – the heart of pure static theory – marks out the difficult relationship between orthodoxy and heterodoxy. But what lies behind the scene to which this last difficult relationship belongs?

What really distinguishes theoretical economics from economic theory is not their more or less explicit reference to 'reality', but rather the articulations of the 'sphere of reality' that we want to describe in *time*, by means of economic categories.[47] According to the static theory, the theoretical frame is the result of the abstraction from the

45   T. Cozzi, *Teoria dello sviluppo economico*, Il Mulino, Bologna, 1984, p.148.
46   M. Weber, 'Die "Objektivität" sozialwissenschaftlicher und sozialpolitischer Erkenntnis', *Archiv für Sozialwissenschaft und Sozialpolitik*, 1904, vol.19, afterwards in *Gesammelte Aufsätze zur Wissenschaftslehre*, hrsg. von J. Winckelmann, J.C.B. Mohr (P. Siebeck), Tübingen, 1988, p.149.
47   R. Teboul, 'Temps et dynamique dans l'oeuvre de J.A. Schumpeter', *Revue Française d'Economie*, 1992, vol.7, 3, pp.75–93; A. Châteauneuf-Maclès, 'Time and Rationality in Schumpeter's Construct', in Arena and Dangel-Hagnauer (ed. by), *The Contribution of Joseph Schumpeter to Economics*, pp.106–23.

instantaneous conditions of reality itself, and it can be utilized only for a moment. In fact, to the variation of the extent of the 'sphere' of reality, does not correspond the same scenario multiplied by scale. Rather, we obtain a 'sphere' characterized by different relationships, within which economic phenomena cannot be described according to the laws of pure static theory. Being only formal, these laws can explain neither ethical intentions nor psychological variables; rather, they should realize the distinction between what Weber defines as *knowledge* and *evaluation*: 'der Unterscheidung zwischen Erkennen und Beurteilen'.[48] Borrowing the same terminology utilized by Ernst Mach in his *Mechanick*,[49] the modernity of Schumpeter's approach resides in this anti-metaphysical distinction. The term 'pure' is utilized here in opposition to apriori; it is what, according to determined rules, can be represented. As the essence of these laws is logical and not statistical, their foundations can only be located in a rational system, unconnected to any causal assumption typical of natural sciences. The claim: 'As all that happen is subjected to a causal law [*dem Kausalgesetze unterworfen*], so also in the sphere of economic science exact laws [*exakte Gesetze*] should exist' – does not demonstrate anything, Schumpeter says. In fact, 'the issue whether the causal interdependence [*die Kausalzusammenhänge*] with which we deal is simple enough to allow the enunciation of general proposition that are sufficiently interesting remains open'.[50]

It is in this way that Schumpeter underlines the distance that separates his approach from the empiristic indeterminateness of the classics, who deduced the laws from what they defined as causes of economic phenomena – so generating, from an apparent terminological imprecision, a fatal confusion:

48   Weber, 'Die "Objektivität" sozialwissenschaftlicher und sozialpolitischer Erkenntnis', p.155.
49   Following Weber, Schumpeter would underline the anti-metaphysical character of the nexus between 'rational' and 'empirical' (*Theorie der wirtschaftlichen Entwicklung*, Dunker & Humblot, Berlin, 1934⁴, reprint 1997, p.88, footnote 1; Engl. trans. by R. Opie: *The Theory of Economic Development*, Harvard University Press, Cambridge MA, 1959, p.57, footnote 1, henceforth *TED*).
50   *DW*, p.XIV.

With regard to phenomena, we shall not speak of a cause [*von 'Ursachen' der Erscheinungen*] – he wrote –, but rather of functional relations [*von funktionelle Beziehungen*] among them, and this, moreover, with much more precision. The concept of function [*Funktionsbegriff*], meticulously elaborated by mathematics, has a clear and unequivocal content that the concept of cause has not [...].[51]

This means that 'pure' economy aims at interpreting economic data defined by their exchange relations among individuals. The nature of these data cannot be observed 'until the ultimate motivation'. To think in causal terms would imply too many philosophical questions and few economic answers. 'Pure' economics is interested in results that 'derive from certain exchange relationships: in this way, functional, not causal, relations impose themselves'.[52] The method informing theoretical economics consists of the description of a system made of 'functional relations occurring among the elements of the said system via the shortest and most valid possible formulae'.[53] It consists of an analytical-formal procedure that, analysing the relations among the economic actors, allows the establishment of the limits of the admitted variations in terms of the quantity of goods within a short time, so as to allow the shift from a situation of equilibrium to the subsequent, without abandoning the static model. Via this method, it is possible to analyse an economic datum during its modification, but only in order to identify laws underlining the 'univocal determination of variations'. Certainly, they are concrete variations, upon which the method can only express a formal judgement. In Schumpeter's words 'the concrete movements [*die konkreten Bewegungen*] depend upon concrete data [*von konkreten Daten*] and our formal reasoning is not sufficiently equipped to make them understandable'.[54]

The delimitation inherent to the static character of the model of general equilibrium derives from its formal connotation; but notwithstanding this, the delimitation is not an insurmountable obstacle.

51   *DW*, p.47. Cf. E. Cassirer, *Substanzbegriff und Funktionsbegriff*, B. Cassirer Verlag, Berlin, 1910.
52   *DW*, p.47.
53   The reference to the Machean *Denkökonomie*, explicitly recalled by Schumpeter in his *History of Economic Analysis*, is clear.
54   *DW*, p.446.

In effect, it represents the very problem that leads to the definition of the method of variation. There is no gap between effective economic variation and its formal explanation. Simply, such a gap imposes some limits: it imposes the margins of an acceptable variation, so that its extent would not entail a discharge from the static model. Any other presumption, Schumpeter assures, would inevitably produce a fracture with regard to the assumptions underpinning economic gnoseology. If it were not so, the earlier mentioned distinction between *theoretische Ökonomie* and *ökonomische Theorie* would become unjustified. If the method of variation would be unable to grasp the essential logical fracture generated by the difference between a static model and a dynamic model, then it would become impossible to grasp the difference between a 'pure', 'formal', theoretical economics, and economic theory. If the specific attributions – above all temporal[55] – that differentiate a static model from the theory of development were absent, how would it be possible to discuss about the properties inherent to a model of general economic equilibrium? Schumpeter's reply is sufficiently obvious: 'development and all that belongs to its realm escape our consideration; essentially, within a system of pure economics there is no room for development [...] This is the most painful limitation, that naturally and unavoidably stems from the essence of our system'.[56]

In view of this reply, it is possible to restate that the relationship between orthodoxy and heterodoxy that pervades *Das Wesen* is certainly characterized by the introduction of a modern economic gnoseology,[57] which follows the unequivocal indication according to

55   Cf. R. Frisch, 'On the Notion of Equilibrium and Disequilibrium', *The Review of Economic Studies*, 1935–1936, vol.3, 1.
56   *DW*, p.186.
57   The modernity of Schumpeter's methodological approach is clearly underlined by Y. Shionoya ('Schumpeter and the Idea of Social Science', pp.91 ff.; Id., 'Instrumentalism in Schumpeter's Economic Methodology', *History of Political Economy*, 1990, vol.22, 2), who considers *Das Wesen* as a theoretical methodological work and Schumpeter as an advocate of a kind of 'instrumentalism', according to which the theories are not 'descriptions', but rather 'tools' to carve out useful results that, as such, cannot be said neither true nor false (cf. J.A. Schumpeter, 'Theoretical Problems of Economic Growth', now in *Essays*, ed.

which 'within our system there is no room for development, not only *because* within it any tendency for development is not admitted and because, moreover, it would destroy the data that are indispensable to us, but also because the effect that could be explained in terms of pure economics and therefore static, are devoid of any interest, being in a context where other data are more relevant'.[58] It might be said that Walras – 'the most famous among the theoreticians' – is indispensable for understanding exactly what *theoretische Ökonomie* can (only) describe; but, in order to understand what modern capitalism is, Marx – a 'certain' Marx – is surely more useful. As such, the *Methodenstreit* should be seen as a mistaken approach to the issue concerning the nature of theoretical economics. It is incomprehensible, Schumpeter observes, that the representatives of economic theory take it as exclusively deductive. In what sense is it deductive? In the way in which the same can be said regarding any other exact science, such as astronomy, for example, a science in which 'nobody can deny neither its empirical character nor its foundation upon facts. How are things exactly?':

> Although the theoretical building seems quite independent, nonetheless it wholly rests upon the observation of the facts [*auf Tatsachenbeobachtung*], whose necessity and influence stretch beyond what is generally believed. The seminal point from which anything depends upon consists of the distinction between two different aspects of the matter: on the one side we have the arbitrariness of principle [*die prinzipielle Willkürlichkeit*] of our theory upon which its system is based upon and, on the other, the fact that it adapts itself to the phenomena and is conditioned by them, something that alone allows the theory to have meaning and value.[59]

by R.V. Clemence, Addison-Wesley, Cambridge 1951; new Edition with an 'Introduction' by R. Swedberg, Transaction Publisher, New Brunswick and Oxford, 1989, p.232). To influence Schumpeter's methodological approach were Mach's doctrine, Poincarré's 'conventionalism', and Vaihinger's 'finctionalism'. In particular, on the relevance of Mach's epistemology upon Vienna's intellectual environment, see M. Cacciari, *Krisis. Saggio sulla crisi del pensiero negativo da Nietzsche a Wittgenstein*, Feltrinelli, Milano, 1976, pp.29–43.

58   *DW*, p.462.
59   *DW*, p.533. On this passage, Machlup's remarks are still relevant ('Schumpeter's Economic Methodology', p.96).

At this point, it would be superfluous to underline how the 'arbitrariness of the principles' indicates the 'relativity' rather than the 'generality' of the principle itself.[60] The confutation of a formal *ratio* that presumes to define a definitive economic language, able to fill the gap between the economic datum and its representation, shows not only the inessentiality of the *Methodenstreit*, but also, and above all, the possibility of widening the gulf from the neoclassical rationalistic fundamentalism – and, in perspective, from any harmonic 'vision' of the economic business cycle. It has been persuasively observed that the distinction between statics and dynamics does not put in place a mere extension of the general theory of economic equilibrium via the introduction of dated variables instead of variables without time. In fact, Schumpeter's attempt is much more radical, although in doing so he credited to the theory of general economic equilibrium narrower margins then the ones it has in reality.[61] Now, apart from the complex development achieved by the contemporary economic science on the specific topic, what does Schumpeter's radical operation consist of? The answers to this question can be found in chapter III, section one of *Das Wesen*.

3. Statics and dynamics

As we have seen above, Schumpeter argues that his entire reasoning assumes the existence of a determinate possession of goods, 'whose quantity is at the disposal of an economic agent in a determinate moment in time'. For this reason, 'the result of the analysis is valid only for that moment, or, at best, for the immediate subsequent instant'. Accordingly, it has been pointed out that the utility functions

60   Cf. Egidi, *Schumpeter. Lo sviluppo come trasformazione morfologica*, pp.19–26.
61   L. Costabile, 'Metodo della scienza e economic theory in Schumpeter. Note su *L'essenza e i principi della economia teoretica'*, *Studi Economici*, 1986, vol.29, 2, p.156.

'should only refer to one and only one instant'. Furthermore, regarding the exchange relations, 'the same warning has been underlined'.[62] So, being the result an instantaneous image, one might ask: why this choice?:

> Immediately, it should be said that to focus upon one and only one instant, or upon a very brief interval of time, is meant to keep unchanged the parts of which the description of reality is made of for the longest possible period of time. If we would have chosen to consider a longer period of time, this decision would have clashed with facts because, as we can easily see, in them changes occur to the point of changing the entire system, and in the face of such a change the initial circumstances would vanished entirely. [...] Can all these factors related to our thesis be said to be mere devices [*nur Redensarten*] that should be overlooked? Obviously, not.[63]

However, as 'at least in the case of the "pure" economic we face a pivotal and definitive limitation', this answer involves relevant theoretical implications. In short, if there are many things that, although being outside the realm of economy, 'are of fundamental relevance for the economist'; and if his science does not allow him to say anything about these many things; then, we are obliged to consider them as immutable. This 'does not compromise the utilization of our result, but only in the short term'. Furthermore, 'that these things might be subjected to change is something clearly observable':

> Certainly, also in this case our formal propositions [*formalen Gesetze*] remain valid, but they lose any interest in the face of those changing in the background conditions [*Grundlagen*] of economy. Our system of equilibrium is shaky. A new equilibrium will be found, but what will be its characteristic and through which processes it will manifest itself, we cannot say. [...] This involves great problems, such as, for example, those concerning the distribution of income [...].[64]

In the face of new *Grundlagen*, the *theoretische Ökonomie* has nothing to say about *these* economic problems. Economic science is therefore subdivided into two distinct realms: 'our exact system' –

62 *DW*, p.176.
63 *DW*, p.177.
64 *DW*, p.179.

230

where theoretical economics is 'pure' representation –, and the one comprehensive of those 'great problems'. These latter, although 'economic by definition', escape 'our exact system', without escaping the sphere of influence of economic science. In effect, they are the subject-matter of the economic theory. Thus, the distinction between theoretical economics and economic theory derives from the fundamental distinction between statics and dynamics, which 'are not only concerned with different problems, but also, dealing with a different material, utilize a different method'. Is there a sharp border between the two? Schumpeter avoids answering in general terms. Certainly, if with regard to the theory of price and its important application, the static methodology seems to be sufficiently equipped, when we deal with the phenomenon of development, the picture changes entirely, as the system of 'pure' economics is devoid of development. This is its specific limit, and it represents a relevant problem, especially if we consider that development is the most important phenomenon to which 'we aim at finding a solution'.

The first element that cannot be analysed in terms of statics is saving in relation to the formation of capital. To verify whether saving might be the object of the static analysis – Schumpeter observes – it is necessary to see whether it is possible to utilize the scheme of exchange: it is necessary to have a saving fund and a value function – both perfectly definable. A static analysis can indeed explain the 'univocal determination of the saving fund, its dependency on the other elements of the system, and even the possibility of considering it a goods similar to all others [...].' Furthermore, it is possible 'to infer determinate laws of movements of the saving fund'.[65] However, the crucial question – not 'logically' crucial (according to theoretical economics), but 'practically' crucial (according to economic theory) – is: can the theory of saving 'explain the formation of capital?' Once again, Schumpeter's answer is negative, as in order to allow such a formation, a change 'in all the value functions', a dynamic process of development – about which *theoretische Ökonomie* cannot be but silent – should occur. The conclusion is as follows:

65   *DW*, p.304.

Only small savings, [...], whose investment is not taken into consideration and that do not particularly affect the economic course can, in principle, be studied in the static economy, otherwise it would cease to be static. Especially the rise of new capital – and this is true whatever significance we assign to the term – expresses an essential dynamic modality, which can only be explained with regard to the problems of development: any attempt to put it into the sphere of static would miserably fail.[66]

It might be said that it makes no sense to analyse saving according to the parameters of static analysis as, from this point of view, nothing relevant can be said about 'the formation of new capitals'. For the same reason, being the analysis of profit linked to that of saving, the former shares the same destiny as the latter. Thus, the question becomes the following: can the saving explain the formation of capital? Besides the capitalization, is there any other efficient cause able to explain the formation of capital? Certainly – Schumpeter says –, it consists of 'the gains deriving from business', including speculative activities and entrepreneurial gains, which are made possible by the fact that competition is not as free as it is usually said.

Hence, if saving is not the result of capitalization, then it should be produced and, as such, should not be immediately consumed. As no one 'consumes immediately the gains deriving from industrial activity', what is essential for the formation of capital is profit. However, in a static economy, in which nothing is left to chance and where free competition pushes the gain to the level of cost, it cannot be contemplated. Essentially, profit is a phenomenon deriving from the process of development.[67] In other words, saving does not explain the formation of capital:

We can conclude that the formation of a patrimony [die Vermögensbildung] is not a static process and, furthermore, cannot be explained via saving. The same can be maintained concerning the creation of capital [von der Schaffung von Kapital] intended as the ensemble of the produced means of production. The latter do not spring out of saving, this is a matter of fact. They are the result of the efforts that destroy the state of equilibrium of our system and that cannot be

66   DW, p.306.
67   DW, p.310.

satisfactorily explained by economics as far as it will develop inside the static realm. Not only these efforts, but also their results are destined to change the entire 'system'.[68]

Within static analysis – Schumpeter argues –, there is another element that finds no explanation: namely, interest – a controversial statement that, after the publication of *Theorie der wirtschaftlichen Entwicklung*,[69] would generate a lively debate. It is worth noting that against the interpretative tradition that conceived of interest as a reward for the specific contribution given by a productive factor,

68 *DW*, pp.310–11.
69 The *querelle* developed as a result of E. von Böhm-Bawerk's remarks ('Eine "dynamische" Theorie des Kapitalzinses', *Zeitschrift für Volkswirtschaft, Sozialpolitik und Verwaltung*, 1913, Bd.22, pp.599–639), to which Schumpeter vividly replied ('Eine "dynamische" Theorie der Kapitalzinses: Eine Entgegnung', *Zeitschrift für Volkswirtschaft, Sozialpolitik und Verwaltung*, 1913, Bd.22, now in *Aufätze zur Ökonomischen Theorie*, J.C.B. Mohr (Paul Siebeck), Tübingen, 1952, pp.411–51). In this regard, the classical references are: L. Robbins, 'On a Certain Ambiguity in the Conception of Stationary Equilibrium', *Economic Journal*, 1930, vol.40, 158; D. Warriner, 'Schumpeter and the Conception of Static Equilibrium', *Economic Journal*, 1931, vol.41, 161; P.A. Samuelson, 'Dynamics, Statics and the Stationary State'; G. Haberler, 'Schumpeter's Theory of Interest', in *Schumpeter social scientist*, pp.72 ff. See also: F. Perroux, *La pensée économique de Joseph Schumpeter. Les dynamiques du capitalisme*, Droz, Genève, 1965, pp.131 ff.; P.A. Samuelson, 'Paradoxes of Schumpeter's Zero Interest Rate', *Review of Economics and Statistics*, 1971, vol.53, 4; Id. 'Schumpeter as an Economic Theorist', in H. Frisch (ed. by), *Schumpeterian Economics*, Praeger Publishers, New York, 1982, pp.1–27; A. Oakley, *Schumpeter's Theory of Capitalist Motion. A Critical Exposition and Reassessment*, Elgar, Aldershot, 1990, pp.144 ff. Specificity and limits of Schumpeter's position are well identified by N. De Vecchi (*Schumpeter viennese*, Bollati-Boringhieri, Torino 1993, p.158) and T. Cozzi ('Sviluppo e ciclo: l'eredità di Schumpeter', in Filippini, Porta (a cura di), *Società, sviluppo, impresa*, p.124, footnote 3), who refers to Schumpeter's statement concerning the circular flow: 'Readers who hold any theory of interest according to which that phenomenon would be present also in a perfectly stationary state (which the writer does not believe) are free to insert here also interest as a payment for the productive service which the particular theory chosen holds to be responsible for it.' (J.A. Schumpeter, *Business Cycles. A Theoretical, Historical and Statistical Analysis of the Capitalist Process*, McGraw-Hill, New York and London, 1939, p.41 – henceforth *BC*).

Schumpeter believes that interest is a part of profit. At the heart of this belief is the idea that interest is connected to industrial activity, something that cannot be explained within a static framework. *'The essential phenomenon is interest deriving from credit [der Zinn für Darlehen], that serves for the creation of new industries, new organizational forms, techniques, commodities [...]'.*[70] But where does credit come from? Not necessarily from given assets of a given lender; there can and should be another way. 'First of all, he could lend *money*; this would not carry essential mutations, *but the question would be greatly altered if he would create money; if, for example, he would issue banknotes or allow an opening of credit'.*[71] At what point have we arrived? – Schumpeter rhetorically asks. At the monetary market [*Geldmarkt*], hence, to establish that 'the origin of interest resides in the development and credit processes and that it is in a specific relationship with progress'.

70   *DW*, p.417.
71   *DW*, pp.417–18. On this decisive aspect see F. Machlup, 'Forced or Induced Savings: An Exploration into Its Synonyms and Homonyms'; W.F. Stolper, 'Monetary Equilibrium and Business Cycles Theory'; both in *Review of Economic Statistics*, 1943, vol.25, 1; A.W. Marget, 'The monetary Aspect of the Schumpeterian System', *Review of Economics and Statistics*, 1951, vol.33, 2; E. Schneider, 'The Nature of Money: On a Posthumous Publication by J.A. Schumpeter', *German Economic Review*, 1970, vol.8, 4; G. Tichy, 'Schumpeter's Monetary Theory. An Unjustly Neglected Part of His Work', in C. Seidl (ed. by), *Lectures on Schumpeterian Economics*, Springer-Verlag, Berlin, 1984, pp.135–8; P.J. Shah, L.B. Yeager, 'Schumpeter on Monetary Determinacy', *History of Political Economy*, 1994, vol.26, 3; M. Reclam, *J.A. Schumpeter's 'credit' theory of money*, University of Michigan Press, Ann Arbor, 1987; A. Graziani, 'Il *Trattato della moneta* di J.A. Schumpeter', in *Scritti in onore di Giuseppe De Meo*, Facoltà di Scienze Statistiche, Roma 1978, vol.1; M. Messori, 'Aspetti monetari della teoria di Schumpeter: la creazione bancaria di mezzi di pagamento', *Note economiche*, 1984, vol.17, 3; Id., 'Financement bancaire et décision de production', *Economie et Société*, 1986, 8–9; Id., 'L'offre et la demande de crédit chez Schumpeter', *Cahiers d'Économie Politique*, 1987, 13; R. Bellofiore, 'Money and Development in Schumpeter', *The Review of Radical Political Economics*, 1985, vol.17, 1–2; L. Berti, M. Messori, 'Introduzione' in J.A. Schumpeter, *Trattato della moneta capitoli inediti*, ESI, Napoli, 1996.

The formation of capital, interest, entrepreneurial profit and crisis are all phenomena that 'pure' economics cannot but fail to explain. Nevertheless, these phenomena should be recognized as 'economical', and no other discipline can claim them as its own. In effect, economic science intended as *ökonomische Theorie*, distinct from *theoretische Ökonomie*, can conveniently group them together, 'so that to these phenomena can be given a unique name: dynamics'. The *punctum saliens* is finally identified. In Schumpeter's own words:

> The sphere of our theme grows in our hands: a particularly important element is credit. In fact, nothing impedes talking about it within the realm of statics, but we believe that such an operation would bring about mere definitions or trivialities; its importance resides in its belonging to dynamics, movement, development [...].[72]

Saving, formation of capital, profit, interest and credit: the monetary terms that go beyond the statics are aligned in a row.[73] What is

---

72   *DW*, p.619.

73   It is necessary to recall the importance of Schumpeter's project of writing a treatise on money, in which his desire would have been to expose in a systematic fashion what in the *Theorie* of 1912 he defined as credit theory of money. Nurtured in the mid 1920s, for several reasons the project was aborted, whilst in 1930 Keynes' *Treatise on Money* was published. Schumpeter thought he had been anticipated in what he had to say, to the point that he would have claimed that the sole remaining thing to do was to get rid of the manuscript on money, as it was no longer useful [Schneider, *Joseph A. Schumpeter: Life and Work of a Great Social Scientist*, p.33; Id., *The Nature of Money. On a posthumous publication by Joseph A. Schumpeter*. However, the conditional is necessary here, because Ch. Seidl has provided sufficiently good reasons for sustaining the idea that Schumpeter was informed about Keynes' work ('Schumpeter addressing Keynes', *History of Economic Ideas*, 1996, vol.4, 3; see J.A. Schumpeter, *Briefe / Letters*, ausgewählt und hrsg. von U. Hedtke und R. Swedberg, Mohr Siebeck, Tübingen, 2000, pp.178–81)]. The posthumous judgements concerning Schumpeter's *Treatise* would be greatly affected by such an alleged claim (already recalled in A. Smithies, 'Memorial of J.A. Schumpeter'). A balanced position is that of A Graziani, who wrote: '[...] non si può disconoscere che, sia pure in un insieme di trattazioni differenti, le idee centrali dell'opera di Schumpeter si ritrovano anche nel *Trattato* di Keynes. [...] Ma se Keynes risulta superiore sul piano del nitore formale, Schumpeter lo supera largamente per ampiezza di vedute e per profondità di analisi.' ('Il

235

still absent is the key function, the entrepreneur who, thanks to his 'will', represents the fulcrum of innovation, around which dynamics processes gravitates. Hence, the soul of dynamics is still absent. Anyhow, the gnoseological skimming cannot be considered at as a mere methodological problem. Never utilized in an instrumental way, though utilized sometimes as an antithetical point of reference, Schumpeter's interpretation of statics refers undoubtedly to Walras' theoretical architecture; when the antithesis concerns the notion of development, however, he would not refer to a generic Historicism, but rather to Marx.[74] At any rate, though correct from a his-

Trattato sulla moneta di J.A. Schumpeter', pp.465–6). On the events concerning *Das Wesen des Geldes* (hrsg. von F.K. Mann, Vandenhöck und Ruprecht, Göttingen, 1970), see Tichy, 'Schumpeter's Monetary Theory', pp.135–8; M. Messori, 'Nota ai testi', in J.A. Schumpeter, *Trattato della moneta capitoli inediti*; Id., 'The Trials and Misadventures of Schumpeter's *Treatise on Money*', *History of Political Economy*, 1997, vol.29, 4.

74   No matter how debatable Schumpeter's interpretation of Marx might be, it is undeniable that he knew deeply Marx's doctrine better than any other economist (R.L. Heilbroner, 'Was Schumpeter Right?', *Social Research*, 1981, vol.48, 3). At any rate, there was a significant precedent close to Schumpeter's upbringing: E. v. Böhm-Bawerk, 'Zum Abschluß des Marxschen System', in O. v. Boenigk (ed. by), *Staatswissenschaftliche Arbeiten. Festgabe für Karl Knies*, Haering, Berlin, 1896. No less important were the researches provided by the Austromarxismus (cf. N. Leser, *Zwischen Reformismus und Bolschewismus. Der Austromarxismus als Theorie und Praxis*, Böhlau, Wien-Frankfurt-Zürich, 1968; AA. Vv., *Austromarxismus*, Europäische Verlagsanstalt, Frankfurt am Main and Wien, 1970), with which Schumpeter shared a fundamental experience (G. Haberler, 'Schumpeter, Ministre des Finances: 15 mars–17 octobre 1919', *Economie Appliquée*, 1950, vol.3, 3–4, 1950; W.F. Stolper, 'Schumpeter's Ministerial Days', *History of Economic Ideas*, 1995, vol.3, 1). On the relationship between Schumpeter and Marx, cf. S. Tsuru, 'Business Cycles and Capitalism: Schumpeter vs. Marx', *Annals of Hitotsubashi Academy*, 1952, vol.2, 2; P. Sylos Labini, 'Il problema dello sviluppo econ-omico in Marx ed in Schumpeter', in *Problemi dello sviluppo economico*, Laterza, Bari, 1977, pp.19–73; J.E. Elliott, 'Marx and Schumpeter on Cap-italism's Creative Destruction: A Comparative Restatement', *Quarterly Journal of Economics*, 1980, vol.95, 1; Id., 'Schumpeter and Marx on Capitalist Transformation', *Quarterly Journal of Economics*, 1983, vol.98, 2; E. März, '*Die Theorie der wirtschaftlichen Entwicklung* von J.A. Schumpeter in ihrer Beziehung zum Marxschen System', *Wirtschaft und Gesellschaft*, 1980, vol.6, 3

toriographical point of view,[75] this synthesis might seem perhaps too simplistic. So, in order to clarify, we may say: the primeval distinction between statics and dynamics implies the formal separateness between theoretical economics and economic theory; what such separateness refuses – and the *Variationsmethode* renders baseless – is a simplistic codification of the existing relations between a static explicative *ratio*, dynamics and empirical phenomena. The *Methodenstreit* appears to be inessential as it missed all the crucial points.

In any case – taking the gulf that separates *Das Wesen* and *Theorie* as given, and beyond the above mentioned codifications –, what is fundamental for our reasoning are the *differences* that it is already possible to identify in early Schumpeter, and which would play a pivotal role *within* his theory of economic development. These differences – that can be synthesized in the complex relationship between endogenous and exogenous factors – confirm, though implicitly, that the primary aim of the 'uncertain' method of variation was not that of guaranteeing, in comparative terms, the specific realm of static analysis, but rather that of constantly indicating its intrinsic and peculiar limitedness. Better still, the very same distinctive character of such a method allows the foundation of the evoked disjunction between the Economical and the Political upon the criterion of *scientific representability* – a criterion that only the endogenous, not the exogenous factors, can satisfy. In order to comprehend, on the one side, the obvious limits inherent to the

(afterwards in März, *J.A. Schumpeter*, pp.23–39); J.B. Foster, 'Theories of Capitalist Transformation: Critical Notes on the Comparison of Marx and Schumpeter', *Quarterly Journal of Economics*, 1983, vol.98, 2; R.L. Heilbroner, 'Economics and Political Economy: Marx, Keynes, and Schumpeter', *Journal of Economic Issues*, 1984, vol.18, 3; N. Rosenberg, 'Schumpeter and Marx: How Common a Vision?', in R.M. Mac Leod (ed. by), *Technology and the Human Prospects. Essays in Honour of C. Freeman*, Pinter Publisher, London, 1986, pp.197–213; W. Semmler, 'Marx and Schumpeter on Competition, Transient Surplus Profit and Technical Change', *Economie Appliquée*, 1984, vol.37, 3–4; D. Cavalieri, N. De Vecchi, R. Faucci, A. Graziani, 'Schumpeter e Marx: una tavola rotonda', *Quaderni di storia dell'economia politica*, 1983, vol.1, 3; R. Faucci, (a cura di), 'Schumpeter / Marx. Sistemi teorici a confronto', *Quaderni di storia dell'economia politica*, 1984, vol.2, 1–2.
75   See Schumpeter's 'Preface' to the Japanese edition of *TED*.

method of variation and, on the other, its apparently paradoxical tendency to move, via an indirect epistemological transposition, towards *ökonomische Theorie*, two aspects become essential: money and time.

The problem – that we shall evaluate in its consequential development – can only be resolved by verifying whether money and time can be contemplated by the theoretical statute of 'pure' economics. Whilst regarding time Schumpeter's answer is explicitly negative, when he deals with money the matter becomes more complicated. In fact, the static model of economic equilibrium does not deny the formal existence of money. However, the way in which such a model considers it, is quite insufficient. Money can find a place within the static scheme, but its role is limited to carrying out the function of unit of account and medium of exchange. As Schumpeter himself suggests in *Das Wesen*, this approach attributes to money a mere exterior aspect, as if it were a veil wrapping economic phenomena, which does not permit considering 'that a part of its essence surviving in that discharged veil'.

For this reason, because money is not a variable connected to the simple purchasing power within given exchange relations, such an attribution is illusory. The specificity of money resides in its ability to potentially assume the functions of monetary capital, credit, elements that trigger the process of development, destabilizing the system of exchange relations. If it is true that, in principle, the neoclassical model does not exclude money, it is also true that it does not provide a theory where money, being able to influence the real phenomena beyond the pure relationship of exchange, might play an essential role. Thus, as soon as a dynamic theory of money – whose nature is extraneous to any static hypothesis concerning the general economic equilibrium model – is identified, the method of variation shows its limits. In respect of monetary economics, in fact, this method can only re-propose two theoretical issues: firstly, the extraneity of economic science – be it *theoretiche Ökonomie* or *ökonomische Theorie* – to the nineteenth century methodological-causal canons belonging to natural sciences; and, secondly, the heuristic value inherent to the static model, in which money is not intended as bank credit aimed at financing the process of development.

From this point of view, rather than referring to the *Theory* of 1912, it may be more useful to refer to a lesser known, but nonetheless seminal work: *Das Sozialprodukt und Rechenpfennige*.[76] Here, the influence of Walras' work is evident and enables Schumpeter to define the role of money within the circular flow.[77] In effect, in Schumpeter's eyes, the Walrasian *opus* represents the apex reached by both *theoretische Ökonomie* and the general equilibrium model. In it, money is no longer conceived of as an isolated phenomenon, exactly because, in the circularity of the economic flow, the constant presence of money in the process of exchange follows. But, in spite of this, in this process it is still impossible to derive a theory of money able to affect the real economic phenomena. Hence, as payments occur at fixed point in time, from an epistemological point of view, the method of variation remains a valid instrument. However, so conceived, money is simply the certification of a realized production, devoid of any autonomy generating development. The situation is different when we drop the curtains on the static scenario and, above all, when we abandon the hypothesis 'that the role of the banks is only that of a conductor and medium of passive adjustment to a commodity process, and that the banks merely help the flow of commodities by creating its monetary complement'.[78] In this case, in fact, it is possible to make a distinction between paper currency guaranteed by the State and bank money. This latter is 'an independent determinant of movements of the price level and of our product sum which are not based on conditions in the world of commodities'.[79] As such, the bank money

76 J.A. Schumpeter, 'Das Sozialprodukt und die Rechenpfennige: Glossen und Beiträge zur Geldtheorie von heute', *Archiv für Sozialwissenschaft und Sozialpolitik*, 1917–1918, vol.44, pp.627–715; afterwards in *Aufätze zur Ökonomischen Theorie*, pp.31–117; 'Money and the Social Product', trans. by A.W. Marget, *International Economic Papers*, 1956, vol.6, pp.148–211.

77 On Schumpeter's notion of *Kreislauf* – according to which human beings follow habits and experience – cf. Perroux, *La pensée économique de Joseph Schumpeter*, pp.66–7; M. Brouwer, *Schumpeterian Puzzles. Technological Competition and Economic Evolution*, Harvester Wheatsheaf, New York, 1991, pp.7–13; Oakley, *Schumpeter's Theory of Capitalist Motion. A Critical Exposition and Reassessment*, pp.54–79.

78 Schumpeter, *Money and the Social Product*, p.209 (*Das Sozialprodukt*, p.712).

79 Ibid., p.208 (*Das Sozialprodukt*, p.711).

generates forced savings, whose results serve for the expansion of production.

In order to explain the specific functions inherent to the creation of bank money, what is fundamental is the definition of a monetary theory of credit. 'The essence of modern credit – Schumpeter says – lies in the creation of such money. It is the specifically capitalistic method of effecting economic progress. It gives scope to the *capitalistic function* of money'.[80] This is the heresy addressed in the *Theory*; a heresy from which Schumpeter's distinction between the monetary theory of credit and the credit theory of money derives.[81] Whilst the former, developing 'the theory of the network of credit 'payments' from the case of payment in specie, assigns to legal-tender money a *logically* privileged position';[82] the latter characterizes a dynamic monetary theory, according to which monetary fluxes, as they are capital, produce 'concrete' effects. This function presupposes the partial endogeneization of the quantity of money and, by consequence, the critique of the traditional formulations of the quantitative theory.[83] Following this path, a new market assumes a fundamental importance: the monetary market, which is the capital market, the 'headquarters of the capitalistic system'.[84]

> Naturally, we might also include this kind of market in the picture of the unchangeable cycle [*des gleichbleibenden Kreislauf*] of economy, but nothing interesting would come about and no one in this economy would see the quintessential of peculiar phenomena or would link, to the concept of market, the simple events of registration of the national accounting that there occur. In this sense, it owes to development not only its theoretical and practical

---

80 Ibid., p.206 (*Das Sozialprodukt*, p.707).
81 *HEA*, p.717. Significantly, such a distinction is explicitly mentioned by S. De Brunhoff with regard to Marx (*La monnaie chez Marx*, Ed. Sociales, Paris, 1973).
82 *HEA*, p.719.
83 L. Berti, M. Messori, 'Introduzione' in Schumpeter, *Trattato della moneta capitoli inediti*, pp.LIX–LX. Cf. also Oakley, *Schumpeter's Theory of Capitalist Motion*, pp.155–61.
84 *TED*, p.126 (*Theorie*, p.205).

importance but also its existence, although once it exists it would also embrace the monetary processes of the cycle [*die Geldvorgänge des Kreislauf*].[85]

The existence of a monetary market cannot find a place in a static model, because it conceives of money as mere proof of a realized production. As soon as it becomes necessary to deal with the perspective entailed by development – explainable only in dynamic terms –, the heuristic value of the neoclassical modelling loses its power, becoming absolutely limited.

Following this train of thought, we should return back to the distinction, fundamental in terms of method, between *theoretische Ökonomie* and *ökonomische Theorie*. According to this distinction, money assumes the character of a theoretical discriminant. Better still, it is the shift from a static conception of money, belonging to theoretical economics, to a dynamic one involving economic theory that produces the changing of all the parameters, above all the temporal ones. Obviously, within the new dynamic model, the relevance of the method of variation fades away. Nevertheless, it would be too simplistic to merely point out the impasse without acknowledging that the *epistemological difference* inherent to this method necessarily would relapse upon the theory of development, generating – as we shall see – a substantial *dyskrasía*.

Before this, however, we have to deal with the second factor characterizing the theory of development, namely, temporal dynamics, with regard to which, the method of variation has virtually nothing to say as, by definition, 'pure' economics does not contemplate the evolution of the temporal paradigm. Nonetheless, because in the theory of development we find problems that the same epistemological projections provided in the *Variationsmethode* helped to raise, a careful evaluation of its constitutive elements is not pleonastic. We shall limit the investigation to the effects generated by the

85   Schumpeter, *Das Wesen des Gelds*, pp.308–9. For a more detailed overview of Schumpeter's critique to the categories of demand and supply of credit, see M. Messori, 'Il credito nel modello di Schumpeter', pp.293–305; Id., 'Aspetti monetari della teoria di Schumpeter: la creazione bancaria di mezzi di pagamento'; De Vecchi, *Schumpeter viennese*, pp.46–52.

dynamic interplay of money and innovation, trying to understand the methodological consequences that follow.

The interplay between money, entrepreneurial skills and new technical conditions destabilizes the neoclassical idea of the market. In fact, this interplay implies the fading away of both the static character and the reductive hypothesis of a balanced growth system. The instability of the system is produced by innovation, underpinned by a liquidity generated *ex novo*. It affects market conditions, relationships among firms, previous economic functions, modes of development and the senescence of the economic system. As Schumpeter says, 'since entrepreneurial activity upsets the equilibrium of the system [...], a revision of values of all the elements of the system becomes necessary and this, for a period of time, means fluctuations and successive attempts at adaptation to changing temporary situations'.[86]

There is no plausible reason why within the capitalistic system the new possible combinations of economic factors and capable entrepreneurs able to make these combination effective should not constantly occur. The capitalistic entrepreneurial character is as such because it clearly distinguishes those who are able to realize, more or less quickly, plans of innovation supported by bank credit, from those who are unable to do so. However, this does not imply a simple redistribution of resources, but rather the modification of their productive functions. Not only does it imply a non homogeneous dynamization of all the technical and organizational conditions, the interaction of innovations expressed in different sectors and, thereby, the constant modification of the relative prices and demand; it also implies further innovations, the generation of a particularly accelerated development/crisis cycle. In Schumpeter's idea, all this is enough to look suspiciously at the allocative criteria inherent to a simple mercantile economy, where 'there is no "capital"; or, otherwise expressed, capital does not fulfil its characteristic function', since 'the various forms of general purchasing power do not constitute capital there; they are simply exchange media, a technical means for carrying out the customary exchanges'.[87]

86   *BC*, p.135.
87   *TED*, p.121 (*Theorie*, pp.172–3).

Thus, the dynamic interplay of money and innovation becomes an element inseparable from the temporal dimension. Consequently, the hypothesis to which the neoclassical modellization linked the role of money becomes unacceptable. It is unacceptable to confine money to the realm of 'pure' exchange, as its capitalistic function is that of being, *potentialiter*, monetary capital, intended as the anticipation to the entrepreneur of the funds he needs to introduce an innovation that cannot but happen through time. The very nature of the above process shows the dynamic interplay of money and innovation. Hence, only facing money of account can we hypothesize a static model that can be analysed via *theoretische Ökonomie*. Vice versa, when money is linked not to its pure equivalent function, but rather to its credit function, the simple mercantile society cannot but be replaced by the capitalistic business cycle and its dynamic instability: equilibrium – (innovation) – prosperity – recession – depression – recovery – new equilibrium. The 'forms' of money, as they represent the discriminant between statics and dynamics, become the propulsive element of the separation between the analytical sphere belonging to theoretical economics and that belonging to economic theory. At the same time, the 'forms' of money delimitate the 'meaning' of the method of variation: whilst the static models of general equilibrium regard only an instantaneous account, money is the link between present and future, its effects on development can only be evaluated in time. The fundamental distinction between *theoretische Ökonomie* and *ökonomische Theorie* is accomplished. But the 'long wave' this distinction generates in the theory of development gives rise to a *dyskrasía*.

On this crucial point, we believe that a short reformulation of the problem on the grounds of what has been said is necessary. The gnoseological framework of *Das Wesen* presents two complementary distinctions: on the one side, between theoretical economics and economic theory and, on the other, between statics and dynamics. Both can claim a link, although weak, with the method of variation. Analytically speaking, at best, it might aspire to a definition of comparative statics model; but what is more interesting, at least in the terms in which the problem is posed by the young Schumpeter, is the fact that such a method is a *distinctive method*, able to separate what is formally traceable to a pure theoretical economics from what is not.

Although this argumentation might seem circular, it is easy to grasp a more ambitious epistemological attempt, aimed at distinguishing what is the 'representable field' of the Economical from what is not, so as to preserve its specific rationality. Now – this is the point – this distinction is not only aimed at separating *theoretische Ökonomie* from *ökonomische Theorie*. In effect, this distinction operates also within a dynamic model – *within* economic theory –, because the very same theory of development requires a distinction between en-dogenous and exogenous factors. In this theoretical context, a rigorous deduction, which moves from the method of variation to reach this clear distinction, is unthinkable. In epistemological terms, however, there is a certain similarity of intents. It is certainly true that Schum-peter interprets 'facts' belonging to economic theory starting from their unavoidable exogenous 'conditioning', but it is also true that his rational intent is to distinguish their dynamics from all that is devoid of a strictly economic *ratio*. The exogenous represent, at any rate, a threat to the rationality of the 'economic discourse': not because it is not pertinent to it, but exactly because it is pertinent to *this* discourse, without being rationally representable via economic categories.

It is evident that, among the exogenous factors, the Political plays a fundamental role, because decisive is the relationship between economy and politics. With regard to this relationship, notable scholars advanced the meaningful idea of separateness. Arthur Smithies, for example, shows that Schumpeter was 'tormented' by such a problem up until his death, probably understanding the para-doxical value of his obstinate attempt to keep the Economical and the Political separated. On the other hand, it is *Capitalism Socialism and Democracy* that reaffirms such a distinction. Thus, before demon-strating why and how such a distinction, far from being a simplistic invocation of principle, is resolved into an *impolitical radicalism*,[88] we shall focus our attention upon the way in which the problem is dealt with in *Capitalism Socialism and Democracy*, so as to leave aside once and for all the hypothesis of a Schumpeter *totus politicus*.

---

88   On the philosophical category of *impoliticus*, see R. Esposito, *Categorie dell'impolitico*, Il Mulino, Bologna, 1988.

4. Schumpeter, the political?

According to Schumpeter, both efficiency and expansion of the capitalist economic system are unproblematic assumptions. The results historically obtained and those that may be expected are such as to exclude any systematic decrease of the rate of profit and the progressive pauperization of the worse-off class. In other words, it is 'by virtue of its mechanism that the capitalistic process progressively raises the standard of life of the masses'.[89] This confirms that, as they serves to make money, the selective criteria that allow the rise of bourgeois class cannot be questioned, even in the case that those competitive forms discussed by Marshall and Wicksell fade away.

In sharp contrast to the monopolistic and oligopolistic theories of imperfect competition that flourished around the 1930s,[90] Schumpeter assumes a conception of competition no longer based upon the reduction of prices, but rather upon dynamic innovative processes.[91] In the capitalistic society, what is important is 'the competition from new commodity, the new technology, the new source of supply, the new type of organization (the largest-scale unit of control for instance) – competition which commands a decisive cost or quality advantage and which strikes not at the margins of the profit and the outputs of the existing firms but at their foundations and their very lives'.[92] Hence, there is a strong basis for the belief that the better quality of life of the masses is to be attributed to big business:

89   J.A. Schumpeter, *Capitalism, Socialism and Democracy*, Allen & Unwin, London, 1955, p.68, henceforth *CSD*.
90   Schumpeter refers to the contributions of E.S. Chamberlin (*Theory of Monopolistic Competition*, Harvard University Press, Cambridge MA, 1933) and of J. Robinson (*The Economic of Imperfect Competition*, Macmillan, London, 1933), on which cf. G.L.S. Shackle, *The Years of High Theory. Invention and Tradition in Economic Thought*, Cambridge University Press, Cambridge, 1967.
91   J.A. Schumpeter, 'Science and Ideology', *The American Economic Review*, 1949, vol.39, 2, pp.357–8.
92   *CSD*, p.84.

Thus it is not sufficient to argue that because perfect competition is impossible under modern conditions [...] the large-scale establishment or unit of control must be accepted as a necessary evil inseparable from the economic progress [...]. What we have got to accept is that it has come to be the most powerful engine of that progress and in particular of the long-run expansion of total output not only in spite of, but to a considerable extent through, this strategy which looks so restrictive when viewed in the individual case and from the individual point of time.[93]

From an economic point of view, capitalism has worked and works. What we ought to ask, however, is if it will work in the near future. The political stance of *Capitalism, Socialism, and Democracy* is enveloped in this question.

According to Schumpeter, there are no economic reasons for which capitalism might collapse. Nothing induces us to believe that new innovations cannot be reached, or that the progressive satisfaction of needs will stop the expansion of the demand. On the contrary, it is possible to think that the increase of wages will determine new modes of consumption. The very same diffusion of monopolistic behaviours might favour innovation, rather than inhibit it. Economically speaking, capitalism has worked, most probably, will work; but the conditions that allow its existence in the future do not merely depend upon economic 'variables'. Here is the point.

Capitalism is the realized rational civilization, 'the propelling force of the rationalization of human behaviour': 'the economic pattern is the matrix of logic'. Not only modern industry, technology, and economic organization spring out of the capitalistic enterprise, 'but all the features and achievements of modern civilization are, directly or indirectly, the products of the capitalist process. They must be included in any balance sheet of it and in any verdict about its deeds or misdeeds'.[94] Modern science, arts, the life-style, democracy, are the mature fruits of modern capitalism, the most rationalistic and anti-

---

93   *CSD*, p.106. As P. Sylos Labini noted, what can be observed is that Schumpeter's position on monopoly is changed from the one provided in 1912 in his *TDE*; and the doubts that arise about the efficacy of his notion of competition to tame in the long-run the power of monopolistic concentration are well founded (*Problemi dello sviluppo economico*, p.67).

94   *CSD*, p.125.

246

heroic civilization. Is this sufficient – in conjunction with the possibility of a development that can be reasonably expected – to assure the future of capitalism? No, Schumpeter has no doubts:

> Things economic and social move by their own momentum and the ensuing situations compel individuals and groups to behave in certain ways whatever they may wish to do – not indeed by destroying their freedom of choice but by shaping the choosing mentalities and by narrowing the list of possibilities from which to choose. If this is the quintessence of Marxism then we all of us have got to be Marxists. In consequence, capitalist performance is not even relevant for prognosis. Most civilizations have disappeared before they had time to fill to the full the measure of their promise. Hence I am not going to argue, on the strength of that performance, that the capitalist intermezzo is likely to be prolonged. In fact, I am now going to draw the exactly opposite inference.[95]

Might the wants of humanity some day be so completely satisfied that little motive would be left to push productive effort still further ahead? A similar state of satisfaction is far from being achieved and, even before this, is unnecessary to hypothesize. On the other hand, many social and productive negative effects that would follow such a hypothesis might also follow from the present forms of development. Progress itself is subjected to a mechanization that negatively affects the entrepreneurial functions and, more generally, the whole of capitalistic society, quite as a hypothetic halt of the economic progress. As a result, in order to grasp the essential elements constituting the crisis of capitalistic civilization, we have to refer to the *social classes theory* rather than to the economic functioning of the theory of development.

According to Schumpeter, in particular, it is necessary to focus our attention upon the nexus rank/function, the idea of social prestige connected to leadership, and the representation of power as it is exerted by the capitalistic class in virtue of its *Weltanschauung*.[96] In fact, none of these three elements seem able to withstand the 'great

95   *CSD*, pp.129–30.
96   J.E. Elliott, 'Schumpeter's Theory of Economic Development and Social Change: Exposition and Assessment', *International Journal of Social Economics*, 1985, vol.12, 67, pp.6–33; A. Martinelli, *Economia e società. Marx, Weber, Schumpeter, Polany, Parsons*, Comunità, Milano, 1987, p.73.

transformation' produced by big business. The entrepreneurial functions replace the will and the individual action of the entrepreneur, whose leadership comes to an end; innovation becomes routine; technological progress develops by means of specialized teams; property is dematerialized and the bourgeois is deprived of its function. In short, it is the *political socialization* that contaminates the pure economic logic of capitalism.

Eliminating the 'protective strata', destroying 'its own defences', the capitalistic process 'creates a critical frame of mind, which after having destroyed the moral authority of so many other institutions, in the end turns against its own' – and the fortress is politically disarmed. Being an instrument of a 'secular improvement', capitalism should defend itself from those who have already condemned it to death. Nevertheless, its rationality is limited. 'Political criticism cannot be met effectively by rational argument. From the fact that the criticism of the capitalist order proceeds from critical attitudes of mind, i.e., from an attitude which spurns allegiance to extra-rational values, it does not follow that rational refutation will be accepted'.[97] And it would be meaningless to think that this exclusively derives from real or alleged evils endured by a determinate social class. Rather, 'capitalism inevitably and by virtue of the very logic of its civilisation creates, educates and subsidizes a vested interest in social unrest'. New media, mass schooling, public companies, irreversibly, endanger the element of continuity between the old and new elite.

Certainly, in an irreversible manner; in fact, in Schumpeter opinion, whatever shape the shifting process might take, capitalism is irreversibly doomed to succumb or, better still, to become 'other'.[98] And this 'other' is socialism: not intended as a value, but rather as rationality. Actually, Schumpeter is convinced that such a transformation process is a tendency – and this is important, because it is one thing to say that something represents a tendency and to forecast

---

97   *CSD*, p.144. Cf. K. Acham, 'Schumpeter – The Sociologist', in Seidl (ed. by), *Lectures on Schumpeterian Economics*, p.165.
98   W.F. Stolper argued: 'Schumpeter thought that the transition might be undramatic and gradual and, I might add, perhaps not even noticed' (*J.A. Schumpeter: The public life of a private man*, p.105).

its conclusion, but something else is to say when this will happen. Furthermore, he underlines that, as industrial integration is far from being accomplished and competition is still an important factor, such a process of transformation cannot occur in less than a century. However, we cannot speak of effective counter-tendencies, but rather of resistances; and this is what makes socialism an unavoidable perspective.[99] In short, the divide between bourgeois values and the capitalistic mentality is generated by two 'plates', whose motion is determined by the modern push towards security, equality and regulation (economic engineering).[100] To think that it is possible to guide capitalism to become 'other' is absolutely illusory; in fact, this is exactly what will give sway to those 'subversive tendencies' that underpin the march into socialism.

It is worth noting that Schumpeter is concerned here with *these* concrete and given 'subversive tendencies', rather then with the 'advent of socialism'. It is certainly not by accident that in *The March into Socialism* he expresses great preoccupation with regard to the post-war inflation. In effect, he is convinced that inflation is 'one of the most powerful factors that make for acceleration of social change', to the point that a state of perennial inflationary pressure 'will have, qualitatively, all the effects of weakening the social framework of society whilst strengthening subversive tendencies' within it. Moreover, given the post-war institutional framework, the standard remedies might be worse than the evil. First of all, to act on the volume of the bank-lending via interest rates or via the supply restriction would not bring about the same results that one might expect in 'a world in

99   It is rather important, however, the reference to the pastoral encyclical *Quadragesimo anno* and to the catholic corporatism made in 'The March into Socialism' (*The American Economic Review*, vol.40, 1950, May). Cf. J. Solterer, '*Quadragesimo Anno*: Schumpeter's Alternative to the Omnipotent State', *Review of Social Economy*, 1951, vol.9, 1; D.L. Cramer, C.G. Leathers, 'Schumpeter's Corporatist Views: Links among his Social Theory, *Quadragesimo anno* and Moral Reform', *History of Political Economy*, 1981, vol.13, 4.

100 Cf. A. Salsano, *Ingegneri e politici*, Einaudi, Torino, 1987; Id., *L'altro corporativismo. Tecnocrazia e managerialismo tra le due guerre*, Il Segnalibro, Torino, 2003.

which everything was entirely flexible', and where one could accept that the reduction of the interest rate reduced the volume of economic operations, monetary wage and employment. 'Surely these effects would not materialize at present and, if they did, they would immediately provoke government action to neutralize them'.[101] Secondly, an eventual price control 'may result in a surrender of private enterprise to public authority, that is, in a big stride toward the perfectly planned economy'.[102] Hence, a constant inflationary pressure 'can play an important part in the eventual conquest of the private-enterprise system by the bureaucracy', to the extent that '[a] situation may well emerge in which most people will consider complete planning as the smallest of possible evils'.

The day of reckoning with the already diffuse Keynesian progressivism is made absolutely explicit. The politically regulated capitalism – aimed at enforcing stabilizing policies so as to impede recession and depression, establishing a higher level of equality in the income distribution, public controlling of the labour market, slogan antitrust, welfare policies –, *this* Labourist capitalism is so seriously compromised that in Schumpeter eyes it cannot survive. And even if it would find its way, it would end up denying the 'scheme of values' that the spirit of capitalism assumes as embodied in 'the civilization of inequality and of the family fortune'. It is not by accident that one of the main reasons for which *Capitalism, Socialism, and Democracy* reached a noteworthy diffusion was due to its disenchanted political reflection upon democracy,[103] considered as a political method without an ultimate aim in itself, an instrument to make 'political decisions' in a given historical situation and in the absence of any

101 Schumpeter, 'The March into Socialism', now in *CSD*, p.423.
102 Ibid., *CSD* p.424.
103 This way of thinking would inspire many research projects, among which the so-called 'economic theory of democracy'. For example, A. Downs wrote: 'Schumpeter's profound analysis of democracy forms the inspiration and foundation for our whole thesis (...).' (*An Economic Theory of Democracy* Harper & Row, New York, 1957, p.29). On the relevance of Schumpeter's political studies, see G. Urbani, 'J.A. Schumpeter e la conoscenza empirica dei fenomeni politici', in Filippini, Porta (ed. by), *Società, sviluppo, impresa*, pp.87 ff.

'value'.[104] It is from this *absence* that we should try to define democracy as a method rather than as an aim in itself – Schumpeter says. Democracy assumes that the individual is able to reckon the relative validity of his own beliefs, showing the necessary determination to support them with no hesitation. Hence, as a decision-making method, democracy requires, above all, that it be explicit *how* these decisions are taken and *by whom*.

To define democracy as the government of the people is therefore a baseless claim. Such a definition, in fact, has as many meanings as are the possible combinations between *demos* and *kratein*. And, above all, it assumes as clear what is not: if *kratein* belongs to *demos*, how can this latter technically govern? In order to give an answer to this question, Schumpeter provides a brief (and confused) critical survey of the eighteenth century political philosophy.[105] The aim of his endeavour is to contest the idea of 'common good'. Essentially, Schumpeter's critical remarks concern the possibility of the existence of an 'individual volition' – even prior to a harmonic 'general will'. Thus, he claims that it is necessary to turn things up side down, considering 'the deciding of issues by the electorate secondary to the election of the men who are to do the deciding'.[106] From here, the step towards the 'competitive struggle for power and office'[107] is very short. In other words, for the Austrian economist, democracy is a

104   *CSD*, p.242. It is worth noting that Schumpeter's contemporaries were far from understanding his position: cf. D.M. Wright, 'Schumpeter's Political Philosophy', *Review of Economic Statistics*, 1951, vol.33, May, pp.152–7.
105   For a critical reading cf. C. Pateman (*Participation and Democratic Theory*, Cambridge University Press, Cambridge, 1970, p.18), who noted that if the way in which Schumpeter characterized what he himself defined 'classical' theory of democracy had been correct, he would have certainly been right. Sadly, he not only misinterpreted the claims of the so-called classical theoreticians, but also overlooked that he was dealing with two different streams of thought on democracy. Cf. also J.P. Plamenatz (*Democracy and Illusion*, Longman, London 1973, p.96) who, regarding the Schumpeterian critique to classic theory of democracy, labelled it as follows: it is 'ignorant and inept, and is worth discussing only because it has been taken seriously'.
106   *CSD*, p.269.
107   *CSD*, p.282. Cf. R.A. Dahl, *A Preface to Democratic Theory*, The University of Chicago Press, Chicago, 1956.

modus procedendi that 'produces legislation and administration as by-products of the struggle for political office'.[108] The competitive nature of this struggle defines a line of thought according to which the competition for leadership gives rise to democratic processes regulated by simple procedures.[109] It is therefore a mistake to think of democracy in semantic terms, as an ideal, towards which a political regime ought to tend.[110] There is no common good, there is no ensemble of an individual's volitions from which the general will would derive. People do not govern and do not chose their politicians, but accept them instead of others.[111] This is a further reason to contest the basis of economic Labourism.

Of this theory of democracy 'without ideals' it has been said that it 'forms the magnificent centrepiece of the political analysis in *Capitalism, Socialism, and Democracy*';[112] a book that – as it has been noted by Joan Robinson – 'is worth the whole parrot-house of contemporary orthodoxies, right, left, or centre'.[113] Both judgements are correct, of course. No one, however, says how the political reasoning of Schumpeter as 'great economist' indicates the main character of his *impoliticalness*.[114] What is the point upon which Schumpeter *politicus* insists? Could it be a critical but governable relationship between the economic and political spheres? It seems not. Does it evoke perhaps an *Untergang des Abendlandes*? Again, the answer is negative. What Schumpeter was trying to show is much more linear and radical. It rests, simply and entirely, upon the impossibility of separating what,

108 *CSD*, p.286.
109 Cf. R. D'Alimonte, 'Sulla teoria della democrazia competitiva', *Rivista italiana di scienza politica*, 1977, vol.7, 1, pp.3–26.
110 G. Sartori, *Democrazia e definizioni*, Il Mulino, Bologna, 1972, p.6.
111 M. Stoppino, 'Democrazia e classe politica: un confronto tra Schumpeter e Mosca', in *Studi in onore di C.E. Ferri*, Giuffrè, Milano, 1973, vol.1, p.551.
112 Swedberg, *J.A. Schumpeter*, p.162.
113 J. Robinson, 'J.A. Schumpeter Capitalism, Socialism and Democracy', *Economic Journal*, 1943, vol.53, June, pp.381–3. See also W. Fellner, 'March into Socialism, or Viable Postwar Stage of Capitalism?', in A. Heertje (ed. by), *Schumpeter's Vision. Capitalism, Socialism and Democracy after 40 years*, Praeger Publisher, New York, 1981, p.46.
114 See A. Zanini, *Schumpeter impolitico*, Istituto della Enciclopedia Italiana, Roma, 1987.

both for practical and theoretical reasons,[115] ought to be separated: the concept of the Economical and the concept of the Political. The irrationality of the exogenous element reaches its apex here, as its political rationality manifests itself, economically, as 'un-representable'. Therefore, Schumpeter *totus politicus* represents, at best, a misinterpretation.

5. The logos of economic theory

It is easy to understand how this may appear as a paradox. Nonetheless, more complex, but also more indicative, is to understand the reasons for this apparent, paradoxical incongruence, according to which those that are unescapable elements of the economic theory are considered as extrinsic to it. Anyway, the issue becomes less paradoxical if we bear in mind two elements. Firstly, Schumpeter's detachment from the neoclassical tradition was never sharp: neither from a doctrinal (microeconomics), nor from an ethical and political point of view. Secondly, Schumpeter's interest in Marx – motivated by a problematic affinity regarding themes such as money and development – stemmed from an assumption according to which he considered the Marxian *Kritik* as 'the vision of the economic evolution intended as a particular process generated by the economic system itself.'[116] This meant to assign an historical value to Marx *vis-à-vis* the neoclassical modelling, but at the price of misrepresenting his original, political intention. In other words, the disjunctive relationship between the Economical and the Political does not generate a sort of paradox of the economic theory, but the economic theory *qua theoria*.

This position has deep roots. Between the end of the nineteenth and the beginning of twentieth century, economic science, through the

---

115 It should not be forgotten what Schumpeter wrote in 'Depressions. Can We Learn from Past Experience?', in AA.VV., *The Economics of the Recovery Program*, Whittlesey House-McGraw Hill, New York-London, 1934.
116 Schumpeter, *Theorie*, p.XXIII.

mature formulations of the dominant neoclassical School, not only privileged certainties that the 'pure' disciplines were looking at with suspicion, but also, upon these alleged certainties, it built massive theoretical architectures. The growing utilization of mathematical language, along with the definition of general equilibrium models, showed a solid trust in the formal *ratio*, exactly when the 'pure' disciplines were doubtful of their own 'theorems'. Without being extraneous to it, Schumpeter does not sympathize with the neoclassical tradition. In this regard, it is not strange that what appears paradoxical ends up by producing a sort of regeneration of the method of variation, understood as an epistemological 'intention', simultaneously aimed at *indicating* and *distinguishing* the representable 'field' of the Economical, in order to preserve its rational specificity with regard to the un-representable *Politicus*.

Certainly, the resurfacing of the epistemological intentions informing the method of variation occurs only after this latter has specifically and definitively traced the limits of the heuristic value of the static model of general equilibrium. It is only at this point that the strenuous effort to preserve the *intentio* of the method of variation intended as 'controllable' economic paradigm, its *epistemological relevance*, emerges with clarity. In effect, if this paradigm was true for *theoretische Ökonomie*, in epistemological terms, it should also be partially true for *ökonomische Theorie*: both constitute the *logos* of the economic science. So, more than a paradox, we can see an unsolved twofold relationship. The 'logical' character of the economic theory sets aside its 'historical' character, ending up by wrapping with its 'purity' economic science as a whole: theoretical economics and economic theory.

The Economical and the Political in Schumpeter are disjointed: this can be said without hesitation. Schumpeter *politicus* of experience, of the cycle, appears to be a mere theoretical abstraction provided by notable scholars, rather than a self-evident interpretation. The confutation of the pure competition model via the distinction between statics and dynamics, although relevant, is strictly pertinent only to the *logos* of the Economical: it has no political breath. This is not only a methodological issue, obviously, but the matter does not change. For Schumpeter, a synthesis between the Economical and the

Political – or, better still, between economic logic and political rationality – cannot be represented at an analytical level. Economic science, divided into *theoretische Ökonomie* and *ökonomische Theorie*, limits itself in order to provide a simple alternative expressed in chronological-theoretical terms. Economic science can be intended either as a mere logical structure (statics), or as the chronological representation of what is empirically representable in time (dynamics). It has often been observed that development and innovation are dynamic concepts, and, as such, they are really representable. No less 'real', however, is the Political, that includes both, and that Schumpeter considers as an exogenous accident, destined to affect the 'truth' of the economic cycle but, not for this reason, so as to be logically representable. Why is there this discrepancy?

Certainly, it is imputable to Schumpeter's analytical approach, within which the Political is both scientifically unrepresentable and logically unthinkable. For him, its logical obscurity is equal to the clarity of its real presence. The transparency of the Political is crystalline, but the economical logic grasps in that transparency only a veiled existence, of which nothing can be said, besides the fact that it is logically unspeakable and, according to an economic *recta ratio*, irrational. Such an unspeakableness represents a problem that needs an adequate reflection. Schumpeter is not enchanted by the exactness of the *Naturwissenschaft*; however, the functional logic approach is, in its relative scepticism and 'fictionality', discretely reductive, *impolitical*: delimitated by 'logic' and 'reason'. And where the 'principle of reason' cannot arrive, where there is no longer *Erkenntniß*, possible *Vorstellung*, only an *Erleuchtung* can be found.[117] This latter, however, is no more than a prophecy that gives rise to an unsolved relationship: the impossible representation of the Political is relative to its unspeakableness and, by contrast, to its ineluctability.

In order to grasp the intermediate passages leading to the *impolitical* and its entrepreneurial functions, once again it is necessary to

---

117 The language I use here is intentionally Schopenhauerean (*Die Welt als Wille und Vorstellung*, in *Sämtliche Werke*, hrsg von A. Hubscher, Brockhaus, Wiesbaden, 1972, Bd.2, p.485). Cf. M. Cacciari, *Pensiero negativo e razionalizzazione*, Marsilio, Padova, 1978, pp.147 ff.

dwell upon Schumpeter's analytical approach. Regarding this, privileged places are the first chapter of *Theorie* and chapters I, II and IV of *Business Cycles*. In order to trace back the elements generating the disjunction between the Economical and the Political it is sufficient to look at the simple definition of 'economic fact'. It is apparent how Schumpeter's methodological choice was pondered. The 'economic fact' is not defined in a positivistic fashion, in its *being given*, but rather in its pure, relational, and conceptual representativeness. Once the economic activity is conceived of 'as conduct direct towards the acquisition of goods', what is in itself definable is defined: what remains is only a relational representation, supported by conceptual abstraction. In Schumpeter's words: 'The designation of a fact as economic [*eine Tatsache als wirtschaftlicher*] already involves an abstraction, the first of the many forced upon us by the technical condition of mentally copying reality [*die technischen Notwendigkeiten der gedanklichen Nachbildung der Wirklichkeit*]'.[118]

Consequently, the representation of the 'technical conditions of mentally copying reality' imposes a restrictive effect. First of all, we may think of these conditions as a linguistic bottleneck, as a habitual postulate stemming from the scientific-disciplinary rigorousness. In reality, it is something else that determines these conditions. In Schumpeter's eyes, the analysis of any economic fact 'neither comes to a natural full stop [*auf einen natürlichen Schlußpunkt*], nor stumbles upon a cause [*auf eine 'Ursache'*], that is an element which does more to determine other elements than it is by them determined'.[119] As an economic fact it 'is never exclusively or purely economic', the sole possible delimitation we can utilize is 'the concept of economic conduct', which, however, entails the already mentioned definition of conduct 'directed towards the acquisition of goods'. Hence, in order to avoid a vicious circle, it is indispensable to solve two issues: firstly, it is necessary to know the point to which the conceptual representation of the Economical can arrive at and, secondly, we have to analyse the point from which such a conceptual representation is no longer possible.

118   *TED*, p.3 (*Theorie*, p.1).
119   *TED*, pp.7–8 (*Theorie*, p.6).

Concerning this, Schumpeter is extremely clear: any 'economic fact' is *an sich* indefinable, in its being a *datum*, it is always 'spurious'. That is, if we assume it in its contextual and environmental complexity, it becomes impossible not only to define, scientifically and logically, the relations of which it is made, but also to delineate the process of its causation: the backwards limit beyond which it is logically meaningless to proceed. Schumpeter says: 'When we succeed in finding a definite causal relation [*einen bestimmten Kausalzusammenhang*] between two phenomena, our problem is solved if the one which plays the 'causal' role [*des 'Grundes'*] is non-economic'.[120]

It is in this way that the Austrian economist answers to the first of the two questions posed above: finding the extreme limit of the conceptual representation of the Economical. Beyond this point, economics as a science, 'logical analysis', is speechless. For Schumpeter, beyond this point there is the unfathomable exogenous: 'for our purpose – he says – it is yet permissible to draw a line between the phenomena directly incident to the working *of* the economic system and the phenomena produced by other social agencies acting *on* the economic system [...]'.[121] The unfathomable exogenous is represented by the problem posed by the Political, logically unspeakable, unfathomable, according to the *recta grammatica* inherent to the economic *ratio*.

It should be noted, however, that the hiatus between endogenous/exogenous, logical/Political, rational/irrational, is not the result of a choice. Schumpeter does not choose, in a neoclassical fashion, to set aside the Political; it is rather the logical type of the economic representation to condemn the Political to be an exogenous *datum*. The Austrian economist does not forget the Political at all, but his interest lies in the physiology rather than in the environmental pathology of the economic corpus. The external factors explain much of the economic fluctuations, and they might explain them entirely – he says. 'Similarly, there is no sense in looking for a single reason why men die, for there is obviously a great variety of reasons. But there is both sense and interest in the question whether and why death

120   TED, pp.4–5 (*Theorie*, p.3).
121   BC, p.7.

would come about, in the absence of all lesions, by virtue of the working of the human organism or the cells of which it consists'.[122] In plain terms, only in this way is it possible to conceive of a functional interaction among internal causes. Although it does not exclude the existence of the exogenous, this interaction can avoid it without losing its own logical rigorousness. This is the sole 'logical type' adequate to the economic 'question of causation'. The Political, not by definition, but consequentially to the assumed 'logical type', is the 'exterior', and with regard to it economic science is speechless, exactly because its paradigm, in order to be representable, should be impolitical.

Although it may seem, here Schumpeter is not referring to the *theoretische Ökonomie* – where such an analytical scenario was defined *de facto* –, but to the *ökonomische Theorie*, whose origin lies in the analysis of development and innovation. In the above mentioned chapters of *Business Cycles*, we can find unequivocal indications of this. We find not only a pre-Weberian claim concerning the exogeneity of the Political, but also the explicit assertion that the theory of development, hence the economic theory, is epistemically other in respect of what is an external cause regarding it: the Political, *in primis*. It is not by chance that the so-called 'question of causation', which has nothing to do with the principle of causality inherent to *Naturwissenschaft*, is defined bearing in mind these epistemic parameters. Only after having identified the tools of analysis adequate to the concept of the economic representation can we carve out 'a model or schema' of the economic process able to overcome the check represented by 'what we may term Nonsense Induction' or 'Spurious Verification'; a checkmate deriving from the utilization of an inadequate model, deduced from other disciplines and, therefore, built around improper tools. Model or schema – 'first approximation', Schumpeter says – should entirely claim their purity: 'When we look at the skeleton, we behold the picture of a distinct process in time which displays functional relations between its constituent parts and is logically self-contained'.[123]

---

122   *BC*, p.34.
123   *BC*, p.138.

Needless to say, Schumpeter is well-aware of the distance between 'first approximation' and 'reality'. However, via such an 'approximation', he believes himself to be able to represent the *economic pars* of that reality, without giving anything up to the *unrepresentable whole*. He believes himself to be able to effectively represent the endogenous apart from the exogenous, the Economical apart from the Political:

> It is a long way from this schema to the point of junction with historical fact. Innumerable layers of secondary, incidental, accidental, and 'external' fact and reaction among all of them and reactions to reactions cover that skeleton of economic life [...]. But the writer must have been sadly lacking in expository skill if the reader does not recognize the common sense and the realistic counterpart of this theoretical world [...].[124]

A simple allusion to common sense is obviously not sufficient. More interesting is the explicit reference to a purely logical model with regard to the external perturbations, and hence, to the epistemological link proposed, backwards, with the method of variation, where, thirty years before *Business Cycle*, Schumpeter established, in antithesis to the neoclassical modelling, his ideal logical type. In effect, although the context is entirely different, it recalls what we can define as a 'closed model of causation'.

According to Schumpeter's understanding of the economic science, the distinction between *theoretische Ökonomie* and *ökonomische Theorie* is given in term of temporal variables: in the former, time is a pure 'spatial fiction', in the latter it is expressed chronologically. Now, if theoretical economics excludes *a priori* the possibility to provide an account of the exogenous variables, economic theory, although it assumes them within it, can only offer a partial account of them. Thus, though in a different way, both refer to time as a theoretical-logical structure. It is this aspect that makes *theoretische Ökonomie* and *ökonomische Theorie* understandable only within a 'closed model of causation'. In fact, even though the interactions among economic variables are far from being easily explicable, however, from a theoretical point of view, as all these variables are

124 *BC*, pp.137–8.

endogenous, it is possible to give a rational representation of each of them.

It is possible to give a rational representation of all the possible interactions among economic variables exactly because their references exhaust themselves within the logical-economical sphere. And this is true not only for the domains of *theoretische Ökonomie*, but also for the entire domain of economic science, representable – via a 'first approximation' – as a closed theoretical model. In order to have an indirect confirmation of this, it is sufficient to consider what an open causation model is. Schumpeter is perfectly conscious that reality (the social environment) is given as an ensemble of open models of causation. Nonetheless, as they do not have a backwards point of reference, they are scientifically un-representable, and therefore alien to the logic of the Economical.

More precisely, we ought to consider that the functional structure of these models avoids the concept of cause *stricto sensu*. Causation – rather than *causa causans* – only means the logical limit inherent to the possibility of interaction among endogenous variables, their incompatibility with the exogenous. But also in this way, a possible opening towards the exogenous by the endogenous, of the Economical towards the Political, would generate an unmanageable complexity within the functional relations and their consequent interactions. Once again, under these circumstances, we would face the impossibility of discerning the endogenous from the exogenous, the Economical from the Political. Exactly for this reason it is possible here to remark upon the persistence of parts of the epistemological intentions that inform the method of variation. As they are logically determined, hence representable, only the *internal variables* can generate *determinate variations*. Vice versa, what is exogenous, indeterminate, is logically un-representable. Not because it is illogical *in se*, but rather because it is irreducible to the *recta grammatica* of the logical-economical analysis. It follows that the fundamental distinction between statics and dynamics is underpinned by the distinction between endogenous and exogenous, Economical and Political.

It is Schumpeter himself who underlines the magnitude of the difference, the hiatus occurring between logical-endogenous-time and historical-exogenous-time. Certainly, in spite of the *impasse*, he believes that an approximate – though logically adequate to reality – model could prevail thanks to its determinacy, its representability that, in turn, is directly proportional to the indeterminacy of the exogenous, to the unrepresentability of the Political. Nevertheless, as the 'historical phase' to which Schumpeter refers is an 'empirical', statistical one, also considering the 'three approximations' discussed in *Business Cycles*, the framework remains unchanged. As Schumpeter says: 'We have accomplished then what we, as economists, are capable of in the case in question and we must give place to other disciplines'.[125]

The *Zurechnung* represents the modern impossibility of the causal method to be relevant as a tool able to distinguish both the endogenous and the exogenous elements in their entirety. As such, it is a functional, logical mechanism. There are few, if any, doubts that the context within which the *Zurechnung* manifests itself is the one sketched by authors like Menger, Weiser, Böhm-Bawerk. It is therefore worth noting how the theoretical coordinates are similar to the ones that, in the sphere of the *Methodenstreit*, allowed the reflections of more than a generation of economists – from Schmoller to Menger – and that influenced the development of the whole political, economic, juridical, and sociological debate, until the definition of Weber's *Wertfreiheit*. Therefore, the 'pro-positive' aspect of Schumpeter's modelling should be intended as a refusal to utilize spurious analytical schemes, invalidate by problematic objects that are not *wertfrei*. The very same aspects, however, go far beyond the exclusion of what is influenced in term of value, to the point of excluding what is exogenous to the economic discipline and, therefore, logically impossible to be represented. Hence, the 'pure model' informing *Business Cycles* is not only a 'first' approximation.

Via a strained but reasonable interpretation, it might be possible to say that Schumpeter is, certainly in his own way, a sort of direct interpreter – a 'mediator' – of the distance separating Kelsen's abstraction and Weber's historical and social understanding. What is 'representable', in fact, is a rational mediation between the impossible 'natural' economic reasoning and the 'social' indeterminacy of the Political. It is an approximation legitimated by the degree of truth that

125 *TED*, p.5 (*Theorie*, p.3).

can be logically expressed within the domain of the economic science. Consequently, 'purity' is unable to 'save', neo-classically, the economic theory. Rather, it 'exposes' its significance up to a reasonable limit, in the hope of preserving what remains of economic theory *after* the definition of economic dynamics. The price to pay for this mediation is the *impoliticalness*: namely, the awareness of the inevitable presence of the Political, of its ineluctability, without being able to rationally represent it, as it is a 'logical factor' economically unrepresentable, exogenous. The *concept of rational*, whose logical limit is represented by the empirical, is the distinctive threshold.[126]

Schumpeter's concept of rational helps us to clarify his role as a 'mediator', because it not only preserves the purity of the method, but also indicates what it should be protected from. It simultaneously indicates the difference between endogenous and exogenous and the peculiarities that allow us to distinguish one from the other. We should bear in mind, however, that the concept is not *given*; it has its own genesis, which should be traced, as there is not an immediate identification between the rational and the empirical. In Schumpeter, rationality has its own genesis and a logical autonomous existence, which precedes the said identification. This latter is an intermediate result rather than a methodological assumption. The autonomy of rationality, as it provides the basis for *theoretische Ökonomie*, goes beyond any insignificant verification. It is the very same epistemological basis informing the method of variation. However, if it is true that this latter allows the distinction between statics and dynamics within the endogenous-logical sphere, it is nonetheless true that in economic theory the 'pure' autonomy related to the concept of rational reveals itself as insufficient. Its identification with the empirical is therefore unescapable. Such an identification is, in fact, indispensable for explaining concrete phenomena and for restraining the influence of what is historically determined. In reality, a further distinction is possible. In effect, although the 'object' of economic theory, the dynamic process, can be defined via a merely logical process of 'first approximation', 'second' and 'third' approximations reinforce the

126 Concerning the anti-metaphysical nexus between 'rational' and 'empirical', cf. *supra* footnote 53.

credibility of this dynamic process. But exactly this confirms our thesis. What is considered to be logical, the 'pure model', seeks a point of reference in the empirical, in a series of repeatable verifications, so as to be distinguished from the exogenous-Politicus.

In brief, it can be said that, belonging only to the Economical, it is via the method of variation that the concept of rationality allows us to draw a border line separating statics from dynamics as well as the sphere of theoretical economics from that of economic theory. Furthermore, the identification between the rational and the empirical enables us to pave the way for the fundamental distinction between endogenous and exogenous, inscribing both *theoretische Ökonomie* and *ökonomische Theorie* in the sphere of the endogenous. Here, the empirical, pertinent solely to economic theory, serves to distinguish this latter from what is historically determined, although, in mere logical terms, at 'first approximation', economic theory is rationally autonomous from any verification – indispensable, instead, to underpin the so-called second and third approximation. Thus, the interpretation provided by those scholars who saw in Schumpeter's distinction between Walras' 'pure' economics and the empirical – not always distinct from what is historical – the more seminal contribution of the Austrian economist, seem correct. It is correct, but not sufficient.

Certainly, it is reasonable to think that there is nothing more contradictory than to combine the rational and the empirical. However, the point in question is not a concept of 'purity' *à la* Kelsen. For this reason, we said that Schumpeter's theory represents a sort of mediation between Kelsen's abstraction and Weber's historical sense. Nevertheless, in Weber, Schumpeter grasps simply what is the empirical, not the Political – and as 'mediator' he proposes a median solution. In our opinion, it consists of attempting to preserve the 'purity' of the Economical from the sphere of the exogenous that is the closest to it, inbuilt in it: the Political. This is not a neo-classical solution, but, exactly for this reason, the empirical should be identifiable with the rational, as the rational *per se* is unable to go beyond the neoclassical modelling, whilst the exogenous, the Political, 'says too much', becoming incomprehensible, irrational in its clarity. Eventually, Schumpeter's mediation resembles the one he himself

263

puts into place between Walras and Marx. In order to preserve the Economical avoiding being trapped into the neoclassical gate, the rational is obliged to accept a series of empirical verifications. This is the only way that would allow us to think about dynamics without appealing to the Political. This is the sole and unique non-bourgeois way to read Marx: to invoke his truth apart from the logical unrepresentability of the *Politicus*:

> If we think about it, – Schumpeter wrote –, we shall understand that it is not a paradox when we claim that an economic explanation of history [*eine ökonomische Erklärung der Geschichte*], such as Marx's attempt, strictly speaking does not belong to economics, as what in this theorization pertains to economics is only the claim according to which the elements to which the development of society can be traced back are essentially of an economic nature. Sadly, this is not an economic explanation, as it operates not according to an *economic method*, with theorems and concepts, and, with regard to the interpretation of the economic phenomena, it is irrelevant.[127]

The ineluctability of the Political is this: it represents that upon which it is impossible to build a 'rational discourse'; but this 'logical' impotence explicitly gives a full acknowledgement of the Political, to its disenchantment. It is not a choice, but an opening towards the limit of what is logically representable, of what is utterable. In the end, it is the ineluctability of the Political that determines its unspeakableness and transparency, its imposition as an ensemble of relationships, its not-disappearing, if not as a result of a drastic overlapping with the Economical. In the face of this, to be speechless involves the abyss of prophecy – or silence. Schumpeter opts for the former, to the point of thinking about the future in terms of the past. The synthesis that emerges rests entirely upon his revolutionary interpretation of the business cycle, innovation, and entrepreneur[128] – whose existence,

127 *TWE*, p.84.
128 The enterpreneur – wrote with an impressionistic flavour E. März, (*Joseph Schumpeter*, p.40) – 'ist der Demiurg des wirtschaftlichen Fortschritts, die persona dramatis der sozi-ökonomischen Entwicklung, der Träger des gesell-schaftlichen Wandels schlechthin'. Wide and very articulate is the bibliography on the topic: among others, see E. Haeussermann, *Der Unternehmer: Seine Funktion, seine Zielsetzung, sein Gewinn*, Kohlhammer, Stuttgart, 1932, pp.21–

however, *singularly given*, is rationally determined 'before' the Web-erian *politicus*.

At any rate, between the *theoria* and these *socio*-logical figures, there is no discontinuity. The ineluctability of the Political is the result of an economical-functional *modus*, which transforms the logical representation into a sort of rational 'protection', aimed at distin-guishing the endogenous from the exogenous. Now, that such a 'protection' ends up with isolating the relevant heterodoxy of Schum-peter, to the extent that it renders his consequent 'political prophecy' legitimate, is a matter of fact. And, paradoxically, of such a prophecy we are obliged to grasp only the rational side, as it is a clear indication of the crisis of a 'pure' project, empirically corroborated, in its own terms 'modern', impolitically resolved into the endogenous. The Schumpeterian entrepreneur represents the paradigm of this crisis.

It is not by chance that the first difficulty that one encounters in understanding the figure of the entrepreneur is its 'economical' *defin-ition*. Although Schumpeter is clear about the essential functions of the entrepreneur, his/her sociological characteristics are obscure and

30; Y. Brozen, 'Business Leadership and technological change', *American Journal of Economics and Sociology*, 1954, vol.14, 6; E.A. Carlin, 'Schum-peter's Constructed Type: the Entrepreneur', *Kyklos*, 1956, vol.9, 1; Perroux, *La pensée économique de Joseph Schumpeter*, pp.81–102; L.A. O'Donnell, 'Rationalism, Capitalism and the Entrepreneur: The Views of Veblen and Schumpeter', *History of Political Economy*, 1973, vol.5, 1; Y. Breton, 'La théorie schumpeterienne de l'entrepreneur ou le problème de la connaissance économique', *Revue Economique*, 1984, vol.35, 2; J. Hagedoorn, 'Innovation and Entrepreneurship: Schumpeter Revisited', *Industrial and Corporate Change*, 1996, vol.5, 3; S.M. Kanbur, 'A Note on Risk Taking, Entre-preneurship, and Schumpeter', *History of Political Economy*, 1980, vol.12, 4; P. Swoboda, 'Schumpeter's Entrepreneur in Modern Economic Theory', in Seidl (ed. by), *Lectures on Schumpeterian Economics*, pp.17–30; L.V. Marco, 'Entrepreneur et innovation: les sources françaises de Joseph Schumpeter', *Economies et Sociétés*, 1985, vol.19, 10; E.J. O'Boyle, 'On the Person and the Work of the Entrepreneur', *Review of Social Economy*, 1994, vol.52, 4, Winter; E. Santarelli, E. Pesciarelli, 'The Emergence of a Vision: The Development of Schumpeter's Theory of Entrepreneurship', *History of Political Economy*, 1990, vol.22, 4; F.M. Scherer, M. Perlman (ed. by), *Entrepreneurship, technological innovation, and economic growth: Studies in the Schumpeterian tradition*, University of Michigan Press, Ann Arbor, 1992.

difficult to define. However, rather than raising ambiguities, such an elasticity indicates the prominence of an action 'logically' definable apart from the contingent and historical situations.[129] That is, not only is it difficult to establish who the entrepreneur is, but it is also irrelevant. This is because, in spite of the evidence, the entrepreneur is not a figure belonging merely to the capitalistic mode of production. To be consequentially explicit, we should be satisfied with a circular deduction, if not of a tautologically defined identity.

The entrepreneur is one who is able to innovate, and only up until he/she is able to do so. Hence, no one can be said to be an entrepreneur for his/her entire life, and no one can be said to be only an entrepreneur. An innovation is subjected to the 'truth' of the cycle; by analogy, the entrepreneur cannot subtract him/herself from that 'truth'. When he/she, in order to govern it, is unable to turn the *Kreislauf* upside down, he/she loses his/her defined social identity. Thus, he/she is a transitory figure: he/she is an entrepreneur only *pro tempore*. Nevertheless, with regard to this transitoriness, what is unequivocal is the distance between the entrepreneurial functions and property. Even more explicit is the irreducible, singular character of the entrepreneurial practices: practices that are singular and transient in time. Consequently, although all this is unequivocally 'modern', to it further terminological elasticity follows. Given the singular, functionally circular, socially fluctuating nature of the entrepreneurial practices, it is neither possible to identify an abstract subject to whom to ascribe them, nor to define and trace back the Function of such a subject to a social identity. What remains of that subject is only a transient singularity, a *Nomen*.

A metaphysical terminology is necessary here. It is helpful to grasp the difference between a transient subject, defined by his/her empirical singularity, and an abstract subject, socially reproducible in its abstractness, and therefore having a role that reproduces and modifies its historical functions. This is the 'logical' apotheosis of what is empirical. There is no contradiction between the emergence of

---

129   J.A. Schumpeter, 'Unternehmer', in *Handwörterbuch der Staatswissenschaften*, in *Handwörterbuch der Staatswissenschaften*, Fisher, Jena, 1928, vol.8, pp.467–87.

the entrepreneurial contingent singularity and the pre-eminence of his/her 'logical' function in a particular historical context. The former, in fact, is always empirically determinated, chained to a *Nomen*, to a transient subject, entrepreneur only *pro tempore*. However, the function that a transient subject interprets without embodying it, fails to preserve the subject's *Nomen*. The Schumpeterian 'impolitical entrepreneur' manifests him/herself in the 'logical' apotheosis of his/her function; but, as he/she is constrained to an individuality, he/she exhausts his/her specific 'modern intention'. Coherently, the same remunerative model attached to the impolitical entrepreneur, the profit, is a 'functional return', although 'it would not always be safe to locate the entrepreneurial function according to the criterion of accrual'.[130] Such a location is possible only within a family business, where the institutional sphere is non existent, where there are no shareholders who can decide upon the redistribution of the net gains. At present, however – Schumpeter laconically admits –, the entrepreneurial reality is dominated by institutionalized firms, rather than by entrepreneurial skills referable, as functions, to *different*, because they are *singular*, subjects. All this is well represented by the dominance of an impersonal, capitalistic collective reason – *der Sozialismus des Kapitals*, as Marx said.

Schumpeter's epistemological pessimism is turned into an ethical pessimism; subtracting the space to the entrepreneurial singularity, capital and institutionalized firms render innovation autonomous. The figure of a 'pure' entrepreneur, 'pure' singular Function enjoying a *Nomen*, powerful 'theoretical fiction' that we find as such from *Theorie* to *Business Cycles*, loses its physiognomy and dissolves. The *impolitical entrepreneur* is wrapped by a Modernity at this point touched by the collective representation of abstract subjects. If the Schumpeterian entrepreneur was able to exert 'individual leadership acting by virtue of personal force and personal responsibility for success', at present he/she is losing his/her importance and the pace of this process is destined to accelerate in the future. 'Rationalized and specialized office work will eventually blot out personality, the calculability result, the "vision". The leading man no longer has the

130   *BC*, p.106.

opportunity to fling himself into the fray. He is becoming just another office worker – and who is not always difficult to replace'.[131] The economic progress has no longer a subject having a *Nomen*, the entrepreneurial function is depersonalized, automatized; the property is 'dematerialized', 'defunctionalized'. Administrators, managers, and the like are turned into functionaries. 'Crumbling Walls' means, first of all, the crumbling of the entrepreneurial functions that, in any case, always refer to an individuality. Personality and will are even less relevant within an environment shaped by economic transformation. Progress tends to be 'depersonalized', 'automatized', to undermine personal and individual will and action. 'Innovation itself is being reduced to routine. Technological progress is increasingly becoming the business of teams of trained specialists who turn out what is required and make it work in predictable ways'.[132] These are the real critical factors.

The Weberian imprinting – bureaucratization, rational discipline *versus* charisma – is apparent. However, Schumpeter is anchored to a categorization that cannot do away with the individuality of the entrepreneur. His/her function is individual, and when it is transformed into mere technical function, rational organization, *officium*, loses its characteristics. This is because Weber's *officium* is a profession that requires a specific training and that follows general rules (more or less fixed and exhaustive) that can be learned. What was 'form of individual leadership acting by virtue of personal force and personal responsibility for success' tends to fade away, undermining the function and the social position of the entrepreneur. But this ends up affecting the entire bourgeois class structure, as '[e]conomically and sociologically, directly and indirectly, the bourgeoisie therefore depends on the entrepreneur and, as a class, lives and will die with him'.[133] Given that it is via its own realization that the capitalistic enterprise tends to automatize progress, it tends to become superfluous. The bureaucratized big firms, in replacing small and medium enterprises, not only expropriate the owners, but also replace the

131 *CSD*, p.133.
132 *CSD*, p.132.
133 *CSD*, p.134.

entrepreneur and expropriates the bourgeoisies of their peculiar function. The capitalistic process, after having dismantled the feudal institutional structure, now tends to demolish its own structure, the specific interest of property, as well as the private character of economic activity. 'Dematerialized, defunctionalized and absentee ownership does not impress and call forth moral allegiance as the vital form of property did. Eventually there will be *nobody* left who really cares to stand for it – nobody within and nobody without the precincts of the big concerns'.[134] Thus, an isomorphic relationship between entrepreneur and innovation no longer exists.

It is not an exaggeration to claim that for Schumpeter the capitalistic system was destined to disappear as a result of the loss of meaning associated to the entrepreneurial singularity. The total lack of comprehension of the Weberian *politicus* brings him to grasp but not to accept the modern nexus between the Political and innovation enacted by collective subjects. The same is true concerning the functional character of a socially displayed meaning of action, which transposes the processes of innovation into society as a whole. It is this operation that occurs in Modernity: concentration, socialization, redefinition of the Political. The Schumpeterian singularity, therefore, remains wrapped within such a 'modern logic', because it is constrained by the apotheosis of the genius, of his irrational charisma. The epistemological pessimism as impossible ethical disposition becomes an 'esthetical tension', stretched towards a singular Function, denied by that to which is no longer possible to assign a 'singular name' in the development process.

In the modern age, the meaning of crisis resides in a collective transposition of any subjectivity into economic planning, into a commensuration of any 'logical analyses' to the 'political discourse'. The modern spirit entailed by the Schumpeterian notion of innovation was only a powerful anticipation of this process. After Marx, that of Schumpeter was the sharpest characterization of the relationship occurring between science and development, but subjectified through Schopenhauer's rather than Weber's *grammatica*. That is, the prophecy of development would try to realize itself denying the role of

134   *CSD*, p.142.

what made it possible: the *Sozialisierung*. *Ex post*, this prophecy – anchored to a theoretical, 'logical time' via a singular entrepreneurial function, always 'empirically' referred to a *Nomen* – would show its capacity to interpret but not to accept the historical shift occurring between the First and the Second World War.

Socialization, rather than being the critical limit of the capitalistic system, represents its vital sources: something that the mature Schumpeter understood, without fully accepting it. In the long term, in fact, the processes of innovation would presuppose a combined action, the multiplication of approaches, the flexibility of the systems, and the legitimacy of different languages. The economic system would end up by producing innovation, even apart from big organization and bureaucratic management. Neither the market nor the State could govern such an innovation entirely. In this 'epochal' context, far from being a passive instrument, innovation would become an active instrument of a diffuse, rather than planned, *Sozialisierung*.

Schumpeter's reflection upon the entrepreneurial *Individualität* is far from being able to provide a satisfactory answer to the above problems: firstly, due to its *impoliticalness*, and secondly due to its logical contingency. In spite of his belief, the problem would have been not the fall of the tension of a serialized and bureaucratized innovation, but rather, *mutatis mutandis*, the impossibility of governing its maximum diffusion. Certainly, these considerations are allowed only *after* Schumpeter; but they not only say something about the determined historicity of Schumpeter's model. They call for a rethinking of the context – logical-temporal and political – of his theory of development, celebrated as the final alternative to Walras' fictions. They call into question the structural limitation of Schumpeter's political approach, or better still, his impoliticalness; finally, they suggest a rethinking *in toto* of the nexus between the Economical and the Political. In short, they suggest the rethinking of a fundamental epistemological passage concerning modern economic science, acknowledging to the Schumpterian *opus* the due crucial role.

6. Economic science and ideology

Is economics a science? Schumpeter was constantly puzzled by such a question. If there is a *continuum* that cuts across his reflections, this is certainly represented by his preoccupation to keep 'science' separate from 'ideology',[135] so as to establish a clear distinction between the Economical-endogenous and the Political-exogenous. This preoccupation is always present. Outstandingly synthesized in *Science and Ideology*, it occupies the first part of the monumental *History of Economic Analysis*.[136] Undoubtedly, dealing with Schumpeter as an historian of economic analysis requires prudence.[137] Nonetheless, it is undeniable that – as Richard Swedberg noted – Part I of the *History of Economic Analysis* 'does not only hold the key to an understanding of Schumpeter's *History* but to his whole work in Economics'. In effect, it is possible to identify in it the *fil rouge* that cuts across the entire Schumpeterian *opus*.[138] But what does this *fil rouge* consist of? In short, according to Schumpeter, when the researcher is willing to present the processes that legitimize economic science *qua* science, a fundamental obstacle should be surmounted: the ideology as bias. What is required is 'the miracle of knowing what we cannot know'.[139] In this sort of Scholastic enigma, the disjunction between the Economical and the Political is perfectly synthesized. Nonetheless, the Schumpeterian reflection upon the nature of economic science and its

---

135   Cf. Shionoya, 'Schumpeter and the Idea of Social Science', pp.54 ff.
136   But between the two works there are many differences: R. Faucci, V. Rodezno, 'Did Schumpeter change his Mind?', pp.43–9.
137   The Schumpeterian philology is very problematic and therefore we are not dealing with a 'canonically' conceived history. This has been noted by F.H. Knight, 'J.A. Schumpeter *History of Economic Analysis*', *Southern Economic Journal*, 1955, vol.21, 3; even clearer was L. Robbins, 'Schumpeter *History of Economic Analysis*', *Quarterly Journal of Economics*, 1955, vol.69, 1. Cf. also L. Beinsen, 'Schumpeter as an Historian of Economic Doctrine', in Seidl (ed. by), *Lectures on Schumpeterian Economics*, pp.173 ff.; L.S. Moss (ed. by), *Joseph A. Schumpeter, Historian of Economics*, Routledge, London and New York, 1996.
138   Swedberg, *J.A. Schumpeter*, p.180.
139   Schumpeter, 'Science and Ideology', *CSD*, p.351.

foundations confirms the reasons why this disjunction does not represent a trivial hypostasis, but rather a real theoretical problem.

As it is known, Schumpeter begins by clarifying that the history of the economic analysis is the history of the analytical, or scientific aspects of economic thought. Moving from the conviction that, differently from other scientists, the historian of economic analysis does not deal with a well-defined object, Schumpeter claims that 'the very ideas of economic analysis, of intellectual effort, of science, are 'quenched in smoke', and the very rules or principles that are to guide the historian's pen are open to doubt and, what is worse, to misunderstanding'.[140] Obviously, the indeterminacy of the object, caused by superabundance rather than absence of specific attributes, represents an essential problem. But why study the history of economic science?

The answer is articulated in four points. Firstly, because scientific analysis does not proceed according to a linear movement, and its methods and problems are always historically determined, they 'cannot be fully grasped without a knowledge of the previous problems and methods to which they are the (tentative) response'.[141] Secondly, the study of the history of economic science allows us to find 'new inspiration' and a useful interpretation of its non-linear development, enabling the researcher to locate those efforts that produced results and those that did not achieve relevant outcomes. Thirdly, economic history – exactly as any other science – teaches us the myriad of ways in which the human brain works, '[i]t displays logic in the concrete, logic in action, logic wedded to vision and to purpose'. Finally, what the history of economic science makes possible is the description of 'what may be called the process of the Filiation of Scientific Ideas – the process by which men's efforts to understand economic phenomena produce, improve, and pull down analytic structures in an unending sequence'.[142]

But, again, is economics a science? According to Schumpeter, the answer depends upon what we intend by science. If by science we

140   *HEA*, p.3.
141   *HEA*, p.4.
142   *HEA*, p.6.

mean 'any field of knowledge that has developed specialized fact-finding and interpretative techniques or inference (analysis)', there are few, if any, who doubt that economics enjoys the rank of science. However, although it utilizes specific languages and techniques, it is very difficult to define Economics, 'because common-sense knowledge goes in this field much farther relatively to such scientific knowledge as we have been able to achieve, than does common-sense knowledge in almost any other field'. The economic field resembles a tropical forest rather than a building erected according to a blueprint. As it is 'an agglomeration of ill-coordinated and overlapping fields of research', it is closer to medicine rather than to acoustics.[143] Within it, the scientific economist moves according to peculiar criteria that differentiate him from those who think in economic terms *without* knowing specific techniques and languages, which, in turn, stem from the ability to dominate the fields of knowledge that constitute economic analysis: namely, 'history', 'statistics', 'economic sociology' and 'economic theory'.

Let us focus our attention upon this latter, whose 'analytical instrumentalism' is clearly re-stated with a terminology similar to the one utilized in *Das Wesen* to describe economic gnoseology:

> Economic theory does something entirely different. It cannot indeed, any more than can theoretical physics, do without simplifying schemata or models [...] So far as our present argument is concerned, the things (propositions) postulates or assumptions or even principles, and the things (propositions) that we think we have established by admissible procedure are called theorems. [...] Now, hypotheses of this kind are also suggested by facts [...] but in strict logic they are arbitrary creations of the analyst. They [...] are mere instruments or tools framed for the purpose of establishing interesting results.[144]

Thus, the theory has become the 'box of tools' of which Joan Robinson spoke. However, compared with the perspective delineated in *Das Wesen*, the methodological instrumentalism here defined undergoes a radical change. Schumpeter no longer distinguishes between *theoretische Ökonomie* and *ökonomische Theorie*. Such a

---

143   *HEA*, pp.9–10.
144   *HEA*, p.15.

distinction has reached its aim with the delineation of a dynamic theory of development, which has revealed itself *toto coelo* not only distinguished but also radically different from the neo-classical theory. Nevertheless – as we have seen –, in the theory of development, the *theoria* 'expanded' itself to the point of risking to establish the explicit predominance of its historically determined nature. This brings about an unavoidable redefinition of 'the problem of theory', destined to amplify – as it is easy to grasp – the 'problem of ideology'. In fact, in order to be dynamic in Schumpeterian terms, the theory becomes historically characterized by the utilization of specific languages and techniques – what is due not only to their scientific evolution or the researcher intentions, but also to the character of 'social science' that such a theory assumes.

But what can be the meaning of Schumpeter's statement according to which economic history is the most important field among those constituting economic science, and if he had decided to return back to study he would have opted to choose economic history? Clearly, in Schumpeter's mind economic history dominates the unitary process of the historical time. '[T]he historical report cannot be purely economic but must inevitably reflect also "institutional" facts that are not economic: therefore, it affords the best method for understanding how economic and non-economic fact *are* related to one another and how the various social sciences *should* be related to one another'.[145] However, can this be the 'path' of a 'pure' theoretician well-aware of the historical conditioning to which all theories are subjected and, just for this reason, interested in identifying, in the history of the analysis, the 'analytical aspect' of economic thought?

To provide a sole response to this question seems to be reductive and unsatisfactory. We could and should mention the different contexts of the research, the external factors (e. g. the US in 1940 was not comparable to Vienna at the beginning of the century), and those related to the evolution of the discipline: it is sufficient here to mention Schumpeter's aversion to Keynesian policies. But this is not enough. Schumpeter's program of research does not seem to be modified, but rather unfinished, for the simple reason that it was

145   *HEA*, p.13.

impossible to accomplish it. In this perspective, the meaning of history, of the historical nature of the economic processes and the disciplines related to the theory, rather than an involution towards Schmoller's historicism, represents the unsolved issue of an economic science historically determined far beyond the 'vision' of the researcher. Nevertheless, the reference to the Weberian *Wertfreiheit*, although opportune, in itself would appear insufficient, since *value judgements*, even if they might create ideologies, cannot be traced back to them:

> An economist's value judgements often *reveal* his ideology but they *are not* his ideology: it is possible to pass value judgements upon irreproachably established facts and the relations between them, and it is possible to refrain from passing any value judgements upon facts that are seen in an ideologically deflected light.[146]

On the basis of this distinction, it is reasonable to say that the researcher's value judgement could represent the premise for an ideological solution. However, what constitutes the problem is the peculiar statute of economics – and the necessary 'incursions' of other disciplines in it –, not the easily unmaskable ideological intention of the researcher. On the other hand, the fact that between value judgements and statements 'that are seen in an ideologically deflected light' there is an affinity and a concrete complementarity, makes it possible that value judgements develop the basis upon which, for example, the distinction between the 'history of economic thought' and the 'history of economic analysis' becomes feasible. In effect, whilst the former displays 'the close association that exists within the attitudes of the public mind [...] with the kind of problems that at any given time interest analysts, and form the general attitude or spirit in which they approach their problems'; the latter, although taking for granted 'the general environment of economic thought in which, at various times, analysts did their work', never assumes the historical changes as its object. This is the nucleus of Schumpeter's argument:

146   *HEA*, p.37.

The development of analytic work, [...], displays a characteristic property which is completely absent from the historical development of economic thought in our sense and also from the historical succession of systems of political economy. This property may best be illustrated by an example: from the earliest times until today, analytic economists have been interested, more or less, in the analysis of the phenomenon that we call competitive price. When the modern student meets the phenomenon on an advanced level of his study, [...], he is introduced to a number of concepts and problems [...]. But the student will also discover before long that a new apparatus poses and solves problems for which the older authors could hardly have found answers even if they had been aware of them. This defines in a common-sense and at any rate a perfectly unambiguous manner, in what sense there had been 'scientific progress' [...].[147]

Thus, is it possible to claim that, once having established the existence of these distinctions, and defined 'the process of Filiation of the scientific ideas', the ideological threat towards the results of economic analysis would disappear? Because any analytical effort begins only after having realized the 'vision' of those phenomena that are subjected to our perception, the answer is negative. The 'vision' is a pre-analytical cognitive act,[148] as it is by its means that we can decide *before* if a phenomenon has any interests at all. This implies a process of analysis and selection on the part of our imagination or common sense. After this:

The first task is to verbalize the vision or to conceptualize it in such a way that its elements take their place, with names attached to them that facilitate recognition and manipulation, in a more or less orderly schema or picture. But in doing so we almost automatically perform two other tasks. On the one hand, we assemble further facts in addition to those perceived already, and learn to distrust others that figured in the original vision; on the other hand, the very work of constructing the schema or picture will add further relations and concepts to, and in general also eliminate other from, the original stock. Factual work and 'theoretical' work, in an endless relation of give and take [...] will eventually produce *scientific models*.[149]

---

147   *HEA*, p.39.
148   Although here we are following the claim expressed in *History*, it should be recalled that in 'Science and Ideology' Schumpeter operated a further distinction between pre-analytic and pre-scientific. Cf. Faucci, Rodezno, 'Did Schumpeter change his Mind?'.
149   *HEA*, p.42.

All this, however, cannot assure that ideology would not influence this 'transformation', as it is part of the pre-analytic cognitive act. When applied to the development of knowledge and scientific processes, ideologies are biases out of our control and are much more dangerous than our value judgements. They are not mere lies, 'they are truthful statements about what a man thinks he sees'.[150] Different from exact sciences, according to which biases can only influence the choice of the problem and the ways in which the inquiry can be conducted, social sciences offer results that might be contested, as they are connected to the researcher's class relations. In order to identify the ideological influences, it is therefore necessary to examine the scientific procedure through which we interpret the perception of a group of correlate phenomena. The 'vision' – it is worth repeating – is a pre-analytical cognitive act, but indispensable for the analytical work itself. It is an act that encourages the research and analysis of reality, verifying what in the act itself is ideologically characterized. As Alessandro Roncaglia observes, for Schumpeter the analytical work is not only the mere elaboration of formal theorems, but also the elaboration of a 'conceptual apparatus' aimed at representing reality.[151] In fact, if it is true that our ideologies stem from the pre-analytical cognitive act, it is also true that it is the necessary condition of our scientific work, and 'that the rules of procedure that we apply in our analytic work are almost as much exempt from ideological influence as vision is subject to it': 'they tend to crush out ideologically conditioned error from the visions from which we start'.[152]

Now, independently from the ways in which one analyses the different analytical passages, in what constitutes the *fil rouge* of Schumpeter's tormented reflection, what is totally absent is a rigorous definition of 'ideology'[153] and, consequently, an acceptable relativization of the problem.[154] This is the result of the fact that

150 Schumpeter, 'Science and Ideology', *CSD*, p.349.
151 Roncaglia, *Schumpeter*, p.100.
152 *HEA*, p.43.
153 Swedberg, *J.A. Schumpeter*, p.181.
154 R.L. Meek's, 'Is Economics Biased? Heretical View of a Leading Thesis in Schumpeter's History', *Scottish Journal of Political Economy*, 1957, vol.4.

Schumpeter's reflection is an attempted synthesis between a static explicative *ratio*, dynamics, empirical phenomena, and historical-social elements. This synthesis is irremediably marked by the distinction between exogenous and endogenous factors. Perhaps, it might be said that Schumpeter the analyst is obliged to distinguish what Schumpeter the historian of the analysis is obliged to declare undistinguishable: the nexus between the Economical and the Political. It is such a clear contradiction that makes Schumpeter's thought an expression unequivocally 'modern', after all.

The *Methodenstreit*, as we have seen, was for Schumpeter inessential, as it did not reach *this* crucial point. Nonetheless, the complementarity that he invokes between economic history, statistics, theory, and economic sociology offers the grounds for a 'scientific environment' so wide that it would become quite difficult to submit it to a sufficiently clear and distinct analytical criteria. On the other hand, it is the 'mode of production' of economic science (and therefore the *Wissenssoziologie* applied to the relationship between ideas and social structures)[155] that represents the problem: not apart from the individual's intentions, but often beyond them. Needless to say, from now on the problem can no longer be represented in terms of the difference between *theoretische Ökonomie* and *ökonomische Theorie*, but rather in terms of what remains of the theoretical character of economic science as a whole. To invoke the predominance of Weber's *Sozialökonomie* is certainly meaningful, but it runs the risk of becoming an elegant escape from the *crucial problem*, although it is Schumpeter himself that legitimizes such an operation.

In the end, Schumpeter was captured by his own 'vision' of economic science,[156] probably more deeply than he would have cared to admit: equally to Marx or Keynes. Equal to them, this feature constitutes the essential tract of Schumpeter's 'inactuality' – in Nietzschean terms –, as well as his magnitude. 'The miracle of knowing what we cannot know' is certainly a difficult target to be

155   Swedberg, *J.A. Schumpeter*, p.180.
156   Cf. the interesting remarks by Y. Shionoya, 'The Science and Ideology of Schumpeter', *Rivista internazionale di scienze economiche e commerciali*, 1986, vol.33, 3.

achieved, because ideology is not a mere lie, but a substantial and 'truthful statement about what a man thinks he sees'. This said, if we were to conclude that, given this awareness, Schumpeter was a mere social scientist[157] rather than a 'great economist', this would be tantamount to turning his doctrine upside down, moving from a different 'vision' of economic science and from a radical incomprehension of the tormented relationship between the Economical and the Political: between what for him is logically demonstrable via hypothesis, languages, rational theories empirically underpinned, and what appeals not only to another rationality, another discursive order, but also to 'values' that should not be of interest for economic science. Nonetheless, it is true that the empirical foundations, necessary to underpin the analytical hypothesis, are irremediably historical – and, for this reason, influenced by 'values'. Certainly, it is this that requires the reaffirmation of the necessity of an analytical separation between the Economical and the Political; but, exactly for this reason, this also confirms that the problem is *here*, not elsewhere.

157　A similar paradox can be found in Elliott's interpretation ('Schumpeter's Theory of Economic development and Social Change'). But see also A.W. Dyer, 'Schumpeter as an Economic Radical: An Economic Sociology Assessed', *History of Political Economy*, 1988, vol.20, 1, 1988; H.E. Jensen, 'J.A. Schumpeter on Economic Sociology', *Eastern Economic Journal*, 1985, vol.11, 3.

Chapter IV
Synthesis
John M. Keynes: uncertainty and normation

1. Introduction

No one has been able to influence modern economic thought as much as Keynes has. Significantly, both *splendeurs et misères* of his *opus* have been advanced and negated.[1] As usually happens, the assumptions from which the interpreters moved often influenced their judgement.[2] It is sufficient here to mention the endless *querelle* concerning the so-called neoclassical synthesis.[3] At any rate, *after* Keynes, no one has been able to provide a convincing analysis of the capitalistic

---

1   P. Samuelson's opinion is paradigmatic. He argued that *The General Theory* 'is a badly written book', 'arrogant, bad-tempered, and polemical'. 'Flashes of insight and intuition intersperse tedious algebra. An awkward definition suddenly gives way to an unforgettable cadenza. When finally mastered, its analysis is found to be obvious and at the same time new. In short, it is a work of genius' ('Lord Keynes and the *General Theory*', *Econometrica*, 1946, vol.14, 3, pp.187–200, afterwards in R. Lekachman (ed. by), *Keynes' General Theory. Reports of Three Decades*, Macmillan, London, 1964, pp.318–19).
2   For example, at the end of 1960s, D. Winch, discussing 'the precise nature of Keynes' contribution', posed a series of questions such as: 'Did Keynes' contribution consist in the proof of "under-employment equilibrium", the abolition of Say's Law, or in the overthrow of the quantity theory of money?'. They were rhetoric questions, to which followed this statement: '[...] the most straightforward way of interpreting the *General Theory* is in terms of the policies to which it lends support [...]' (*Economics and Policy*, Walker & Company, New York, 1970, pp.170–1).
3   Besides R.W. Clower's famous, although not 'neutral', contribution ('The Keynesian Counter-revolution: a Theoretical Appraisal', *Schweizerische Zeitschrift für Volkswirtschaft und Statistik*, 1963, vol.79, March, pp.8–81), see W. Young, *Interpreting Mr. Keynes. The IS-LM Enigma*, Polity Press, Cambridge, 1987; T.D. Togati, *Keynes and the Neoclassical Synthesis: Einsteinian versus Newtonian Macroeconomics*, Routledge, London and New York, 1998.

economic system apart from his interpretation. The attempt to reopen a further general discussion on this matter does not fit the purpose of this final chapter. Our ambition is much more humble. It derives from a question that has been previously posed many times: what is – if it exists at all – the nexus between Keynes' early epistemological research and the social philosophy pervading his entire *opus*, and which finds its most vivid expression in chapter XXIV of *The General Theory* (henceforth *GT*)? Needless to say, this question has been posed mainly with regard to the evolution of Keynes' method. However, in the attempt to push our reflection to a deeper level, the same question should be also advanced with regard to what might be defined as Keynes' *normative intention*. With normative intention we are referring to a 'practical acting' that, although it is not reducible to ethics, is linked to possible 'political choices'[4] that are ethically connoted.[5] An 'acting' according to which the exigency of regulating the 'uncertainties' characterizing the economic cycle in the aftermath of the First World War would have been perceived not as a contingent but rather as a *strategic choice*. It is for this reason that, in term of political philosophy, Keynes' strategy would play a pivotal role in the epochal disenchantment that would culminate in the crisis of the liberal State-form.[6]

4   With the locution 'political choice', we refer to the action of *taking a decision*, not only in comparison with other possible choices, but also with the 'choice' not to take any decision.

5   On this matter, R. Skidelsky ('Keynes's Philosophy of Practice', in R.M. O'Donnell (ed. by), *Keynes as Philosopher-Economist*, Macmillan, London, 1991, p.118) wrote: 'His conception of economic statesmanship is much more solidly rooted in his theory of probability than in his theory of ethics'.

6   It is worth mentioning the attention that in the mid 1920s notable German scholars placed upon Keynes *politicus*. They referred to what he wrote in his 'Introduction' to H. Wright's book (*Die Bevölkerung*, Springer, Berlin, 1924; the 1923 first edition belonged to the series *Cambridge Economic Handbooks*): cf. M. Scheler, *Probleme einer Soziologie des Wissens, Gesammelte Werke*, hrsg. von M.S. Frings, Francke Verlag, Bern-München, 1960, Bd. 8, p.189. Obviously, the Keynes they were referring to was the pamphletist, well-known for his polemic position at the Versailles Conference. Keynes, 'einer der klarsten Beobachter und Beurteiler' – E. Troeltsch wrote – understood 'das die Weltwirtschaft nicht durch Machpolitik, sondern nur durch gegen gegenseitige

In the last three decades, a renewed interest in Keynes' *A Treatise on Probability* (henceforth *TP*) gave sway to a new field of research aimed at analysing the many connections between the epistemological model informing *TP* and the uncertainty characterizing *GT*.[7] Superficial agreements apart, the interpretative differences among the scholars are sometime noticeable.[8] Nevertheless, what in our opinion has been undervalued is a decisive question: namely, how is it possible to transpose a 'relative knowledge'[9] – and the consequent 'regional epistemological model' inherent in a delimitated *corpus of*

Verständigung und Solidarität aus schwersten Erschutterüngen und Lähmungen befreit werden kann' [*Spektator Briefe: Aufsätze über die deutsche Revolution und die Weltpolitik, 1918–1922*, F.C.B. Mohr (P. Siebeck), Tübingen, 1924, p.264. On this matter cf. R. Racinaro, 'Hans Kelsen e il dibattito su democrazia e parlamentarismo negli anni Venti-Trenta', in H. Kelsen, *Socialismo e stato*, De Donato, Bari, 1978]. All this indicated the centrality of the *normative issue* raised as a problem of *political government* after the end of the First World War.

7   This is a very different situation from the one described, at the end of the 1960s, by I. Hishiyama ('The Logic of Uncertainty according to J.M. Keynes', *Kyoto University Economic Review*, 1969, vol.39, 1, pp.22–44), who argued that not even in the most accredited interpreters of Keynes could we find a trace of the relationship between the *Treatise* and the *General Theory*. However, among various exceptions, I would like to mention the clear *incipit* by G.L.S. Shackle, 'Keynes and the Nature of Human Affairs', *Weltwirtischaftliches Archiv*, 1956, vol.87, 1, pp.93–107; now in *The Nature of Economic Thought. Selected Papers 1955–1964*, Cambridge University Press, London, 1966.

8   See M. Dardi, 'Interpretazioni di Keynes: logica del probabile, strutture dell'incerto', *Moneta e credito*, 1991, 173, pp.59–88 (but see also A. Carabelli's indirect reply, 'Uncertainty and Measurement in Keynes: Probability and Organicness', in S. Dow, J. Hillard (ed. by), *Keynes, Knowledge and Uncertainty*, Elgar, Aldershot, 1995, pp.137–60). Particularly relevant is the distinction between 'atomism' and 'methodological organicism' (see *infra*). More in general, cf. S. Dow, 'Keynes Epistemology and Economic Methodology', in O'Donnell (ed. by) *Keynes as Philosopher-Economist*, pp.144–67; T. Lawson, 'Uncertainty and Economic Analysis', *Economic Journal*, 1985, vol.95, December, pp.909–27; O.F. Hamouda, J.N. Smithin, 'Some Remarks on "Uncertainty and Economic Analysis"', *Economic Journal*, 1988, vol.98, March, pp.159–64.

9   With the adjective 'relative' we intend, etymologically, 'related-to' a delimited corpus of knowledge. The same meaning is attributed to the substantive 'relativity'. So, what is relative is not relativistic.

knowledge[10] – into a 'practical system' of regulation, a normative social philosophy?[11] The idea that this transposition mirrors the evolution of some ethical and esthetical values expressed, between continuities and differences, by philosophers, artists, and writers like Henry Sidgwick, George E. Moore, Duncant Grant and Virginia Woolf,[12] is the most obvious, even if it involves a risk. As Keynes'

10   As the definition might appear to be obscure, it might be worth specifying that with the adjective 'regional' (and the substantive 'regionality') we shall qualify a contextual epistemological model, inherent in a delimitating, 'regional', corpus of knowledge, which, in turn, circumscribes 'the various degrees of rational belief about a proposition', on the basis of what Keynes defines as 'our circumstances'; namely, on the basis of that contextual *corpus of knowledge* within which the distance between certainty and probability is expressed via argumentative propositions.

11   Regarding this, R. Skidelsky's comment is important (*John Maynard Keynes. II. The Economist as Saviour 1920–1937*, Macmillan, London, 1992, p.57): 'Substantial as it is, the *Treatise on Probability* is a mere fragment of a larger design for a philosophy of practice which Keynes sketched out half playfully in the summer of 1905. In some notes he called "Miscellanea Ethica", he had proposed a "complete ethical treatise" divided into the two divisions of "Speculative and Practical Ethics"'. As maintained by A. Fitzgibbons (*Keynes's Vision*, Clarendon, Oxford, 1988, p.62), 'Practical Ethics' indicated a mediation between Moore and Burke (J.M. Keynes, *The Political Doctrines of Edmund Burke*, 1904, UA/20/3; Id., *Miscellanea Ethica*, 1905, UA/21, The John Maynard Keynes Papers, King's College Library, Cambridge). For an overview see S. Marzetti Dall'Aste Brandolini, 'Bene morale e condotta giusta: la politica economica di John Maynard Keynes', in S. Marzetti Dall'Aste Brandolini, R. Scazzieri (ed. by), *La probabilità in Keynes: premesse e influenze*, Clueb, Bologna, 1999, pp.139–87; S. Helburn, 'Burke and Keynes', in B.W. Bateman, J.B. Davis (ed. by), *Keynes and Philosophy. Essays on the Origin of Keynes's Thought*, Elgar, Aldershot, 1991, pp.30–54; J.B. Davis, 'Keynes's Critiques of Moore: Philosophical Foundations of Keynes's Economics', *Cambridge Journal of Economics*, 1991, vol.15, 1, pp.61–77. For a different point of view, see R.M. O'Donnell, *Keynes: Philosophy, Economics and Politics*, Macmillan, London, 1989, pp.108–12.

12   On this regard, in 1938, Keynes wrote: 'Our apprehension of good was exactly the same as our apprehension of green, and we purported to handle it with the same logical and analytical technique which was appropriate to the latter. Indeed we combine a dogmatic treatment as to the nature of experience with a method of handling it which was extravagantly scholastic. Russell's *Principles of Mathematics* came out in the same year as *Principia Ethica*; and the former,

284

interests were political rather than esthetical,[13] it is quite difficult to see in him only a genial dandy *à la* Bloomsbury.[14] Keynes' thought reached peaks that overshadowed what in the Cambridge of the beginning of the century was 'genial' or more simply 'frivolous'.[15] In short, an investigation into this terrain would lead us to reckon that the usual historiographical coordinates are rather insufficient. And although the 'landing point' – the crisis of the liberal State-form in the aftermath of the First World War – is well-known, it still seems decisive to understand Keynes' normative thought.

In other words, what we shall suggest is an 'argumentative complication' of the link that, as *a fil rouge*, connects *TP* and *GT* on the basis of the relationship – more or less accentuated – between the *logic* informing *TP* and the *uncertainty* characterizing *GT*. However, in order to give a full account of this decisive link, it is necessary to

in spirit, furnished a method for handling the material provided by the latter' (*My Early Beliefs, CWK*, X, pp.438–9). Y. Shionoya ('Sidgwick, Moore and Keynes: A Philosophical Analysis of Keynes's "My Early Beliefs"', in Bateman, Davis (ed. by), *Keynes and Philosophy*, pp.6–29; on Sidgwick's position cf. also S. Collini, D. Winch, J. Burrow, *That Noble Science of Politics*, Cambridge University Press, Cambridge, 1983, pp.279–307) has noted that the perspective delineated in *My Early Belief, de facto*, entailed the problem of identifying what, in Keynes, represents the relationship between ethics and politics, and particularly, between ethical intuitionism and political consequentialism. It is a non-utilitarian consequentialism, that concerns 'the provision of rules'. Cf. J.B. Davis, *Keynes's philosophical Development*, Cambridge University Press, Cambridge, 1994.

13   Here, we are intentionally stretching the meaning of J. Robinson's thesis: 'What has become of the Keynesian Revolution?', in M. Keynes (ed. by), *Essays on John Maynard Keynes*, Cambridge University Press, Cambridge, 1975, p.128.

14   Cf. S.P. Rosenbaum (ed. by), *The Bloomsbury Group*, Croom Helm, London, 1975; D. Crabtree, A.P. Thirlwall (ed by), *Keynes and the Bloomsbury Group*, Macmillan, London, 1980; V.P. Mini, *Keynes, Bloomsbury and The General Theory*, Macmillan, London, 1991.

15   Cf. P. Allen, *The Cambridge Apostles. The Early Years*, Cambridge University Press, Cambridge, 1979; R. Deacon, *The Cambridge Apostles: a History of Cambridge University Press's élite intellectual Secret Society*, Royce, London, 1985; W.C. Lubenow, *The Cambridge Apostles, 1820–1914. Liberalism, Imagination, and Friendship in British Intellectual and Professional Life*, Cambridge University Press, Cambridge, 1998; Collini, Winch, Burrow, *That Noble Science of Politics*, pp.341–63.

comprehend in the first instance what underpins it and, perhaps, simplifies it: namely, the radical critique to *laissez-faire*. In fact, Keynes' philosophical approach, besides stigmatizing what in a pure market model does not work, questions both the *epistemological* and *normative* roots of a baseless *lex naturae* upon which an improbable economical and political *ordre naturel* ought to be based.

Keynes' reasoning rests upon an ethical and epistemological belief according to which, as the 'regionality' of the processes of knowledge concerning economics is socially determined, its 'natural foundation' is 'unthinkable'. Here, more than anywhere else, it is possible to grasp the framework in which uncertainty is included: namely, the interaction between the 'regionality' inherent to the modern epistemological functionalism and the unthinkable 'natural foundation' of any social order. In effect, together and specifically, they point out the uncertainty that distinguishes a 'monetary economy' from a 'neutral economy'. As a result, according to Keynes, what is needed is, firstly, a reduction of uncertainty via the identification of efficacy monetary instruments and, secondly, the determination of those political choices able to solve the problems that a monetary policy alone cannot solve.

Thus, the 'argumentative complication' that we shall propose derives from Keynes' very same approach. Here it is where the normative horizon, which is political,[16] imposes itself and where the relationship between 'function' and 'norm' – which characterizes an 'epistemic regionality' freed from the idea of a *Substanzbegriff*[17] –

16   E. Screpanti and S. Zamagni wrote: 'Non crediamo di esagerare se sosteniamo che questo [come dimostrare l'erroneità della *Treasury view*] fu uno dei temi principali del dibattito di politica economica da cui emerse la rivoluzione keynesiana' (*Profilo di storia del pensiero economico*, Nis, Roma, 1991, p.227). On the *Treasury view*, fundamental remains *Can Lloyd George do it?* (*CWK*, IX, pp.86–134), the message of which is well summarized by the following statement: 'To bring up the bogy of inflation as an objection to capital expenditure at the present time is like warning a patient who is wasting away from emaciation of the danger of excessive corpulence' (Ibid., p.118). On this issue, cf. P. Clarke, *The Keynesian Revolution in the Making, 1924–1936*, Clarendon, Oxford, 1988, pp.47 ff.; 142 ff.

17   Reference is made here to Cassirer's epistemological synthesis (E. Cassirer, *Substanzbegriff und Funktionsbegriff*, B. Cassirer Verlag, Berlin, 1910), where

manifests itself as a consequence of the impossible 'natural foundation' of any social order.[18] It is Keynes *politicus* the *trait d'union* between 'relative knowledge' and uncertainty.[19] He deals not only with the changing psychology of the 'animal spirits',[20] but also, and repeatedly, with the choices made – or omitted – by the main political

the overcoming of the concept of substance throught the logical-mathematical research that, starting from Frege and Russell, would give rise to the doctrine of functions, is delineated. Regarding the role exerted by Cassirer's functionalism (on which I myself stressed in my *Keynes: una provocazione metodologica*, Bertani, Verona 1985; but cf. A. Carabelli, *On Keynes's Method*, Macmillan, London, 1988, p.288, footnote 3), cf. A. Janik, S. Toulmin, *Wittgenstein's Vienna*, Weidenfeld and Nicolson, London, 1973.

18   As we pointed out in the previous chapter, in his maturity, also Schumpeter confronted himself with the problems posed by the impossible natural foundation of the political order, but advancing totally opposite conclusions. Equally important to recall is Kelsen's *Society and Nature: a Sociological Inquiry* (The University Press of Chicago Press, Chicago, 1943), in which the author argued against the legitimacy of an interpretation of society based upon a 'natural causality'. The epistemological intention is the same: the refusal of considering what pertains to social science via a causality inherent to natural sciences.

19   The expression 'politicus' used here is borrowed directly from G. Ferrari Bravo ('Politicus. J.M. Keynes nella prima guerra mondiale', in A. Agnati, A. Covi, G. Ferrari Bravo, *I due Keynes*, Cleup, Padova, 1983, pp.26–76), who underlined 'quel capitale fraintendimento dell'azione keynesiana entro il Tesoro', namely, 'la tenace rappresentazione di Keynes come un funzionario isolato nella sfera di ottimismo irrealistico e di ingenuità tipica dello scienziato, che ha preso largamente piede sia nella storiografia inglese sia in quella statunitense del periodo e costituisce l'antecedente logico del giudizio diffuso sul suo 'fallimento'. The author's statement, historically grounded, is this: 'Keynes è un funzionario del Tesoro. A differenza degli altri economisti che si affollano entro l'*Economic Section*, era un funzionario del Tesoro anche *prima* del dibattito teorico rovente degli anni Trenta e l'assunzione che sta alla base di questo studio è che, in senso lato, lo sia stato sempre' (*Keynes. Uno studio di diplomazia economica*, Cedam, Padova, 1990, pp.216 and 221). As R. Skidelsky wrote: 'Taking his life as a whole, Keynes was a successful, not a tragic hero – an Odysseus rather than an Achilles' (*John Maynard Keynes. III. Fighting for Britain 1937–1946*, Macmillan, London, 2000, p.XVI).

20   A. Dow, S. Dow, 'Animal Spirits and Rationality', in T. Lawson, H. Pesaran (ed. by), *Keynes' Economics. Methodological Issues*, Croom Helm, London and Sidney, 1985, pp.46–65; R. Marchionatti, 'On Keynes's animal spirits', *Kyklos*, 1999, vol.52, 3, pp.415–39.

and economical institutions. Certainly, these choices do not eliminate the problems relative to individual behaviour; more simply, they have to deal with a 'systemic' uncertainty[21] that requires a synthesis between the Economical and the Political.

2. Epistemic probability

When, in 1921, Keynes published *TP* he had already gained an international reputation, mainly due to his being a member of the British delegation at the Versailles Conference. His *The Economic Consequences of the Peace* was a worldwide success. Nevertheless, in spite of the achieved reputation, the publication of *TP* – to which Keynes dedicated almost fifteen years – did not received the due attention. Neglected for a long time, only recently has its theoretical relevance been fully acknowledged. As a result of the multiplying of significant interdisciplinary studies,[22] economic scientists have recognized in it the first formulation of the central idea that would later inform *GT*: namely, uncertainty.[23] This latter, indeed, is related to the 'regional

21 Carabelli, *On Keynes's Method*, p.213.
22 Cf. F. Vicarelli, 'Dall'equilibrio alla probabilità: una rilettura del metodo della teoria generale', in Id. (a cura di), *Attualità di Keynes*, Laterza, Roma-Bari, 1983; Lawson, Pesaran (ed. by), *Keynes' Economics. Methodological Issues*; Carabelli, *Keynes on Method*; O'Donnell, *Keynes: Philosophy, Economics and Politics*; Id. (ed. by), *Keynes as Philosopher-Economist*; R. Rossini Favretti (a cura di), *Il linguaggio della Teoria generale. Proposte di analisi*, Patron, Bologna, 1989; A. Marzola, F. Silva (a cura di), *John M. Keynes. Linguaggio e metodo*, Lubrina, Bergamo, 1990; Bateman, Davis (ed. by), *Keynes and Philosophy*; Davis, *Keynes's philosophical Development*; Dow, Hillard (ed. by), *Keynes, Knowledge and Uncertainty*; Marzetti Dall'Aste Brandolini, Scazzieri (a cura di), *La probabilità in Keynes*.
23 Cf. Robinson, 'What has become of the Keynesian Revolution?', p.125. Among many different perspectives, it is worth recalling first of all G.L.S. Shakle'works (on which cf. E.R. Weintraub, '"Uncertainty" and the Keynesian Revolution', *History of Political Economy*, 1975, vol.7, 4, pp.530–48; for a different point of view, see M. Stohs, '"Uncertainty" in Keynes' *General Theory*', *History of*

288

epistemological model' that was defined in *TP*. As we have already mentioned, with 'relative knowledge' we intend a knowledge strictly linked to a given analytical context, to which it is referred to and within which it is produced as a logical and linguistic model. Within this framework, the Keynesian concept of 'probable' gives rise to an epistemological model that underpins 'relative knowledge', of which the long-term expectations represent the extreme outcomes. In fact, these latter are based upon interpretative models that cannot provide an exhaustive representation of the object of knowledge, given the irreducible degree of uncertainty that can be qualified and understood only beyond the 'probable' neoclassical risk.[24]

Generally speaking, the critic always acknowledged Keynes' great cultural polyhedric: his active participation in the Bloomsbury circle represents a sort of historiographical *topos*.[25] However, it is not difficult to see that too frequently this *topos* has been handled super-ficially, as a fashionable operation. Keynes' polyhedric was often assumed as an aura surrounding a 'great' personality, rather than an element influencing his theoretical research.[26] In the last three decades, however, this approach has radically changed. There is no inter-preter that fails to mention that Keynes' Cambridge was the same where Russell and Wittgenstein played a crucial role. Not only the 'first', but also the 'second' Wittgenstein, for whom it was illegitimate

Political Economy, 1980, vol.12, 3, pp.372–82). See also J.A. Kregel, 'Economic Methodology in the Face of Uncertainty: The Modelling Methods of Keynes and the Post-Keynesians', *Economic Journal*, 1976, vol.86, 346, pp.209–25; J.A. Kregel, E. Nasica, J.A. Kregel, 'Alternative Analyses of Uncertainty and Ration-ality: Keynes and Modern Economics', in Marzetti Dall'Aste Brandolini e Scazzieri (a cura di), *La probabilità in Keynes*, pp.115–38; Lawson, 'Uncertainty and Economic Analysis'; Id., 'Probability and Uncertainty in Economic An-alysis', *Journal of Post-Keynesian Economics*, 1988, vol.11, Autumn, pp.38–63; G. Lunghini, G. Rampa, 'Conoscenza, equilibrio e incertezza endogena', *Econ-omia politica*, 1996, vol.13, 3, pp.435–75.

24   Cf. Kregel, 'Economic Methodology in the Face of Uncertainty: the Modelling Methods of Keynes and the Postkeynesian'.

25   On this regard, see R. Skidelsky, *John Maynard Keynes. I. Hopes Betrayed 1883–1920*, Viking Penguin, New York, 19862, pp.242 ff.

26   This assumption makes a sharp distinction between R. Skidelsky's interpre-tation and the more traditional ones.

to think that a univocal transcription of the logical relations between 'language' and 'world' were possible. Apropos, it is worth recalling the letter quoted in Harrod's account:[27]

J.M. Keynes to Duncan Grant: '12th November 1912: Wittgenstein is a most wonderful character – [...] – and extraordinarily nice. I like enormously to be with him.[28]

Although he underlined that Wittgenstein 'exerted a dominating influence over the younger generation of philosophers', it is true that Harrod leaves this matter suspended. He says nothing about Wittgenstein's possible influence upon the Keynesian *opus* that comes to life at the same time as Wittgenstein's rethinking, which was in turn stimulated – according to Georg H. von Wright[29] – also by the critiques provided by the young Piero Sraffa.[30] Anyhow, at present, it is well-accepted that the cognitive strategy defined by Keynes in economic thought is the same that characterized Wittgenstein's late works, in particular, *On Certainty*.[31]

Although the reasons lying beneath this complex friendship should not be emphasized, it would be erroneous to ignore the philosophical contexts in which Keynes' model of 'relative knowledge'

27   Cf. R.F. Harrod, *The Life of John Maynard Keynes*, Macmillan, London, 1951, p.161.
28   As Skidelsky noted (*John Maynard Keynes*, II, pp.290–1), for Keynes, the friendship of the 'Divine Fool' was not always easy to accept.
29   Cf. N. Malcolm, *Ludwig Wittgenstein*, Oxford University Press, Oxford, 1954.
30   Cf. P. Albani, 'Sraffa and Wittgenstein. Profile of an Intellectual Friendship', *History of Economic Ideas*, 1998, vol.6, 3, pp.151–73.
31   In these very same terms it is possible to interpret the distinction between 'ontology and the conditions of our knowledge', suggested by A. Carabelli, 'Keynes on Cause, Chance and Possibility', p.160. On the relationship between Keynes' thought and Wittgenstein, see J.B. Davis, *Keynes's philosophical Development*, pp.71–2; 117–19. A different opinion is that of R. Skidelsky (*John Maynard Keynes*, II, pp.67 ff.), according to whom 'Keynes's enterprise was a product of the pre-war Cambridge way of doing philosophy'. Although it is an historically correct interpretation, it remains difficult to accept it *in toto*, as we shall try to show. Cf. also M. Hesse, 'Keynes e il metodo dell'analogia', in R. Simili (a cura di), *L'epistemologia di Cambridge 1850–1950*, Il Mulino, Bologna, 1987, pp.197–220.

took shape.[32] From *TP* onwards, it would be represented as a model that configures the 'epistemological regionality' of *any* corpus of knowledge – which is, *ex definitione*, always contextual.[33] In short, Keynes' epistemic probability provides the basis not only for the long-term expectations theory that would characterize *GT*, but also, and even before, for his corrosive critique to the jusnaturalistic assumptions lying at the basis of *laissez-faire*.

In the opening of *TP* Keynes wrote:

> The terms *certain* and *probable* describe the various degrees of rational belief about a proposition [...]. All propositions are true or false, but the knowledge we have of them depends on our circumstances; and while it is often convenient to speak of propositions as certain or probable, this expresses strictly a relationship in which they stand to a *corpus* of knowledge, actual or hypothetical, and not a characteristic of the propositions in themselves.[34]

This is an *introitum* of a rare efficacy. A proposition is certain or probable, true or false, as it refers to a specific corpus of knowledge. As it assumes relevance only insofar as it is the enunciation of a determinate argument, it has a mere '*pro*-positive' character. It might be certain or probable, true or false, but it cannot establish a definitive truth. Hence, certain and probable are possible attributes of a proposition only insofar as this latter is related to a specific corpus of knowledge. In fact, '[a] proposition is capable at the same time of varying degrees of this relationship, depending upon the knowledge to which it is related, so that it is without significance to call a proposition probable unless we specify the knowledge to which we are relating it'.[35] In these terms, Keynes emphasizes the limit beyond which a proposition loses its meaning. If 'the knowledge to which it is related' is not specified, it becomes impossible to understand the sense of the proposition.

---

32   Cf. F. Varese, 'Keynes 'apostolo' della probabilità', in Rossini Favretti (a cura di), *Il linguaggio della Teoria generale*, pp.46–51.
33   M. Lombardi, 'Keynes ovvero dell'economia non-euclidea', *Studi Economici*, 1981, 15.
34   J.M. Keynes, *A Treatise on Probability*, Macmillan, London, 1921, *CWK*, VIII, pp.3–4; henceforth *TP*.
35   *TP*, *CWK*, VIII, p.4.

Thus, the theory of probability is connected with that part of knowledge 'which we obtain by argument'[36] – not only, but essentially by it –,[37] 'and it treats of the different degrees in which the results so obtained are conclusive or inconclusive'.[38] It follows that the argumentative propositions cannot assume any degree of conclusive logical exhaustivity.[39] In fact, it is due to this non-exhaustivity that we may define an analytical framework within which the inquiry is carried out. The logical 'productivity' of what is probable regards 'the degree of belief which it is *rational* to entertain in given conditions',[40] and the rationality of the inquiry rests upon the 'rational grounds for assertions which are not conclusively demonstrated'.[41] Evidently, where there is certainty it makes no sense to invoke a relationship of probability, as no degree of rationality has to be shown. It follows that only when there is no possibility to establish an exhaustive 'I know' in respect of the object of knowledge, is it meaningful to establish a relationship of probability with regard to an argumentative proposition.[42]

Therefore, as this is the 'given condition' of that part of knowledge 'which we obtain by argument' and that characterizes its 'epistemological regionality', it follows that there is not a unique model of knowledge, but a multiplicity of 'regional models', a multiplicity of analytical-relational models. If the proposition is 'ambiguous', this is due to the rational proliferation of models and knowledge: 'A *definition* of probability is not possible, unless it contents us to define degrees of the probability-relation by reference to degrees of rational belief'.[43] This impossibility expresses the cognitive value of what is probable, expressing, at the same time, the 'utility' of its being limited

---

36   Ibid., *CWK*, VIII, p.3.
37   Ibid., *CWK*, VIII, p.12.
38   Ibid., *CWK*, VIII, p.3.
39   Carabelli's distinction (*On Keynes' Method*, p.145) between 'a logic of the formal type' and 'an ordinary discourse logic' is sound.
40   *TP*, *CWK*, VIII, p.4.
41   Ibid., *CWK*, VIII, p.5.
42   Regarding this, we should mention Wittgenstein's critique to Moore, advanced in *On Certainty*.
43   *TP*, *CWK*, VIII, p.8.

knowledge. With his usual clarity, Wittgenstein – although critical of Keynes' 'technicality' – would say: '(The theory of probability is connected with the fact that the more general, i.e. the more incomplete, description is more likely to fit the facts than the more complete one)'.[44]

The limit of knowledge is established by the context to which the degree of probability is referred to. Not only the limit imposed by the 'relative knowledge', but also the method is contingent. In fact, what is probable, before being the result of knowledge *by* argumentative propositions, is knowledge *of* propositions. Obviously, this is possible 'as the result of contemplating the object of acquaintance', but it is essentially expressed 'by argument',[45] moving from a secondary to a primary proposition. Significantly, when Keynes is obliged to provide a definition of the objects with which we can become acquainted via direct propositions, he admits the difficulty of the task. Regarding this, he wrote: 'It is not easy to say'; 'It is not possible to give a clear answer'. Moreover, recalling Hume's lesson, he is obliged to consider the complication deriving from the acting of memory.[46] Also for this reason, he takes a 'logical' leap. From this moment onwards, in fact, the impossible exhaustivity of what is probable – that is, the outcome of the relationship between secondary and primary propositions – with regard to the certainty, becomes of fundamental importance.

However, Keynes' subdivision of knowledge into *certainty* and *probability* is only apparent. In fact, different degrees of certainty are expressed in terms of different degrees of probability, which do not allude to a definitive and final truth. It is worth noting that, according to Keynes, what is probable is essentially 'relative': 'Between two sets of propositions, therefore, there exists a relation, by virtue of which, if we know the first, we can attach to the latter some degree of rational belief. This relation is the subject-matter of the logic of probability'.[47]

---

44   L. Wittgenstein, *Philosophische Bemerkungen*, hrsg. von R. Rhees, Blackwell, Oxford, 1964, p.115; *Philosophical Remarks*, translated into English by R. Hargreaves and R. White, Blackwell, Oxford, 1975, p.115.
45   *TP, CWK*, VIII, p.12.
46   Ibid., *CWK*, VIII, p.15. See also Carabelli, *On Keynes's Method*, pp.64 ff.
47   *TP, CWK*, VIII, pp.6–7.

What cannot be grasped here, the degree of certainty necessary to reach the maximum probability, is simply what is not relative to the 'sets of proposition', to the contextual knowledge. At this point, once again, the limit concerning relative knowledge is explicit. As Mauro Lombardi wrote, Keynes' theoretical model, assuming the existence of a plurality of interacting decisional centres, cannot propose itself as a definition of a univocal concatenation of quantities conceptually represented.[48] In short, 'relative knowledge', as knowledge *of* and *by* argumentative prepositions, either accepts such a possible limit, or renounces any cognitive criterion.

We have seen the way in which Keynes characterizes the propositions as instruments of a *given* knowledge, delimitable between argumentative probability and certainty. Carrying on the inquiry, we have to deal with the fundamental relationship between the probable and the certain: this is the very same relationship that informs the method as 'principle of indifference'. Keynes describes this relationship as follows: 'The peculiarity of certainty is that knowledge of a secondary proposition involving certainty, together with knowledge of what stands in this secondary proposition in the position of evidence, leads to *knowledge of*, and not merely *about*, the corresponding primary proposition'.[49] Thus, there is certainty when the secondary proposition includes, besides what is explicitly in it, the certain intended as what leads to knowledge of the corresponding primary proposition. The situation is different when the secondary proposition includes a degree of probability lower than certainty. In this case, knowledge 'leads only to a *rational belief of the appropriate degree* in the primary proposition'.[50]

Hence, it is possible to demonstrate the strict link between inferential method and 'relative knowledge'. In this light, *TP* can indeed be seen as an epistemological *tractatus*,[51] which is devoted to

48   Lombardi, 'Keynes e l'economia non-euclidea', p.92.
49   *TP, CWK*, VIII, p.15.
50   Ibid., *CWK*, VIII, pp.15–16.
51   We believe that this is the sense in which I. Hacking refers to 'epistemic probability' (*The Emergence of Probability. A Philosophical Study of Early Ideas about Probability, Induction and Statistical Inference*, Cambridge University Press, Cambridge, 1975, p.73).

measure the gulf, in terms of probability, between maximum probability and the different degrees of certainty, between 'knowledge *of*' and 'knowledge *about*'. 'The knowledge present in this latter case I have called knowledge *about* the primary proposition or conclusion of the argument, as distinct from knowledge of it'[52] – Keynes wrote. That is, the relativity of the argumentative propositions expresses the essence of a 'relative knowledge', only probable, with regard to a 'certain knowledge'.[53] In Keynes' own terms: 'Of probability we can say no more than that it is a lower degree of rational belief than certainty; and we may say, if we like, that it deals with degrees of certainty. Or we may make probability the more fundamental of the two and regard certainty as a special case of probability, as being, in fact, the *maximum probability*'.[54]

The probable refers to the degrees of certainty – and this presupposes the relative 'value' of any acquired knowledge. This does not imply the impossibility of comparing the different kinds of acquired knowledge and their relative possibilities. To compare the different possibilities via their degrees of certainty, so as to establish an interaction between different kinds of knowledge – although with

---

52 *TP*, *CWK*, VIII, p.16.
53 What is here not under discussion – and here is relevant Dardi's 'Interpretazioni di Keynes', (p.74), regardless whether we agree or not with his general interpretation – is that it is the issue concerning the truth of a 'primary proposition' that is unsolvable and not the objective rationality of the argumentation. [It is relevant what has been written by B. De Finetti about Keynes' *Treatise* ('Cambridge Probability Theorists', *Manchester School of Economics and Social Studies*, 1985, vol.53, 4, pp.348–63): 'Primary would be those assertions which do not contain probability evaluations; secondary are those which contain them. For me an assertion containing probability evaluations is without sense if one is not given (at least implicitly) the subject. He who evaluates the probability']. In other words, for Keynes, the different kinds of 'regional knowledge' are not such because they are subjective; their numerical incomparability has nothing to do with their non-rationality. Nevertheless, this does not mean that it is possible to inscribe Keynes' theory within a rationalistic model *stricto sensu*. In fact, those who claim this are obliged to admit that in the *Treatise* we are confronted with 'some unspecified connection between logic and reality' (O'Donnell, *Keynes: Philosophy, Economics and Politics*, p.105).
54 *TP*, *CWK*, VIII, p.16.

no intention of achieving, cumulatively, an exhaustive knowledge – is both possible and necessary. But such a possibility cannot aim at transforming *quality* into *quantity*. The comparison involves 'calculation', the research of a higher degree of a numerically ascertainable certainty. Here, however, Keynes faces an obvious problem: because any 'relative knowledge' entails a proper and undeniable 'regional statute', the comparison might hide the assumption of identifying, via 'calculation', a superior degree of certainty, able to exclude any other degree. In other words, the 'measure' includes the concept of number.

If this were the case, however, the whole Keynesian 'discourse' would become a *contradictio in adjecto*. Keynes, in fact, excludes that the main characteristic of what is probable is the possibility of being numerically measurable:[55]

> By saying that not all probabilities are measurable, I mean that it is not possible to say of every pair of conclusions, about which we have some knowledge, that the degree of our rational belief in one bears any numerical relation to the degree of our rational belief in the other; and by saying that not all probabilities are comparable in respect of more and less, I mean that it is not always possible

---

55   Keynes proposed the same idea in *Ethics in Relation to Conduct* (1904), in *The John Maynard Keynes Papers*, UA/19/2/6. Regarding this, decisive is the objection advanced by F.P. Ramsey (*The Foundations of Mathematics and other Logical Essays*, ed. by R.B. Braithwaite, Routledge & Kegan, London, 1931, pp.160–1): 'When it is said that the degree of the probability relation is the same as the degree of belief which it justifies, it seems to be presupposed that both probability relations, on the one hand, and degrees of belief on the other can be naturally expressed in terms of numbers, and then that the number expressing or measuring the probability relation is the same as that expressing the appropriate degree of belief. But if, as Mr. Keynes holds, these things are not always expressible by numbers, then we cannot give his statement that the degree of the one is the same as the degree of the other such a simple interpretation, but must suppose him to mean only that there is a one-one correspondence between probability relations and the degrees of belief which they justify. This correspondence must clearly preserve the relations of greater and less, and so make the manifold of probability relations and that of degrees of belief similar in Mr Russell's sense. I think it is a pity that Mr Keynes did not see this clearly, because the exactitude of this correspondence would have provided quite as worthy material scepticism as did the numerical measurement of probability relations'.

to say that the degree of our rational belief in one conclusion is either equal to, greater than, or less than the degree of our belief in another.[56]

If the relations between variables that are not algebraically deducible do not exclude the possibility of a comparison, then they affirm that such a comparison can be numerical only in a very small number of cases.[57] Thus, we may say that the 'limit' of a system of relational knowledge (whose articulation is given by the difference between 'knowledge *of*' and 'knowledge *about*' as a result of the method by argument) lies in the impossibility of a numerical comparison between different relations of probability.[58] This represents at the same time the limit and the strength of Keynes' system. In fact, the principle of indifference as the unique 'comparative paradigm' adequate to a 'regional' cognitive strategy, annulling the distance between the adequacy of the method and the *value* of the 'relative knowledge', makes explicit the 'regionality' of this latter, apart from any cumulative hypothesis.

3. Indifference and normation

The relevance of this operation is evident. Avoiding any unessential methodological dispute, it aims to unify 'method' and 'knowledge'. Although in the early 1920s it was undoubtedly difficult to attribute a 'technical' value to the mere revisiting of the principle of indifference, however, it might be said that this was a marginal problem. Keynes' innovative contribution should be rethought beyond the probabilistic 'technique[59] – if it is true, at least, that, regardless the many ideal

---

56 *TP*, *CWK*, VIII, p.37.
57 Ibid., *CWK*, VIII, pp.39–40.
58 On this point, B. Russell (*The Mathematical Gazette*, 1922, July, pp.119–25) concentrated his critique.
59 In 'Keynes and the Nature of Human Affairs', Shackle wrote: '*Probability* was a bad title for the earlier book, since it suggested the essentially arithmetical procedures by which knowledge and certainty can be attained in such matter as

debts, he moved away exactly from the Russellian analytical tradition.[60] When, among the many pages written by Russell, we read that 'what matters in mathematics, [...], is not the intrinsic nature of our terms, but the logical nature of their interrelations' – because 'the only thing of importance about a relation is the cases in which it holds, not its intrinsic nature'[61] – it is easy to understand how much Keynes owed to this philosopher who, in 1921, had already published fundamental works. Nonetheless, denying any privileged heuristic character to the logical-mathematical relation, Keynes determined a fracture that Russell pointed out when he reviewed *TP*.

In the same way Keynes paid off his debt to Laplace. Once we understand that the 'logical relation'[62] for Keynes represents the disenchantment of science towards the equal possibility of *all* languages – where the logical-mathematical, and even more the economic one, is *only one* among others, and *not the sole* exact language –, the intrinsic classicism of the principle of indifference becomes absolutely irrelevant. If the process of knowledge suffers from indeterminacy, if certainty is that maximum probability towards which we have to aspire without metaphysical conviction, and if the method is merely a contextual expression of different probabilities, it follows that the '*calcolemus*' loses its privileged role. In fact, the

insurance. Instead, that book is concerned with the bases, the meaning and the proper scope of *judgement* in human affairs [...]'. And Carabelli (*On Keynes's Method*, p.10) wrote: 'Though far from being a mere 'internal' exercise in the theory of probability, the core of his work was primarily philosophical and gnoseological'.

60   Cf. Carabelli, *On Keynes's Method*, pp.134 ff.
61   B. Russell, *Introduction to the Mathematical Philosophy*, Allen & Unwin, London, 1975[14], pp.59–60.
62   Logico-subjective theory, would lately say K. Popper, *The Logic of Scientific Discovery*, Hutchinson, London, 1968, p.149. As Hacking (*The Emergence of Probability*, p.147) noted, although Keynes' theory was grounded 'on a measure of objectivity', often it has been defined by its critics as 'subjective'. Also I. Scardovi spoke of an inclination towards subjectivism, 'Keynes e la probabilità: una sintassi dell'uncertainty', in Marzetti Dall'Aste Brandolini, Scazzieri (a cura di), *La probabilità in Keynes*, pp.27. Cf. V. Fano, 'Keynes, Carnap e l'intuizione induttiva', in Marzetti Dall'Aste Brandolini e Scazzieri (a cura di), *La probabilità in Keynes*, pp.73–89.

'logical plays,' besides being all possible, are also all equally rational. Indifference, therefore, lies in this *rational indeterminacy*, rather than in a logical equiprobability – and Wittgenstein ceases to be a 'shadow':

> If, however, one wanted to give something like a rule here [*etwas Regelartiges*], then it would contain the expression 'in normal circumstances' [*unter normalen Umständen*]. And we recognize normal circumstances but cannot precisely describe them. Almost, we can describe a range of abnormal cases.[63]

Keynes' definition of the principle of indifference, although more than classic, induces *consequences* that allude to a similar radical doubt:

> The principle of indifference asserts that if there is no *known* reason for predicating of our subject one rather than another of several alternatives, then relatively to such knowledge the assertions of each of these alternatives have an *equal* probability. Thus *equal* probabilities must be assigned to each of several arguments, if there is an absence of positive ground for assigning *unequal* ones.[64]

Even if he is aware of the paradoxes that the assumed categorical function of indifference might generate,[65] such awareness does not diminish the belief that, although the possible outcomes might be paradoxical, they are nonetheless *fruitful*. Better still, even if the contradictory articulation is not hidden, Keynes believes that valid modifications of the 'principle' can be attained anyhow. On these grounds, it is possible to claim that the principle of indifference is simply an efficacious hypothesis.

This hypothesis is supported by the fact that where – according to Keynes' terminology – the relation $a/h = \frac{1}{2}$ is not satisfied, the inapplicability of the principle, not invalidating the principle in itself, delimitates only the case in which it is not valid, in conformity with the 'regional epistemological model', upon which only 'relative

---

63 L. Wittgenstein, *Über Gewissheit – On Certainty*, hrsg. von G.E.M. Anscombe und G.H. von Wright, Blackwell, Oxford, 2003, p.6.
64 *TP*, *CWK*, VIII, p.45.
65 Cf. ibid.

knowledge' can be based. The efficacy of the principle stems from the relativity of a logical system of probability, whose object 'is to enable us to know the relations' that cannot be clearly perceived, via other relations 'which we can recognise more distinctly', so as to convert 'vague knowledge into more distinct knowledge'.[66] Thus, the principle of indifference is not a *clavis universalis*. Rather, it represents the *cesuram* between different probabilities. It is a 'comparative model', exactly because – to borrow Wittgenstein terminology – 'we recognize normal circumstances, but cannot precisely describe them'.

Now, among the variety of relations of probability that can be compared, two are essential. The first, 'in which the evidence is the same and the conclusions different', the second, 'in which the evidence is different but the conclusion the same':[67]

> In symbolic language we may wish to compare x/h with y/h, or x/h with x/h_1h. We may call the first type judgements of *preference*, or, when there is equality between x/h and y/h, of *indifference*; and the second type we may call judgements of *relevance*, or, when there is equality between x/h and x/h_1h, of *irrelevance*. In the first we consider whether or not x is to be preferred to y on evidence h; in the second we consider whether the addition of h_1 to evidence h is relevant to x.[68]

Whilst in the former case 'we consider whether or not x is to be preferred to y on the evidence of h; in the second we consider whether the addition of h_1 to evidence h is relevant to x'[69] – something that can occur only if $x/h \neq x/h_1h$, because if $x/h = x/h_1h$, h_1 is obviously irrelevant. Thus, as it is impossible to provide the definition of the principle of indifference without simultaneously providing a definition of the judgement of irrelevance, which is a judgement of comparison, the principle of indifference rests upon a comparison. 'We must first determine what parts of our evidence are relevant on the whole by a series of judgments of relevance [...] – Keynes wrote. If this relevant evidence is *of the same form* for both alternatives, then the principle

---

66   Ibid., *CWK*, VIII, p.57.
67   Ibid., *CWK*, VIII, p.58.
68   Ibid.
69   Ibid.

authorises a judgement of indifference'.[70] As we shall see later, the relationship between *evidence* and *probability* represents a seminal passage, as it underpins the concept of 'weight of arguments', to which the long-term economic expectations are referred to.[71]

Therefore, the relation of indifference can be expressed through what is relevant, because it is *different*. With no paradox, the 'epistemic relativity' follows the 'epistemological rigidity' attached to the principle of indifference, which establishes the 'logical' impossibility to compare probabilities of a different nature. 'In short, the principle of indifference is not applicable to a pair of alternatives, if we know that either of them is capable of being further split up into a pair of possible but incompatible alternatives of the same form as the original pair'.[72] However, such impossibility allows us to see how the rigidity of the probabilistic model does not characterize an 'exhaustive', but rather a 'relative' knowledge. The impossibility cannot exclude exactly what is 'utterable' via other methods or languages.

To borrow the well-known Baconian formulation, one could say that the comparison as *advancement of learning* is valid only in particular realms. Through it, the meaning of *calcolemus*, the 'number' as privileged language and expression of the rigidity of a knowledge according to which everything should be 'logically' aimed at to a certain and 'cumulative process', shows its limits. Thus, with

---

70   Ibid., *CWK*, VIII, p.60.
71   'As the relevant evidence at our disposal increases, the magnitude of the probability of the argument may either decrease or increase, according as the new knowledge strengthens the unfavourable or the favourable evidence; but *something* seems to have increased in either case –, we have more substantial basis upon which to rest our conclusion. I express this by saying that an accession of new evidence increases the *weight* of an argument. New evidence will sometimes decrease the probability of an argument, but it will always increase its "weight".' (*TP*, *CWK*, VIII, p.77). Cf. J. Runde, 'Keynesian Uncertainty and the Weight of Argument', *Economic and Philosophy*, 1990, vol.6, 2, pp.275–92; A. Vercelli, 'Peso dell'argomento e decisioni economiche', in Marzetti Dall'Aste Brandolini e Scazzieri (a cura di), *La probabilità in Keynes*, pp.91–113; L. Jonathan Cohen, 'Dodici domande sul concetto di peso in Keynes', in Simili (a cura di), *L'epistemologie di Cambridge 1850–1950*, pp.221–44.
72   *TP*, *CWK*, VIII, p.66.

the introduction of *his* version of the principle of indifference, Keynes operates a deep sectioning of rationality. He says: 'Logical priority has no absolute signification, but is relative to a specific body of knowledge [...]'.[73] In this regard, it is relevant to observe the presence of a odd note in chapter XXI of *TP*, where, defining as valid the principle of uniformity 'when applied to events only differing in their positions in time or space',[74] Keynes adds the following question: 'Is this interpretation of the principle of the uniformity of nature affected by the doctrine of relativity?'.[75] Although such a question is obviously rhetorical, it synthesizes the different aspects of the 'regional episte-mological model', to which, in economic terms, a normative model would coherently follow.

Certainly – to say nothing about the role played by Sraffa, who would trigger Wittgenstein's interest in common language –, the temptation to interpret *TP* on the basis of Keynes' subsequent ac-knowledgement of Frank Ramsay's critique should not be under-valued.[76] As Alessandro Vercelli noted, if it is true that in this acknowledgement a clear demarcation point between rational choice (based upon 'objective' criteria) and irrational choice (based upon 'subjective' criteria) disappears, it is also true that, for this reason, Keynes would be stimulated to reflect upon the demarcation zone between the rational and the irrational, that is, upon the grey zone characterized by the interaction between subjective beliefs (ex-pectations) and inter-subjective beliefs (conventions).[77] At any rate,

73   Ibid., *CWK*, VIII, p.127.
74   Ibid., *CWK*, VIII, p.276.
75   Ibid.
76   Ramsey reviewed *A Treatise on Probability* in *The Cambridge Magazine*, 1922, January, pp.3–5. Later Keynes would observe: '[…] So far I yield to Ramsey – I think he is right' (*CWK*, X, 338–339). Cf. R.B. Braithwaite, 'Keynes as a Philosopher', in M. Keynes (ed. by), *Essays on John Maynard Keynes*, pp.241–2. But see *supra*, footnote 55.
77   Vercelli, 'Peso dell'argomento e decisioni economiche', p.107. The author, criticizing M. Dardi's position, maintains that the evolution of Keynes' thought 'non intacca le linee essenziali della sua teoria della probabilità'. Rather unconvincing are the arguments proposed by R.M. O'Donnell, 'Continuity in Keynes's Conception of Probability', in D.E. Moggridge (ed. by), *Perspectives on the History of Economic Thought*, Elgar, Aldershot, 1988, vol.4, p.64; Id.,

we believe that the argumentative continuity is guaranteed not by the fact that the probability is based upon comparative judgements, but by the further limits that the *comparative possibilities* should always take into consideration. Hence, although Keynes' acknowledgement of Frank Ramsay's critique is relevant and fundamental, it does not question the decisive epistemological aspect: that is, the 'regionality' of any 'relative knowledge' is reasserted, as the probable 'is that which it is rational for us to believe'.[78] The non-exhaustivity generates uncertainty, apart from the chosen logic.[79]

It is not difficult to see that the epistemological conclusions to which the analysis of the foundations of *TP* lead are to be found within the Cambridgean landscape. However, the conclusions reached by *this* Keynes go far beyond such a landscape. They cannot be understood merely referring to Russell and Wittgenstein, as they should be framed within the wider epistemological debate occurring in Europe during the 1920s.[80] Widening the Cambridgean hendiadys of 'logical' and 'ethical', Keynes widened the English tradition. Differing from both Russell – who researched the mathematical perfectibility of the 'logic' – and Wittgenstein – who would radicalize the impossible transcription of the unspeakable – Keynes, similarly to

Keynes: Philosophy, Economics and Politics, pp.141–8. O'Donnell's thesis is criticized by B.W. Bateman, 'The Elusive Logical Relation: An Essay on Change and Continuity in Keynes's Thought', in Moggridge (ed. by), *Perspectives on the History of Economic Thought*, vol.4, pp.73 ff.

78   *TP*, *CWK*, VIII, p.339.
79   In these terms, the critique to the 'logicistic interpretation' (Carabelli, 'Keynes on Cause, Chance and Possibility', p.166) becomes stronger and, at the same time, less exposed to the accusation deriving from the fact that it privileges 'an ordinary discourse logic'. Cf. Vercelli ('Peso dell'argomento e decisioni economiche', p.100): 'Concludo osservando che la distinzione tra "probabilità" e "uncertainty" non può dunque essere interpretata come dicotomia tra due modalità dell'uncertainty di prim'ordine, bensì come distinzione tra due ordini gerarchici di misura dell'uncertainty; la *probabilità* si riferisce alla misura dell'uncertainty di prim'ordine, mentre l'*uncertainty* in senso stretto si riferisce a quella di second'ordine misurata dal peso dell'argomento'.
80   Cf. Scardovi, 'Keynes e la probabilità: una sintassi dell'uncertainty', pp.25–32.

Kelsen the interpreter of Vaihinger and Cassirer,[81] would solve 'relative knowledge' in normation. If, in order to exclude from the juridical field any 'natural foundation' of the *Grundnorm*, Kelsen had recurred to functional epistemology, in order to exclude from the economic field any alleged 'natural foundation' of the economic equilibrium, Keynes would recur to 'relative knowledge'. In any case, what is 'natural' gives rise to a logically 'impossible function'. The consequent absence of exhaustive, ethical, and epistemic assumptions explains why the probable 'is that which it is rational for us to believe'. Certainly, 'it is not rational for us to believe that the probable is true; it is only rational to have a probable belief in it'. Anyhow, it is from here that 'the hypothesis on which it is rational for us to act' follows.[82]

The epistemological explication of the *Funktionsbegriff* unifies theoretical 'efforts' and 'disciplines', rendering *a posteriori* licit the institution of what historiographically might appear merely eclectic: for example, the comparison between Kelsen and Keynes.[83] Anyway, their respective contributions to the definition of the scene of 'progressive European thought' are well-known. Thus, it is easy to guess the degree of affinity that can be inferred from a synoptical comparison between their respective epistemological models and from the consequent foundation of a 'normative acting'. Both in Kelsen and Keynes, a stimulating paradox is delineated: an overlapping between the relative epistemological model and normation, between functional and normative knowledge. In both authors, the missed legitimation of the idea of equilibrium as 'natural' model requires a normation: formal, in one case, practical in the other. The normative dimension is clear and unescapable: it is the basis for a modern ruled democracy. This explains why Hayek would criticize both Kelsen's juridical positivism and Keynes' economic doctrine. [84] In the realm of social

81 The first edition of *Hauptprobleme der Staatsrechtslehre* is dated 1911. Cf. M.G. Losano, *Forma e realtà in Kelsen*, Comunità, Milano, 1981.
82 *TP, CWK*, VIII, p.339.
83 See Zanini, *Keynes: una provocazione metodologica*.
84 Cf. F.A. von Hayek, *Law, Legislation and Liberty*, University of Chicago Press, Chicago 1982.

science, in other words, the relative knowledge, intended as a projection of a 'regional epistemology', can only manifest itself as logical comprehension and practical normation.

From this interlacing emerges, between the end of the nineteenth and the beginning of the twentieth century, the trasversality of European 'models of thought'. Less obvious, instead, at least historiographically speaking, is the contribution of Keynes' economic doctrine to these 'models'. Even if there is no doubt that Keynes' approach is paradigmatically normative and regulative, it is however correct to wonder in which sense it is so. Is this due to contingent reasons, or does it embody an instance that, in different terms and autonomously, it can be found in other contemporary theoretical answers to the European crisis of the 1920s and 1930s? This is the sense of the comparison between Keynes and Kelsen, as exactly in Keynes' idea of the State it becomes fully mature what 'was invoked by those theoreticians of normativism whose analysis focused upon the relationship between validity and efficacy and that, similarly to Kelsen, had transformed the *Stufenbau* into a circular structure of legitimation'.[85]

This circularity would have challenged the very foundations of the whole neoclassical and liberal political system. At the basis of Keynes' reasoning there were two objectives to be reached: the demolition of the neoclassical method,[86] and the confutation of what in it was a naturalistic residual, that is, the 'system of needs' both in the acceptation of the contractualistic *ordre naturel*, and in that which informed the old neoclassical liberalism. But how could these objectives be reached? Essentially, moving from the delimitation of the field of action of the concepts of 'equilibrium' and 'nature'. This is the seminal point. Keynes, at least starting from *The End of Laissez-faire*, would determine the baselessness of the tendential equilibrium

85   A. Negri, 'Keynes e la teoria dello stato nel '29', in R. Faucci (a cura di), *John Maynard Keynes nel pensiero e nella politica economica*, Feltrinelli, Milano, 1977, pp.49–50.
86   Regarding this, see A. Carabelli, 'La metodologia della critica della teoria economica classica', in Marzola, Silva (a cura di), *John M. Keynes. Linguaggio e metodo*, pp.141–84.

of the neoclassical functional relations, making it possible to overturn the previous political and economic theories. He would show that only by setting aside the concept of equilibrium could the economic theory be qualified as an open model, based upon a 'relative knowledge', necessarily underpinned by normative instruments, so as to cope with the uncertainty inherent to it.

This is not an aporetical outcome. The aim to be reached is not 'practical' because it is empirical; rather, it is 'practical' as it is finalized to a normative action theoretically conscious and grounded, formulated on the basis of the changing relationship among individual and collective economic subjects. Here we find the many 'psychological laws' in their interlacing with long-term expectations. In this articulation, the method underpinning a system whose equilibrium would be automatically determined – as the behaviour of the subjects would be the explication of expectations concerning 'natural' needs – should be reasonably set aside. As it has been noted, in Keynes it is possible to identify the last representative of the great cultural tradition initiated by Weber and Kelsen.[87] The contraposition to the identification of *ordre naturel* and norm – sustained, for example, by Mach, Pearson, Weber and Kelsen – is complementary to the one offered by Keynes in respect of the neoclassicals (Hayek in particular), against which his refusal of a mechanical adjustment of investment to full-employment saving is underpinned by the refusal to consider the investments as variable rather than a function.[88] This, in conjunction with the experience of the 'great crisis', induced Keynes to think in a deeper way upon the objective and subjective conditions that made it possible to realize, as norm, the decisions about investment in the capitalistic system.[89]

This latter observation allows us to open an important parenthesis to explain why in Keynes the term 'norm' does not hold the usual meaning – from which the adjective 'normal' – and how, instead, it assumes a meaning strictly connected to what necessitates 'normation'. So conceived, it becomes possible to make explicit the

87 Negri, 'Keynes e la teoria dello stato nel '29', p.42.
88 F. Vicarelli, *Keynes. L'instabilità del capitalismo*, Etas, Milano, 1977, p.169.
89 Ibid. p.140.

way in which the normative method overcomes the neoclassical theoretical context. Norm, for Keynes, is not a substantive from which the adjective 'normal' derives, but rather it is the instrument upon which 'it is rational for us to act' – from which it derives the 'government' of what is *not* normal. The linguistic difference expresses a different epistemological context; in this case, it expresses the overcoming of the neoclassical relationship between 'event' and 'law', 'economic datum' and 'scientific abstraction'. It is Marshall, in the 'Preliminary Survey' of his *Principles*, who places the emphasis upon this issue, defining what can be said to be economic law (or norm). Reckoning as perfect the equivalence between 'law' and 'norm' – to the point of considering useful the substitution of the former with the latter[90] – he defines economic law as 'the course of action which may be expected *under certain conditions* from the members of an industrial group'; a course of action that is 'the *normal* action of the members of that group relatively to those conditions'.[91] If 'economic law' is synonymous with 'economic norm', and if 'normal action' is synonymous with 'economic law', it follows that 'normal action' and 'economic norm' overlap. It should be said that to Marshall the 'relativity' of what is normal was perfectly clear. [92] 'In all these cases – he says – normal results are those which may be expected as the outcome of those tendencies which the context suggests; or, in other words, which are in accordance with those "statements of tendency", those Laws or Norms, which are appropriate to the context'.[93] In this

90   'Corresponding to the substantive "law" is the adjective "legal". But this term is used only in connection with "law" in the sense of an ordinance of government; not in connection with "law" the sense of a statement of relation between cause and effect. The adjective used for this purpose is derived from "norm", a term which is nearly equivalent to "law", and might perhaps with advantage be substituted for it in scientific discussions.' (A. Marshall, *Principles of Economics*, Macmillan, London, 1959, p.28).
91   Ibid.
92   Ibid., pp.27–30.
93   Ibid., p.30. Significantly, M. Dardi (*Il giovane Marshall: accumulazione e mercato*, Il Mulino, Bologna, 1984, p.222 and p.228) wrote: '(...) il campo di applicazione del concetto di normale finisce praticamente per coincidere con quello di equilibrio (...)'; but he further added: 'La normalità dell'equilibrio è

context, however, the 'relativity' can always be resolved as average in the 'measurability' of the tendencies of human actions, that occur along the temporal axis represented by the 'long-term'. 'The raison d'être of economics as a separate science is that it deals chiefly with that part of man's action which is most under the control of measurable motives [...]'.[94] In this sense, Marshall's theory should be intended as temporal commensuration of the verifiability and measurability of economic phenomena. 'These considerations point to the great importance of the element of time'[95] – Marshall says –, as '[t]he actual value at any time, [...] the market value as it is often called, is often more influenced by passing events and by causes whose action is fitful and short lived, than by those which work persistently. But in long-terms – he carries on –, these fitful and irregular causes in large measure efface one another's influence; so that in the long run persistent causes dominate value completely'.[96]

This is one of the key assumptions of the neoclassical universe, of which – although with a lot of doubts,[97] Keynes would notice[98] – Marshall was one of the main architects.[99] In this universe, normation consists of the solution of what is temporary (short-period prices) in 'persistent causes' (long-period prices). In other words, what for Marshall is 'relative', is thought of as a function of the possible stability, as a 'normal' condition – according to a 'norm': 'law'. Only

la garanzia che concorrenza e consuetudine funzionano in pieno accordo, ovvero che il mercato e le altre istituzioni sono fra loro ben bilanciati'.

94   Marshall, *Principles*, p.32. On the concept of 'separate science' cf. Winch's essay, in Collini, Winch, Burrow, *That Noble Science of Politics*, pp.311–37.

95   Marshall, *Principles*, p.289.

96   Ibid., p.291. J. Robinson would observe: 'Long-run equilibrium is a slippery eel' (*Economic Philosophy*, Watts, London, 1962, p.81).

97   On the complexity of Marshall's doctrine see D. Winch's already quoted essay, and the more recent P. Groenewegen, *Soaring Eagle: Alfred Marshall 1842–1924*, Elgar, Aldershot, 1995; T. Raffaelli, *Marshall's Evolutionary Economics*, Routledge, London, 2003.

98   J.M. Keynes, *The General Theory of Employment, Interest and Money*, Macmillan, London, 1936, henceforth *GT*, *CWK*, VII, p.19.

99   'Marshall had a foxy way of saving his conscience by mentioning exceptions, but doing so in such a way that his pupils would continue to believe in the rule' (Robinson, 'What has become of the Keynesian Revolution?', p.124).

what is tendentially stabile, in fact, is hypothetically subjected to a 'measure'. The 'parallel axiom' informing the neoclassical theory derives from here.

Now, that such an axiom seems to Keynes inevitably partial is well-known. In his eyes, this is so as the methodological neoclassical approach transforms what is relative as a function of equilibrium. On the contrary, what is relative for Keynes is so exactly because it renders highly problematic the very same ideas of stability and equilibrium. The variation of what is relative is not 'linear-temporal'; it represents the simultaneous movement of different contexts in the same temporal instant. Thus, the meaning of the variation triggered in this universe cannot be traced back to stability, but rather to its opposite, to the instability of infra-systemic relations. The variation is not 'relative' in comparison with a tendentially absolute Marshallian temporal flow; rather, there are multiple variations of economic aggregates, as a result of the simultaneous mutation of systemic variables.[100]

In this sense, the base-axiom of the neoclassical equilibrium – pivotal to his method – is nullified in its essence. Obviously, 'the conclusion that the *costs* of output are always covered in the aggregate by the sale-proceeds resulting from demand, has great plausibility' – Keynes wrote. In the same way, he argued that 'it is indubitable that the sum of the net increments of the wealth of individuals must be exactly equal to the aggregate net increment of the wealth of the community'. It is plausible, but *only if* 'there is a nexus which unites decisions to abstain from present consumption with decision to provide for future consumption; whereas the motives which determine the latter are not linked in any simple way with the motives which determine the former'.[101] In short, although relevant, the Marshallian 'statements of tendency' is insufficient, as the tendential identity

100 P. Barotta, T. Raffaelli (*Epistemologia ed economia*, Utet, Torino, 1988, p.162) wrote: 'Il tempo cessa di essere il *continuum* marshalliano di derivazione kantiana e diventa successione discontinua di eventi nella quale l'opera di riforma, l'azione consapevole, non può che limitarsi al contingente, sempre che riesca a sottrarlo alle incertezze che si profilano all'orizzonte e che incalzano fino a indurre all'inazione e alla paralisi'.
101 *GT, CWK*, VII, pp.20–1.

between acquired and spent income is untenable. In order to be so, in fact, this identity necessitates the absolutization of what is merely possible. In a sense, the neoclassical method mirrors the 'limits' of the Newtonian universe, whose axioms cannot but investigative what is relative to an 'economic space' modelled according a temporal *continuum*.

In the attempt to reform this 'universe', Keynes detached himself from the neoclassical 'mechanics'. From this point of view, the tendential identity between acquired and spent income is the *topos* against which *GT* would address its critique. Absolutely consequent, therefore, is the distance initially posed between Marshall's understanding of 'normal' and Keynes' understanding of 'normative'. Evidently, both adjectives derive from the same term, but whilst for the former the norm represents the accomplishment of what is temporarily relative, for the latter, it indicates the necessity to keep *within* the critical threshold what inevitably pushes itself always beyond any equilibrium. The difference is crystalline. *TP* is not a 'probabilistic' episode, but rather the epistemological substrate underpinning modern macroeconomic knowledge.

4. An improbable '*ordre naturel*'

Certainly, the distance between Keynes and Marshall is appreciable *a posteriori*, after the publication of *GT*. However, already in 1924, in his obituary for the *magister*, sketching his respectful but irreversible confutation of Marshall's theory, Keynes highlighted some of the most salient traits of that distance. As is well-known, the obituary was published immediately after *A Tract on Monetary Reform* (henceforth *MR*) that, in turn, was followed by another two short but seminal essays: *The Economic Consequences of Mr. Churchill* and *The End of Laissez-faire*. Thought out within the post-war context, the obituary singled out the motivations that would have led Keynes to confute the neoclassical 'philosophy', of which Marshall was considered the key

310

figure of the Cambridge tradition – no matter how problematic and refined his position was.[102] In short, although the eulogy represented a clear acknowledgement of the *magister*'s theoretical greatness,[103] some doubts began to emerge.[104]

In Keynes' eyes, the assumptions informing the neoclassical theory could not explain the post-war events which characterized the world economic system. In his opinion, the breakdown of the market automatisms represented the most relevant result stemming from the monetary storm that ensued post-war reconstruction. Thus, the analysis of inflation and distribution induced Keynes to consider the effects of the changes in the general level of prices with respect to the role played by economic actors within the system of accumulation and re-distribution of wealth. Certainly, the theoretical fracture had not yet reached a fully mature formulation. Nonetheless, Keynes already refused the central assumption underpinning the neoclassical model: namely, the assumed neutrality of money with respect to the real economics.[105] 'Nowhere do conservative notions consider themselves more in place than in currency' – affirmed Keynes –, 'yet nowhere is the need of innovation more urgent'.[106] The monetary instability thrown light upon the failure of the pure market model and the

---

102   Cf. E. Eshag, *From Marshall to Keynes: An Essay in the Monetary Theory of Cambridge School*, Blackwell, Oxford, 1963, pp.128–44. On Marshall's Cambridge see G. Becattini, 'Alfred Marshall e la vecchia scuola economica di Cambridge', in Id. (a cura), *Il pensiero economico: temi, problemi e scuole*, Utet, Torino, 1990, pp.275–310.

103   A.G. Gruchy, 'J.M. Keynes' Concept of Economic Science', *Southern Economic Journal*, 1949, vol.15, January, pp.249–66.

104   B. Corry observed: 'For Keynes and his 'circus' it was the Cambridge tradition that had to be destroyed if the revolution was to succeed' ('Keynes in the History of Economic Thought: Some Reflections', in A.P. Thirlwall (ed. by), *Keynes and Laissez-faire*, Macmillan, London, 1978, p.8).

105   'It would thus seem reasonable to recognize "topical" aspects such as the 1914 Crisis and Keynes participation in war-time finance and commodity markets on behalf of the British Treasury as relevant to his subsequent monetary analysis' (J.A. Kregel, 'Expectations and Relative Prices in Keynes' Monetary Equilibrium', *Economie Appliquée*, 1982, vol.35, 3, pp.449–65).

106   J.M. Keynes, *A Tract on Monetary Reform*, Macmillan, London, 1923, henceforth *MR*, *CWK*, IV, p.xiv.

political system within which that model was referred to. Keynes developed these considerations already in 1923, before the obituary. This explained why it could not hide the emerging distance between two very different theoretical paradigms.

In the few pages dedicated to a synthetic reconstruction of the salient tracts of Marshall's economic theory, Keynes recognized that, thanks to his *magister*, the unnecessary controversy 'about the respective parts played by demand and by cost of production in the determination of value was finally cleared up'; he recognized that Marshall established, via the equilibrium point of demand and supply, 'a whole Copernican system, by which all the elements of the economic universe are kept in their places by mutual counterpoise and interaction', wages and profits included, both subsumed 'under the general laws of value, supply and demand'.[107] Above all, Keynes recognized that Marshall had correctly emphasized the importance 'of the element of time', as well as 'the conception of the "long" and "short" period'. However, what Keynes added, sounded like a deathly embrace: 'Nevertheless, this is the quarter in which, in my opinion, Marshall analysis is least complete and satisfactory, and what remains most to do'.[108] In other words, this was tantamount to questioning the Marshallian long-period normal value – a task that Keynes fully accomplished in *GT*.

107 We should bear in mind that, thanks to Keynes' invitation, P. Sraffa's 'The Laws of Returns under Competitive Conditions' was published in 1926 (*Economic Journal*, vol.36, 144, pp.67–84). In this regard, Skidelsky (*John Maynard Keynes*, II, p.290) wrote: 'Still, it remains a puzzle that the two escape routes from Marshallian orthodoxy – the one associated with Sraffa and imperfect competition, the other with Keynes and effective demand – never converged in Keynes's lifetime, though leading disciples like Kahn and Joan Robinson were heavily involved in both "revolutions"'. See also Id., 'Keynes e Sraffa: un caso di non-comunicazione', in R. Bellofiore (a cura di), *Tra teoria economica e grande cultura europea: Piero Sraffa*, F. Angeli, Milano, 1986, pp.73–84; D. Cavalieri, 'Keynes e Sraffa. Premesse, sviluppi ed esiti della critica di Cambridge', in AA.Vv., *Keynes in Italia*, Ipsoa, Milano, 1984, pp.165–72. A different point of view is expressed by A. Roncaglia, *La ricchezza delle idee*, Laterza, Roma-Bari, 2003, p.496.

108 Keynes, *Alfred Marshall*, *CWK*, X, pp.205–7.

The distance separating Keynes from the different neoclassical models developed itself in the progressive abandonment of a conceptual approach informed by hypotheses such as normal conditions, equilibrium, equality between costs and long-period prices – hypotheses already confuted by the post-war crisis, of which the neoclassical model could say nothing. At that point, the shift of paradigm reached its full maturity. Already in 1919, Keynes began to frame the problem concerning the European economic reconstruction via interpretative categories radically different from the traditional ones. As is well-known, at the Versailles Conference his voice went unheard; but few months later, in *The Economic Consequences of the Peace*, with his eloquent and efficient prose, he stigmatized the myopia of the winners. At any rate, it would be wrong to believe that in examining the German war debit, his aims were confined to a sterile polemic against the improbable assessments of damages proposed by the winners. At the heart of Keynes' position there was the belief that, after the frontal collision between the two main European economic superpowers, the ascendant phase of the nineteenth century capitalism had reached its end. This hypothesis is confirmed by the attention that Keynes would place in the following years upon the monetary difficulties generated by post-war reconstruction. The refusal of the neoclassical assumption according to which money would have had to be neutral with respect to the play of the market could not be an isolated intuition. Although in 1919 inflation appeared to Keynes still as an historical 'accident', it was already correlated to the post-war *system of accumulation*. Moreover, between 1922 and 1923, hence before the obituary, Keynes refined his position: inflation and unemployment became widespread both in Germany and Austria. In his eyes, the monetary movements, rather than being neutral, appeared to be the main causes of the crisis. The mentioned doubts found evident references.

Keynes' conclusion represents an important landing point. Nevertheless, it is necessary to recall that he had had notable predecessors. It is impossible not to mention the Cambridgean context, where Dennis H. Robertson, for example, already in 1922, described the dissimilar course between investment and saving with regard to the increase of prices and the formation of induced saving.[109] Even before, it should be mentioned Knut Wicksell's *Geldzins und Güterpreise* (1898), where the discussion upon the instability of the general level of prices focused upon the inflationary process generated by both firms indebtedness and the dissimilarity between the natural rate and the monetary rate of interest.[110] Hence, we may say that Keynes operated in an already awakened theoretical terrain. In any case, apart from the identification of the best historiographical approach necessary to interpret Keynes' doubts, what is paradigmatic is that it was the nature of the monetary fluxes that led him to a rethink – which is global already in *MR*[111] – explicitly aimed at the confutation of the neoclassical system. From Keynes' point of view, the monetary instability characterizing the post-war period posed tangible problems (inflation and unemployment) and a sharp theoretical alternative (inflation/deflation). From this moment onwards, Keynes began to measure the distance between himself and the Cambridgean tradition, giving shape to his doubts. The monetary storm following the First World War strongly affected the general level of prices, aggregate demand, and saving. For Keynes, this was in-dicative of the need for newer and deeper explanations. According to the neoclassical scheme, the change in the general level of prices would

---

109   Concerning the complex and fundamental relationship between Robertson and Keynes, cf. Skidelsky, *John Maynard Keynes*, II, pp.272 ff.; J.R. Presley, *Robertsonian Economics*, Macmillan, London, 1979; Id., 'J.M. Keynes and D.H. Robertson: Three Phases of Collaboration', *Research in the History of Economic Thought and Methodology*, 1989, vol.16, 4, pp.31–46.

110   'Apart from Mr. Robertson, it was probably Wicksell who exercised most influence on these early stages of Mr. Keynes' though. Keynes was mainly instrumental in securing the translation of *Geldzins und Güterpreise* into English and its publication by the *Royal Economic Society'* (E.A.G. Robinson, *John Maynard Keynes – 1883–1946*, in Lekachman (ed. by), *Keynes' General Theory. Reports of Three Decades*, p.52).

111   Skidelsky argued: (*John Maynard Keynes*, II, p.160): 'Beneath both the technical and the ironic drapery of the *Tract* were a series of connected propositions which were to inspire Keynes's economic work for the rest of his life. Economic health was too important to be left to *laissez-faire*. Economic management, which had already started, must become part of the modern science of government, not the tool of vested interests'. For a different opinion, see M. De Cecco, *Moneta e impero*, Einaudi, Torino, 1979, pp.20–1.

have had to lead to an automatic adjustment of monetary wages. Vice versa, it produced the destabilization of the value of money, rendering the whole economic system unstable. In the face of what was happening, the orthodox theory, excluding aprioristically the influence of monetary events upon the real variables affecting the economic system, was simply a baseless hypostasis.

'What moral for our present purpose should we draw from this?' – Keynes asks. And he carries on: 'Chiefly, I think, that it is not safe or fair to combine the social organisation developed during the nineteenth century (and still retained) with a *laissez-faire* policy towards the value of money'.[112] In fact, it is the decisive change of the monetary prices of goods and services that indicates the relevance of money. Concerning this, Keynes is peremptory: 'Unemployment, the precarious life of the worker, the disappointment of expectation, the sudden loss of savings, the excessive windfalls to individuals, the speculator, the profiteer – all proceed, in large measure, from the instability of the standard of value'.[113] The concrete effects of such instability are inexplicable by the simplistic logic of *laissez-faire*. Inflation and deflation, producing different outcomes for different earners, affect the accumulation processes. A change in the general level of prices 'generally affects different classes unequally, transfers wealth from one to another'.[114] Inflation means an unfair re-distribution of income for wage earners in favour of entrepreneurs and profit makers – that are favoured, among other factors, by the devaluation of the debt. Deflation means re-evaluation of public and private debt, unemployment, nominal growth of the value of capital, a front of a real process of de-accumulation. 'Thus inflation is unjust and deflation is inexpedient'.[115]

In these terms, Keynes underlines the partiality of the neo-classical model. Faced with inflationary trauma, he demonstrates the fallacy of the theorem supporting the automatic adjustment of the nominal wages, indicating their rigidity; he grasps the inefficacy of

---

112   *MR, CWK*, IV, p.16.
113   Ibid., *CWK*, IV, p.xiv.
114   Ibid., *CWK*, IV, p.1.
115   Ibid., *CWK*, IV, p.36.

the re-balancing effect exerted by relative prices in allocating resources in an efficient manner.[116] Furthermore, considering the instability of money as one of the main causes of the great perturbations affecting the economic system, he not only refuses the alleged neutrality of money, but also explicitly questions the distributive mechanism of the market. In so doing, he recognizes the capitalist social organization as irremediably unstable. As the individualistic nature of capitalism '*presumes* a stable measuring-rod of value, and cannot be efficient – perhaps cannot survive – without one',[117] Keynes' first proposal would be the government of the standard value money. But only one year after, on the grounds that one 'of the most interesting and unnoticed developments of recent decades has been the tendency of big enterprise to socialise itself',[118] he would recognize the relative efficacy of that sole proposal. The regulation of money guaranteed stability, this was certain; but what did one have to say with regard to an economic system that was no longer decipherable through the neoclassical assumptions, and within which money was the main element upon which the economic relationships rested upon? Fausto Vicarelli is right in pointing out that this question showed a generalized dissatisfaction towards the behavioural rule inspired by the principle of *laissez-faire*.[119] The Keynesian doubts had become certainty.

Keynes' progressive distance from Marshall's economics and the passage to a more mature analysis of the apories inherent to the market philosophy can be found in *The End of Laissez-faire*. This work represents the beginning of what might be defined as the 'ascending phase' of Keynes' revolution.[120] It is for this reason that particular attention should be paid to the texts written between 1924 and 1926. The historical-theoretical and the critical-polemic analytical

116 Vicarelli, *Keynes*, p.61.
117 *MR, CWK*, IV, p.36.
118 J.M. Keynes, *The End of Laissez-faire*, *CWK*, IX, p.289. It is here worth recalling that this work was the result of two conferences held in 1924; published as a pamphlet in 1926, it would subsequently find its place in *Essays in Persuasion*, Macmillan, London, 1931.
119 Vicarelli, *Keynes*, p.61.
120 Cf. D.E. Moggridge, *Keynes*, Fontana, London, 1976, pp.74 ff.

316

levels informing these works provide the basis upon which a 'normative knowledge' rests, operating not against but rather in favour of the market.[121] Undoubtedly, the path – whose first leg would be represented by *A Treatise on Money* (henceforth *TM*) – is not straightforward. However, the control of saving proposed in *The End of Laissez-faire* represents a clear advancement if compared to the control of the value of money proposed in *MR*. Being explicitly anchored to investment, it anticipates the analysis of the relationship between savings and investments, which ought to be 'normalized' via the control of the rate of interest. The bridge is built: it is impossible to reform an economic system based upon the *laissez-faire* assumption apart from a *criterion of normation*. Already in 1924, this was Keynes' belief. The following step, *TM*, would be conceived starting from this normative background.

A chain of negative statements, intentionally apodictic, illustrates Keynes' shift:

> Let us clear from the ground the metaphysical or general principles upon which, from time to time, *laissez-faire* has been founded. It is *not* true that individuals possess a prescriptive 'natural liberty' in their economic activities. There is *no* 'compact' conferring perpetual rights on those who Have or to those who Acquire. The world is *not* so governed from above that private and social interest always coincide. It is *not* so managed here below that in practice they coincide. It is *not* a correct deduction from the principles of economics that enlightened self-interest always operates in the public interest. Nor is it true that self-interest generally *is* enlightened; more often individuals acting separately to promote their own ends are too ignorant or too weak to attain even these.[122]

---

121   We should bear in mind what, in *The End of Laissez-faire*, Keynes wrote concerning Marxist socialism ('illogical' and 'dull' doctrine) and State socialism, unable to grasp 'the significance of what is actually happening'. Cf. M. Cranston, 'Keynes: His Political Ideas and Their Influence', in Thirlwall (ed. by), *Keynes and Laissez-faire*, pp.110 ff.

122   Keynes, *The End of Laissez-faire*, *CWK*, IX, pp.287–8. M. Freeden's interpretation of this passage (*Liberalism Divided. A Study in British Political Thought, 1914–1939*, Oxford University Press, Oxford, 1986, pp.157–8), although acute, seems to undermine the decisive aspect; namely, that between natural 'individualism' and the identification of an enlightened *self-interest* 'socially oriented' there is a wide gulf.

It would be difficult to disagree on the fact that, already in 1924, Keynes produced a fracture with respect to the neoclassical tradition. In *The End of Laissez-faire*, deepening his reflection upon the changing of the socio-institutional arrangements of the economic system, he grasps the essential, basic aspects of such a change. Certainly, the progressive maturation of the normative hypothesis is still subjected to the hiatus between 'observation' and 'interpretation'. Keynes grasps the impossible efficacy of *laissez-faire* without proposing radical alternatives at the level of economic theory. Indicative of this hiatus is the attempt to ground a 'new course' upon the distinction between the individual and the collective sphere – *Agenda* and *Non-Agenda* of government –, so as to re-formulate the socio-economic organization on the basis of 'semi-autonomous bodies within the State': 'the ideal size for the unit of control and or-ganisation – Keynes affirms – lies somewhere between the individual and the modern State'.[123] In any case, it is this perspective that reveals the wealth of *The End of Laissez-faire*. Besides in a not fully devel-oped and thereby still weak argumentations concerning economic policy, this can be seen mainly in the progressive attention paid to *political action*, which is a deliberate *normative acting*. The explicit reference to the influence that can be exerted upon investment via the 'government' of the saving indicates the strict connection, the in-dispensable synthesis, between economics and politics.[124]

His past experience as a civil servant compelled Keynes to single out the blindness of the governments that, as a result of their adhering to worn-out orthodoxies, were incapable of understanding the radical change informing the new phase of development of the world economic system.[125] Nevertheless, it is fairly evident that, in the mid 1920s, Keynes' 'vision' still does not hold the clarity that only the

123 Keynes, *The End of Laissez-faire*, *CWK*, IX, p.288. See A. Cairncross' com-ment: 'Keynes and The Planned Economy', in Thirlwall (ed. by), *Keynes and Laissez-faire*, pp.44–5.
124 As Screpanti and Zamagni observed, 'ciò che conta è l'idea che lo stato debba assumersi il compito del "*concerted and deliberate management*" della econ-omia, sia pure attraverso l'uso di un limitato numero di strumenti politici' (*Profilo di storia del pensiero economico*, p.230).
125 Ferrari Bravo, *Keynes. Uno studio di diplomazia economica, passim*.

acquisition and the final theoretical systematization of the mechanisms of government of a capitalistic social system would guarantee.[126] Taking this for granted, it is also clear that his interests went far beyond the simple logical apories inherent to the market model. That Keynes' intent was predominantly political it is proved by his fight against the 'Treasury view'. This claim is made explicit in *The End of laissez-faire*. In its being a sort of transitional point, this pamphlet touches the political intents of *GT*. In a short work that precedes the *magnum opus*, we can read: 'For me, therefore, it is impossible to rest satisfied until I can put my finger on the flaw in that part of the orthodox reasoning which leads to the conclusions which for various reasons seem to me to be unacceptable. I believe that I am on my way to do so'.[127]

Undoubtedly, the confutation of the orthodox apories can only be understood as a radical transformation of the economic theory, whose political meaning, however, cannot be hidden. This intention is made clear in *The Economic Consequences of Mr. Churchill*, where Keynes wrote:

> Nine times out of ten, nothing really serious does happen – merely a little distress to individuals or to groups. But we run a risk of the tenth time (and are stupid into the bargain), if we continue to apply the principles of an economics, which was worked out on the hypotheses of *laissez-faire* and free competition, to a society which is rapidly abandoning these hypotheses.[128]

At any rate, it has always been overlooked that this confutation stems from a theoretical reasoning that, rather than being merely economical, is philosophical and therefore political. Keynes is absolutely clear on this, to the point of excluding that *laissez-faire* were a product of economic science. It is worth noting that the work of 1924 moves from the analysis of the philosophical variants incorporated into *laissez-faire*: namely, individualism, hedonism, utilitarianism,

---

126 On this aspect, see Skidelsky, *John Maynard Keynes*, II, ch.7.
127 J.M. Keynes, 'Poverty in Plenty: is the Economic System Self-Adjusting?', *The Listener*, 21.XI.1934 (*CWK*, XIII, p.489).
128 J.M. Keynes, *The Economic Consequences of Mr. Churchill*, afterwards in *Essays in Persuasion*, *CWK*, IX, p.224.

jusnaturalism and Darwinism. What Keynes provides here is a simultaneous confutation of both *laissez-faire* and contractualism, via a 'normative knowledge' aimed at the confutation of the alleged *ordre naturel* that underpins them. We have repeatedly claimed that Keynes' regulative approach develops throughout all his theoretical experience. Now, *The End of the Laissez-faire* represents a decisive, though intermediate, passage, in which Keynes synthesizes not only the relative maturity of his theoretical revolution, but also the certainties reached via his acquaintance with the philosophical and epistemological basis informing economic science. In this respect, the critique that *TP* addresses to the alleged *ordre naturel* of knowledge is decisive.

Very carefully, Keynes reconstructs the way through which the principle of *laissez-faire* arrived at dominating economic theory.[129] He excludes that it belongs to the foundations of economics. He claims that the economists were simply responsible for the vulgarization of that principle, whose origin is philosophical, perhaps ideological, but certainly not scientific. Keynes' polemic is at same time both deep and irreverent. The thesis proposed is drastic, and not always easy to accept. However, the historiographical aspect – besides being legitimately debatable – has a relative importance. Keynes speaks to his contemporaries. Beyond the correctness of the attributions, he grasps the essence of the problem: first of all, he underlines the correlation and, subsequently, the ideological identity between *laissez-faire* and jusnaturalistic *ordre naturel*. The many bodies of thought that contributed to the making of such an identity are evaluated, although not always in the correct manner. There is, first of all, Hume and Locke's individualism, 'no more than a scientific study of the consequences of the rational self-love'. Then, there is utilitarianism, a sort of 'mathematical law of indifference' applied to social utility;

---

129 This reconstruction can certainly raise legitimate historical perplexities. Two different points of view concerning the existence of an 'age of *laissez-faire*' are provided by G.S.R. Kitson Clark (*An Expanding Society; Britain, 1830–1900*, Cambridge University Press, Cambridge, 1967, ch.8) and by E.J. Hobsbawm (*Industry and Empire. An Economic History of Britain since 1750*, Penguin Books, Harmondsworth, 1968, ch.12). For an overview see A.J. Taylor, *Laissez-faire and State Intervention in Nineteenth-century Britain*, Macmillan, London, 1972.

finally, there is Rousseau's naturalism, which 'took the Social Contract from Locke and drew out of it the General Will'. Different, if not opposite approaches, which at the end of the eighteenth century would converge in Adam Smith's prophetic 'invisible hand'. Keynes wrote:

> Suppose that by the working of natural laws individuals pursuing their own interests with enlightenment in conditions of freedom always tend to promote the general interest at the same time! Our philosophical difficulties are resolved – at least for the practical man [...]. To the philosophical doctrine that government has no right to interfere, and the divine that it has no need to interfere, there is added a scientific proof that its interference is inexpedient.[130]

And it is not paradoxical that to the above 'list' Keynes added Darwinism. In fact, if the economists 'were teaching that wealth, commerce, and machinery were the children of free competition', Darwinism would have shown that 'the free competition had built man'.[131] Besides, it should be noted that this occurred in a specific historical context, within which progress was supported by the entrepreneurs' pioneering initiative carried out against the ineptitude of public administration. The material progress 'between 1750 and 1850 came from individual initiative, and owed almost nothing to the directive influence of organised society as a whole'. Hence, if both the individualism embraced by the political philosopher and the ideology of the divine or social harmony were pointing at *laissez-faire*, and if the politicians' ineptitude was a matter of fact, then the fortune of the Manchesterism was easily explained by the multiplicity of these causes.

In this landscape, it is certain that the economists accepted the individualistic assumption 'because it is the simplest, and not because it is the nearest to the facts'. Accordingly, they were embedded into a wider cultural context within which they end up by assuming 'that there must be no mercy or protection for those who embark their capital or their labour in the wrong direction'. And for this reason it is simply natural that 'the giraffes with the longest necks starve out those whose necks are shorter'. In fact, on the basis of 'the method of trial

130 Keynes, *The End of Laissez-faire*, *CWK*, IX, pp.274–5.
131 Ibid., *CWK*, IX, p.276.

and error "at the margin"', it can be thought that what attains 'the ideal distribution of the instruments of production', concerns also 'the ideal distribution of what is available for consumption'. Thus, to the ideal of natural selection, the need 'for unlimited private money-making as an *incentive* to maximum effort' is simply complementary. The basic assumption is the very same: 'Profit accrues, under *laissez-faire*, to the individual who, whether by skill or good fortune, is found with his productive resources in the right place at the right time'.[132] The complications, when they are recognized, arrive later in time, and furthermore are discharged by those for whom the simplified hypothesis described 'does represent what is "natural" and therefore ideal'.[133]

It is certain that Keynes tried to diminish the responsibilities of economic doctrine with regard to the rise of the market ideology. Probably, this was a wise choice that allowed him to reduce to the minimum serious professional contrasts. 'He sought targets for attack, to the neglect of the profound wisdom of the great men, Locke, Hume, Rousseau, Bentham, Burke, Paley, Malthus, Darwin, whose names bespeckled his pages' – wrote Harrod.[134] But it is also clear that Keynes' polemic attitude, though unfair, was the best possible strategy in order to reach his purpose. Notwithstanding his attempts to keep to the minimum the contrasts, his theoretical approach was characterized by a proper *philosophical intention*, aimed at demolishing the assumptions concerning both rational egoism and social Darwinism. We have already quoted the sequence of negative statements that Keynes utilizes in order to demonstrate the philosophical, juridical, and economic baselessness of *laissez-faire*. If we extrapolate those statements and join them together, we obtain a definitive repudiation of the ideology of natural right: 'natural liberty', 'compact', aprioristic coincidence between 'private and social interest' – this is Keynes' terminology – are purely fiction, absolutely arbitrary and ideological constructions. Keynes is sharp here, and any comment is superfluous.

132   Ibid., *CWK*, IX, pp.282–4.
133   Ibid., *CWK*, IX, pp.284–5.
134   Harrod, *The Life of John Maynard Keynes*, p.355.

We should ask, however: are those ideological constructions merely arbitrary?

5. The crisis of the liberal state of right

The issue is twofold. If Keynes' intention had been purely exegetic, the result would have been a mere acknowledgement of the fact that a group of hypotheses, developed in a specific context, was no longer adequate. But what Keynes pointed out was not the inadequacy of the traditional theory, but rather its baselessness – a precise value judgement. 'It is *not* true'; 'There is *no* "compact"'; 'It is *not* a correct deduction': in this way he stigmatized the 'political forms' inferred from 'natural right'. This was tantamount to saying that the hypotheses upon which the liberal State of right grounded its legitimacy were compromised to the point of jeopardizing their concrete, historical, variants.

Given the above, it is possible to say that Keynes' interest was not merely that of highlighting the inadequacy of the neoclassical model, but rather to urgently find an alternative to it: both at theoretical and practical level.[135] Nevertheless, it should be pointed out that the regulation of the relationships between saving and investments would have appeared insufficient without an adequate rethinking of both juridical and political institutions. Certainly, from an analytical point of view, the difficulty of keeping together the *concepts* of 'civil society', 'economic system' and 'political institution' shows that Keynes' research was in progress. However, the fact that he regarded the market as an economic and political structure, within which the decisions have always had two sides, explains why he considered *laissez-faire* as an hypothesis which is only partially economic. Its double character, in fact, reveals why any decision is political (as it concerns economics), as well as economical (as it is

135   In *Am I liberal?* written in the August 1925, this is made very clear (*CWK*, IX, p.301).

political). Without the consciousness of such an assumption, the *laissez-faire* as a 'natural doctrine' cannot be confuted.

The End of the laissez-faire grasps, fixes, and begins to dismantle such a circular structure. Intended as a theoretical hypothesis, the neoclassical market model – which is not a caricature of *laissez-faire*, but its most refined interpreter – enjoys the same logical strength of any other economic model. To attempt to confute it via a purely logical operation is possible, but inadequate. As Giorgio Lunghini observed, 'the beauty of Marshall's *Principles* – that of the new "Economics" are a sort of scientific constitution – is that of all bourgeois constitutions, where there is all and its contrary'.[136] There are few, if any, who doubt that already in 1926 Keynes was coming to terms with this 'circularity'. It should be said, however, that this could happen also because the principles informing the Keynesian epistemological model began to assume the normation as the sole 'practical' alternative with regard that 'circularity'. Thus, the approach to economic reality – which can never be 'logically' determined – was fixed, in its poliysemy, via a deliberate normative acting. It was not the logical structure of the market model that appeared as incorrect, rather, it was its efficacy that was irrelevant.[137] As a result, the *normative acting* – the sphere of the 'political choice' – became a deliberate *practical acting* that, rather than nullifying, qualified the efficacy of the 'relative knowledge' facing uncertainty.

Are we attributing too much importance to *The End of the Laissez-faire*? It might be the case, but we believe that it is here and in *The Economic Consequence of Mr. Churchill* that Keynes establishes,

---

136 G. Lunghini, *La crisi dell'economia politica e la teoria del valore*, Feltrinelli, Milano, 1977, p.19.

137 Cf. J. Robinson, *Essays in the History of Economic Growth*, Macmillan, London, 1962. Robinson's decisive critique to the neoclassical modelling has been stigmatized for its 'nihilistic consequences', which would lead to conclusions contrasting with Keynes' highly eclectic approach (see A. Coddington, 'Keynesian Economics: the Search for First Principles', *Journal of Economic Literature*, 1976, vol.14, 4, pp.1258–73). This argument is not particularly convincing: it is not a matter of 'fundamental principles' abstractly determined, but of models that operate on the ground of assumptions that are not only more or less logical, but also more or less pertinent to the analysed economic reality.

for the first time, the relationship between 'relative knowledge' and 'economic normation': the complementarity between Market and Norm. If we consider that *MR* was published in 1923, and if we bear in mind that – as confirmed by Donald E. Moggridge – starting from the June of 1924, Keynes began to work at *TM*,[138] then, the role of *The End of the Laissez-faire* becomes evident. In a sense, it represents the necessary introduction to the wider reflection on money that would definitively characterize Keynes' notion of economic knowledge as macroeconomic knowledge. From this perspective, the main writings composed between 1924 and 1926 would have to be merged together. If *The End of Laissez-faire* deepens the critique to the logical-philosophical assumption informing the market system, *The Economic Consequence of Mr. Churchill* appears to be an alternative program of economic policy, in which the neoclassical system – intended as a concrete, but not contingent model – should be confuted through 'practical' objections. The two works permeate one another, representing, in the intertwining between the critique of the historical-theoretical assumptions and the confutation of the concrete economic policy, the first moment of juxtaposition *and* integration between Market *and* Norm.

If in *The End of laissez-faire* it is possible to see the theoretical sketch of what the Keynesian revolution would consist of, in *The Economic Consequences of Mr. Churchill* it is possible to find Keynes' full awareness of the monetary relations underpinning both social and economic systems. At this intermediate point in time – between *MR* and *TM* – Keynes radicalizes his critique. The pure market model was, in his eyes, a dangerous and devastating ideology: the British economic policy was proving the truth of this statement. Theory and market praxis, during Churchill's cabinet, had reached a threshold beyond which the alternative became clear-cut. 'The truth is that – Keynes says – we stand midway between two theories of economic society'; and it is false that 'in the end, unless there is a social upheaval, 'the fundamental adjustments' will duly take place'.[139]

138   Cf. D.E. Moggridge, 'From the *Treatise* to *The General Theory*: An Exercise in Chronology', *History of Political Economy*, 1973, vol.5, Spring, pp.72–88.
139   Keynes, *The Economic Consequences of Mr. Churchill, CWK*, IX, pp.223–5.

Keynes' prose has something of the Classics' *esprit*. To prove this claim it is sufficient to notice that 'social upheaval' that characterizes *any* economic policy. We should not believe that Keynes was questioning the most elementary class interests, which he always and fully acknowledged.[140] Simply put, quite differently from 'Queen Baldwin', in the face of deflationary expectations that would have had follow the restoration of the alleged automatisms of the golden standard,[141] he indicated, as the sole remedy, an economic and monetary regulation. The English crisis occurred in 1926 would pose this kind of alternative.[142]

140 'I can be influenced by what seems to me to be justice and good sense; but the *class* war will find me on the side of educated *bourgeoisie*' [Keynes, *Am I Liberal?*, (*CWK*, IX, p.297)]. On Keynes's elitism, cf. Cranston, 'Keynes: His Political Ideas and Their Influence', p.114; M.L. Pesante, *Economia e politica*, Angeli, Milano, 1986, pp.64 ff. In particular, Freeden (*Liberalism Divided. A Study in British Political Thought, 1914–1939*, pp.154 ff.) has pointed out that Keynes' liberalism 'was dispersed over a wider range of the ideological spectrum than was the case with most liberals at the time'. And furthermore: 'Keynes's curious mix of statism and individualism remained all along one of the hallmarks of his thought, emphasizing once again that while his ideological predilections were certainly centrist-liberal, if not slightly to the right of that, he had not been caught up in the progressive liberal backlash against the state which was set in motion by the war' (ibid., p.171). On Keynes' liberalism see also O'Donnell, *Keynes: Philosophy, Economics and Politics*, pp.316–21; A. Peacock, 'Keynes and the Role of the State', in D. Crabtree, A.P. Thirlwall (ed. by), *Keynes and the Role of the State*, Macmillan, London, 1993, pp.3–32.

141 On the end of the gold standard, see De Cecco, *Moneta e impero*, pp.174 ff.; B. Eichengreen (ed. by), *The Gold Standard in Theory and History*, Methuen, New York and London, 1985, pp.141–225. On Keynes' monetary thought evolution cf. D.E. Moggridge, S. Howson, 'Keynes on Monetary Policy, 1910–1946', *Oxford Economic Papers*, 1974, vol.26, 2; D. Patinkin, *Keynes' Monetary Thought: A Study of its Development*, Duke University Press, Durham, 1976; P. Alessandrini, 'Keynes e la politica monetaria internazionale', in Faucci (ed. by), *John Maynard Keynes nel pensiero e nella politica economica*, pp.177–201; for a general overview, Clarke, *The Keynesian Revolution in the Making, 1924–1936*.

142 M. Gobbini, 'Lo sciopero generale inglese del '26', in AA. Vv., *Operai e stato*, Feltrinelli, Milano, 1972, pp.55–68. On Keynes' position see Skidelsky, *Keynes*, II, pp.272 ff.

Above all, it would show that the decisions concerning monetary policy and, in particular, the revaluation of sterling, could only be the fruit of a choice intrinsic to a monetary economy, with inevitable repercussions upon wages, employment, accumulation, and re-evaluation of the debt.[143] Keynes' position regarding the opportunity to return back to the gold standard was well-known. Even before the publication on *The Evening Standard* of the three articles that would form *The Economic Consequences of Mr. Churchill*, he clearly expressed his position in a series of writings that appeared in *The Nation*, between March and April 1925. In these works – not to mention the famous *Notes* published in the same year on *The Economic Journal*[144] – the issue was posed as indissolubly connected to the critique previously addressed to the neoclassical model. The return to the gold standard was conceived of as an obvious, but ruinous, consequence stemming from that analytical model. 'The gold standard, with its dependence on pure chance, its faith in "automatic adjustments", and its general regardlessness of social detail, is an essential emblem and idol of those who sit in the top tier of the machine'.[145]

The extent to which the battle against the re-evaluation of sterling was felt – to the point of the most irreverent sarcasm – has been repeatedly noted. As Harrod underlined, the target of Keynes' battle was not Churchill, but rather the entire apparatus presiding over British economic policy. Better still, the target was the tradition to which that apparatus was blindly referring. In addition, in dealing with the economic crisis and the choices that such a crisis was destined to exacerbate, Keynes was absolutely alone – Ralph G. Hawtrey's

---

143 Cf. D.E. Moggridge, *The Return to Gold, 1925: The Formulation of Economic Policy and Its Critics*, Cambridge University Press, Cambridge, 1969; Id., *British Monetary Policy 1924–1931*, Cambridge University Press, Cambridge, 1972; S. Pollard (ed. by), *The Gold Standard and Employment Policies between the Wars*, Methuen, London, 1970; Winch, *Economics and Policy*, pp.75 ff.; K.P.G. Matthews, 'Was Sterling Overvalued in 1925?', *Economic History Review*, 1986, II s., 4, pp.572–87.

144 J.M. Keynes, 'The Committee on the Currency. Notes and Memoranda', *The Economic Journal*, 1925, June, *CWK*, XIX, pp.371–8.

145 Keynes, *The Economic Consequences of Mr. Churchill*, *CWK*, IX, p.224.

position was emblematic. He did not underestimate the measure designed to redress the balance of payment; on the other hand, his proposal to return back – via a consensual mediation – to the system of relative prices established before the introduction of the revaluation of sterling was the opposite of what the monetary authorities had chosen.

Keynes' widely studied arguments were the following. A ten per cent revaluation of the sterling, being unable to automatically bring about a proportional and generalized reduction of money wages, interests paid, and production costs, would have implied first of all a ten per cent reduction in the receipt of export industries. This would have entailed – further than unemployment – a wage decline; however, not proportional to the decrease, certainly inferior, of the cost of living. If, according to Keynes, the unemployment produced within the export industries sector and the reduction of real wages was assured, the rest was not. In fact, the viscosity of monetary wages would have rendered their generalized reduction problematic so far as the same would not have happened also in non-export industries. But this would have been paradoxical, as the realization of such a strategy would have required a deliberate increase of the level of unemployment also in the 'protected' industries via a credit squeeze. The mechanism, Keynes concluded, would have been circular and, moreover, totally inequitable on social grounds, and therefore unacceptable:

> Nor can the classes, which are first subjected to a reduction of money wage, be guaranteed that this will be compensated later by a corresponding fall in the cost of living, and will not accrue to the benefit of some other class. Therefore they are bound to resist so long as they can; and it must be war, until those who are economically weakest are beaten to the ground.[146]

It is clear that the 'midway between two theories of economic society' did not indicate simply two different ways of understanding the *same* reality via the *same* theory, but rather a change of paradigm. While Keynes insisted upon the impossibility of reabsorbing the unemployment generated by a credit squeeze, the advocates of the neoclassical model reaffirmed that a compression of monetary wages

146   Ibid., *CWK*, IX, p.211.

would have guaranteed, via an automatic adjustment of the market price of labour force, the decrease of the frictional unemployment so generated. A middle path between these positions was impossible. Either the variation in the value of money was considered as neutral – so that real economic variables tended towards an automatic re-balancing –, or turning upside down the previously established relative relationships of value, the very same variations was considered able to modify the general shape of the economic system. To this alternative – to which he had already provided an answer in *MR* – Keynes added a further variable, 'unknown' to the neoclassical model and determined by specific erroneous monetary choices: namely, unemployment. In this way, confuting its alleged automatic decrease, he buried the neoclassical model with a memorable epitaph:

> We are depending for the reduction of wages on the pressure of unemployment and of strikes and lockouts; and in order to make sure this result we are deliberately intensifying the unemployment. [...] The proper object of dear money is to check an incipient boom. Woe to those whose faith leads them to use it to aggravate a depression![147]

This solution was indeed paradoxical, but not for the neoclassical tradition. In fact, according to this tradition, the role of money, monetary wages, and unemployment were not ignored *ex definitione*; rather, what it excluded was the possibility that they might be able to subvert their aprioristic relationships tending towards equilibrium. In its duplicity, the relevance of Keynes' fracture with the philosophy underpinning the pure market model is for this reason superior to any other: it is a theoretical and epistemological fracture, bearer of a new paradigm based upon a relative-normative approach. What, according to the neoclassical model, was a consequent result, for Keynes, as it involved a different degree of verifiability, was only possible and not necessary.

Thus, the idea of leaving the automatic rebalancing of the socio-economic relationships to market mechanisms appears to be as arbitrary, untenable. Since the economic system is not self-adjusting, the market as a mere allocative instrument is a dangerous fiction. The

147 Ibid., *CWK*, IX, p.220.

mere economic maximization upon which the neoclassical model rests upon is an absolutization of an ethically fragile aim[148] that, once confuted, shows its incapacity to master economical uncertainty and social instability. That is why Keynes' analysis can only invoke the relevance of normative criteria. Assuming the implications involved by social mobility, individual expectations, and economic uncertainty, Keynes' 'epistemological regionality' manifests itself as normation. This provides the grounds for an unequivocal conclusion: 'For my part I think that capitalism, wisely managed, can probably be made more efficient for attaining economic ends than any alternative systems yet in sight, but that in itself it is in many ways extremely objectionable'.[149]

For this reason, as Axel Leijonhufvud observed, Keynes's diagnosis 'is not just based on "positive" economic analysis free of normative ingredients. Policy judgements enter in from the very start'.[150] Normation should be able to transpose into 'practical choice' what in itself is 'relative knowledge'. In short, the confutation of the neoclassical system occurs when to 'uncertainty' is opposed a 'decision' that ought to be able to anticipate the effects of the economic actors' expectations. This is the point reached by Keynes, as it is illegitimate to assume 'that our vast machine should crash along, with regard only to its equilibrium as a whole'.[151] The pure market process might become a fatal illusion, 'and the tragedy of our situation lies in the fact that, from the misguided standpoint which has been officially adopted, this course is theoretically justifiable'.[152]

In the face of the unprecedented crisis that followed the end of the First World War and that characterized both the 1920s and 1930s,

---

148 Hence, Keynes argues that: '[...] the fiercest contests and the most deeply felt divisions of opinion are likely to be waged in the coming years not round technical questions, [...], but round those which, for want of better words, may be called psychological or, perhaps, moral' (Keynes, *The End of Laissez-faire*, *CWK*, IX, p.293).

149 Ibid., *CWK*, IX, p.294.

150 A. Leijonhufvud, *On Keynesian Economics and the Economics of Keynes*, Oxford University Press, London, 1968, p.344.

151 Keynes, *The Economic Consequences of Mr. Churchill*, *CWK*, IX, p.223.

152 Ibid., *CWK*, IX, p.219–20.

the neoclassical model was heavily conditioned by its being linked to 'static microeconomics based squarely on the equimarginal rule'.[153] Keynes could not but disassociate himself from this tradition of thought. He was not the only one who arrived at this conclusion via the analysis of the role of money.[154] No one, however, had been able to generate such a wide 'paradigmatic fracture'.[155] On this matter, Schumpeter's judgement is significant. In fact, although he underlines that next to GT should be mentioned, among others, the contributions of the Swedish School and Richard Kahn,[156] in his opinion, Keynes' originality essentially stems from a true paradox. His contribution is macrostatic and not macrodynamic – Shumpeter says –, however, it would become relevant for 'the impulse it gave to macrodynamics'.[157] The existence of that paradox – also represented by the shift from the dynamic approach that informs TM to the macrostatic approach that would inform GT – is certain. At any rate, it would be difficult to understand this passage if we would see in it a mere change of perspective. We have to ask ourselves, in fact, whether, for Keynes, 'macroeconomics' might mean *only* what the later economic theory would have identified with this term. We might think of Paul A.

---

153 M. Blaug, *Economic Theory in Retrospect*, Cambridge University Press, Cambridge, 1997, p.281.

154 It is sufficient here to mention Schumpeter's *opus* and the so-called Swedish School interpreter of Wicksell. Cf. G. Myrdal, *Monetary Equilibrium*, W. Hodge, London, 1939; G.L. Shackle, *The Years of High Theory. Invention and Tradition in Economic Thought*, Cambridge University Press, Cambridge, 1967. As G. Myrdall (*Against the Stream: Critical Essays in Economics*, Pantheon, New York, 1972, pp.4–5) noted: '[...] the Keynesian revolution [...] was mainly an Anglo-American occurrence. In Sweden, where we grew up in the tradition of Knut Wicksell, Keynes' works were read as interesting and important contributions along a familiar line of thought, but not in any sense as a revolutionary breakthrough'. For a synthesis, see B. Hansen, 'Unemployment, Keynes, and the Stockholm School', *History of Political Economy*, 1981, vol.13, 2, pp.256–77.

155 W.J. Barber, *A History of Economic Thought*, Penguin Books, Harmondsworth, 1967.

156 J.A. Schumpeter, *History of Economic Analysis*, Allen & Unwin, London, 1955, pp.1173–4.

157 On this issue, similar is G. Haberler's opinion: '*The General Theory* after Ten Years', in S.E. Harris, *The New Economics*, A. Knopf, New York, 1947.

Samuelson's definition, according to which macroeconomics 'examines the overall level of a nation's output, employment, prices, and foreign trade'.[158]

To provide an answer is as easy as it is hazardous. However, it is realistic enough to claim that it is exactly Keynes' insistence on the crisis of the liberal State that renders his economic theory dynamic, although it is conceived of as regulation in the short term. Such regulation would represent the real challenge to economic theory of the mid 1930s. But, already in the confutation of the neoclassical market mechanisms, the dynamic effects are commensurate to their aim, in particular, with regard to the economic analysis of the capitalist system intended as a monetary economy. Beyond the neoclassical barter,[159] in fact, the economic *ratio* can be entirely explained only according to an analytical approach for which money, further than being the link between past and future, is the essential moment of social relations.

In the works composed between 1924 and 1926, this can be seen with clarity in the macroeconomic and monetary relationships that occur between price stability, value of money, monetary wages, aggregate demand, and employment. We have seen how Keynes considered inflation as a perverse mechanism of income redistribution, and how much he believed that the revaluation of sterling was a turning up side down of the relative quote of the social income

---

158   P.A. Samuelson, *Economics*, McGraw-Hill, New York, 1992[14], p.396.
159   Cf. K. Arrow and F.H. Hahn, *General Competitive Analysis*, Oliver and Boyd, Edinburgh, 1971, p.338. Emblematic, on this regard, is Keynes' critique to Pigou, contained in a letter dated the 5th of January 1930: 'My main hesitation arises out of a doubt as to whether the method of abstraction by which you first of all deal with the problems in terms of a barter economy, and then at a later stage bring in monetary considerations, is a legitimate means of approach in dealing with a short-period problem of this kind, the characteristics of which are, or may be, hopelessly entangled with features arising out of monetary factors'. Exactly six months later, Pigou would write the famous letter published in *The Times*, arguing for a massive program of public works (Skidelsky, *John Maynard Keynes*, II, pp.366–7). This tells us how wide the gulf was separating Keynes and the 'Professor', and that such a distance was not due to a generic socio-political preoccupation, but rather to a *theoretical difference* between a 'neutral' and a 'monetary' approach.

subdivided among and within the classes. This required a radical alternative; it required defeating the diffidence toward the regulation of money. It required a normative criterion. Because '[i]t is not true that our former arrangements have worked well' – Keynes wrote in 1923 –, thus 'we must make it a prime object of deliberate State policy that the standard value' in terms of which the 'investments' are expressed 'should be keep stable'.[160]

Now, it is this normative approach that makes Keynes' statics anomalous, although in the passage in the long run this would create many well-known problems. It is sufficient to recall the relevance, in social terms, attributed to two fundamental monetary relationships: the one involving entrepreneurs and wage earners, and the one between productive capital and financial capital.[161] They are macroeconomic and monetary relations,[162] inevitably dynamic, within which norma-tion ought to guarantee both the adaptability of the viscosity of the monetary wage and an adequate relationship between finance and investments. On the other hand, it is exactly for this reason that the State, the normation intended as dynamic element that intervenes in the monetary fluxes, would be in turn incorporated into a 'general representation'.[163] Money and State are the two extremes within which normation is given.

It is correct to think that Keynes' belief reached its maturation through different stages. However, it seems possible to affirm that a similar outline was already elaborated in 1926, because it is legitimate to think that from 1924 onwards his engagement with *TM* allowed him to clarify the relationship between State and money. 'Various inter-esting reflections occur in this connection' – Harrod wrote. 'One is how early (1924) Keynes had completed the outline of the public policy which has since been specifically associated with his name –

160 *MR*, p.20 (*CWK*, IV, p.16).
161 M. Messori, 'Aspetti monetari della domanda effettiva', in A. Graziani, C. Imbriani, B. Jossa (a cura di), *Studi di economia keynesiana*, Liguori, Napoli, 1981, pp.235–99.
162 A. Graziani, 'Keynes e il *Trattato sulla moneta*', in Graziani, Imbriani, Jossa (a cura di), *Studi di economia keynesiana*, p.223.
163 S. De Brunhoff, *Etat et Capital*, Presses Universitaires de Grenoble, Grenoble, 1976.

credit control to eliminate the credit cycle, State-sponsored capital development [...]'.[164] This confirms that Keynes came to the confutation of the neoclassical model imposing money as an essential determinant of the economic system. Thus, before anything else, it is money that should be subjected to normation, as it is with respect to money and for it that the economic system expresses its fundamental variations.[165] In this way, what for the neoclassical economists was microanalysis of a barter economy, with Keynes becomes macroanalysis of a monetary economy;[166] what was intended as microstatics, becomes macrodynamics. This is the result of the assumption according to which monetary policies are the instrument for economic policies, beyond any alleged 'natural' and 'normal' automatism concerning economic market relations. And this assumption presupposes the government of the primary source of uncertainty: money.

6. Fundamental equations or perilous paths?

Considering the writings that according to a contingent taxonomy might be defined as 'minor', we have arrived at touching on the themes belonging to the maturity of Keynes' economic 'discourse'. For this reason, we have previously stressed upon the relevance of *MR*. In fact, some of the 'minor writings' that we have taken into

164 Harrod, *The Life of John Maynard Keynes*, p.350. In 1946 E.A.G. Robinson wrote: '[...] never, so far as I remember, did Keynes in later life devise an economic tool purely for its own sake rather than to solve an immediate practical problem in the application to government of the methods of economic analysis; his absorbing interest in politics and government made Keynes, in the very best sense of those words, a political economist' (*John Maynard Keynes – 1883–1946*, p.23).

165 L. Berti (a cura di), *Moneta, crisi e stato capitalistico*, Feltrinelli, Milano, 1978.

166 On the controversial aspect concerning the microfoundation of macroeconomics, cf. G. Lunghini and G. Rampa, 'Il falso problema dei fondamenti microeconomici', in C. Gnesutta (a cura di), *Uncertainty, moneta, aspettative, equilibrio. Saggi per Fausto Vicarelli*, Il Mulino, Bologna, 1996, pp.113 ff.

consideration are based, at least partially, upon this work. Assuming that from 1924 onwards a new phase had begun, it is possible to see how these 'minor writings' delineated the passage between *MR* and *TM*. This could happen on the basis of a shift from the concept of 'stability of the general level of prices' to a 'system of relative price'. Now, as this shift expresses the evolution of the normative hypothesis with regard to money, it is important to spend some time on the matter.

For Keynes, an adequate monetary stability is the first goal to be achieved in the post-war context. As a result, in *MR*, the traditionalism of the gold standard is seen as unsustainable and politically danger-ous.[167] The economic stability based on the gold standard is only a mere illusion. When it is no longer money of account, in fact, money is not a mere variable referring to its 'intrinsic value' – which is, anyhow, a bizarre concept, as the value of money is a relative convention, expressed through the relationship between the same money and the general system of prices. The different purchasing power of money, inflation and deflation, are monetary phenomena economically relevant, intrinsic to the changing of the monetary prices of goods and services, rather than implausible variations in the 'intrinsic value' of money.

Not by chance, during the aftermath of the First World War, these phenomena showed their autonomy with respect to the policies based upon the central reserve of gold, implying a radical income re-distribution and an increase in the consumption standard and ag-gregate demand. As these subversions appeared ruinous for the maintenance of a stable socio-economic framework, they required new criteria of monetary regulation. The injustice 'to those who in good faith have committed their savings to title to money' was apparent. 'But injustice on such a scale has further consequences' – Keynes argued. Thus, an effective monetary stability was required.

---

167   'With the existing distribution of the world's gold, the reinstatement of the gold standard means, inevitably, that we surrender the regulation of our price level and the handling of the credit cycle to the Federal Reserve Board of the United States' (*MR, CWK*, IV, p.139).

In theoretical terms, the problem is not represented by inflation or deflation *per se*. Rather, the problem exists because money is not a simple *numeraire*, but an instrument whose role renders the economic process dynamic. If 'the capacity of the investing class to saving' is eroded, 'the atmosphere of confidence which is a condition of the willingness to save'[168] is destroyed. Intended as simple nominal variation, inflation is simply unjust; but as it affects the relationships between real economic variables, it generates even further problems. Above all, it hides the distinction between capital and income, as the 'increasing *money* value of the community's capital goods obscures temporarily a diminution in the real quantity of the stock'.[169] Conversely, a deflationist process 'may inhibit the productive process altogether';[170] the consequent 'general fear' is concrete economic variation, which produces unemployment and disaccumulation. Between inflation and deflation, Keynes' choice is notoriously sharp. At any rate, the 'ideal' consists of assuring 'that there shall never exist any confident expectation either that prices generally are going to fall or that they are going to rise'.[171] So, in order to reach the stability of the general level of prices – and of value of money – it is necessary to control 'the standard of value that, whenever something occurred which, left to itself, would create an expectation of a change in the general level of prices, the controlling authority should take steps to counteract this expectation by setting in motion some factors of a contrary tendency'.[172]

It is apparent that the main preoccupation expressed in *MR* concerns the possibility of reaching a monetary stability not bound to the gold standard. A stability that should be achieved via an economic policy able to guarantee, through the mediation of the banking system and the Treasury, a certain constancy of expectations of the market actors. From this perspective, the necessity to establish a central banking authority, able to regulate the liquidity and the relationship

168   Ibid., *CWK*, IV, p.29.
169   Ibid., *CWK*, IV, p.27–8.
170   Ibid., *CWK*, IV, p.34.
171   Ibid., *CWK*, IV, p.35.
172   Ibid.

336

between savings and investments, emerges. In fact, the mere restoration of the gold standard 'certainly will not give us complete stability of internal prices and can only give us complete stability of the external exchange if all other countries also restore the gold standard'.[173]

Therefore, what *MR* shows is, on the one side, the unavoidable monetary character of the capitalistic economy – to be regulated by well-thought out policy on the part of the Treasury – and, on the other, the structural instability of the general level of prices as a monetary indicator. The relationship between *normation* and *monetary policy* is clear. What remains unclear, however, is the 'relative value' of *any* monetary policy. This is the reason why the banking policies and the Treasury strategies run the risk of appearing yet undifferentiated with regard to their impact on the different monetary realities expressed by the system of relative prices. From this perspective, Keynes' contribution can be seen as still partially intrinsic to the dominant theory. Nevertheless, after the publication of *The End of Laissez-faire* – where Keynes confuted the pure market philosophy – can the reflection concerning the stability of the general level of prices be sufficient to develop an adequate monetary theory? Evidently, the answer is negative, although the condemnation of the return to the gold standard heralds other important developments. Thus, if *MR* opens up the road to the 'minor writings' composed between 1924 and 1926, these latter would show the limits of *MR* at the beginning of the 1930s. Concerning these, nothing is more explicit than a passage of *TM*, where we can read: 'I see no *meaning* in an assumption to the effect that the purchasing power of money is *equal* for different classes of the community'.[174] Compared to *MR* the perspective is entirely changed.

One should think of the way in which the opening of *TM* analytically deals with the relationship between the level of prices and the purchasing power of money. The starting point is obviously the same: the absence of an 'intrinsic value' of money. However, the

173 Ibid., *CWK*, IV, p.132.
174 J.M. Keynes, *Treatise on Money*, Macmillan, London, 1930; henceforth *TM*, *CWK*, V, p.88.

change of perspective is evident, because this relationship is no longer expressed in absolute, but rather in relative terms:

> To act in such a case on the assumption that all classes of prices are affected more or less in the same way by a change 'on the side of money' is, as we have said above, to assume away the very phenomenon which we are our to investigate. The fact that monetary changes do not affect all prices in the same way, in the same degree, or at the same time, is what makes them significant.[175]

This is, furthermore, what makes the definition of a general level of prices of secondary importance.[176] Obviously, the purchasing power of money should be related to the general level of prices. This latter, however, is not representative of the different 'types of expenditures' that are possible with respect to various goals belonging to the different classes constituting the collectivity. The locution 'prices level' is meaningful only if it is assumed as a partial indicator, as the 'price of a composite commodity which is representative of some type of expenditure.'[177] In fact, the value of the 'composite commodity' is different with regard to the expectations that should be satisfied. The way in which different monetary incomes are spent changes, 'because there is a change in what distribution of expenditure between different objects is the most economical means of attaining the purpose'.[178] In short, it is not possible to identify a sole parameter to which to relate the general level of prices, or what Edgeworth defined as the 'objective mean variation of general prices', around which the different prices of single commodities gravitate. Simply put, there are 'all the various, quite definite, conceptions of price-levels of composite commodities [...]'.[179] With regard to this, *MR* said too little – and only with reference to the different impact of the inflationary/deflationary mechanisms on the distribution of income. Its overcoming, therefore, expresses an adequate valorization of the system of relative prices and,[180] above all, the different ways in which the consumer goods

175 Ibid.
176 Graziani, 'Keynes e il *Trattato sulla moneta*', p.217.
177 *TM*, I, *CWK*, V, p.47.
178 Ibid., I, *CWK*, V, p.85.
179 Ibid., I, *CWK*, V, p.76.
180 Cf. Graziani, 'Keynes e il *Trattato sulla moneta*', p.218.

338

prices and the capital goods prices are defined. It is not accidental that the differences between relative prices 'are at once the test and the measure of the social disturbances which are occurring'.[181]

In order to establish the value of money, this situation imposes us to make reference to the 'relative relationships' between the assumed composite commodities and, therefore, to the magnitude of the 'compensatory movements'. '[I]n the case of prices a movement in the price of one commodity necessarily influences the movement in the prices of other commodities, whilst the magnitude of these compensatory movements depend on the first commodity as compared with the importance of the expenditure on the commodities secondary affected'.[182] In this sense, the analytical objective is twofold. On the one hand, it is necessary to emphasize the primary role of relative prices and the difficulties intrinsic to the hypothesis according to which the value of money would be fixed on the basis of a mere numerical instrument represented by the general level of prices; on the other, it is necessary to show how the variation in the relative prices, as it modifies the prices level (quantity given *ex post*), is relevant – even if it is assumed to be perfectly proportional. Hence, it is absolutely mistaken to assume 'that there is a meaning of price level, as a measure in some sense or another of the value of money, which retains its value unaltered when only *relative* prices have changed'.[183] In fact, the level of prices 'is itself a function of relative prices and liable to change its value whenever, [...], relative prices have change', because this change 'has in itself affected the price level'.[184] To sum up, it is the existence of the relative prices that characterizes the functioning mechanism of the capitalistic economy as a monetary economy.

For this reason, their variations, which in turn affect the level of prices when the social composition of the composite commodity change, inform a theory of the purchasing power of money that is based upon relative prices and that includes their variation. It is

181   *TM*, I, *CWK*, V, p.84.
182   Ibid., I, *CWK*, V, p.77.
183   Ibid., I, *CWK*, V, p.77.
184   Ibid.

reasserted, however, that a numerical comparison of prices that assumes to identify the level of the purchasing power cannot escape the difficulty that 'arises whenever we ask whether one thing is superior in degree to another *on the whole*, the superiority depending on the resultant of several attributes which are each variable in degree but in ways not commensurable with one another'.[185] For Keynes, in fact, what is 'relative' cannot be mediated. In this sense, the reference to *TP* is not symptomatic, but explicit: 'The difficulty is the same as that I have discussed in my *Treatise on Probability* [...]'[186] – Keynes maintains.

It might seem that a reconstruction of the evolution of Keynes's monetary theory would be marginal if compared to our problem; that is, it might seem that the relationship between *money* and *normation* should not imply a particular analysis of the role played by the relative prices system. This would be, however, an extrinsic objection. There is no doubt, in fact, that it is the existence of such a system that describes the alternative between hoarding and investment, imposing an active and normative role to the credit control policy via the interest rate policy. So conceived, the relative prices system serves also to explain the role of money in the distribution of monetary incomes and in the determination of profit.

Money connects 'past' and 'future', the temporal coordinates that lie at the very basis of the economic system and upon which normation should be able to exert its power. Through them, the relative prices system functions as a paradigm, as a sliding axis between the consumer goods and capital goods sectors, within which the decisions are autonomously made, determining the rate of profit adequate to the difference between investments and savings. Monetary stability, based upon this difference, is thus expressed by the relative prices system, in which the decisions taken by entrepreneurs, consumers, and the world of finance are all reciprocally distinct. The fundamental problem concerning the monetary theory – Keynes says – is 'to exhibit the causal process by which the price level is determined, and the method of

185 Ibid., I, *CWK*, V, p.88.
186 Ibid., I, *CWK*, V, p.88, footnote 2.

transaction from one position of equilibrium to another'.[187] Therefore, production and consumption are related, so as to define a theory of the general level of relative prices, according to which the fundamental problem refers to those 'past' and 'future' characterizing the economic system and within which the relationship between productive capital and financial capital is expressed.

What the so-called fundamental equations indicate is the fact that 'the price level of consumption goods is entirely independent of the price level of investment goods',[188] which are connected *de facto* to the choices made by the financial and banking capital, rather than to the production costs. This is the way in which the monetary character of the capitalistic economy allows us to identify, on the one hand, the sharp separateness between the determination of the level of consumption and the typology of investments and, on the other hand, to explain the dependency of the productive capital on the financial capital in the determination of the capital goods prices. It might be said that the relative prices system expresses, at the same time, the *separateness* and the *interdependence* that characterize the whole economic system and that, exactly for their character, point out as necessary the *monetary normation*.

Significantly, the truism of the fundamental equations – 'nothing but a detour and blind alley', Samuelson said[189] – indicates the very existence of the rate of profit and the reason why the relative prices system can only describe a dynamic situation in the purchasing power of money: 'In truth, the gold standard is already a barbarous relic'.[190] In comparison with *MR*, nevertheless, the monetary normation is more explicit here. Its different manifestations can be traced back to a model according to which the monetary policy consists of the stabilization of both the value of money and the rate of profit in the realm of a monetary economic system considered as a whole. The central

---

187   Ibid., I, *CWK*, V, p.120.
188   Ibid., I, *CWK*, V, p.123.
189   Samuelson, 'Lord Keynes and the *General Theory*', p.328. Regarding the critiques addressed to the *Treatise* and its 'fundamental equations', see Skidelsky, *John Maynard Keynes*, II, pp.444 ff.
190   *MR*, *CWK*, IV, p.138.

role of the credit policies is clearly related to the investment choices and to the alternative that these policies might bring about. In this sense, the credit policies play the role of *normative institution*, and the rate of interest represents the *limit* of their normative power.

The instrument that the credit intermediation can utilize is represented by the regulation of the funds saving via the rate of interest. The investment is encouraged when the prospective yield is higher than the rate of interest paid by the investor in order to dispose of the necessary credit. Vice versa, an increase in the rate of interest 'tends – other things being equal – to make the rate of investment [...] to decline relatively to the rate of saving',[191] hence, to make unstable the relationship between investments and savings. The concrete consequence in terms of a price decrease and unemployment is easily understandable (at least if the relationship is seen in its essential linearity); even prior, however, what we can infer at a theoretical level is the specific role of money, as it permits us to link together those 'past' and 'future' that characterize a monetary economy.

We have already said that in the monetary essence of the capitalistic economy we can see one of the main contributions produced by the Keynesian revolution. By the same token – Keynes assures – this does not deny but rather gives meaning to the role of the productive capital, clearly bound to financial capital, but nonetheless in relation to the expected return. What triggers the change, in fact, is linked to the action of the entrepreneurs, carried out 'under the influence of the actual enjoyment of positive or negative profits',[192] because it is the expected profit or loss that triggers the spring. Anyhow, it is true that according to such a forecast the banking system not only can, but also should act via its normative instruments, aiming at an approximate identity between the market rate of interest and the natural rate of interest.[193] If the price of credit is less onerous, the investment is encouraged, the prices level increases, profit is

---

191 *TM*, I, *CWK*, V, p.139.
192 Ibid., I, *CWK*, V, p.141.
193 Cf. K. Wicksell, *Geldzins und Güterpreise*, Fisher, Jena, 1898; on this matter see also G. Giovannetti, 'The Role of the Rate of Interest: From Wicksell to Keynes' Treatise on Money', *Economic Notes*, 1984, vol.1, 1, pp.66–85.

made, a higher competition in the capital goods, and therefore a higher rate of return, is expected. All this will occur until, in the long-period, the equilibrium will be reproduced, as prosperity and depression express the fluctuation of the credit policies. Finally, this shows how 'the influence of the rate of interest on the price level operates by its effect on the rate of investment [...]'.[194]

Now, what we want to emphasize is the way in which this relationship represents one of the strongest links connecting real economic choices and monetary choices. In the previous pages we have indicated the main reasons for this. However, it is now time to see how this link allows us to interpret the normation, which we have identified as the *method* and the *essence* of Keynes' economic theory. At this point, that the rate of interest expresses the *monetary normation* is evident. Certainly, it cannot be asserted 'that the banking system is the *only* factor in the situation – the *net* result depends on the policy of the banking system in conjunction with all kinds of other factors'.[195] Nevertheless, Keynes does not say to what additional factors he is referring to; and this induced him to conclude, perhaps simplistically, that the banking system 'can, by coming in as a balancing factor, control the final outcome'.[196] The normative acting is therefore essentially consigned to the rate of interest as a *last resource* of the normative institution embodied in the banking system. Of course, it is not possible to trace back the complexity of the economic system solely to the normative power of the banking policies; however, within such a complex framework, the banking system represents the pivot, the *starting point* from which the control 'of the final outcome' becomes possible – according to Keynes' expression.

This gives rise to two analytical models. The first is 'fictional' and therefore highly abstract. In it, value and cost of capital are equal to saving and profit is equal to zero. The second is 'critical', and it is represented by the impossible closing of the so-called credit cycle. The first model is 'fictional', as it assumes that the banking policy is effectively able to determine, via a market rate of interest tending

194 *TM*, I, *CWK*, V, p.177.
195 Ibid., I, *CWK*, V, p.164.
196 Ibid., I, *CWK*, V, p.165.

towards the natural rate of interest, the relationship between cost of investments and volume of saving.[197] The second is 'critical', as it assumes that the above is not at all a guaranteed result, and that, in an open economy, the reduction in the rate of interest might even involve a capital flight, in front of which the monetary normation would be insufficient. Given these complications, the rate of interest is a sort of *last resource*, provided that the banking system might be able and willing to utilize it in the most adequate and rational manner. On the other hand, operating *de facto* within an international economic structure, an equilibrium system of relative prices also requires the elasticity of the money rate of efficiency earnings of the productive factors.

The ensemble of these conditions can be grasped in the so called credit cycle, where 'a disturbance initially due to monetary factors will soon set up some disturbance on the investment side, and similarly a disturbance due to investments factors is likely, as we shall see, to cause some modification to monetary factors'.[198] Hence, there is a sort of reversibility, of which the credit cycle offers an adequate synthesis, revealing what are the limitations to which the rate of interest as a normative banking instrument is subjected when it is not referred to a simple 'fictional' model. This does not lead to the abandonment of this monetary instrument, but rather to the exigency of its focalization.[199] Such an exigency arises from the necessity to give a less uncertain shape to the theory of investment. Exigency that would become urgent above all after the publication of *TM*. At any rate, already in Book IV of *TM* it appears clear that the 'fictional' model would inevitably be destined to be confuted by the 'critical' model. In fact, the relevance of chapters XVII–XVIII imposes itself as

---

197 Keynes would return on this in *GT*: 'I had, however, overlooked the fact that in any given society there is, [...], a *different* natural rate of interest for each hypothetical level of employment'. So, 'the system could be in equilibrium with less than full employment' (*CWK*, VII, pp.242–3).

198 *TM*, I, *CWK*, V, p.248.

199 See Messori, 'Aspetti monetari della domanda effettiva', where a wide and qualified bibliography is included.

a result of the weight that Keynes attributes to the variations in investments intended as critical factors.[200]

Particularly in chapter XVIII, the phases characterizing the economic cycle are synthesized, and the causes and effects of the cyclical fluctuations in investment are analysed. The analytical terms recall the 'fictional' model, but they reach their synthesis in the shift towards the 'critical' model represented by the credit cycle. Of this latter Keynes provided the following definition: 'We now define the *credit cycle* to mean the alternations of excess and defect in the cost of investments over the volume of saving and the accompanying seesaw in the purchasing power of money due to these alternations'.[201] As noted by Augusto Graziani, once we fix our attention upon the expansive phase of the economic cycle, only the following alternative is given: either the total output is stable and investments increase to the detriment of the production of consumer goods; or the increment of investment generates a net increment of the total output. This is the general case – provided that there are unemployed production factors –, as it is the variation in the total investments that determines the start of the credit cycle.

If it is assumed that the volume of the total output is determined by aggregate demand, the problem concerns both the relationship between consumption and saving and the one between investment and saving. It concerns the relationship between aggregate demand and saving, the salient tracts of which have already been clarified by Keynes in the previous pages of *TM*. Thus, within this framework, the imbalance produced by the fluctuation in the investments is restated, as 'the decisions which determine saving and investment respectively are taken by two different sets of people influenced by different sets of motives'. Furthermore, '[n]ot only are the decisions made by different sets of persons; they must also in many cases be made at different times'.[202] If the variation in investments would imply an automatic variation in saving, no imbalance would be produced; what would vary would only be the relationship between the quota of investments

200 Keynes, *TM*, II, ch. 27. Cf. Vicarelli, *Keynes*, pp.113–14.
201 *TM*, I, *CWK*, V, p.249.
202 Ibid., I, *CWK*, V, p.250–1.

and the quota of consumption with respect to the total income as a whole – whilst the total employment and the total output would remain the same, assuming that the investment in fixed capital would not generate unemployment. However, this situation is only a 'fictional' hypothesis; so, it is needed to assume that both investment and saving represent entities not necessarily dependent in their reciprocal movements.

It is superfluous to note that this 'relationship' is governed by the rate of interest. In fact, insofar as the difference between the market rate and the natural rate of interest is particularly relevant, the changing of investments produces imbalance.[203] As a result, within the credit cycle the rate of interest distinguishes the 'fictional' from the 'critical' model, determining the effective primacy of the former upon the latter. The same relevance of the definition of a relative prices system in view of the determination of the value of money and of its stability resides here. Moreover, the irrelevance of a gold monetary stability is made perfectly clear, as the terms of the matter rest upon both the expansive capacity of the economic system, and the fluctuations of investment with regard to their relationships with savings. Once again, money is re-confirmed to be that temporal 'past' and 'future' of the economic process, for and in which the entrepreneurial activity makes explicit its expectations of profit. The banking system acts with respect to those temporal determinations. It can do so, *normatively*, operating via the *instrument* that influences the determination of the rate of saving and the regulation of the relationship between saving and investment. So, the rate of interest is the *last resource* of the monetary normation, the limit of the Keynesian normation before the definitive assumption of the State as *political guarantee* in the determination of effective demand.[204]

---

203 'Ogni qual volta si verifica una caduta nei rendimenti attesi degli investimenti netti, il tasso d'interesse naturale si abbassa; se il tasso di mercato non si abbassa anch'esso con eguale prontezza, gli investimenti cadono al di sotto dei risparmi e una depressione si mette in moto' (Graziani, 'Keynes e il *Trattato sulla moneta*', p.226).
204 Cf. Clarke, *The Keynesian Revolution*, pp.256–310.

The relevance and the role of this *last resource* have been questioned. Nevertheless, it is difficult to exclude that the rate of interest is, in the long run, an element of hope for Keynes. The hope here expresses the belief to weld together the choices concerning the expectations of the productive capital, those connected to the financial capital, and those inherent to the relationships between social collectivity and money. Hence, it becomes simply consequential that the banking system and the Treasury policies represent a sort of 'catalyst' – and Keynes' contribution is even more original if we think how rich was the tradition in which he operated. Its originality resides in that 'utopian pessimism', in that oxymoron, that would reach its full maturation in *GT*. 'There is, indeed – Keynes wrote in the 1930s – no possibility of intelligent foresight designate to equate savings and investment unless it is exercised by the banking system. [...] Yet hitherto the banking system has been mainly preoccupied with a different objective'.[205] Such a pessimism, however, still involves the hope that the banking system could operate in the due manner.

At any rate, Keynes' idea that the regulation of the credit cycle via the rate of interest could *only* be obtained under *given* conditions, explained the reasons why the same cycle should be assumed as a 'critical' model – in which the limit embodied by the rate of interest could be broken *de facto*, to the point of being *normatively* insufficient. Certainly, this specifies the role of the monetary regulation that the banking system holds in a 'fictional' model, but, on the other hand, it specifies also the difficulties of synthesizing, via the same regulation, the monetary choices in their being linked to investments. In other words, Keynes' pessimism interprets the problematic side of *TM*, which leads towards an indispensable political-Statual normation. From this point of view, the credit cycle shows both limits and hopes of a monetary policy *für sich*. If we look at Keynes' reasoning, this becomes apparent:

(i) The increased investment may take place, without any change in the total volume of output, by the substitution of the production of capital goods in place

205   *TM*, I, *CWK*, V, p.251.

of consumption goods; in this case the increase of investment will not materialise until after the elapse of a production period.

(ii) The increased investment may take the form of an increase of working capital corresponding to an increased total output due to an additional production of capital goods superimposed on the existing output; in this case the increase of investment will begin from the outset, being first of all in the shape of working capital and, after the elapse of a production period, in the shape of fixed capital.

(iii) The increased investment may take the form of an increase of working capital corresponding to an increased total output due to an additional production of consumption goods being superimposed on the existing output; in this case the increase of investment will only continue for the duration of a production period.[206]

Now, both (ii) and (iii) require an increased volume of money that 'may be furnished for the industrial circulation as the result of a decrease of the financial circulation'. However, if an adequate banking policy is not put in place, the risk of a crisis becomes very high, because the inflation generated by windfall profit, via competition would produce an income inflation that would require, in order to sustain the industrial circulation, a higher volume of money. This would increase the rate of interest, with the consequence of reducing new investments with respect to saving. 'The reaction from the boom will not merely have brought back prices and profits to the normal, but an era of business losses and subnormal prices will have commenced'.[207] As a result, the equilibrium of the 'fictional' model brings about, *de facto*, the crisis.

It is true that the above presupposes an indifferent banking system. In fact, if this latter were able to govern money according to the criterion $I = S$, the credit cycle would not occur. This is what Keynes, in the opening of chapter XXII, defines 'the normative side of our subject'.[208] At this point, however, one cannot avoid asking to what 'critical point' the limit constituted by the rate of interest as normative instrument might arrive. Operating in an open economy, it might be that the reduction of the rate of interest determines capital

206 Ibid., I, *CWK*, V, pp.252–3.
207 Ibid., I, *CWK*, V, p.261.
208 Ibid., II, *CWK*, VI, pp.3–4.

flight and consequent overseas investments. And if this were the case, we would face the following alternative: to stimulate employment regardless of the fact that the prospective yield might result inferior to the rate of interest; or to accept unemployment. If we decide to accept the former hypothesis, as Keynes notoriously suggested, then we also ought to contemplate a political system promoting social investments and adequate fiscal policies. Hence, the monetary normation, although technically unexceptionable in a 'fictional' model, in a 'critical' model must be integrated by investments support policies. This does not reduce the normative power that can be exerted by the monetary system via the discount rate and the rate of interest.[209] It simply shows the *social complexity* of a monetary economy.

7. Effective demand and 'political supply'

One of the first issues posed in the opening of *GT* is the relationship with *TM*. In the attempt to clarify the changes occurring, Keynes try to justify first of all why in *GT* money has lost the centrality previously held. This is a matter of argumentative opportunity – he seems to say – justified by 'a natural evolution in a line of thought which I have been pursuing for several years'. However, in a sort of self-critique, he continues saying: 'When I began to write my *TM* I was still moving along the traditional lines [...]. When I finished it, I had made some progress towards pushing monetary theory back to becoming a theory of output as a whole'. The primary fault was 'that I failed to deal thoroughly with the effects of *changes* in the level of output'. The

---

209   It is worth recalling the influence of Keynes' experience within the Macmillan Committee (cf. Skidelsky, *John Maynard Keynes*, II, pp.343 ff.; Clarke, *The Keynesian Revolution in the Making*, pp.103–24), if it is true, as Skidelsky pointed out (p.362), that the *General Theory* 'was, in part, a response to the objections of the Bank and the Treasury to his proposals.' As Skidelsky underlined (p.365), the so-called 'Henderson's shift', facing what he himself wrote in *Can Lloyd George Do It?*, would be emblematic.

fundamental equations 'were an instantaneous picture taken on the assumption of a given output'. The dynamic development 'was left incomplete and extremely confused'.[210]

Keynes' judgement is peremptory, but it neglects what is missing in the passage from *TM* to *GT*. According to Graziani, for example, some essential interpretative keys concerning the role of money would be missed.[211] If, in *GT*, money is explicitly considered from the point of view of demand, the same cannot be said concerning the financing of supply. To this removal it follows that the propulsive role of money would no longer be related to the total industrial activity, but rather to the sole production of capital goods. Further nodal differences between the two seminal works concern the theory of prices. Whilst, in *TM*, the relative prices system constituted the fundamental theoretical point, *GT* recuperates the marginalistic approach, which ignores *de facto* the essential distinction between capital goods prices and consumer goods prices. This implies the impossibility of reaching an eventual rebalancing between demand and supply of the consumer goods via the prices system. In fact, if the entrepreneurs decide the amount of investments, they do not decide the amount of consumer goods, now established by the propensity to consume.

Certainly, as Keynes remarks, the definitive shift of attention towards the relationship between employment and output should be considered, because in this relationship 'money enters into the economic scheme in an essential and peculiar manner'. The role of money is therefore restated, but this does not confute the impression that what is gained on the side of the 'theory of production' is partially lost on the side of the 'theory of money'. This is due to the fact that in the sphere of the former the role of the financing of production is no longer considered in a clear and distinct manner. As a result, the shift involves a price, but this is compensated by a new theory of crisis, that

---

210   *GT, CWK*, VII, p.XXII.
211   A similar point of view has been expressed by R.F. Harrod, 'Mr. Keynes and Traditional Theory', *Econometrica*, 1937, vol.5, 1. A very different opinion is provided by Vicarelli, *Keynes*, pp.86 ff. On the comparison between *TM* and *GT*, see Shackle, *The Years of High Theory. Invention and Tradition in Economic Thought*.

now Keynes links to the liquidity preference or, better still, to the transfer of profits in liquid cash. With regard to this latter, the sole monetary policy is no longer effective, even if the banking system would operate according to the most rational principles.[212] In short, it is only in *GT* that Keynes reaches the full consciousness of the limits inherent to the manoeuvre that the monetary instruments can exert and, specifically, of those limits inherent to the determination of the rate of interest. This represents Keynes' final detachment from the neoclassical model; it is the definitive refusal of the law of markets.[213]

At any rate, to interpret the shift from *TM* to *GT* simply as a theoretical evolution, would be insufficient. As Samuelson pointed out, '[w]hile Keynes did much for the Great Depression, it is no less true that the Great Depression did much for him'.[214] In other words, the effects of the Great Depression confirmed the worst forecasts deducible from the *normal functioning* of the capitalist business cycle. To think of *GT* as a reply to the Russian revolution and the insurrections of the 1920s, which occurred both in Europe and in the United States, is therefore stimulating but reductive. In the mid 1930s, Keynes' problem was represented not only by the necessity to govern the last effects of the Great Depression, but also by the urgency to govern those 'variables' that would have been able to lead to a new and possibly deeper crisis. Thus, it would be wrong to interpret *GT* as a simple description of the past. It might seem more correct to claim that from the catastrophe that had characterized the beginning of the 1930s, Keynes drew an exact theoretical comprehension of the general phenomena that would have been able to trigger a future and deeper crisis.

As a result, the control of demand and employment, besides giving rise to a theoretical revolution, should be intended as a powerful *political innovation*. According to Keynes, unemployment always in-

212   See also A. Graziani, 'Moneta senza crisi', *Materiali filosofici*, 1983, 7, pp.95–112.
213   Cf. A.H. Hansen, A *Guide to Keynes*, McGraw-Hill, New York, 1953.
214   Samuelson, 'Lord Keynes and the *General Theory*', p.329; but see also D. Dillard, 'The Pragmatic Basis of Keynes's Political Economy', *Journal of Economic History*, 1946, vol.6, November, pp.121–52.

volves two aspects. What is important is not only to avoid or control it, in order to impede wide demand fluctuations; but, also, it is essential to stabilize the whole social framework within which unemployment is determined. Mass production and demand support measures require a discipline aimed at stabilizing both economic and political supply[215] on the basis of the new systems of social relationship now in place.[216] What would be defined as a 'ruled democracy' cannot be inferred simply from the 'calculation' of the economic variables that the State would have to support. Rather, it express a political and social over-determination exerted by the State with regard to the macroeconomic relations that the political system would have to govern. In fact, in Keynes, the 'economic aspect' represents only one side of the coin. The other is represented by the control of social re-production, regarding which the effective demand stability is crucial, because the existence of capitalism as 'political supply' is connected to it. In this way, the

215 It is superfluous to say that, with the locution 'political supply', we do not intend to refer to the vast literature comprising, among others, K.J. Arrow (*Social Choice and Individual Values*, Wiley & Sons, New York, 1951), A. Downs (*An Economic Theory of Democracy*, Harper & Row, New York, 1957), J.M. Buchanan, G. Tullock (*The Calculus of Consent*, The University Press of Michigan Press, Ann Arbor, 1962). Rather, we are implicitly referring to T.H. Marshall, *Citizenship and Social Class* (1949), in Id., *Sociology at the Crossroad*, Heinemann, London, 1963.

216 From an historiographical point of view, Keynes' theoretical revolution has been repeatedly associated both with Taylorism and Fordism (B. Coriat, *L'atelier et le chronomètre*, C. Bourgois Editeur, Paris, 1979; A. Salsano, *Ingegneri e politici*, Einaudi, Torino, 1987), and the constitutional models that, in the post Second World War period, would formulate a new relationship between juridical formalism and social sphere (cf. R. Schlesinger, *Central European Democracy and its Background: Economic and Political Group Organisation*, Routledge & Keagan, London, 1953). On this matter, see E. Forsthoff, *Rechtsstaat im Wandel*, W. Kohlhammer Verlag, Stuttgart, 1964, pp.27–62; and A. Negri, *La forma stato. Per la critica dell'economia politica della Costituzione*, Feltrinelli, Milano, 1977, pp.27–110, who particularly insists on the 'costituzionalizzazione del lavoro'. With regard to the possibility of defining Keynes as a 'social economist', see K.P. Cochran, 'Why a Social Economics?', *Review of Social Economy*, 1979, vol.37, April, pp.121–32; H.E. Jensen, 'Some Aspects of the Social Economics of John Maynard Keynes', *International Journal of Social Economics*, 1984, vol.11, 3–4, pp.72–91.

effective demand becomes the formal epicentre of the Keynesian theoretical system, and to it the many social and economic tensions must be traced back.[217]

From an analytical point of view, it is well known that the notion of effective demand rests at the heart of *GT*. Effective demand is connected to the functional character of both aggregate demand and aggregate supply, intended as functions of employment. But we shall not dwell upon this. It is sufficient to say here that the critical point is represented, on the one side, by the permanence of *autonomous decisions* concerning the sector of consumer goods and that of capital goods, and, on the other, by the relationship between saving and investments.[218] This latter relationship restates the normative relevance of the rate of interest, as the amount of current investment 'depend[s] on the relation between the schedule of the marginal efficiency of capital and the complex of rate of interest [...]'.[219] It is worth noting that these conditions, *de facto*, reunite both monetary regulation and social normation under the concept of effective demand, from which depend not only the rate of employment, but also the reproducibility of the capitalistic system of accumulation.

With respect to the above, it is certainly possible to underline the lesson of the Great Depression; but, even before, it should be underlined that it is the derived and innovative concept of 'involuntary unemployment' which gives meaning to the normative character of effective demand. This character would be widely confirmed, as Moggridge recalled, in a series of articles that Keynes published on *The Times* in 1937, and in which the attention was 'concentrated on the avoidance of future fluctuations in demand'.[220] According to the neoclassical theory, as the supply determines its own demand, any point of the demand curve would correspond to the effective demand. According to Keynes, instead, '[w]ide variations are experienced in

217 G. Lunghini, 'La *Teoria generale* come trappola teoretica', in Graziani, Imbriani, Jossa (a cura di), *Studi di economia keynesiana*, pp.99–100.
218 On this relationship, see F. Caffè, *Teorie e problemi di politica sociale*, Laterza, Bari, 1970, pp.20–1. The author underlines how in this relationship it is possible to grasp what is in common between *TM* and *GT*.
219 *GT*, *CWK*, VII, p.28.
220 Moggridge, *Keynes*, p.110.

the volume of employment without any apparent change either in the minimum real demand of labour or in its productivity'.[221] Thus, there should be only one point of the aggregate demand curve that indicates the effective demand and, *above all*, nothing can guarantee that full employment corresponds to such a point. Rather, it is underemployment that is more likely to occur. As a result, the probable fall of the consumer demand would induce a flexion of the aggregate demand, a fall in the investments and a further decrease of the rate of employment. This well-known schizophrenia represents the effective critical point of the capitalist system, and on these grounds it is possible to claim that the concept of effective demand enjoys a normative value.

However, also with regard to investments the effective demand synthesizes the monetary essence of the whole inter-capitalistic relationship. In fact, the relationship between aggregate income and the variation in investments indicates that the increase of these latter, through stimulating production, induces an increase of the disposable income from which the necessary saving for financing of investment derives. Assuming that an increase in employment might be absorbed given a determinate 'situation of technique',[222] the effective demand would necessarily tend to increase. We have already said that investments are linked *de facto* to the expected return and, with regard to their financing, to the interest rate. Thus, the monetary normation should focus its action upon the variations in demand and upon the increase/decrease of its normative efficacy with regard to the levels of employment. In fact, under-employment equilibrium, with respect to which the effective demand ought to increase in order to express its effect as social normation, is indeed made explicit in the relationship between productive capital and finance.

As Marcello Messori wrote, the role played by finance shows that the underemployment equilibrium is not a mere possibility, but rather a *chronic* characteristic, intrinsic to the *normal functioning* of

221 *GT, CWK*, VII, p.9.
222 But see P. Sylos Labini, *Oligopolio e progresso tecnico*, Einaudi, Torino, 1972, pp.205–6.

the capitalistic economy and its social division into classes.[223] Hence, we might say that the effective demand qualifies the very same monetary normation as *social normation*. The relationship between productive capital and financial capital represents the key for understanding the first cause of the underemployment equilibrium, upon which the level of effective demand should exert its normative effect. The trade cycle is represented by the fluctuations of investments with respect to the aggregate real income. These fluctuations, affecting the standard of consumption, can be described according to the effective demand variation. That is, demand determines the outcome expectations. This allows us to synthesize the essence of the Keynesian trade cycle with regard to the critical relationship between marginal efficiency of capital and the long-term interest rate, as the incentive to invest depends upon the relation between the schedule of marginal efficiency of capital and rates of interest.[224]

In short, the marginal efficiency of capital is defined by Keynes as 'the relation between the prospective yield of a capital-asset and its supply price', that is, as 'that rate of discount which would make the present value of the series of annuities given by the returns expected

223   Messori, 'Aspetti monetari della domanda effettiva', p.282. On the 'finance motive' cf. A. Graziani, 'The Debate on Keynes' Finance Motive', *Economic Notes*, 1984, 1, pp.5–33; A. Asimakopulos, 'The Role of Finance in Keynes' *General Theory*', *Economic Notes*, 1985, 3, pp.5–16; A. Graziani, 'Keynes' Finance Motive: A Replay', *Economic Notes*, 1986, 1, pp.5–9; J.A. Kregel, 'Il finanziamento in Keynes: dal *Trattato* alla *Teoria generale*', in A. Graziani, M. Messori (a cura di), *Moneta e produzione*, Einaudi, Torino, 1988, pp.59–71.

224   On the ambiguities intrinsic to the concept of marginal efficiency of capital there is a vast literature. Among others, Joan Robinson observed: 'There is another element of *The General Theory* which is more dubious; this is the conception of the marginal efficiency of capital. It seems to contain an undigested lump of what Keynes called classical theory. In one sense it means merely the expected rate of profit on investments that businesses are planning to make, but in another sense it means the real return to the economy as a whole that an increment of capital will bring' (Robinson, 'What has become of the Keynesian Revolution?', p.129). Two different approaches are provided by P. Garegnani (*Valore e domanda effettiva*, Einaudi, Torino, 1979, pp.70 ff.) and Lunghini (*La crisi dell'economia politica e la teoria del valore*, p.63).

from the capital-asset during its life just equal to its supply price'.[225] Evidently, any single capital expresses a marginal efficiency, and only the agglomeration of singular kinds of capital expresses the marginal efficiency of the 'social capital'. It is inevitable that, at this point, the rate of interest 'holds the role of villain of the piece that impoverishes nations'[226] – as Schumpeter said. In fact, the problem resides in the identification of the causes that make possible the variation of the marginal efficiency of capital, which, in turn, 'depends on the rate of return expected to be obtainable on money if it were invested in a *newly* produced asset'.[227]

Furthermore, since this return is expressed in prospective yields, it becomes also inevitable that it is influenced by the variations of the rate of interest. In general terms, the increase in investments – assumed as hypothetically homogeneous – reduces marginal efficiency, 'partly because the prospective yield will fall as the supply of that type of capital is increased, and partly because, as a rule, pressure on the facilities of producing that type of capital will cause its supply price to increase [...]'. 'In other words, the rate of investment will be pushed to the point on the investment demand-schedule where the marginal efficiency of capital in general is equal to the market rate of interest'.[228] In a different way, the maintenance of liquid stocks would be the most likely result. 'It follows – Keynes concludes – that the inducement to invest depends partly on the investment demand-schedule and partly on the rate of interest'.[229]

This simple 'economical mechanic', however, has not yet explained the critical relationship between the stability of the marginal efficiency of capital and the middle-social profitability of the investment. In fact, the problem is not represented by the simple maximization of marginal efficiency, but rather by its *social regulation*: what the rate of interest is unable to guarantee, what the sole monetary normation cannot obtain. In other words, individual expectations aim

225   *GT*, *CWK*, VII, p.135.
226   Schumpeter, *The History of Economic Analysis*, p.1176.
227   *GT*, *CWK*, VII, p.136
228   Ibid., *CWK*, VII, pp.136–7.
229   Ibid., *CWK*, VII, p.137.

at maximizing the marginal efficiency; however, this raises an issue that goes far beyond the normation realized by the rate of interest, as the instability of the capitalistic system cannot be governed until the different prospective marginal rates of profit are not brought back to the middle efficiency of the *Kapital im allgemeinen*.

Thus, two points are crucial here. If, on the one hand, the determination of the marginal efficiency of capital represents the dynamic, and therefore unstable, essence of the trade cycle, on the other, the relationship between marginal efficiency of capital and rate of interest emphasizes that the monetary and conflictual character of the capitalistic economy requires its social integration: a *plan of control*. It is not accidental that the marginal efficiency of capital, in its relationship with the rate of interest, indicates the limit inherent to the monetary manoeuvre regarding long run expectations. It is this that underlines the possible role to be assigned to the State in sustaining investment, indicating exactly in the dynamics of expectations the main feature of the capitalistic system of accumulation.

8. Im Lauf der Zeit

After having dedicated chapter V of *GT* to short-term expectations – 'upon the basis of which a producer estimates what he will get for a product when it is finished if he decides to begin producing it to-day with the existing plant [...][230] –, Keynes dedicates chapter XII to the analysis of long-term expectations:

> The considerations upon which expectations of prospective yields are based are partly existing facts which we can assume to be known more or less for certain, and partly future events which can only be forecast with more or less confidence. Amongst the first may be mentioned the existing stock of various types of capital-assets and of capital-assets in general and the strength of the existing consumers' demand for goods which require for their efficient production a relatively larger assistance from capital. Amongst the latter are future changes

---

230   Ibid., *CWK*, VII, p.148.

in type and quantity of the stock of capital-assets and in tastes of the consumer, the strength of effective demand from time to time during the life of the investment under consideration, and the changes in the wage-unit in terms of money which may occur during its life.[231]

In short, with regard to the uncertainty generated by future events, Keynes argues that 'the state of long-term expectation' does not differ from a 'state of psychological expectation'.[232] And it is at this very point that we find the fundamental statement according to which '[i]t will be foolish, in forming our expectations, to attach great weight to matters which are very uncertain.' In other words, the locution 'very uncertain' is not equivalent to what, in *TP*, Keynes defined as 'very improbable'. In fact, we should take into consideration here an unknown probability.[233] Hence, there is no inference between primary and secondary proposition, as the former, being related to future events, for which 'there is no scientific basis on which to form any calculable probability whatever', is radically undecidable.[234]

Regarding this, the Keynesian exegetics reached notable virtuosities. At any rate, as we have already noted, it would be meaningless to deny that – on the basis of the distinction between what is very improbable and what is very uncertain – Keynes is identifying here a 'grey area' characterized by the interaction between subjective beliefs (expectations) and inter-subjective conventions.[235] On the other hand, as this new perspective is not intended to question the 'regionality' of any 'relative knowledge', it seems correct to argue that the *epistemological approach* characterizing *TP* is unchanged. If it is true that

231   Ibid., *CWK*, VII, p.147.
232   See also the critical remarks provided by G. Hodgson ('Persuasion, Expectations and the Limits to Keynes', in Lawson, Pesaran (ed by), *Keynes' Economics. Methodological Issues*, pp.10–45), who placed the emphasis 'on the institutional frameworks which both influence and constrain economic action in the real world'.
233   R. O'Donnell, 'Keynes's Weight of Argument and its Bearing on Rationality and Uncertainty', in Bateman, Davis, *Keynes and Philosophy*, pp.82–3.
234   J.M. Keynes, 'The General Theory of Employment', *Quarterly Journal of Economy*, 1937, vol.51, February, pp.209–23, *CWK*, XIV, p.114.
235   Vercelli, 'Peso dell'argomento e decisioni economiche', p.107.

the non-esaustivity of a contextual knowledge always generates uncertainty, it follows that what 'is rational for us to believe'[236] is not only what is probable, but also what is *conventionally* considered as a sort of epistemological barrier in respect of the irrational *tout court*.[237] As Tony Lawson observes, 'the convention of assuming the existing state of affairs will continue unless there is definite news to the contrary is legitimately applied on essential epistemic grounds'.[238]

In explaining the fallibility of long-term forecasts, Keynes underlines that the projection of the 'facts about which we feel somewhat confident' heavily affects the formation of the long-term expectation. Its state 'does not depend, therefore, on the most probable forecast we can make. It also depends upon the *confidence* with which we make this forecast – on how highly we rate the likelihood of our best forecast turning out quite wrong'.[239] Accordingly, the impact of confidence upon economic phenomena derives from the fact that particularly great is its influence upon the schedule of the marginal efficiency of capital, 'which is the same thing as the investment demand-schedule'. Long-term expectations can only rest upon psychological expectations, partially bound by what happened in the past; in turn, exactly because there is not 'much to be said about the state of confidence *a priori*',[240] what happened in the past can only generate a psychological expectation. In a society dominated by 'private business of the old-fashioned type', the decision to invest was 'largely irrevocable'. 'But the Stock Exchange revalues many investments every day and the revaluations give a frequent opportunity to the individual

236   *TP*, *CWK*, VIII, p.339.
237   Regarding this, Vicarelli ('Dall'equilibrio alla probabilità: una rilettura del metodo della *Teoria generale*', p.298) wrote: 'La maggiore incertezza degli elementi su cui si formano le aspettative riduce la "fiducia" ma è neutrale sulla probabilità, e quindi sul grado di credenza razionale che è possibile assegnare a certi eventi futuri sulla base della loro relazione con dati eventi osservati'.
238   T. Lawson, 'Economics and Expectations', in Dow, Hillard (ed. by), *Keynes, Knowledge and Uncertainty*, pp.94–5. Cf. also E.G. Winslow, 'Organic Interdependence, Uncertainty and Economic Analysis', *Economic Journal*, 1989, vol.99, 398, pp.1173–82.
239   *GT*, *CWK*, VII, p.148.
240   Ibid., *CWK*, VII, p.149.

(though not to the community as a whole) to revise his commitments'. The development of organized markets makes it possible that the daily revaluations 'inevitably exert a decisive influence on the rate of current investments'. Hence, only a *tacit convention* can provide a sufficiently robust ground upon which it would be possible to base any forecast.[241] 'The essence of this convention – though it does not, of course, work out quite so simply – lies in assuming that the existing state of affairs will continue indefinitely, except in so far as we have specific reasons to expect a change'.[242] Clearly, the fiction is consciously explicit and compatible only 'with a considerable measure of continuity and stability in our affairs, *so long as we can rely on the maintenance of the convention*'.[243]

As it is legitimate to assume that, in general terms, the factors of indeterminateness of long-term expectations are connected to the modification of the capitalistic socio-economic structure, it follows that it is difficult to make reference only to economic factors in the strictest sense of the term. First and foremost, it is the complexity of a social system, within which entrepreneurial and financial structures continuously change, that determine the heterogeneity of both the causes and effects. Hence, 'the gradual increase in the proportion of the equity in the community's aggregate capital investment', certainly connected to an entrepreneurial structure that was no longer Marshallian – Keynes says –, decreases both knowledge and control of people, 'who do not manage and have no special knowledge of the circumstances, either actual or prospective, of the business in question'. By the same token, day-to-day fluctuations of profits 'tend to have an altogether excessive, and even absurd, influence on the market', generating repercussions 'as the result of a sudden fluctuation of opinion due to factors which do not really make much difference to the prospective yield [...]':

> But – Keynes underlines – there is one feature in particular which deserves our intention. It might have been supposed that competition between expert professionals, [...], would correct the vagaries of the ignorant individual left to

241   Cf. Davis, *Keynes's Philosophical Development*, pp.124 ff.
242   *GT, CWK*, VII, p.152.
243   Ibid.

360

himself. It happens, however, that the energies and skill of the professional investor and speculator are mainly occupied otherwise. For most of these persons are, in fact, largely concerned, not with making superior long-term forecasts of the probable yield of an investment over its whole life, but with foreseeing changes in the conventional basis of valuation a short time ahead of the general public.[244]

Those who speculate do so placing their hopes on a favourable change of the conventional basis of valuation, rather than upon the prospective yield. Consequently, the so-called fetish of liquidity leads to a paradox. 'As the organisation of investment markets improves, the risk of the predominance of speculation does, however, increase'.[245] The more severe the effects induced by the fetish of liquidity, the more unjustified they appear, and the more the normative value of the conventional basis of valuation are destroyed by them. Expectations generate further expectations, that produce uncertainty *de facto*, the impossible automatism of an economic system no longer able to sustain the greatest fiction: the idea that there is a necessary virtuous correlation between profit, risk and social system:

> There is no clear evidence from experience that the investment policy which is socially advantageous coincides with that which is most profitable. It needs *more* intelligence to defeat the forces of time and our ignorance of the future than to beat the gun.[246]

But the paradox, stemming from 'a good Benthamite calculation', concerns not only the fetish of liquidity. There is also another kind of instability. It derives directly from intrinsic characteristics of human nature, according to which 'a large proportion of our positive activities depends on spontaneous optimism rather than on a mathematical expectation, whether moral or hedonistic or economic'.[247] An

244 Ibid., *CWK*, VII, p.154. It has been noted that it is not uncertainty that stems from instability, 'piuttosto, l'incertezza, vista come proprietà del sistema di interazione congiunturale, può generare instabilità' (Lunghini, Rampa, 'Conoscenza, equilibrio e incertezza endogena', p.471).
245 *GT, CWK*, VII, p.158. Cf. Dillard, 'The Pragmatic Basis of Keynes's Political Economy'.
246 *GT, CWK*, VII, p.157.
247 Ibid., *CWK*, VII, p.161.

enterprise based upon long-term valuations is beneficial to the community as a whole; however, only when reasonable calculations are sustained by 'animal spirits' able to set aside the 'thought of ultimate loss' will the individual enterprise reveal its adequacy. This implies that economic prosperity directly depends upon a political and social atmosphere 'congenial to the average business man'. In the seminal article published in 1937, after having argued once again that with the locution 'uncertain knowledge' he was not merely referring to the possibility to distinguishing 'what is known from what is only probable', Keynes observes:

> Around these matters there is no scientific basis on which to form any calculable probability whatever. We simply do not know. Nevertheless, the necessity for action and for decision compels us as practical men to do our best to overlook this awkward fact and to behave exactly as we should if we had behind us a good Benthamite calculation of a series of prospective advantages and disadvantages, each multiplied by its appropriate probability, waiting to be summed.[248]

The variety of techniques thought *ad hoc* essentially consists of assuming 'that the present is a much more serviceable guide to the future than a candid examination of the past experience would show it to have been hitherto'; hence, in assuming that the present kinds of judgements rest 'on a *correct* summing up of future prospects, so that we can accept it as such unless and until something new and relevant comes into the picture'. Finally, knowing 'that our individual judgment is worthless', 'we endeavour to conform with the behaviour of the majority or the average'. As a result, the diffusion of conventional judgements, based upon an uncertain basis and subjected to abrupt and sharp changes, occurs. Vice versa, the orthodox theory, assuming a *stricto sensu* calculable future, 'leads to a wrong interpretation of the principles of behaviour which the need for action compels us to adopt, and to an underestimation of the concealed factors of utter doubt, precariousness, hope and fear'.[249] In short, if long-term expectations can only guarantee a range of possible prospective yields, only con-

248 Keynes, 'The General Theory of Employment', *CWK*, XIV, p.114.
249 Ibid., *CWK*, XIV, p.122.

fidence can sustain the decision to invest. Below, we shall briefly return to this matter.

Before doing so, it is worth recalling how effective demand synthesizes the wholeness of an economic trade strongly affected by the state of expectation. This is said in chapter XXII of *GT*, and subsequently confirmed in the famous article published in 1937, where Keynes, in order to determine the employment relative to a given effective demand, stressed the relevance attributed to the fluctuations in the marginal efficiency of capital and in the rate of interest. The nexus between demand and employment synthesizes the complexity of economic trade and, simultaneously, explains the importance of its stability, that should be reached via policies sustaining the function of aggregate investment, and a gradual reduction in the marginal efficiency, so as to support the propensity to consume. In Keynes' words: '[w]hilst aiming at a socially controlled rate of investment with a view to a progressive decline in the marginal efficiency of capital, I should support at the same time all sorts of policies for increasing the propensity to consume'.[250]

It has been advanced that with his theory of aggregate demand Keynes would partially obliterate the conflictual character of the capitalistic system. This might be correct; but what is more important is that around effective demand, Keynes coagulates the (dis)-functioning of the capitalistic system as a whole, challenged not because of its unfair allocation of resources, but rather because of the impossible automatism of its process of accumulation. It might be an exaggeration to claim that, regardless of the fact that one likes it or not, Keynes' ideology has no importance; at any rate, it is true that 'Keynes is the sole modern economist concerned, in his own way, with the fundamental and indeterminable relationship occurring between composition and distribution of surplus. A fundamental relationship that, for reasons that are as obvious as neglected, is indeterminable, because the determinants of at least one, and certainly the most important, components of surplus intended as effective demand, are

---

250   *GT*, *CWK*, VII, p.325.

indeterminable'.[251] And it is such an indeterminacy which pushes effective demand beyond pure economic reasoning.

Any sphere of the economic system should be shaped according to a 'vision' that in first instance is primarily social and then economic. Keynes' distance from the neoclassical aim is synthesized by this assumption. Only the social stability of the economic relations can guarantee a relative stability of the system *en général*. And it is consequential that in Keynes' mind this ought to be reached via the control of the two components that determine aggregate demand. On the other hand, it is necessary to be very careful in order not to incur a twofold over-simplification. Although it might seem that the sole problem is represented by a sort of 'social calculation' of aggregate demand, it should not be forgotten that the control upon demand presupposes the stability in the investment supply and that – given its dependency from the credit system (self-financing always enjoyed a marginal role) – an efficient monetary policy is similarly indispensable. If the capitalist system rests upon a monetary economy, the liquidity preference represents, always and anyway, its spectre. This is why any possible decision taken by a single investor attempting to reach the maximum marginal efficiency is not necessarily the most apt decision. And we should not underrate the fact that the policies determining the rates of interest are chronically insufficient to stimulate or to control the course of marginal efficiency; and, although efficient, they run the risk of being inadequate whereby, in particular situations, investment policies are not directly underpinned by the State. At the end of chapter XII of *GT* Keynes wrote:

> For my own part, I am now somewhat sceptical of the success of a merely monetary policy directed towards influencing the rate of interest. I expect to see the State, which is in a position to calculate the marginal efficiency of capital on long view and on the basis of the general social advantage, taking an ever greater responsibility for directly organising investment [...].[252]

251   G. Lunghini, 'Teoria economica ed economia politica', in Id. (a cura di), *Produzione, capitale e distribuzione*, Isedi, Milano, 1975, p.XVII.
252   *GT, CWK*, VII, p.164. See also *State Planning* (*CWK*, XXI, pp.84–92).

It is worth mentioning – as we shall see in the last section – that the above reasoning leads to the *vexata quaestio* concerning the tendencies in the long-term and the system of expectations they involve.[253] As Lunghini pointed out, this is Keynes' great ambiguity, towards which, however, it is insufficient to assume that the hiatus between short and long-term is entirely traceable to issues of economic theory *qua theoria*. In fact, regardless of logical aporias present in the Keynesian 'open model',[254] in the long-run the sole meaningful choices are those inspired by the *social philosophy* that for Keynes represents the *fulfilment* of his 'critical economic theory'[255] – even if, and exactly because, its aim is 'to deal with long-term problems as they were short term problems'.[256] In *GT*, in fact, questions to which the sole economic discipline cannot provide satisfactory answers are intentionally raised. Nevertheless, it is due to its *critical character* that Keynes' theoretical building cannot but be commensurated, conceptually, with the problem represented by the action of the State – and, therefore, thought *beyond* the liberal State and its alleged automatisms. In other words, it is not an 'ethical surplus' that defines the *critical character* of the Keynesian reflection. Ethics informs it

253 For example, Axel Leijonhufvud argued that Keynes 'turned his attention away from the traditional preoccupation with long-run tendencies towards the problems of macroeconomic adjustment processes in the short run' (*On Keynesian Economics and the Economics of Keynes*, p.333). For a detailed account of Leijonhufvud's interpretation, see Vicarelli, 'Dall'equilibrio alla probabilità', pp.313–18; G. Martinengo, 'La reinterpretazione del pensiero di Keynes nell'analisi di Leijonhufvud: una formalizzazione critica', in F. Vicarelli (a cura di), *La controversia keynesiana*, Il Mulino, Bologna, 1974, pp.109–42; A. Vercelli, 'Equilibrio e disequilibrio nella *Teoria Generale* di Keynes: il ruolo dei salari monetari e le difficoltà di un metodo di puro equilibrio', in Graziani, Imbriani, Jossa (a cura di), *Studi di economia keynesiana*, pp.107–55). An opinion *toto coelo* different is expressed by Lunghini, *La crisi dell'economia politica*, pp.59–67.
254 M. Gotti, 'La *General Theory* come opera aperta', in Marzola, Silva (a cura di), *John Maynard Keynes. Linguaggio e metodo*, pp.185–227.
255 Cf. H.P. Minsky, *John Maynard Keynes*, Columbia University Press, New York, 1975, pp.145 ff.
256 Lunghini, *La crisi dell'economia politica*, p.64.

from the very outset, but its development, rather than being a conditioning element, becomes even more conditioned.[257]

In this sense, Schumpeter's claim according to which Keynes' approach can only be transposed into a macro-dynamic framework determined by the role of money, enjoys a wider, even if less *technical*, significance. In fact, the prospective yields constituting the essential motivations of the economic actors are given in time, as expectations. However, once established that it is due to the disappearance of those 'neoclassical automatisms' assured by the liberal State that these prospective yields become merely possible, the fundamental issue still remains intact. It is represented by the role of 'political choice' and deliberate action, taken for granted that the sole monetary policies are not able to control the instability of the social system, and that a normal level of investments or a normal rate of accumulation, to which the long run expectation tends to compare itself, does not exist.[258]

9. We have to abate somewhat...

Upon which assumption can the economic actors base their long-term expectations? And furthermore, upon which basis is the long-run prefigurable? Keynes' answer is unequivocal: upon the state of confidence. That is, beyond any 'calculation', the expectations, given their uncertain nature, are guaranteed only by the state of confidence: namely, by its conventional character as it is determinable in the short-run. Evidently, it is fundamental to understand how stable the convention might be. On this matter, Keynes maintains: 'We should not conclude from this that everything depends on waves of irrational psychology. On the contrary, the state of long-term expectation is often steady, and, even when this is not, the other factors exert their

257   See Davis, *Keynes's Philosophical Development*.
258   Vicarelli, 'Dall'equilibrio alla probabilità', pp.314–15.

compensating effects'.[259] However, if we ask what are the foundations for the forecast concerning the 'human decisions affecting the future' – be they personal, political, or economical –, we can see that they 'cannot depend on strict mathematical expectation' but, rather, they are based on 'our motive on whim or sentiments or chance'.[260] In other words, the *convention* rests upon a *conventional base*.

On these grounds, it is unequivocal what Keynes says in the famous letter to Hugh Townshend dated the 7th of December 1938, where, distinguishing between risk premium and liquidity premium,[261] and therefore between what is very improbable and what is very uncertain, he affirms:

> I think it important to emphasise the point that all this is not particularly an *economic* problem, but affects every rational choice concerning conduct where consequences enter into the rational calculation. Generally speaking, in making a decision we have before us a large number of alternatives, none of which is demonstrably more 'rational' than the others, in the sense that we can arrange in order of merit the sum aggregate of the benefits obtainable from the complete consequences of each. To avoid being in the position of Buridan's ass, we fall back, therefore, and necessarily do so, on motives of another kind, which are not 'rational' in the sense of being concerned with the evaluation of consequences, but are decided by habit, instinct, preference, desire, will, etc. All this is just as true of non-economic as of the economic man. But it may well be, as you suggest, that when we remember all this, we have to abate somewhat from the traditional picture of the latter.[262]

Only a few months before, in the midst of his polemic with Jan Tinbergen,[263] Keynes had wrtten to Harrod noticing that economic

259   *GT*, *CWK*, VII, p.162.
260   Ibid., *CWK*, VII, p.163.
261   'I am rather inclined to associate risk premium with probability strictly speaking, and liquidity premium with what in my *Treatise on Probability* I called "weight"' (*To Hugh Townshend, 7 December 1938, CWK*, XXIX, p.293).
262   Ibid., *CWK*, XXIX, p.94.
263   The *querelle* concerned Tinbergen's *Statistical Testing of Business-Cycle Theories. A Method and Its Application in Investment Activity* (League of Nations, Geneva, 1939, vol.1), sponsored by The League of Nations. The aim of the book was 'to test hypotheses about the trade cycle produced by Haberler in his book *Prosperity and Depression*. Keynes was sent it in proof for comment (Skidelsky, *John Maynard Keynes*, II, p.618 ff.). The arguments proposed by Keynes in

science could not be considered as a natural science; rather, as it not only deals 'with introspection and with values', but also 'with mo-

'Professor Tinbergen's Method' (*Economic Journal*, 1939, vol.49, 195, pp.34–51; *CWK*, XIV, pp.306–18) stem from Tinbergen's claim, according to which his analysis was confined to 'measurable phenomena', although he acknowledged the relevance of the non-measurable phenomena, with respect to which his analysis should have been integrated by information inferred 'from other sources' (cf. Tinbergen, *Statistical Testing of Business-Cycle Theories*, p.11). Keynes remarked: 'But how can this be done? He does not tell us. His method of calculating the relative importance of these measurable factors essentially depends on the assumption that between them they are comprehensive. He gives them such regression coefficients that they completely explain the phenomenon under examination. How can they be "supplemented" by other information? If it is necessary that *all* the significant factors should be measurable, this is very important. For it withdraws from the operation of the method all those economic problems where political, social and psychological factors, including such things as government policy, the progress of invention and the state of expectation, may be significant. In particular, it is inapplicable to the problem of business cycle' (Ibid., p.309). Not less important were Keynes' remarks about the fact that Tinbergen's analysis dealt 'with non-simultaneous events and time lags'; in fact, this implied an epistemological aspect extremely important for Keynes: namely, induction. 'Thirty years ago I used to be occupied in examining the slippery problem of passing from statistical description to inductive generalization in the case of simple correlation; and today in the era of multiple correlation I do not find that in this respect practice is much improved' (Ibid., p.315). In this regard, Samuelson's critique would be harsh: 'Keynes' critical review of Tinbergen's econometric business cycle study for the League of Nations reveals that Keynes did not really have the necessary technical knowledge to understand what he was criticizing. How else are we to interpret such remarks as his assertion that a linear system can never develop oscillations?' (Samuelson, 'Lord Keynes and the *General Theory*', p.327, footnote 2). However, that Tinbergen's system were 'open to serious criticisms, about which no more can be said than that they should not blind us to the greatness of this pioneer effort', has also been noted by Schumpeter in his *History* (p.1163). Tinbergen's position – *contra* Keynes – would be subsequently defended by T. Haavelmo ('The Probability Approach in Econometrics', *Econometrica*, 1944, vol.12, July, Suppl.). Only in recent times Keynes' critique has been revaluated: D. Dharmapala, M. McAleer, 'Econometric Methodology and the Philosophy of Science', *Journal of Statistical Planning and Inference*, 1996, vol.49, pp.9–37; H.A. Keuzenkamp, *Probability, Econometrics and Truth. The Methodology of Econometrics*, Cambridge University Press, Cambridge, 2000; Lawson, Pesaran (ed. by), *Keynes' Economics: Methodological Issues*.

tives, expectations, psychological uncertainties', it should be considered as a 'moral science'.[264]

Now, this explains what we have previously defined as the conventional character of the convention, determined by Keynes' insistence on referring uncertainty to sentiments: *motives, instinct* and *preference*. If we stop here, however, Keynes' analysis would appear as a sort of great short-circuit – and such a conclusion is suggested by most of the critics, who, not accidentally, argue for the Marshallian (and therefore Victorian) matrix characterizing the Keynesian political outcomes.[265] That economic science could not be considered as a natural science was certainly maintained by Marshall. Nevertheless, very different would be the *epistemic grounds* and the contextualization upon which, starting from the 1920s, Keynes *politicus* would forge his 'critical economic theory'. It is true that the conventional character of the convention has to do with *motives, instinct* and *preference*; however, in no case is it confined within the singular universe of the action; rather, it is the same uncertainty intended as 'common sentiments' which requires a publicly orientated acting. The 'necessity for action and for decision' imposes itself on the basis of a specific 'critical economic theory', and not upon an 'ethical' surplus: this is the pivotal point and it is not contradictory. Simply, ethics, economy, and politics should stay together, not by a mere overlapping, but rather representing a *synthesis*. As Joan Robinson wrote, Keynes brought back into Economics 'something of the hard-headedness of the Classics'.[266] As for classical authors, also for Keynes the capitalistic system is a structure in movement. Hence, we can say that economic phenomena can never be merely economic. This means neither that we can extrinsically assign an ethical connotation to them, nor that political choice or action is thinkable apart from the economic 'datum' or from the interindividual ethical interaction. The turning

---

264   *To R.F. Harrod, 16 July 1938, CWK*, XIV, p.300.
265   Such a perspective has been provided by E. and H. Johnson, 'The Social and Intellectual Origins of the *General Theory*', *History of Political Economy*, 1974, vol.6, 3, pp.261–77; and by Davis, *Keynes's Philosophical Development*, p.171.
266   J. Robinson, *Economic Philosophy*, p.74.

point lies somewhere else. It is represented by the tireless work of Keynes *politicus* that, after having assumed the impossible 'natural foundation' of any social order, demolished the very same idea of an economic *ordre naturel*, informed by its own alleged, political stability, intrinsic certainties, and forecasts. Thus, the conventional character of the convention, although it synthesizes a state of psychological expectation, is conceived of as the result of a social interaction among individuals and between them and institutions.[267] The confidence rests upon a conventional basis exactly because it cannot invoke any 'value' able to transcend the interaction itself. Accordingly, although any potential political deliberation is connected to the conventional character of the confidence, it is distinct from this latter, because it must appeal to a *normative instance*.

Our initial question was: how an epistemological 'relative' model could be transposed into a 'practical' system of regulation, into a normative 'social philosophy'? We believe that the answer should be articulated bearing in mind that the convention is *tacit* but *public*; as such, it concerns individual subjects in their interrelationships and collective subjects in their public praxis. It might probably be difficult to deny that uncertainty has something to do with the ignorance of the objective distribution, weight of arguments, scarcity of the relevant evidence, etc. It is nonetheless acceptable the idea according to which the common denominator that qualifies the very uncertain events can be found in the fact that they represent 'the result of the interaction between different social actors'.[268] With regard to this interaction, 'the social philosophy towards which *GT* might lead' can only propose

---

267   Here is worth recalling the difference between 'atomism' and 'organicism'. On this matter, A. Carabelli (*On Keynes's Method*, p.213) wrote: 'As the whole did not consist simply of the sum of the parts, the collective result of the actions of single individuals or group, even motivated by common expectations, might be different from what one would expect to obtain from the sum of them. The postulate of homogeneity between parts and whole was criticised by Keynes as the "fallacy of composition", as it obscured the possibility that the whole and the sum of its parts might need to be treated differently. Keynes's attitude was strictly connected with his view of society as an organic unity'.

268   Lunghini, Rampa, 'Conoscenza, equilibrio e incertezza endogena', p.452.

itself as an 'acting' normatively oriented, on the basis of a realized synthesis between the Economical and the Political.

It is worth repeating that, in its radicality, Keynes' critique to *laissez-faire* is not merely confined to the stigmatization of what in the pure market model is not working, but rather it questions the ethical and epistemological groundings of a baseless *lex naturae*, upon which an improbable economical and political *ordre naturel* ought to be based. All this has a precise consequence. Given the monetary rather than the 'neutral' character of the capitalistic system; given, as a consequence, the strategic importance of monetary normation; measured its relative incidence; measured '[t]he outstanding faults of the economic society in which we live and its failure to provide for full employment and its arbitrary and inequitable distribution of wealth and incomes'; what follows is that the 'critical economic theory' produces a *deliberate political acting*, based upon what the economic theory can *rationally* identify. Such a deliberate political acting requires a synthesis between the Economical and the Political, as it is faced with a radical uncertainty that characterizes both 'the economic society in which we live', and the conventional acting, *tacit* but *public*.[269]

The state of confidence and the state of convention constitute the premises but not the limits of the political acting in the long-run. Its essence 'lies in assuming that the existing state of affairs will continue indefinitely, except in so far as we have specific reasons to expect a change'.[270] Thus, its essence is social, in the sense that '[t]he social object of skilled investment should be to defeat the dark forces of time and ignorance which envelop our future'.[271] That is, the political acting is expressed as a possible *normation* in the long run. Its possibility is strongly bound to consistent actions that cannot be considered apart from convention, but that could not hide themselves behind it. And this – assuming that the autonomy characterizing the 'animal spirits' might generate a refractoriness towards any normation

---

269 Cf. C. Marazzi, *E il denaro va. Esodo e rivoluzione dei mercati finanziari*, Bollati Boringhieri-Casagrande, Torino-Bellinzona, 1998, pp.72–80.

270 *GT, CWK*, VII, p.152.

271 Ibid., *CWK*, VII, p.155.

– is not only due to the fact that the autonomous changing of expectations might induce modifications in the state of confidence – and therefore of the convention –, but also, and above all, to the fact that it is upon the political acting that, in the last instance, the maintenance of the legitimacy of capitalism as 'political supply' must be traced back.

The invocation of 'a somewhat comprehensive socialisation of investment' is the most reasonable suggestion in terms of economic policy, intended to reduce the structural uncertainties in the long-run. But it is also an exhortation aimed at making the political acting the interpreter of a certain degree of socialization, of a 'political supply', obviously unthinkable in the tradition of Marshall's Economics. In more appropriate terms, the normative State becomes the Social State, where, in perspective, the Political would no longer be a simple normative condition, but rather a synthetic function that, combined with the administrative function, would constitute the 'political system'.[272]

In short, the main path we have taken is this. We have introduced an 'argumentative complication' concerning the link between *TP* and *GT*, restating the importance of this link and, simultaneously, insisting upon what underpins it: that is, Keynes' critique to *laissez-faire*. We have tried to show that his primary objective was that of questioning the epistemological and ethical foundations of a baseless, economical, and political *ordre naturel*. We have seen that such an operation excludes any 'natural foundation' of economics. The uncertainty characterizing the capitalistic, social, and economic model is therefore the result of the interaction between different kinds of 'relative knowledge', which characterize the forecast processes inherent not only to the changing psychology of the 'animal spirits', but also, and above all, to the choices made or omitted by the main political and economic institutions. More specifically, if it is true that uncertainty is one of the characteristic tracts that for Keynes distinguish a monetary economy from a neutral economy, what follows is, first of all, the necessity to identify adequate monetary instruments and, secondly, the urgency of defining 'political choices' able to reach where the sole monetary

---

272 The explicit reference to N. Luhmann's work ('Politische Planung', *Jahrbuch für Sozialwissenschaft*, 1966, Heft 27, pp.271–96) is intentional here.

policy cannot. The 'argumentative complication' is so resolved in the definition of a normative horizon, not merely monetary, but *explicitly political*, according to which the exigency of the regulation of the economic trade is not a contingent but a structural event.

Undoubtedly, at the very basis of this reasoning it is possible to see the 'Philosophy of Practice' that the young Keynes elaborated in the summer of 1905. At the same time, this reasoning indicates, *lato sensu*, the relevance that should be credited to the epochal knot represented by the epistemological difference between *Substanzbegriff* and *Funktionsbegriff*. In fact, this difference directly concerns the definition of a 'progressive' political philosophy, according to which the fiction of an *ordre naturel* represents an unacceptable price – equal to the inability of recognizing the endogenous and structural character of uncertainty. On these grounds, 'political decision' and 'economic mediation' merge together.[273] In this, the experience of Keynes *politicus* – 'einer der klarsten Beobachter und Beurteiler', Troeltsch wrote – had a role that was *not* merely pragmatic, but rather consciously and radically *synthetic*.

---

273   It is pertinent here to recall Carl Schmitt's fundamental critique to economic liberalism (*Der Begriff des Politischen*, Duncker & Humblot, Berlin, 1963, p.69). According to Schmitt, as it is confined between *heterogenen Sphären – Ethik und Wirtschaft, Geist und Geschäft, Bildung und Besitz –*, Liberalism is unable to grasp what is the peculiar function of *the Political*. It is worth noting that Schmitt's polemic towards the mere 'positivity' informing Kelsen's *Grundnorm* (*Verfassunglehre*, Duncker&Humblot, Berlin, 1928, pp.8–9) – severely criticized on the grounds that it is not based on the *existenziell vorhanden*, which is such as it is *Ursprung eines Sollens*, whose *potestas oder Autorität liegt in seinem Sein* – is for many aspects complementary to his critique to economic liberalism. In turn, Kelsen's reply would qualify as *fiktiv* what to his eyes appeared, in Schmitt's reasoning, as undemostrated *Einheit des Volkes* ('Wer soll der Hüter der Verfassung sein?', *Die Justiz*, 1930–1931, Bd. VI, 11–12, pp.576–628; in H. Kelsen, A. Merkl, A. Verdross, *Die Wiener Rechtstheoretische Schule*, Europa Verlag, Wien, 1968, pp.1873 ff.; part. p.1909).

Bibliography

1. Primary sources

Arendt, H., *The Human Condition*, The University of Chicago Press, Chicago, 1958.

—— *On Revolution*, Penguin Books, Harmondsworth, 1986.

Bentham, J., *Déontologie ou science de la morale*, *Oeuvres*, éd. par E. Dumont, Hauman, Bruxelles, 1840, vol.3.

Berkeley, G., *The Works of George Berkeley Bishop of Cloyne*, ed. by A.A. Luce, T.E. Jessop, Nelson, London, 1950.

Böhm-Bawerk, E. von, 'Zum Abschluß des Marxschen System', in O. von Boenigk (hrsg. von), *Staatswissenschaftliche Arbeiten. Festgabe für Karl Knies*, Haering, Berlin, 1896.

—— 'Eine "dynamische" Theorie des Kapitalzinses', *Zeitschrift für Volkswirtschaft, Sozialpolitik und Verwaltung*, 1913, Bd.22.

Böhm-Bawerk, E. von, Clark, J.B., Menger, C., Schumpeter, J.A., *La teoria austriaca del capitale e dell'interesse. Fondamenti e discussione*, introduzione di N. De Vecchi, Istituto della Enciclopedia Italiana, Roma, 1983.

Butler, J., *The Works of Bishop Butler*, ed. by J.H. Bernard, Macmillan, London, 1900.

Cassirer, E., *Substanzbegriff und Funktionsbegriff*, B. Cassirer Verlag, Berlin, 1910.

Chamberlin, E.S., *Theory of Monopolistic Competition*, Harvard University Press, Cambridge MA, 1933.

Clarke, S., *A Demonstration of the Being and Attributes of God*, James Knapton, London, 1705.

Condillac, E.B. de, *Traité des sensation*, *Oeuvres*, de l'imprimerie de Ch. Houels, Paris, 1798, vol.3.

Condorcet, M.J.A.N. Caritat de, *Esquisse*, in *Oeuvres*, éd. par F. Arago, M.F. O'Connor, Firmin Didot, Paris, 1847–1849, vol.6.

Cumberland, R., *De legibus naturae disquisitio philosophica*, Typis E. Flesher, apud Nathanaelem Hooke, Londini, 1672.

Descartes, R., *Regulae ad directionem ingenii*, in *Oeuvres*, éd. par C. Adam, P. Tannery, Vrin, Paris, 1974, vol.10.

—— *Passion de l'âme*, in *Oeuvres*, vol.11.

Diderot, D., Alembert, J. Le Rond D' (mis en ordre et publie par), *Encyclopédie ou dictionnaire raisonné des sciences, des arts et des métiers*, Impr. des Editeurs, Livourne, 1770–1779: 'Égalité', 'Droit naturel', 'Liberté naturelle', 'Société'.

Diderot, D., *De l'interpretation de la nature*, in *Oeuvres*, éd. par J. Assézat, M. Torneux, Kraus Reprint, Nendeln, 1966, vol.2.

Durkheim, É, *De la division du travail social*, PUF, Paris, 1960.

—— *Les règles de la méthode sociologique*, PUF, Paris, 1960.

Ferguson, A., *An Essay on the History of Civil Society*, Millar, London, 1767.

Frisch, R., 'On the Notion of Equilibrium and Disequilibrium', *The Review of Economic Studies*, 1935–1936, vol.3, 1.

Hayek, F.A. von, *Law, Legislation and Liberty*, University of Chicago Press, Chicago, 1982.

Hegel, G.W.F., *Über die wissenschaftlichen Behandlungsarten des Naturrechts*, in *Gesammelte Werke*, hrsg. von H. Buchner und O. Pöggeler, Meiner, Hamburg, 1968, Bd.4.

—— *Jenenser Realphilosophie I*, in *Gesammelte Werke*, hrsg. von W. Bonsiepen und H. Heede, Bd.8.

—— *Die Phänomenologie der Geist*, in *Gesammelte Werke*, hrsg. von R.P. Horstmann und G.H. Trede, Bd.9.

—— *Die "Rechtsphilosophie" von 1820. Mit Hegels Vorlesungsnotizen 1821–1825*, in *Vorlesungen über Rechtsphilosophie 1818–1831*, hrsg. von K.-H. Ilting, Frommann-Holzboog, Stuttgart-Bad Cannstatt, 1974, Bd.2.

Heidegger, M., *Vorträge und Aufsätze*, Verlag G. Neske, Pfullingen, 1954.

Helvétius, C.A., *De l'Esprit*, in *Oeuvres*, éd. par I. Belaval, G. Olms, Hildesheim, 1969.

Hobbes, Th., *Opera philosophica, quae latine scripsit, omnia*, ed. by W. Molesworth, Scientia Verlag, Aalen, 1961.

—— *The English Works*, ed. by W. Molesworth, Scientia Verlag, Aalen, 1962.

Holbach, P.H.D., Baron d', *Système de la nature*, éd. par I. Belaval, G. Olms, Hildesheim, 1966.

Home, H., Lord Kames, *Essays on the Principles of Morality and Natural Religion*, G. Olms, Hildesheim, 1976.

Hume, D., *A Treatise of Human Nature*, in *The Philosophical Works*, ed. by T.H. Green, T.H. Grose, Scientia Verlag, Aalen, 1964, vol.1.

—— *Philosophical Essays concerning Human Understanding*, in *The Philosophical Works*, vol.4.

—— *Enquiry concerning the Principles of Morals*, in *The Philosophical Works*, vol.4.

—— *Essays, Moral, Political, and Literary*, ed. by E.F. Miller, Liberty Fund, Indianapolis, 1987.

—— *The Letters of David Hume*, ed. by J.Y.T. Greig, Oxford University Press, Oxford, 1932.

Hutcheson, F., *An Inquiry concerning beauty, order, harmony, design*, ed. by P. Kivy, Nijhoff, The Hague, 1973.

—— *A System of Moral Philosophy*, Millar, London, 1755.

Kant, I., *Idee zu einer allgemeinen Geschichte in weltbürgerlicher Absicht*, in *Werke*, hrsg. von W. Weischedel, Wissenschaftliche Buchgesellschaft, Frankfurt, 1968, Bd.11.

Kelsen, H., *Hauptprobleme der Staatsrechtslehre*, J.C.B. Mohr (P. Siebeck), Tübingen, 1911.

—— 'Wer soll der Hüter der Verfassung sein?', *Die Justiz*, 1930–1931, Bd.6, 11–12.

—— *Society and Nature: a Sociological Inquiry*, The University of Chicago Press, Chicago, 1943.

Keynes, J.M., *The Collected Writings of John Maynard Keynes*, ed. by E. Johnson and D. Moggridge, Macmillan, London, 1971 ff.

—— 'Ethics in Relation to Conduct (1904)', in *The John Maynard Keynes Papers*, King's College Library, Cambridge, UA/19/2/6.

—— 'The Political Doctrines of Edmund Burke (1904)', in *The John Maynard Keynes Papers*, UA/20/3.

—— 'Miscellanea Ethica (1905)', in *The John Maynard Keynes Papers*, UA/21.

—— *A Treatise on Probability*, Macmillan, London, 1921 (*CWK*, VIII).

—— *A Tract on Monetary Reform*, Macmillan, London, 1923 (*CWK*, IV).

—— *Am I liberal?* (*CWK*, IX).

—— 'Alfred Marshall 1842–1924', in *Essays in Biography*, Macmillan, London, 1933 (*CWK*, X).

—— 'The Committee on the Currency. Notes and Memoranda', *The Economic Journal*, 1925, June (*CWK*, XIX).

—— 'The Economic Consequences of Mr. Churchill', in *Essays in Persuasion*, Macmillan, London, 1931 (*CWK*, IX).

—— 'The End of Laissez-faire', in *Essays in Persuasion* (*CWK*, IX).

—— *Can Lloyd George Do It?* (*CWK*, IX).

—— *A Treatise on Money*, Macmillan, London, 1930 (*CWK*, V–VI).

—— *State Planning* (*CWK*, XXI).

—— 'Poverty in Plenty: is the Economic System self-Adjusting?', *The Listener*, 21.XI.1934 (*CWK*, XIII).

—— *The General Theory of Employment, Interest and Money*, Macmillan, London, 1936 (*CWK*, VII).

—— 'The General Theory of Employment', *Quarterly Journal of Economy*, 1937, vol.51, February (*CWK*, XIV).

—— *My Early Beliefs* (*CWK*, X).

—— *To R.F. Harrod, 16 July 1938* (*CWK*, XIV).

—— *To Hugh Townshend, 7 December 1938* (*CWK*, XXIX).

—— 'Professor Tinbergen's Method', *Economic Journal*, 1939, vol.49, 195 (*CWK*, XIV).

La Mettrie, J.O., *Oeuvres philosophiques*, G. Olms, Hildesheim, 1970.

La Rochefoucauld, F., *Maximes*, éd. par J. Truchet, Garnier, Paris, 1967.

Locke, J., *An Essay concerning Human Understanding*, ed. by P.H. Nidditch, Clarendon, Oxford, 1975.

377

—— *Two Treatises of Government*, ed. by P. Laslett, Cambridge University Press, Cambridge, 1967.

Malthus, T.R., *Principles of Political Economy*, Kelley, New York, 1964.

Mandeville, B., *The Fable of the Bees: or Private Vices, Publick Benefits*, ed. by F.B. Kaye, Oxford University Press, Oxford, 1924.

—— *A Search into the Nature of Society*, in Mandeville 1924.

Marshall, A., *Principles of Economics*, Macmillan, London, 1959.

Marx, K, Engels, F., *Werke*, Dietz, Berlin, 1956 ff.

Marx, K., *Kritik des Hegelschen Staatsrechts* (*MEW*, Bd.1).

—— *Lohnarbeit und Kapital* (*MEW*, Bd.6).

—— *Grundrisse der Kritik der Politischen Ökonomie*, Dietz, Berlin, 1953.

—— *Zur Kritik der Politischen Ökonomie*, Duncker, Berlin, 1859 (*MEW*, Bd.13).

—— *Das Kapital. Kritik der politischen Ökonomie*, O. Meissner, Hamburg, 1890–1894[4] (*MEW*, Bde.23-5).

—— *Resultate Des Unmittelbaren Produktionsprozesses: (6. Kpl. d. 1 Bd. d. "Kapitals". Entwurf 1863/1864)*, Dietz Verlag, Berlin, 1988.

—— *Theorien über den Mehrwert* (*MEW*, Bd.26, 1–3).

—— *To Engels, 8 December 1857* (*MEW*, Bd.29).

—— *To Engels, 18 December 1857* (*MEW*, Bd.29).

—— *To Engels, 25 December 1857* (*MEW*, Bd.29).

—— *To Engels, 16 January 1858* (*MEW*, Bd.29).

—— *To Engels, 13 January 1859* (*MEW*, Bd.29).

—— *To Weydemeyer, 1 February 1859* (*MEW*, Bd.29).

—— *Capital. A Critique of Political Economy*, trans. by B. Fowkes, Penguin Books, London, 1990.

—— *Grundrisse. Foundations of the Critique of Political Economy*, trans. by M. Nicolaus, Penguin Books, London, 1993.

—— *Theories of Surplus-value*, trans. by E. Burns, Progress Publishers, Moscow, 1969

Marx, K., Engels, F., *Collected Works*, Progress Publishers – Lawrence & Wishart, Moscow and London, 1975 and ff.

Marx, K., Engels, F., *Der Deutsche Ideologie* (*MEW*, Bd.3).

Mclaurin, C., *Discoveries of Sir Isaac Newton*, G. Olms, Hildesheim, 1971.

Menger, C., *Untersuchungen über die Methode der Sozialwissenschaften, und der Politischen Ökonomie insbesondere*, Duncker & Humblot, Leipzig, 1883

—— *Die Irrtümer des Historismus in der deutschen Nationalökonomie*, Hölder, Wien, 1884.

Millar, J., *Observations Concerning the Distinctions of Ranks in Society*, printed for John Murray, London, 1771.

Myrdal, G., *Monetary Equilibrium*, W. Hodge, London, 1939.

Montaigne, M. de, *Essais*, in *Oeuvres complètes*, éd. par R. Barral, P. Michel, Seuil, Paris, 1967.

Montesquieu, C.L. de Secondat, *De l'esprit des lois, Oeuvres*, éd. par A. Masson, Nagel, Paris, 1950.

—— *Lettres Persanes, Oeuvres*, vol.1.

Newton, I., *Principia*, in *Opera*, ed. by S. Horsley, J. Nichols, Londini, 1779, vol.3.

Parsons, T., *The Social System*, Free Press, Glencoe (Ill.), 1959.

Pascal, B., *Pensées*, in *Oeuvres*, éd. par L. Brunschvicg, Hachette, Nendeln, 1977.

Pope, A., *Essay on Man*, in *The Poems of Alexander Pope*, ed. by J. Butt, Methuen, London, 1965.

Ramsey, F.P., 'A Treatise on Probability', *The Cambridge Magazine*, 1922, January.

—— *The Foundations of Mathematics and other Logical Essays*, ed. by R.B. Braithwaite, Routledge & Kegan, London, 1931.

Reid, Th., 'Thomas Reid's Criticism of Adam Smith's Theory of Moral Sentiments', ed. by E.H. Duncan and R.M. Baird, *Journal of the History of Ideas*, 1977, vol.28, 3.

Ricardo, D., *On the Principles of Political Economy and Taxation*, in *The Works and Correspondence of David Ricardo*, ed. by P. Sraffa, Cambridge University Press, Cambridge, 1951–1973.

Robbins, L., 'On a Certain Ambiguity in the Conception of Stationary Equilibrium', *Economic Journal*, 1930, vol.40, 158.

Robinson, J., *The Economic of Imperfect Competition*, Macmillan, London, 1933.

Rousseau, J.-J., *Discours sur l'inégalité parmi les hommes*, in *Oeuvres*, éd. par B. Gagnebin, Gallimard, Paris, 1964, vol.3.

Russell, B., *Introduction to the Mathematical Philosophy*, Allen & Unwin, London, 1919.

—— 'A Treatise on Probability. By John Maynard Keynes', *The Mathematical Gazette*, 1922, July.

Samuelson, P.A., 'Dynamics, Statics and the Stationary State', *The Review of Economics and Statistics*, 1943, vol.25, 1.

Scheler, M., *Wesen und Formen der Sympathie, Gesammelte Werke*, hrsg. von M.S. Frings, Francke, Bern und München, 1973, Bd.7.

—— *Probleme einer Soziologie des Wissens, Gesammelte Werke*, Bd.8.

Schmitt, C., *Verfassunglehre*, Duncker & Humblot, Berlin, 1928.

—— *Der Begriff des Politischen*, Duncker & Humblot, Berlin, 1963.

Schmoller, G., 'Die Schriften von C. Menger und W. Dilthey zur Methodologie des Staat – und Sozialwissenschaften', *Jahrbuch für Gesetzgebung, Verwaltung und Volkswirtschaft im Deutschen Reich*, 1883, Bd.7.

Schopenhauer, A., *Die Welt als Wille und Vorstellung*, Brockhaus, Leipzig, 1859.

Schumpeter, J.A., *Das Wesen und der Hauptinhalt der theoretischen National-ökonomie*, Duncker & Humblot, München-Leipzig, 1908.

—— *Theorie der wirtschaftlichen Entwicklung*, Duncker & Humblot, Berlin, 1934[4].

—— 'Eine "dynamische" Theorie der Kapitalzinses: Eine Entgegnung', *Zeitschrift für Volkswirtschaft, Sozialpolitik und Verwaltung*, 1913, vol.22.

—— *Epochen der Dogmen- und Methodengeschichte*, in *Grundriss der Sozial-ökonomik*, I Abteilung, *Wirtschaft und Wirtschaftswissenschaft*, Mohr (Paul Siebeck), Tübingen, 1914.

—— 'Das Sozialprodukt und die Rechenpfennige: Glossen und Beiträge zur Geldtheorie von heute', *Archiv für Sozialwissenschaft und Sozialpolitik*, 1917–1918, Bd.44.

—— *The Theory of Economic Development*, Harvard University Press, Cambridge MA, 1934.

—— 'Carl Menger', *Zeitschrift für Volkswirtschaft und Sozialpolitik*, 1921, n. S., Bd.1.

—— 'Depressions. Can We Learn from Past Experience?', in AA.VV., *The Economics of the Recovery Program*, Whittlesey House – McGraw Hill, New York and London, 1934.

—— *Business Cycles. A Theoretical, Historical and Statistical Analysis of the Capitalist Process*, McGraw-Hill, New York and London, 1939.

—— 'Science and Ideology', *The American Economic Review*, 1949, vol.39, 2.

—— 'Theoretical Problems of Economic Growth', in *Essays*, ed. by R.V. Clemence, Addison-Wesley, Cambridge MA, 1951.

—— 'The March into Socialism', *The American Economic Review*, 1950, vol.40, May.

—— *Ten Great Economists. From Marx to Keynes*, Allen & Unwin, London, 1952.

—— *Capitalism, Socialism and Democracy*, Allen & Unwin, London, 1954.

—— *Economic Doctrine and Method*, trans. by R. Aris, George Allen & Unwin, London, 1954

—— *History of Economic Analysis*, Allen & Unwin, London, 1955.

—— 'Money and the Social Product', trans. by A.W. Marget, *International Economic Papers*, 1956, vol.6, pp.148–211.

—— *Das Wesen des Geldes*, hrsg von F.K. Mann, Vandenhöck und Ruprecht, Göttingen, 1970.

—— *Trattato della moneta capitoli inediti*, a cura di L. Berti e M. Messori, ESI, Napoli, 1996.

—— *Briefe / Letters*, ausgewählt und hrsg. von U. Hedtke und R. Swedberg, Mohr (P. Siebeck), Tübingen, 2000.

Shaftesbury, A.A.C., *Characteristicks*, John Darby, London, 1732.

Simmel, G., *Philosophie des Geldes*, in *Gesammelte Werke*, Duncker & Humblot, Berlin, 1958, Bd.1.

—— *Grundfragen der Soziologie (Individuum und Gesellschaft)*, de Gruyter, Berlin, 1917.

—— *Kant. Sechzehn Vorlesungen gehalten an der Berliner Universität*, Duncker & Humblot, München-Leipzig, 1924.

Smith, A., *The Glasgow Edition of the Works and Correspondence of Adam Smith*, Clarendon, Oxford, 1976 ff., vol.6.

—— *The Theory of Moral Sentiments*, ed. by A.L. Macfie, D.D. Raphael.

380

—— *An Inquiry into the Nature and Causes of the Wealth of Nations*, ed. by R.H. Campbell, A.S. Skinner, W.B. Todd, vol.2.

—— *Essays on Philosophical Subjects*, ed. by P.D. Wightman, J.C. Bryce & I.S. Ross.

—— *Lectures on Rhetoric and Belles Lettres*, ed. by J.C. Bryce.

—— *Lectures on Jurisprudence*, ed. by R.L. Meek, D.D. Raphael, P.G. Stein.

—— *Correspondence of Adam Smith*, ed by E.C. Mossner, I.S. Ross.

Spinoza, B. *Epist.* L a J. Jelles, 2.6.1674, in *Opera*, hrsg. von C. Gebhardt, C. Winters, Universitätsbuchhandlung, Heidelberg, 1924–1925, Bd.4.

Sraffa, P., 'The Laws of Returns under Competitive Conditions', *Economic Journal*, 1926, vol.36, 144.

Tocqueville, A. de, *L'Ancien régime et la Révolution*, in *Oeuvres complètes*, M. Levy, Paris, 1952.

Toland, J., *Letters to Serena*, Frommann, Stuttgart, 1964.

Troeltsch, E., *Spektator Briefe: Aufsätze über die deutsche Revolution und die Weltpolitik, 1918–1922*, Mohr (P. Siebeck), Tübingen, 1924.

Veblen, T., *The Theory of the Leisure Class*, Kelley, New York, 1965.

Voltaire, *Dictionnaire*, in *Oeuvres*, éd par L. Moland, Garnier, Paris, 1878–1883, vol.22.

—— *Métaphysique de Newton*, in *Oeuvres*, vol.22.

—— *Traité de métaphysique*, *Oeuvres*, vol.22.

Weber, M., *Der protestantische Ethik und der Geist des Kapitalismus* (1904–1905), *Gesammelte Aufsätze zur Religionssoziologie*, Mohr (P. Siebeck), Tübingen, 1978, Bd.1.

—— *Wirtschaft und Gesellschaft*, hrsg. von J. Winckelmann, Mohr (P. Siebeck), Tübingen, 1956.

—— *Gesammelte Aufsätze zur Wissenschaftslehre*, hrsg. von J. Winckelmann, Mohr (P. Siebeck), Tübingen, 1951[2].

Wicksell, K., *Geldzins und Güterpreise*, Fisher, Jena, 1898.

Wittgenstein, L., *Über Gewissheit – On Certainty*, hrsg. von G.E.M. Anscombe und G.H. von Wright, Blackwell, Oxford, 2003.

—— *Philosophische Bemerkungen*, Blackwell, Oxford, 1964.

2. Secondary literature

AA. Vv., *Austromarxismus*, Europäische Verlagsanstalt, Frankfurt a. M.- Wien, 1970.

AA. Vv., *Operai e stato*, Feltrinelli, Milano, 1972.

AA. Vv., *Il newtonianesimo nel Settecento*, Istituto della Enciclopedia Italiana, Roma, 1983.

Aaron, R.I., *John Locke*, Clarendon, Oxford, 1952.

Aglietta, M., Orlean, A., *La violence de la monnaie*, PUF, Paris, 1982.

Ahmad, S., 'Adam Smith's Four Invisible Hands', *History of Political Economy*, 1990, vol.22, 1.

Albani, P., 'Sraffa and Wittgenstein. Profile of an Intellectual Friendship', *History of Economic Ideas*, 1998, vol.6, 3.

Alessandrini, P., *Keynes e la politica monetaria internazionale*, in Faucci 1977.

Allen, P., *The Cambridge Apostles. The Early Years*, Cambridge University Press, Cambridge, 1979.

Allen, R.L., *Opening Doors: The Life and Work of Joseph Schumpeter*, Transaction Publisher, New Brunswick and London, 1991.

Althusser, L., *Pour Marx*, Maspero, Paris, 1965.

Althusser, L., Balibar, E., *Lire Le Capital*, Maspero, Paris, 1965.

Anspach, R., 'The Implications of the Theory of Moral Sentiments for Adam Smith's Economic Thought', *History of Political Economy*, 1972, vol.4, Spring.

Appleby, J., *Liberalism and Republicanism in the Historical Imagination*, Harvard University Press, Cambridge MA., 1992.

Arena, R., 'Schumpeter after Walras: "Economie pure" or "stylized Facts"'?, in T. Lowry (ed. by), *Perspective on the History of Economic Thought*, Elgar, Aldershot, 1992.

—— 'Schumpeter on Walras', in R. Arena and C. Dangel-Hagnauer (ed. by), *The Contribution of Joseph Schumpeter to Economics*, Routledge, London, 2002.

Arestis, P., *The Post-Keynesian Approach to Economics. An alternative Analysis of Economic Theory and Policy*, Elgar, Aldershot, 1992.

Arrow, K.J., *Social Choice and Individual Values*, Wiley & Sons, New York, 1951.

Arrow, K., Hahn F.H., *General Competitive Analysis*, Oliver and Boyd, Edinburgh, 1971.

Ashcraft, R., 'Locke's State of Nature: Historical Fact or Moral Fiction?', *The American Political Science Review*, 1968, vol.62, September.

—— *Locke's Two Treatise on Government*, Allen & Unwin, London, 1987.

Asimakopulos, A., 'The Role of Finance in Keynes' General Theory', *Economic Notes*, 1985, 3.

Backhaus, J.G., 'The German Economic Tradition: from Cameralism to the Verein für Sozialpolitik', in *Political Economy and National Realities*, ed. by M. Albertone e A. Masoero, Fondazione L. Einaudi, Torino, 1994.

Baczko, B., *Lumières de l'utopie*, Payot, Paris, 1978.

Bagolini, L., *La simpatia nella morale e nel diritto*, Giappichelli, Torino, 1975.

—— 'Sulla "Teoria dei sentimenti morali" di Adam Smith', *Rivista internazionale di filosofia del diritto*, 1977, vol.64.

—— *David Hume e Adam Smith*, Patron, Bologna, 1979.

Baldini, A.E., *Il pensiero giovanile di John Locke*, Marzorati, Milano, 1969.

Barber, W.J., *A History of Economic Thought*, Penguin Books, Harmondsworth, 1967.

Barotta, P., Raffaelli, T., *Epistemologia ed economia*, Utet, Torino, 1988.

Bateman, B.W., 'The Elusive Logical Relation: An Essay on Change and Continuity in Keynes's Thought', in Moggridge 1988, IV.

Bateman, B.W., Davis, J.B. (ed. by), *Keynes and Philosophy. Essays on the Origin of Keynes's Thought*, Elgar, Aldershot, 1991.

Becattini, G., 'Alfred Marshall e la vecchia scuola economica di Cambridge', in Id. (a cura), *Il pensiero economico: temi, problemi e scuole*, Utet, Torino, 1990.

Becker, J.F., 'Adam Smith's Theory of Social Science', *Southern Economic Journal*, 1961, vol.28, July.

Begg, D.K.H., *Rational Expectations Revolution in Macroeconomics. Theories and Evidence*, Allan, Oxford, 1982.

Beinsen, L., *Schumpeter as an Historian of Economic Doctrine*, in Seidl 1984.

Bellofiore, R., 'Marx dopo Schumpeter. Il mutamento strutturale del capitalismo come economia essenzialmente monetaria', *Note economiche*, 1984, vol.17, 2.

—— 'Money and Development in Schumpeter', *The Review of Radical Political Economics*, 1985, vol.17, 1–2.

—— 'Introduzione' in *Tra teoria economica e grande cultura europea: Piero Sraffa*, F. Angeli, Milano, 1986.

—— 'A Monetary Labour Theory of Value', *Review of Radical Political Economy*, 1989, vol.21, 1–2.

—— 'Per una teoria monetaria del valore-lavoro. Problemi aperti nella teoria marxiana, tra radici ricardiane e nuove vie di ricerca', in G. Lunghini (a cura di), *Valori e prezzi*, Utet, Torino, 1993.

—— (ed. by), *Marxian Economics: a Reappraisal. Essays on Volume III of Capital*, Macmillan Press, London, 1998.

Bellofiore, R., Realfonzo, R., 'Finance and the Labour Theory of Value. Towards a Macroeconomic Theory of Distribution in a Monetary Perspective', *International Journal of Political Economy*, 1997, vol.27, 2.

Benetti, C., *Smith*, Etas, Milano, 1979.

Benetti, C., Cartelier, J., *Marchands, salariat et capitalistes*, Maspero, Paris, 1980.

Biasco, S., 'Sfruttamento e profitto in Sraffa', in Sylos Labini 1973.

Bishop, J.D., 'Adam Smith's Invisible Hand Argument', *Journal of Business Ethics*, 1995, vol.14, 3.

Bitterman, H.J., 'Adam Smith's Empiricism and the Law of Nature', *Journal of Political Economy*, 1940, vol.48, 4.

Blaug, M., *Economic Theory in Retrospect*, R.D. Irwin, Homewood, 1968.

—— *Karl Marx (1818–1883)*, Elgar, Aldershot, 1991.

Bobbio, N., *Locke e il diritto naturale*, Giappichelli, Torino, 1963.

—— *Da Hobbes a Marx*, Morano, Napoli, 1965.

—— 'Esiste una dottrina marxista dello Stato?', *Mondo Operaio*, 1975, sett.-ott.

Bologna, S., 'Money and Crisis: Marx as Correspondent of the New York Daily Tribune, 1856–57', translated by Ed. Emery, *Common Sense*, 1993, 13 and 14.

Borkenau, F., *Der Übergang vom feudalen zum bürgerlichen Weltbild*, Wissenschaftliche Buchgesellschaft, Darmstadt, 1971.

Braithwaite, R.B., 'Keynes as a Philosopher', in M. Keynes 1975.

Braverman, H., *Labor and Monopoly Capital. The Degradation of Work in the Twentieth Century*, Monthly Review Press, New York and London, 1974.

Breicha, O., Fritsch G., *Finale und Auftakt: Wien, 1898–1914*, Müller, Salzburg, 1964.

Breton, Y., 'La théorie schumpeterienne de l'entrepreneur ou le problème de la connaissance économique', *Revue Economique*, 1984, vol.35, 2.

Brouwer, M., *Schumpeterian Puzzles. Technological Competition and Economic Evolution*, Harvester Wheatsheaf, New York, 1991.

Brown, M., *Adam Smith's Economics*, Croom Helm, London, 1988.

Brozen, Y., 'Business Leadership and technological change', *American Journal of Economics and Sociology*, 1954, vol.14, 6.

Brunner, O., 'Das "ganze haus" und die altereuropäische "Ökonomik"', *Zeitschrift für Nationalökonomie*, 1958, Bd.13.

Buchanan, J.M., Tullock, G., *The Calculus of Consent*, The University of Michigan Press, An Arbor, 1962.

Buckle, S., *Natural Law and the Theory of Property*, Clarendon, Oxford, 1991.

Cacciari, M., *Krisis. Saggio sulla crisi del pensiero negativo da Nietzsche a Wittgenstein*, Feltrinelli, Milano, 1976.

—— *Pensiero negativo e razionalizzazione*, Marsilio, Padova, 1978.

—— *Dialettica e critica del Politico*, Feltrinelli, Milano, 1978.

—— *Dallo Steinhof*, Adelphi, Milano, 1980.

Caffè F., *Teorie e problemi di politica sociale*, Laterza, Bari, 1970.

Cairncross, A., 'Keynes and The Planned Economy', in Thirlwall 1978.

Caldwell, B.J. (ed. by), *Carl Menger and his Legacy in Economics*, Duke University Press, Durham and London, 1990.

Cameron, R., *Banking in the Early Stages of Industrialization*, Oxford University Press, New York, 1967.

—— *Banking and Economic Development*, Oxford University Press, New York, 1972.

Campbell, T.D., 'Adam Smith's Theory of Justice, Prudence, and Beneficence', *American Economic Review*, 1967, vol.57, 2.

—— *Adam Smith's Science of Morals*, Allen & Unwin, London, 1971.

Campbell, R.H., Skinner, A.S., *Adam Smith*, Croom Helm, London, 1982.

Carabelli, A., 'Keynes on Cause, Chance and Possibility', in T. Lawson, H. Pesaran (ed. by), *Keynes' Economics. Methodological Issues*, Croom Helm, London and Sidney, 1985.

—— *On Keynes's Method*, MacMillan, London, 1988.

—— 'La metodologia della critica della teoria economica classica', in Marzola, Silva 1990.

—— 'Uncertainty and Measurement in Keynes: Probability and Organicness', in Dow, Hillard 1995.

Carlin, E.A., 'Schumpeter's Constructed Type: the Entrepreneur', *Kyklos*, 1956, vol.9, 1.

Cassirer, E., *Die Philosophie der Aufklärung*, Mohr, Tübingen, 1932.

—— *Die Platonische Renaissance in England und die Schule von Cambridge*, Studien der Bibliothek Warburg, Hft. 24, Leipzig-Berlin, 1932.

—— *Das Erkenntnisproblem in der Philosophie und Wissenschaft der neueren Zeit*, W. Kohlhammer, Stuttgart, 1957.

Cavalieri, D., 'Keynes e Sraffa. Premesse, sviluppi ed esiti della critica di Cambridge', in AA.Vv., *Keynes in Italia*, Ipsoa, Milano, 1984.

—— 'Plusvalore e sfruttamento dopo Sraffa: lo stato del problema', *Economia politica*, 1995, vol.12, 1.

Cavalieri, D., De Vecchi, N., Faucci, R., Graziani, A., 'Schumpeter e Marx: una tavola rotonda', *Quaderni di storia dell'economia politica*, 1983, vol.1, 3.

Chalk, A.F., 'Schumpeter's Views on the Relationship of Philosophy and Economics', *Southern Economic Journal*, 1958, vol.24, 1.

Charlier, C., 'The Notion of Prudence in Smith's Theory of Moral Sentiments', *History of Economic Ideas*, 1996, vol.4, 1–2.

Châteauneuf-Maclès, A., 'Time and Rationality in Schumpeter's Construct', in Arena and Dangel-Hagnauer 2002.

Châtelet, F., *Histoire des idéologies*, Hachette, Paris, 1978.

Clark, C.M.A., 'Adam Smith and Natural Law', *Quaderni di storia dell'economia politica*, 1988, vol.6, 3.

Clarke, P., *The Keynesian Revolution in the Making, 1924–1936*, Clarendon, Oxford, 1988.

Clower, R.W., 'The Keynesian Counter-revolution: a Theoretical Appraisal', *Schweizerische Zeitschrift für Volkswirtschaft und Statistik*, 1963, Bd.79, March.

Cochran, K.P., 'Why a Social Economics?', *Review of Social Economy*, 1979, vol.37, April.

Coddington, A., 'Keynesian Economics: the Search for First Principles', *Journal of Economic Literature*, 1976, vol.14, 4.

Cohen, L.J., 'Dodici domande sul concetto di peso in Keynes', in Simili 1987.

Colie, R.L., 'Spinoza in England (1665–1730)', *Proc. of the American Phil. Society*, 1963, vol.107, 3.

Colletti, L., *Ideologia e società*, Laterza, Bari, 1969.

Collini, S., Winch, D., Burrow, J., *That Noble Science of Politics*, Cambridge University Press, Cambridge, 1983.

Coriat, B., *L'atelier et le chronomètre*, C. Bourgois Editeur, Paris, 1979.

Corry, B., 'Keynes in the History of Economic Thought: Some Reflections', in Thirlwall 1978.

Costa, P., *Il progetto giuridico*, Giuffrè, Milano, 1974.

Costabile, L., 'Metodo della scienza e teoria economica in Schumpeter. Note su "L'essenza e i principi dell'economia teorica"', *Studi Economici*, 1986, vol.29, 2.

Cousin, V., *Cours d'Histoire de la Philosophie Morale*, in *Oeuvres*, Hauman, Bruxelles, 1841, vol.II.

—— *Philosophie écossaise*, Levy, Paris, 1864.

Cox, R.H., *Locke on War and Peace*, Oxford University Press, Oxford, 1960.

Cozzi, T., *Teoria dello sviluppo economico*, Il Mulino, Bologna, 1984.

—— 'Sviluppo e ciclo: l'eredità di Schumpeter', in Filippini, Porta 1985.

Crabtree, D., Thirlwall, A.P. (ed by), *Keynes and the Bloomsbury Group*, Macmillan, London, 1980.

Cramer, D.L., Leathers, C.G., 'Schumpeter's Corporatist Views: Links among his Social Theory, Quadragesimo anno and Moral Reform', *History of Political Economy*, 1981, vol.13, 4.

Cranston, M., *John Locke. A Biography*, Longmans, London, 1968.

—— 'Keynes: His Political Ideas and Their Influence', in Thirlwall 1978.

Cremaschi, S., *Il sistema della ricchezza*, F. Angeli, Milano, 1984.

Crocker, L.G., *An Age of Crisis: Man and World in Eighteenth Century French Thought*, The John Hopkins Press, Baltimore, 1959.

Cropsey, J., *Polity and Economy*, Nijhoff, The Hague, 1957.

—— 'The Invisible Hand: Moral and Political Considerations', in O'Driscoll 1979.

Cubeddu, R., 'Fonti filosofiche delle "Untersuchungen über die Methode der Sozialwissenschaften" di Carl Menger', *Quaderni di storia dell'economia politica*, 1985, vol.3, 3.

—— *Il liberalismo della Scuola Austriaca. Menger, Mises, Hayek*, Morano, Napoli, 1992.

—— *The Philosophy of the Austrian School*, Routledge, London, 1993.

—— *Tra scuola austriaca e Popper. Sulla filosofia delle scienze sociali*, ESI, Napoli, 1996.

Wood, J.C. (ed. by), *Karl Marx's Economics: Critical Assessments*, Croom Helm, London, 1988, vol.4.

Dahl, R.A., *A Preface to Democratic Theory*, The University of Chicago Press, Chicago, 1956.

Dal Prà, M., *Hume e la scienza della natura umana*, Laterza, Bari, 1973.

Danner, P.L., 'Sympathy and Exchangeable Value: Keys to Adam Smith's Social Philosophy', *Review of Social Economy*, 1976, vol.34, December.

Dardi, M., *Il giovane Marshall: accumulazione e mercato*, Il Mulino, Bologna, 1984.

—— 'Interpretazioni di Keynes: logica del probabile, strutture dell'incerto', *Moneta e credito*, 1991, 173.

Davis, J.B., 'Keynes's Critiques of Moore: Philosophical Foundations of Keynes's Economics', *Cambridge Journal of Economics*, 1991, vol.15, 1.

—— *Keynes's philosophical Development*, Cambridge University Press, Cambridge, 1994.

—— 'Adam Smith on the Providential Reconciliation of Individual and Social Interests: Is Man Led by an Invisible Hand or Misled by a Sleight of Hand?', *History of Political Economy*, 1990, vol.22, 2.

De Beer, E.S., 'Locke and English Liberalism: The Second Treatise of Government in its contemporary setting', in *John Locke: Problems and Perspectives*, ed. by J. Yolton, Cambridge University Press, Cambridge, 1969.

De Brunhoff, S., *Le monnaie chez Marx*, Ed. Sociales, Paris, 1973.

—— *Etat et Capital*, Presses Universitaires de Grenoble, Grenoble, 1976.

De Cecco, M., *Moneta e impero*, Einaudi, Torino, 1979.

De Finetti, B., 'Cambridge Probability Theorists', *Manchester School of Economics and Social Studies*, 1985, vol.53, 4.

De Vecchi, N., *Valore e profitto nell'economia politica classica*, Feltrinelli, Milano, 1976.

—— 'Da Menger ai Viennesi. Il rapporto tra individuo e istituzioni nella spiegazione del processo capitalistico', *Quaderni di storia dell'economia politica*, 1986, vol.4, 3.

—— 'La scuola viennese di economia', in G. Becattini (a cura di), *Il pensiero economico. Temi, problemi e scuole*, Utet, Torino, 1990.

—— *Schumpeter viennese*, Bollati Boringhieri, Torino, 1993.

De Vroey, M., 'La théorie marxiste de la valeur, version travail abstrait. Un bilan critique', in B. Chavance (éd par), *Marx en perspective*, Éd de l'École des Hautes Études en Sciences Sociales, Paris, 1985.

Deacon, R., *The Cambridge Apostles: a History of Cambridge University's élite intellectual Secret Society*, Royce, London, 1985.

Defalvard, H., 'La main invisible: mythe et réalité du marché comme ordre spontané', *Revue d'économique Politique*, 1990, vol.100, 6.

Deleule, D., *Hume et la naissance du libéralisme économique*, Aubier Montaigne, Paris, 1979.

Deleuze, G., *Empirisme et subjectivité*, PUF, Paris, 1953.

—— 'Hume', in F. Châtelet (a c. di), *Histoire de la philosophie*, Hachette, Paris, 1972, vol.4.

—— *Foucault*, Minuit, Paris, 1986.

—— *Le pli. Leibniz et le Baroque*, Minut, Paris, 1988.

Della Volpe, G., *Logica come scienza storica*, Editori riuniti, Roma, 1964.

—— *La filosofia dell'esperienza di Davide Hume*, II, in *Opere*, a cura di I. Ambrogio, Editori riuniti, Roma 1972, vol.2.

—— *Chiave della dialettica storica*, in *Opere*, vol.6.

Demaria, G., 'Studi sull'attività dell'imprenditore moderno', *Rivista internazionale di scienze sociali e discipline ausiliarie*, 1929, n.s., vol.37, 1.

—— *Trattato di logica economica*, Cedam, Padova 1974.

—— 'L'opera e il pensiero di Schumpeter sotto il profilo della di lui teoria dell'interesse', in Filippini, Porta 1985.

Dharmapala, D., McAleer, M., 'Econometric Methodology and the Philosophy of Science', *Journal of Statistical Planning and Inference*, 1996, vol.49.

Dickey, L., 'Historicizing the "Adam Smith Problem"', *Journal of Modern History*, 1986, vol.58, September.

Dillard, D., 'The Pragmatic Basis of Keynes's Political Economy', *Journal of Economic History*, 1946, vol.6, November.

Dobb, M., *Political Economy and Capitalism*, Routledge, London, 1940[2].

Donzelli, F., 'Schumpeter e la teoria economica neoclassica', *Ricerche Economiche*, 1983, vol.37, 4.

Dow, A., Dow, S., 'Animal Spirits and Rationality', in Lawson, Pesaran 1985.

Dow, S., 'Keynes Epistemology and Economic Methodology', in O'Donnell 1991.

Dow, S., Hillard,, J. (ed. by), *Keynes, Knowledge and Uncertainty*, Elgar, Aldershot, 1995.

Downs, A., *An Economic Theory of Democracy*, Harper & Row, New York, 1957.

Dumont, E., *Homo aequalis*, Gallimard, Paris, 1977.

Dunn, J., 'Justice and the Interpretation of Locke's Political Theory', *Political Studies*, 1968, vol.16, 1.

—— *The Political Thought of John Locke*, Cambridge University Press, Cambridge, 1969.

—— 'From Applied Theology to Social Analysis: the break between John Locke and the Scottish Enlightenment', in Hont, Ignatieff 1983.

Dupuy, J.-P., 'De l'émancipation de l'économie: Retour sur "le problème d'Adam Smith"', *L'Année sociologique*, 1987, vol.37.

Dyer, A.D., 'Schumpeter as an Economic Radical: An Economic Sociology Assessed', *History of Political Economy*, 1988, vol.20, 1.

Egidi, M., *Schumpeter. Lo sviluppo come trasformazione morfologica*, Etas, Milano, 1981.

—— 'Schumpeter: la genesi della teoria e le transizioni', *Ricerche economiche*, 1983, vol.37, 4.

Eichengreen, B. (ed. by), *The Gold Standard in Theory and History*, Methuen, New York and London, 1985.

Elliott, J.E., 'Marx and Schumpeter on Capitalism's Creative Destruction: A Comparative Restatement', *Quarterly Journal of Economics*, 1980, vol.95, 1.

—— 'Schumpeter and Marx on Capitalist Transformation', *Quarterly Journal of Economics*, 1983, vol.98, 2.

—— 'Schumpeter's Theory of Economic Development and Social Change: Exposition and Assessment', *International Journal of Social Economics*, 1985, vol.12, 67.

Eshag, E., *From Marshall to Keynes: An Essay in the Monetary Theory of Cambridge School*, Blackwell, Oxford, 1963.

Esposito, R., *Categorie dell'impolitico*, Il Mulino, Bologna, 1988.

Euchner, W., *Naturrecht und Politik bei John Locke*, Europa Verlag, Frankfurt a.M., 1969.

Evensky, J., 'The Evolution of Adam Smith's views on political economy', *History of Political Economy*, 1989, vol.21, 1.

Fagiani, F., *Nel crepuscolo della probabilità*, Bibliopolis, Napoli, 1983.

Fallot, J., *Marx et le machinisme*, Éditions Cujas, Paris, 1966.

Fano, V., 'Keynes, Carnap e l'intuizione induttiva', in Marzetti Dall'Aste Brandolini, Scazzieri 1999.

Faucci, R. (a cura di), *John Maynard Keynes nel pensiero e nella politica economica*, Feltrinelli, Milano, 1977.

—— (a cura), 'Schumpeter / Marx. Sistemi teorici a confronto', *Quaderni di storia dell'economia politica*, 1984, vol.2, 1–2.

Faucci, R., Rodezno, V., 'Did Schumpeter change His Mind? Notes on Max Weber's Influence on Schumpeter', *History of Economic Ideas*, 1998, vol.6, 1.

Ferrari Bravo, G., *Keynes. Uno studio di diplomazia economica*, Cedam, Padova, 1990.

Filippini, C., Porta P. (a cura di), *Società, sviluppo, impresa. Saggi su Schumpeter*, Ipsoa, Milano, 1985.

Finelli, R., *Astrazione e dialettica dal romanticismo al capitalismo. (Saggio su Marx)*, Bulzoni, Roma, 1987.

Fiori, S., *Ordine, mano invisibile, mercato. Una rilettura di Adam Smith*, Utet, Torino, 2001.

Fistetti, F., *Critica dell'economia e critica della politica*, De Donato, Bari, 1976.

Fitzgibbons, A., *Keynes's Vision*, Clarendon, Oxford, 1988.

Forbes, D., 'Sceptical Whiggism, Commerce, and Liberty', in Wilson, Skinner 1975.

Forsthoff, E., *Rechtsstaat im Wandel*, W. Kohlhammer Verlag, Stuttgart, 1964.

Foster, J.B., 'Theories of Capitalist Transformation: Critical Notes on the Comparison of Marx and Schumpeter', *Quarterly Journal of Economics*, 1983, vol.98, 2.

Foucault, M., *Les mots et les choses*, PUF, Paris, 1966.

Fowler, T., *Locke*, Macmillan, London, 1883.

Freeden, M., *Liberalism Divided. A Study in British Political Thought, 1914–1939*, Oxford University Press, Oxford, 1986.

Freeman, A., Carchedi, G., *Marx and non-equilibrium Economics*, Elgar, Cheltenham, 1996.

Fuchs, A., *Geistige Strömungen in Osterreich 1867–1918*, Löcker, Wien, 1949.

Garegnani, P., *Valore e domanda effettiva*, Einaudi, Torino, 1979.

—— *Marx e gli economisti classici*, Einaudi, Torino, 1981.

Galli, C., *Modernità. Categorie e profili critici*, Il Mulino, Bologna, 1988.

Garin, E., 'L'etica di Giuseppe Butler', *Giornale critico della filosofia italiana*, 1932, vol.32, 13

—— *L'illuminismo inglese. I Moralisti*, Bocca, Milano, 1942.

Gay, P., *The Enlightenment: An Interpretation*, Weidenfeld and Nicolson, London, 1967.

Gerschenkron, A., *Economic Backwardness in Historical Perspective*, University of California Press, Berkeley, 1943.

Geuna, M., Pesante M.L. (a cura di), *Passioni, interessi, convenzioni*, F. Angeli, Milano, 1992.

Gill, E.R., 'Justice in Adam Smith: The Right and The Good', *Review of Social Economy*, 1976, vol.34, December.

Gille, B., *La banque en France au XIXe siècle: recherches historiques*, Droz, Genève, 1970.

Ginzberg, E., 'An Economy Formed by Men', in O'Driscoll 1979.

Gioia, V., *Gustav Schmoller: la scienza economica e la storia*, Congedo, Galatina, 1990.

Giovannetti, G., 'The Role of the Rate of Interest: From Wicksell to Keynes' Treatise on Money', *Economic Notes*, 1984, 1.

Giuliani, A., 'Adamo Smith filosofo del diritto', *Rivista internazionale di filosofia del diritto*, 1954, vol.6, 4.

Giuntini, C., 'Scienza newtoniana e teologia razionale: Bentley, Clarke e l'ideologia delle Boyle Lectures', in AA. Vv. 1983.

Gloria-Palermo, S., 'Schumpeter and the old Austrian School', in Arena and Dangel-Hagnauer 2002.

Godbout, J.T., *L'Esprit du don*, Editions de la découverte, Paris-Montréal, 1992.

Goodwin, R.M., 'A Marx Keynes Schumpeter Model of Economic Growth and Fluctuation', in R.H. Day, P. Chen, (ed. by), *Nonlinear dynamics and evolutionary economics*, Oxford University Press, Oxford, 1993.

Gough, J.W., *John Locke's Political Philosophy*, Clarendon, Oxford, 1950.

Gouhier, H., *Les Méditations Métaphysiques de Jean-Jacques Rousseau*, Vrin, Paris, 1970.

Gozzi, G., *Modelli politici e questione sociale in Italia e in Germania fra Otto e Novecento*, Il Mulino, Bologna, 1988.

Grampp, W.D., 'Adam Smith and the Economic Man', *Journal of Political Economy*, 1948, vol.56, 4.

Grassl, W., Smith, B. (ed. by), *Austrian Economics: Historical and Philosophical Background*, Croom Helm, London, 1986.

Gray, J., *Liberalism*, Open University Press, Milton Keynes, 1986.

Graziani, A., 'Il Trattato della moneta di J.A. Schumpeter', in *Scritti in onore di Giuseppe De Meo*, Facoltà di Scienze Statistiche, Roma, 1978, vol.1.

―― 'Keynes e il Trattato sulla moneta', in Graziani, Imbriani, Jossa 1981.

―― 'L'analisi marxista e la struttura del capitalismo moderno', in *Storia del marxismo*, Einaudi, Torino, 1982, vol.4.

―― 'Moneta senza crisi', *Materiali filosofici*, 1983, vol.7.

―― 'The Debate on Keynes' Finance Motive', *Economic Notes*, 1984, 1.

―― 'Keynes' Finance Motive: A Replay', *Economic Notes*, 1986, 1.

―― 'La teoria marxiana della moneta', in C. Mancina (a cura di), *Marx e il mondo contemporaneo*, Editori riuniti, Roma, 1986.

―― 'The Theory of the Monetary Circuit', *Thames Papers in Political Economy*, 1989, Spring.

—— *The Monetary Theory of Production*, Cambridge University Press, Cambridge, 2003.

Graziani, A., Imbriani, C., Jossa B. (a cura di), *Studi di economia keynesiana*, Liguori, Napoli, 1981.

Griswold jr. Ch. L., *Adam Smith and the Virtues of Enlightenment*, Cambridge University Press, Cambridge, 1999.

Groenewegen, P., *Soaring Eagle: Alfred Marshall 1842–1924*, Elgar, Aldershot, 1995.

Groethuysen, B., *Philosophie de la Révolution française*, Gallimard, Paris, 1956.

Grossmann, H., *Das Akkumulation und das Zusammenbruchsgesetz des kapitalistischen Systems*, Verlag Neue Kritik, Frankfurt, 1967.

Gruchy, A.G., 'J.M. Keynes' Concept of Economic Science', *Southern Economic Journal*, 1949, vol.15, January.

Guidi, M.E.L., *Il sovrano e l'imprenditore*, Laterza, Roma-Bari, 1991.

Haakonssen, K., *The Science of a Legislator: The Natural Jurisprudence of David Hume and Adam Smith*, Cambridge University Press, Cambridge, 1981.

Haavelmo, T., 'The Probability Approach in Econometrics', *Econometrica*, 1944, vol.12, July, Suppl.

Haberler, G., 'The General Theory after Ten Years', in S.E. Harris, *The New Economics*, A. Knopf, New York, 1947.

—— 'J.A. Schumpeter: 1883–1950', *Quarterly Journal of Economics*, 1950, vol.64, 3.

—— 'Schumpeter, Ministre des Finances: 15 mars – 17 octobre 1919', *Economie Appliquée*, 1950, vol.3, 3–4.

—— 'Schumpeter's Theory of Interest', in Harris 1951.

—— 'Schumpeter's Capitalism, Socialism and Democracy after Forty Years', in Heertje 1981.

Habermas, J., *Der philosophischen Diskurs der Moderne. Zwölf Vorlesungen*, Suhrkamp Verlag, Frankfurt am Main, 1985.

Hacking, I., *The Emergence of Probability. A Philosophical Study of Early Ideas about Probability, Induction and Statistical Inference*, Cambridge University Press, Cambridge, 1975.

Haeussermann, E., *Der Unternehmer: Seine Funktion, seine Zielsetzung, sein Gewinn*, Kohlhammer, Stuttgart, 1932.

Hagedoorn, J., 'Innovation and Entrepreneurship: Schumpeter Revisited', *Industrial and Corporate Change*, 1996, vol.5, 3.

Halévy, E., *La formation du radicalisme philosophique*, Alcan, Paris, 1901.

Hamouda, O.F., Smithin, J.N., 'Some Remarks on "Uncertainty and Economic Analysis"', *Economic Journal*, 1988, vol.98, March.

Hansen, A.H., *A Guide to Keynes*, McGraw-Hill, New York, 1953.

Hansen B., 'Unemployment, Keynes, and the Stockholm School', *History of Political Economy*, 1981, vol.13, 2.

Hargreaves Heap, S.P., *The New Keynesian Macroeconomics: Time, Belief and Social Interdependence*, Elgar, Aldershot, 1992.

Harris, S.E. (ed. by), *Schumpeter, social scientist*, Harvard University Press, Cambridge MA., 1951.

Harrod, R.F., 'Mr. Keynes and Traditional Theory', *Econometrica*, 1937, vol.5, 1.

—— *The Life of John Maynard Keynes*, Macmillan, London, 1951.

Harvey, D., *The Condition of Postmodernity*, Basil Blackwell, Oxford, 1990.

Häuser, K., 'Historical School and "Methodenstreit"', in Schiera, Tenbruck 1989.

Heertje, A. (ed. by), *Schumpeter's Vision. Capitalism, Socialism and Democracy after 40 years*, Praeger Publisher, New York, 1981.

Heilbroner, R.L., 'Was Schumpeter Right?', *Social Research*, 1981, vol.48, 3.

—— 'Economics and Political Economy: Marx, Keynes, and Schumpeter', *Journal of Economic Issues*, 1984, vol.18, 3.

Helburn, S., 'Burke and Keynes', in Bateman, Davis 1991.

Helburn, S.W., Bramhall, D.F. (ed. by), *Marx, Schumpeter, Keynes: A Centenary Celebration of Dissent*, M.E. Sharpe, Armonk, NY and London, 1986.

Hesse, M., 'Keynes e il metodo dell'analogia', in Simili 1987.

Hicks, J.R., Weber, W. (ed. by), *Carl Menger and the Austrian School of Economics*, Clarendon, Oxford, 1972.

Hintikka, J., 'Was Leibniz's Deity an akrates?', in *Modern Modalities*, ed. by S. Knuuttila, Kluwer Academic, Dordrecht-London, 1981.

Hirschman, A.O., *Exit, Voice and Loyalty*, Harvard University Press, Cambridge MA., 1970.

—— *The Passions and the Interests*, Princeton University Press, Princeton, 1977.

—— *Shifting Involvements. Private Interest and Public Action*, Robertson, Oxford, 1982.

Hishiyama, I., 'The Logic of Uncertainty according to J.M. Keynes', *Kyoto University Economic Review*, 1969, vol.39, 1.

Hobsbawm, E.J., *Industry and Empire. An Economic History of Britain since 1750*, Penguin Books, Harmondsworth, 1968.

—— 'Introduction', in K. Marx, *Pre-capitalist Economic Formations*, Lawrence & Wishart, London, 1964.

Hodgson, G., 'Persuasion, Expectations and the Limits to Keynes', in Lawson, Pesaran 1985.

Hollander, S., *The Economics of Adam Smith*, University of Toronto Press, Toronto, 1973.

—— 'Adam Smith and the Self-Interest Axiom', *Journal of Law and Economics*, 1977, vol.20, April.

Hont, I., Ignatieff, M. (ed. by), *Wealth and Virtue: The Shaping of Political Economy in the Scottish Enlightenment*, Cambridge University Press, Cambridge, 1983.

Howard, M., King, J.E., *Marxian Economics*, Elgar, Aldershot, 1990.

Iacono, A.M., 'Adam Smith e la metafora della "mano invisibile"', *Teoria*, 1985, 5.

Il'enkov, E.V., *Dialektika abstraktnogo i konkretnogo v 'Kapitale' Marksa*, Izdatel'stvo Akademii Nauk SSSR, Moskva, 1960.

Janet, E.P., *Histoire de la science politique dans ses rapports avec la morale*, Levy, Paris, 1913, vol.2.

Janik, A., Toulmin, S., *Wittgenstein's Vienna*, Weidenfeld and Nicolson, London, 1973.

Jàszi, O., *The Dissolution of the Habsburg Monarchy*, The University of Chicago Press, Chicago and London, 1961.

Jensen, H.E., 'Some Aspects of the Social Economics of John Maynard Keynes', *International Journal of Social Economics*, 1984, vol.11, 3–4.

—— 'J.A. Schumpeter on Economic Sociology', *Eastern Economic Journal*, 1985, vol.11, 3.

Johnson, E. and H., 'The Social and Intellectual Origins of the General Theory', *History of Political Economy*, 1974, vol.6, 3.

Johnson, E.A.J., *Predecessors of Adam Smith*, King & Son, New York, 1937.

Johnson, W.M., *The Austrian Mind: An Intellectual and Social History, 1848–1938*, The University of California Press, Berkeley, 1972.

Kanbur, S.M., 'A Note on Risk Taking, Entrepreneurship, and Schumpeter', *History of Political Economy*, 1980, vol.12, 4.

Kendall, W., *John Locke and the doctrine of majority-rule*, The University of Illinois Press, Urbana, 1965.

Keynes, J.N., *The Scope and Method of Political Economy*, Macmillan, London, 1891.

Keynes M. (ed. by), *Essays on John Maynard Keynes*, Cambridge University Press, Cambridge, 1975.

Khalil, E.L., 'Beyond Self-Interest and Altruism', *Economics and Philosophy*, 1990, vol.6, 2.

Kindleberger, C.P., *A Financial History of Western Europe*, Allen & Unwin, London, 1984.

Kitson Clark, G.S.R., *An Expanding Society; Britain, 1830–1900*, Cambridge University Press, Cambridge, 1967.

Knight, F.H., 'J.A. Schumpeter History of Economic Analysis', *Southern Economic Journal*, 1955, vol.21, 3.

Koselleck, R., *Kritik und Krise. Ein Beitrag zur Pathogenese der bürgerlichen Welt*, Alber, Freiburg-München, 1959.

Krahl, H.J., *Konstitution und Klassenkampf*, Verlag Neue Kritik, Frankfurt am Main, 1971.

Kraynak, R.P., 'John Locke: From Absolutism to Toleration', *The American Political Science Review*, 1980, vol.74, 1.

Kregel, J.A., 'Economic Methodology in the Face of Uncertainty: The Modelling Methods of Keynes and the Post-Keynesians', *Economic Journal*, 1976, vol.86, June.

—— 'Expectations and Relative Prices in Keynes' Monetary Equilibrium' *Economie Appliquée*, 1982, vol.35, 3.

—— 'Il finanziamento in Keynes: dal *Trattato* alla *Teoria generale*', in A. Graziani, M. Messori (a cura di), *Moneta e produzione*, Einaudi, Torino, 1988.

Kregel, J.A., Nasica, E., 'Alternative Analyses of Uncertainty and Rationality: Keynes and Modern Economics', in Marzetti Dall'Aste Brandolini, Scazzieri 1999.

Kumar, K., *From Post-Industrial to Post-Modern Society. New Theories of the Contemporary World*, Blackwell, London, 1995.

Kusin, A.A., *Marx e la tecnica*, Mazzotta, Milano, 1975.

Keuzenkamp, H.A., *Probability, Econometrics and Truth. The Methodology of Econometrics*, Cambridge University Press, Cambridge, 2000.

Lamprecht, S.P., *The Moral and Political Philosophy of John Locke*, Columbia University Press, New York, 1918.

Laski, H.J., *Political Thought in England. Locke to Bentham*, Oxford University Press, Oxford, 1950.

Lawson, T., 'Uncertainty and Economic Analysis', *Economic Journal*, 1985, vol.95, December.

—— 'Probability and Uncertainty in Economic Analysis', *Journal of Post-Keynesian Economics*, 1988, vol.11, Autumn.

—— 'Economics and Expectations', in Dow, Hillard 1995.

Lawson, T., Pesaran, H. (ed. by), *Keynes' Economics. Methodological Issues*, Croom Helm, London and Sidney, 1985.

Lecaldano, E., *Hume e la nascita dell'etica contemporanea*, Laterza, Roma-Bari, 1991.

Leijonhufvud, A., *On Keynesian Economics and the Economics of Keynes*, Oxford University Press, London, 1968.

Lekachman R. (ed. by), *Keynes' General Theory. Reports of Three Decades*, Macmillan, London, 1964.

Lemos, R.M., *Hobbes and Locke*, The University of Georgia Press, Athens, 1978.

Leser, N., *Zwischen Reformismus und Bolschewismus. Der Austromarxismus als Theorie und Praxis*, Böhlau, Wien-Frankfurt-Zürich, 1968.

—— (hrsg. von), *Die Wiener Schule der Nationalökonomie*, H. Böhlau, Wien, 1986.

Limentani, L., *La morale della simpatia*, Formiggini, Genova, 1914.

Lindgren, J.R., *The Social Philosophy of Adam Smith*, Nijhoff, The Hague, 1973.

Lombardi, M., 'Keynes ovvero dell'economia non-euclidea', *Studi Economici*, 1981, vol.15.

Losano, M.G., *Forma e realtà in Kelsen*, Comunità, Milano, 1981.

Lovejoy, A.O., *Essays in the History of Ideas*, The John Hopkins Press, Baltimore, 1948.

—— *The Great Chain of Being: a Study of the History of an Idea*, The John Hopkins Press, Baltimore, 1948.

Lubenow, W.C., *The Cambridge Apostles, 1820–1914. Liberalism, imagination, and friendship in British intellectual and professional life*, Cambridge University Press, Cambridge, 1998.

Luhmann, N., 'Politische Planung', *Jahrbuch für Sozialwissenschaft*, 1966, vol.17.

Lukács, G., *Der junge Hegel und die Probleme der kapitalistischen Gesellschaft*, Europa Verlag, Zürich, 1948.

Lunghini, G., 'Teoria economica ed economia politica', in Id. (a cura di), *Produzione, capitale e distribuzione*, Isedi, Milano, 1975.

—— *La crisi dell'economia politica e la teoria del valore*, Feltrinelli, Milano, 1977.

—— 'La Teoria generale come trappola teoretica', in Graziani, Imbriani, Jossa 1981.

—— 'Un "Discorso" contraddittorio: due domande e un poscritto', in Pasinetti 1989.

Lunghini, G., Rampa, G., 'Conoscenza, equilibrio e incertezza endogena', *Economia politica*, 1996, vol.13, 3.

—— 'Il falso problema dei fondamenti microeconomici', in C. Gnesutta (a cura di), *Incertezza, moneta, aspettative, equilibrio. Saggi per Fausto Vicarelli*, Il Mulino, Bologna, 1996.

Mabbott, J.D., *John Locke*, Macmillan, London, 1973.

Macfie, A.L., *The Individual in Society*, Allen & Unwin, London, 1967.

—— 'The Invisible Hand of Jupiter', *Journal of the History of Ideas*, 1971, vol.32, October–December.

Machlup, F., 'Forced or Induced Savings: An Exploration into Its Synonyms and Homonyms', *Review of Economic Statistics*, 1943, vol.25, 1.

—— *Schumpeter's Economic Methodology*, in Harris 1951.

Macintyre, A., *After Virtue. A Study in Moral Theory*, University of Notre Dame Press, Notre Dame Ill., 1981–1984.

Macpherson, C.B., *The Political Theory of Possessive Individualism: Hobbes to Locke*, Oxford University Press, Oxford, 1964.

Malcolm, N., *Ludwig Wittgenstein*, Oxford University Press, Oxford, 1954.

Marazzi, C., *E il denaro va. Esodo e rivoluzione dei mercati finanziari*, Bollati Boringhieri – Casagrande, Torino – Bellinzona, 1998.

Marchionatti, R., 'Sulla significatività del saggio di plusvalore dopo Sraffa', *Economia politica*, 1993, vol.10, 2.

—— 'On Keynes's animal spirits', *Kyklos*, 1999, vol.52, 3.

Marco, L.V., 'Entrepreneur et innovation: les sources françaises de Joseph Schumpeter', *Economies et Sociétés*, 1985, vol.19, 10.

Marget, A.W., 'The monetary Aspect of the Schumpeterian System', *Review of Economics and Statistics*, 1951, vol.33, 2.

Marramao, G., *Austromarxismo e socialismo di sinistra tra le due guerre*, La Pietra, Milano, 1980.

Marshall, T.H., 'Citizenship and Social Class', in Id., *Sociology at the Crossroad*, Heinemann, London, 1963.

Martin, D.A., 'Economics as Ideology: On Making "The Invisible Hand" Invisible', *Review of Social Economy*, 1990, vol.48, 3.

Martinelli, A., *Economia e società. Marx, Weber, Schumpeter, Polany, Parsons*, Comunità, Milano, 1987.

Martinengo, G., 'La reinterpretazione del pensiero di Keynes nell'analisi di Leijonhufvud: una formalizzazione critica', in Vicarelli 1974.

März, E., 'Die Theorie der wirtschaftlichen Entwicklung von J.A. Schumpeter in ihrer Beziehung zum Marxschen System', *Wirtschaft und Gesellschaft*, 1980, Bd.6, 3.

—— *J.A. Schumpeter: Forscher, Lehrer und Politiker*, Oldenbourg, München, 1983.

Marzetti Dall'Aste Brandolini, S., 'Bene morale e condotta giusta: la politica economica di John Maynard Keynes', in S. Marzetti Dall'Aste Brandolini, R. Scazzieri (a cura di), *La probabilità in Keynes: premesse e influenze*, Clueb, Bologna, 1999.

Marzola, A., Silva, F. (a cura di), *John M. Keynes. Linguaggio e metodo*, Lubrina, Bergamo, 1990.

Matthews, K.P.G., 'Was Sterling Overvalued in 1925?', *Economic History Review*, 1986, s. S., 4.

Mazzocchi, G., Villani, A. (a cura di), *Etica, economia, principi di giustizia*, F. Angeli, Milano, 2001.

—— (a cura di), *Alla ricerca di principi di giustizia. Liberal o comunitari*, F. Angeli, Milano, 2002.

May, A.J., *Vienna in the Age of Franz Josef*, University of Oklahoma, Norman, 1966.

Mayer, G., *Friederich Engels. A Biography*, Chapman & Hall, London, 1936.

Mayr, O., *Authority, Liberty and Automatic Machinery in Early Modern Europe*, Johns Hopkins University Press, Baltimore, 1986.

McLellan, D., *Karl Marx his Life and Thought*, MacMillan, London, 1973.

Medio, A., 'L'interesse nella teoria dello sviluppo economico di J. Schumpeter', *Rivista internazionale di scienze economiche e commerciali*, 1968, vol.15, 10.

Meek, R.L., 'Is Economics Biased? Heretical View of a Leading Thesis in Schumpeter's History', *Scottish Journal of Political Economy*, 1957, 4.

—— *Studies in the Labour Theory of Value*, Lawrence & Wishart, London, 1973[2].

—— *Social Science and the Ignoble Savage*, Cambridge University Press, Cambridge, 1976.

Megill, A.D., 'Theory and Experience in Adam Smith', *Journal of the History of Ideas*, 1975, vol.36, 1.

Mehring, F., *Karl Marx, Geschichte seines Lebens, Gesammelte Schriften*, Dietz, Berlin, 1964, Bd.3.

Messori, M., 'Aspetti monetari della domanda effettiva', in Graziani, Imbriani, Jossa 1981.

—— 'Credito e innovazione in Marx, Keynes e Schumpeter', *Politica ed economia*, 1983, vol.14, 4.

—— 'La sequenza Marx-Schumpeter-Keynes: cenni introduttivi', in T. Cozzi (a cura), *Keynes*, Piemonte vivo ricerche, Torino, 1983.

—— 'Teoria del valore senza merce-moneta? Considerazioni preliminari sull'analisi monetaria di Marx, *Quaderni di storia dell'economia politica*, 1984, vol.2, 1–2.

—— 'Aspetti monetari della teoria di Schumpeter: la creazione bancaria di mezzi di pagamento', *Note economiche*, 1984, vol.17, 3.

—— 'Financement bancaire et décision de production', *Economie et Société*, 1986, 8–9.

—— 'L'offre et la demande de crédit chez Schumpeter', *Cahiers d'Économie Politique*, 1987, 13.

—— 'The Trials and Misadventures of Schumpeter's Treatise on Money', *History of Political Economy*, 1997, vol.29, 4.

Mini, V.P., *Keynes, Bloomsbury and The General Theory*, Macmillan, London, 1991.

Minsky, H.P., *John Maynard Keynes*, Columbia University Press, New York, 1975.

Mizuta, H., 'Moral Philosophy and Civil Society', in Wilson, Skinner 1975.

Moggridge, D.E., *The Return to Gold, 1925: The Formulation of Economic Policy and Its Critics*, Cambridge University Press, Cambridge, 1969.

—— *British Monetary Policy 1924–1931*, Cambridge University Press, Cambridge, 1972.

—— 'From the Treatise to The General Theory: An Exercise in Chronology', *History of Political Economy*, 1973, vol.5, Spring.

—— *Keynes*, Fontana, London, 1976.

—— (ed. by), *Perspectives on the History of Economic Thought*, Elgar, Aldershot, 1988, IV.

Moggridge, D.E., Howson, S., 'Keynes on Monetary Policy, 1910–1946', *Oxford Economic Papers*, 1974, vol.26, 2.

Moore, J., Silverthorne, M., 'Gershom Carmichael and Natural Jurisprudence', in Hont, Ignatieff 1983.

Moravia, S., *Filosofia e scienze umane nell'età dei lumi*, La Nuova Italia, Firenze, 1982.

Morishima, M., *Marx's Economics: A Dual Theory of Value and Growth*, Cambridge University Press, Cambridge, 1973.

Morrow, G.R., 'Adam Smith: Moralist and Philosopher', *Journal of Political Economy*, 1927, vol.35, June.

—— *The Ethical and Economic Theories of Adam Smith*, Kelley, New York, 1969.

Moscovici, S., 'A propos de quelques travaux d'Adam Smith sur l'histoire et la philosophie des sciences', *Revue d'histoire des Science et de leurs applications*, 1959, 9.

—— *La machine à faire des dieux. Sociologie et psychologie*, Fayard, Paris, 1988.

Moss, L.S. (ed. by), *Joseph A. Schumpeter, Historian of Economics*, Routledge, London and New York, 1996.

Muller, J.Z., *Adam Smith in his Time and ours*, Princeton University Press, Princeton, 1995[2].

Myrdal, G., *Against the Stream: Critical Essays in Economics*, Pantheon, New York, 1972.

Napoleoni, C., 'Sulla teoria della produzione come processo circolare', *Giornale degli economisti e Annali di economia*, 1960, vol.20, n.s., 1–2.

—— 'La questione delle macchine in Marx', *La rivista trimestrale*, 1970, 31–2.

—— *Lezioni sul Capitolo VI inedito di Marx*, Boringhieri, Torino, 1972.

—— *Smith Ricardo Marx. Observations on the History of Economic Thought*, Blackwell, Oxford, 1975.

—— *Discorso sull'economia politica*, Boringhieri, Torino, 1985.

—— 'Value and Exploitation. Marx's Economic Theory and Beyond', in G. Caravale (ed. by), *Marx and Modern Economic Analysis*, Elgar, Aldershot, 1991.

—— *Dalla scienza all'utopia*, a cura di G.L. Vaccarino, Bollati Boringhieri, Torino, 1992.

Negri, A., 'Problemi di storia dello Stato moderno. Francia: 1610–1650', *Rivista critica di storia della filosofia*, 1967, vol.22, 2.

—— 'Marx sul ciclo e la crisi', *Contropiano*, 1968, 2.

—— *Descartes politico*, Feltrinelli, Milano, 1970.

—— 'Esiste una dottrina marxista dello Stato?', *aut aut*, 1976, 152–3.

—— 'Keynes e la teoria dello stato nel '29', in Faucci 1977.

—— *La forma stato. Per la critica dell'economia politica della Costituzione*, Feltrinelli, Milano, 1977.

—— *Marx beyond Marx. Lessons on the Grundrisse*, translated by H. Cleaver, M. Ryan and M. Viano, ed. by J. Fleming, Bergin & Garvey Publishers, New York, 1984.

—— *Il potere costituente*, SugarCo, Milano, 1992.

Neumann, F., *The Democratic and the Authoritarian State*, Macmillan, London, 1964.

Nikolaevskij, B., Maenchen-Helfen, O., *Karl Marx. Eine Biographie*, J.H.W. Dietz, Hannover, 1963.

Nozick, R., *Anarchy, State and Utopia*, Basic Books, New York, 1974.

O'Boyle, E.J., 'On the Person and the Work of the Entrepreneur', *Review of Social Economy*, 1994, vol.52, 4.

O'Donnell, L.A., 'Rationalism, Capitalism and the Entrepreneur: The Views of Veblen and Schumpeter', *History of Political Economy*, 1973, vol.5, 1.

O'Donnell, R.M., 'Continuity in Keynes's Conception of Probability', in Moggridge 1988, vol.4.

—— *Keynes: Philosophy, Economics and Politics*, Macmillan, London, 1989.

—— 'Keynes's Weight of Argument and its Bearing on Rationality and Uncertainty', in Bateman, Davis 1991.

—— (ed. by) *Keynes as Philosopher-Economist*, Macmillan, London, 1991.

O'Driscoll Jr., G.P. (ed. by), *Adam Smith and Modern Political Economy*, Iowa State University, Ames, 1979.

Oakley, A., *Schumpeter's Theory of Capitalist Motion. A Critical Exposition and Reassessment*, Elgar, Aldershot, 1990.

Olson, R., *Scottish Philosophy and British Physics 1750–1880*, Princeton University Press, Princeton, 1975.

Panzieri, R., 'Sull'uso capitalistico delle macchine', *Quaderni rossi*, 1961, 1.

—— 'Plusvalore e pianificazione', *Quaderni rossi*, 1964, 4.

—— *La ripresa del marxismo leninismo in Italia*, Sapere Edizioni, Milano-Roma, 1973.

Pasinetti, L. (a cura di), *Aspetti controversi della teoria del valore*, Il Mulino, Bologna, 1989.

Pateman, C., *Participation and Democratic Theory*, Cambridge University Press, Cambridge, 1970.

Patinkin, D., *Keynes' Monetary Thought: A Study of its Development*, Duke University Press, Durham, 1976.

Peacock, A., 'Keynes and the Role of the State', in D. Crabtree, A.P. Thirlwall (ed. by), *Keynes and the Role of the State*, Macmillan, London, 1993.

Perri, S., 'La "significatività" del saggio di plusvalore dopo Sraffa', *Rivista internazionale di scienze economiche e commerciali*, 1991, vol.38, 6–7.

—— 'Neovalore e plusvalore', *Economia politica*, 1997, vol.14, 2.

Perroux, F., *La pensée économique de Joseph Schumpeter. Les dynamiques du capitalisme*, Droz, Genève, 1965.

Perroux, F., Schuhl, P.-M. (sous la direction de), 'Saint-simonisme et pari pour l'industrie. XIXe–XXe siècles', *Economies et Sociétés*, IV, 4, 6, 10; V, 7, VII, 1, Droz, Genève, 1970–1973.

Persky, J., 'Adam Smith's Invisible Hands', *Journal of Economic Perspectives*, 1989, vol.3, 4.

Pesante M.L., *Economia e politica*, F. Angeli, Milano, 1986.

Pesciarelli, E., *La jurisprudence economica di Adam Smith*, Giappichelli, Torino, 1988.

—— 'Smith, Bentham and the Development of Contrasting Ideas on Entrepreneurship', *History of Political Economy*, 1989, vol.21, 3.

Pesciarelli, E., Santarelli, E., 'Introduzione', in J.A. Schumpeter, 'Teoria dello sviluppo economico (1911). Cap. II: Il fenomeno fondamentale dello sviluppo economico', *Quaderni di storia dell'economia politica*, 1986, vol.4, 1–2.

Pesciarelli, E., Santarelli, E., 'The Emergence of a Vision: The Development of Schumpeter's Theory of Entrepreneurship', *History of Political Economy*, 1990, vol.22, 4.

Petry, F., *Der soziale Gehalt der Marxschen Werttheorie*, Fischer, Jena, 1916.

Phillipson, T., 'Adam Smith as Civic Moralist', in Hont, Ignatieff 1983.

Pietranera, G., *La teoria del valore e dello sviluppo capitalistico in Adam Smith*, Feltrinelli, Milano, 1963.

—— *Capitalismo ed economia*, Einaudi, Torino, 1972.

Plamenatz, J.P., *Democracy and Illusion*, Longman, London, 1973.

Plessis, A., *La politique de la Banque de France de 1851 a 1870*, Droz, Genève, 1985.

Pocock, J.G.A., *The Machiavellian Moment*, Princeton University Press, Princeton, 1975.

Pollard, S. (ed. by), *The Gold Standard and Employment Policies between the Wars*, Methuen, London, 1970.

Pollock, F., *An Introduction to the History of the Science of Politics*, Macmillan, London, 1920.

Pollock, F., *Automation. Materialien zur Beurteilung der ökonomischen und sozialen Folgen*, Europäische Verlagsanstalt, Frankfurt am Main, 1956.

Popper, K., *The Logic of Scientific Discovery*, Hutchinson, London, 1968.

Porta, P.L., 'I fondamenti dell' ordine economico: 'policy', 'police', 'politeness' nel pensiero scozzese', *Filosofia politica*, 1988, vol.1, 1.

Portinaro, P.P. *La crisi dello jus publicum europaeum*, Edizioni di Comunità, Milano, 1982.

Presley, J.R., *Robertsonian Economics*, Macmillan, London, 1979.

—— 'J.M. Keynes and D.H. Robertson: Three Phases of Collaboration', *Research in the History of Economic Thought and Methodology*, 1989, vol.16, 4.

Preti, G., *Alle origini dell'etica contemporanea. Adamo Smith*, La Nuova Italia, Firenze, 1977².

Racinaro, R., 'Hans Kelsen e il dibattito su democrazia e parlamentarismo negli anni Venti-Trenta', in H. Kelsen, *Socialismo e stato*, De Donato, Bari, 1978.

Rae, J., *Life of Adam Smith*, Macmillan, London, 1895.

Raffaelli, T., 'Human Psychology and the Social Order', *History of Economic Ideas*, 1996, vol.4, 1–2.

—— *Marshall's Evolutionary Economics*, Routledge, London, 2003.

Rancière, J., *Le concept de critique et la critique de l'économie politique*, Maspero, Paris, 1965.

Raphael, D.D., '"The true old Humean Philosophy" and its influence on Adam Smith, in *David Hume: Bicentenary Papers*, ed. by G.P. Morice, Edinburgh University Press, Edinburgh, 1977.

—— *Adam Smith*, Oxford University Press, Oxford, 1985.

Rawls, J., *A Theory of Justice*, Harvard University Press, Cambridge MA., 1980.

Reclam, M., *J.A. Schumpeter's 'credit' theory of money*, University of Michigan Press, Ann Arbor, 1987.

Reichelt, H., *Zur logischen Struktur des Kapitalsbegriffs bei Karl Marx*, Europäische Verlagsanstalt GmbH, Frankfurt am Main, 1970.

Renault, E., *Marx et l'idée de critique*, PUF, Paris, 1995.

Restaino, F., *Scetticismo e senso comune*, Laterza, Roma-Bari, 1974.

Riedel, M., *Studien zu Hegels Rechtsphilosophie*, Suhrkamp Verlag, Frankfurt am Main, 1969.

Robbins, L., *The Theory of Economic Policy in English Classical Political Economy*, Macmillan, London, 1952.

—— 'Schumpeter History of Economic Analysis', *Quarterly Journal of Economics*, 1955, vol.69, 1.

Robertson, J., 'The Legacy of Adam Smith: Government and economic Development in the Wealth of Nations', in R. Bellamy (ed. by), *Victorian Liberalism*, Routledge, London, 1990.

Robinson, E.A.G., 'John Maynard Keynes – 1883–1946', *Economic Journal*, 1947, vol.57, March.

Robinson, J., 'J.A. Schumpeter Capitalism, Socialism and Democracy', "Economic Journal", 1943, vol.53, June.

—— *An Essay on Marxian Economics*, Macmillan, London, 1949.

—— *On Re-Reading Marx*, Students' Bookshops Ltd, Cambridge, 1953.

—— *Economic Philosophy*, Watts, London, 1962.

—— *Essays in the History of Economic Growth*, Macmillan, London, 1962.

—— 'What has become of the Keynesian Revolution?', in M. Keynes 1975.

—— *Collected Economic Papers*, Basil Blackwell, Oxford, 1980, vol.4.

Roncaglia, *Schumpeter. È possibile una teoria dello sviluppo economico?*, Banca Popolare dell'Etruria, Arezzo, 1987.

Rosdolsky, R., *Zur Entstehungsgeschichte des Marxschen 'Kapital'*, Europäische Verlagsanstalt -Europa Verlag, Frankfurt-Wien, 1968.

Rosenbaum, S.P. (ed. by), *The Bloomsbury Group*, Croom Helm, London, 1975.

Rosenberg, N., 'Adam Smith and Laissez-faire Revisited', in O'Driscoll 1979.

—— 'Schumpeter and Marx: How Common a Vision?', in R.M. Mac Leod (ed. by), *Technology and the Human Prospects. Essays in Honour of C. Freeman*, Pinter Publisher, London, 1986.

Rossi, P., 'Le tradizioni di ricerca nella storia della scienza', in AA.Vv. 1983.

Rossini Favretti, R. (a cura di*), Il linguaggio della Teoria generale. Proposte di analisi*, Patron, Bologna, 1989.

Rothschild, E., 'Adam Smith and the Invisible Hand', *American Economic Review*, 1994, vol.84, 2.

Roversi, A., *Il magistero della scienza. Storia del Verein für Sozialpolitik dal 1872 al 1888*, F. Angeli, Milano, 1984.

Rubin, I.I., *Essays on Marx's Theory of Value*, Black Rose, Detroit, 1972.

Runde, J., 'Keynesian Uncertainty and the Weight of Argument', *Economic and Philosophy*, 1990, vol.6, 2.

Salanti, A., 'La teoria del valore dopo Sraffa: una nota', *Rivista internazionale di scienze economiche e commerciali*, 1990, vol.37, 8.

Salsano, A., *Ingegneri e politici*, Einaudi, Torino, 1987.

—— *L'altro corporativismo*, Il Segnalibro, Torino, 2003.

Salvucci, P., *La filosofia politica di Adam Smith*, Argalia, Urbino, 1966.

Samuelson, P.A., 'Schumpeter as a Teacher and Economic Theorist', in Harris 1951.

—— 'Lord Keynes and the General Theory', *Econometrica*, 1946, vol.14, July.

—— 'Paradoxes of Schumpeter's Zero Interest Rate', *Review of Economics and Statistics*, 1971, vol.53, 4.

—— *Economics*, McGraw-Hill, New York 1992[14].

—— 'Schumpeter as an Economic Theorist', in H. Frisch (ed. by), *Schumpeterian Economics*, Praeger Publishers, New York, 1982.

—— '1983: Marx, Keynes and Schumpeter', *Easter Economic Journal*, 1983, vol.9, 3.

Sartori, G., *Democrazia e definizioni*, Il Mulino, Bologna, 1972.

Scardovi, I., 'Keynes e la probabilità: una sintassi dell'incertezza', in Marzetti Dall'Aste Brandolini, Scazzieri 1999.

Scherer, F.M., Perlman, M. (ed. by), *Entrepreneurship, technological Innovation, and economic Growth: Studies in the Schumpeterian tradition*, University of Michigan Press, Ann Arbor, 1992.

Schiera, P., *Il laboratorio borghese. Scienza e politica nella Germania dell'Ottocento*, Il Mulino, Bologna, 1987.

Schiera, P., Tenbruck, F. (hrsg./a cura di), *Gustav Schmoller e il suo tempo: la nascita delle scienze sociali in Germania e in Italia / Gustav Schmoller in seiner Zeit: die Entstehung der Sozialwissenschaften in Deutschland und Italien*, Il Mulino – Duncker & Humblot, Bologna-Berlin, 1989.

Schlesinger, R., *Central European Democracy and its Background: Economic and Political Group Organisation*, Routledge & Keagan, London, 1953.

Schmitt, C., *Politische Romantik*, Duncker & Humblot, Berlin, 1968[2].

—— *Römischer Katholizismus und politische Form*, Theatiner Verlag, München, 1925[2].

—— *Der Hüter der Verfassung*, Duncker & Humblot, Berlin, 1931.

Schneider, E., *J.A. Schumpeter: Leben und Werk einen großen Sozialökonomen*, J.C.B. Mohr (P. Siebeck), Tübingen, 1970.

—— 'The Nature of Money: On a Posthumous Publication by J.A. Schumpeter', *German Economic Review*, 1970, vol.8, 4.

Schneider, L., 'Adam Smith on Human Nature and Social Circumstance', in O'Driscoll 1979.

Schorske, C.E., *Fin-de-siècle Vienna*, Weidenfeld and Nicolson, London, 1980.

Scott, W.R., *Francis Hutcheson, His Life, Teaching and Position in the History of Philosophy*, Cambridge University Press, Cambridge, 1900.

Screpanti, E., Zamagni, S., *Profilo di storia del pensiero economico*, Nis, Roma, 1991.

Seidl, C. (ed. by), *Lectures on Schumpeterian Economics*, Springer-Verlag, Berlin, 1984.

—— 'Schumpeter addressing Keynes', *History of Economic Ideas*, 1996, vol.4, 3.

Seliger, M., *The Liberal Politics of John Locke*, Allen & Unwin, London, 1968.

Semmler, W., 'Marx and Schumpeter on Competition, Transient Surplus Profit and Technical Change', *Economie Appliquée*, 1984, vol.37, 3–4.

Sen, A., *Choice, Welfare and Measurement*, Blackwell, Oxford, 1982.

Sen, A., Williams, B. (ed. by), *Utilitarianism and Beyond*, Cambridge University Press, Cambridge, 1982.

Shackle, G.L.S., 'Keynes and the Nature of Human Affairs', *Weltwirtschaftliches Archiv*, 1956, Bd.87, 1.

—— *The Nature of Economic Thought. Selected Papers 1955–1964*, Cambridge University Press, London, 1966.

—— *The Years of High Theory. Invention and Tradition in Economic Thought*, Cambridge University Press, Cambridge, 1967.

Shah, P.J., Yeager, L.B., 'Schumpeter on Monetary Determinacy', *History of Political Economy*, 1994, vol.26, 3.

Shell, M., *Money, Language and Thought*, University of California Press, Berkeley, 1982.

Shionoya, Y., 'The Science and Ideology of Schumpeter', *Rivista internazionale di scienze economiche e commerciali*, 1986, vol.33, 3.

—— 'Instrumentalism in Schumpeter's Economic Methodology', *History of Political Economy*, 1990, vol.22, 2.

—— 'Schumpeter on Schmoller and Weber: A Methodology of Economic Sociology', *History of Political Economy*, 1991, vol.23, 2.

—— 'Sidgwick, Moore and Keynes: A Philosophical Analysis of Keynes's "My Early Beliefs"', in Bateman, Davis 1991.

Simili, R. (a cura di), *L'epistemologia di Cambridge 1850–1950*, Il Mulino, Bologna, 1987.

Simpson, D., 'Joseph Schumpeter and the Austrian School of Economics', *Journal of Economic Studies*, 1983, vol.10, 4.

Skidelsky, R., *John Maynard Keynes. I. Hopes Betrayed 1883–1920*, Viking Penguin, New York, 1986.

—— 'Keynes e Sraffa: un caso di non-comunicazione', in R. Bellofiore (a cura di), *Tra teoria economica e grande cultura europea: Piero Sraffa*, F. Angeli, Milano, 1986.

—— 'Keynes's Philosophy of Practice', in O'Donnell 1991.

—— *John Maynard Keynes. II. The Economist as Saviour 1920–1937*, Macmillan, London, 1992.

—— *John Maynard Keynes. III. Fighting for Britain 1937–1946*, Macmillan, London, 2000.

Skinner, A.S., *A System of Social Science*, Oxford University Press, Oxford, 1979.

Skinner, Q., *The Foundations of Modern Political Thought*, Cambridge University Press, Cambridge, 1978.

Small, A.W., *Adam Smith and Modern Sociology*, The University of Chicago Press, Chicago, 1907.

Smithies, A., 'Memorial: J.A. Schumpeter, 1883–1950', *American Economic Review*, 1950, vol.40, 4.

Sohn-Rethel, A., *Geistige und körperliche Arbeit. Zur Theorie der gesellschaftlichen Synthesis*, Suhrkamp Verlag, Frankfurt am Main, 1970.

Solterer, J., 'Quadragesimo Anno: Schumpeter's Alternative to the Omnipotent State', *Review of Social Economy*, 1951, vol.9, 1.

Spahn, H.P., 'Marx Schumpeter Keynes: Drei Fragmente über Geld, Zins und Profit', *Jahrbucher für Nationalökonomie und Statistik*, 1984, Bd.199, 3.

Starobinski, J., *Le remède dans le mal*, Gallimard, Paris, 1989.

Steedman, I., *Marx after Sraffa*, New Left Books, London, 1977.

Stephen, L., *History of English Thought in the Eighteenth Century*, Rupert Hall Davies, London, 1962.

Stevenson, L., *Ethics and Language*, Yale University Press, New Haven, 1944.

Stewart, D., *Account of the Life and Writings of Adam Smith* (1794), in A. Smith, *Essays on philosophical Subjects*.

Stohs, M., '"Uncertainty" in Keynes' *General Theory*', *History of Political Economy*, 1980, vol.12, 3.

Stolper, W.F., 'Monetary Equilibrium and Business Cycles Theory', *Review of Economic Statistics*, 1943, vol.25, 1.

—— 'The Schumperian System', *Journal of Economic History*, 1951, vol.11, 3.

—— *Joseph Alois Schumpeter: The Public Life of a Private Man*, Princeton University Press, Princeton, 1994.

—— 'Schumpeter's Ministerial Days', *History of Economic Ideas*, 1995, vol.3, 1.

Strauss, L., 'Anmerkungen zu C. Schmitt, Der Begriff des Politischen', *Archiv für Sozialwissenschaft und Sozialpolitik*, 1932, Bd.67.

—— *The Political Philosophy of Hobbes*, Clarendon, Oxford, 1936.

—— *Natural Rights and History*, The University of Chigaco Press, Chicago, 1953.

Streissler, E., Milford, K., 'Theoretical and Methodological Positions of German Economics in the Middle of the Nineteenth Century', *History of Economic Ideas*, 1993–1994, vol.1–2, 3–1.

Streissler, E., Weber, W. (ed. by), *Carl Menger and the Austrian Economics*, Clarendon, Oxford, 1973.

Streminger G., 'Hume's Theory of Imagination', *Hume Studies*, 1980, vol.6, 2.

Swedberg, R., *Schumpeter. A Biography*, Princeton University Press, Princeton, 1991.

Sweezy, P.M., *The Theory of Capitalistic Development*, Monthly Review Press, New York, 1942.

Swoboda, P., 'Schumpeter's Entrepreneur in Modern Economic Theory', in Seidl 1984.

Sylos Labini, P., *Oligopolio e progresso tecnico*, Einaudi, Torino, 1972.

—— (a cura di), *Prezzi relativi e distribuzione del reddito*, Boringhieri, Torino, 1973.

—— 'Il problema dello sviluppo economico in Marx ed in Schumpeter', in *Problemi dello sviluppo economico*, Laterza, Bari, 1977.

Talamona, M., 'Sviluppo, moneta e credito: la "visione" di Schumpeter e il caso italiano', *Giornale degli economisti e Annali di economia*, 1983, vol.42, 7–8.

Taminiaux, J., *La fille de Thrace et le penseur professionnel*, Payot, Paris, 1992.

Taranto, D., *Abilità del politico e meccanismo economico*, Liguori, Napoli, 1982.

Taylor, A.J., *Laissez-faire and State Intervention in Nineteenth-century Britain*, Macmillan, London, 1972.

Teboul, R., 'Temps et dynamique dans l'oeuvre de J.A. Schumpeter', *Revue Française d'Economie*, 1992, vol.7, 3.

Teichgraeber, R.F., 'Rethinking "Das Adam Smith Problem"', *Journal of British Studies*, 1981, vol.20, Spring.

—— *'Free Trade' and Moral Philosophy*, Duke University Press, Durham, 1986.

Thirlwall, A.P. (ed. by), *Keynes and Laissez-faire*, Macmillan, London, 1978.

Thompson, E., 'The Moral Economy of the English Crowd in the XVIIth Century', *Past and Present*, 1971, vol.50.

Thompson, H.F., 'Adam Smith's Philosophy of Science', *Quarterly Journal of Economics*, 1965, vol.79, 2.

Tichy, G., 'Schumpeter's Monetary Theory. An Unjustly Neglected Part of His Work', in Seidl 1984.

Tinbergen, J., *Statistical Testing of Business-Cycle Theories. A Method and Its Application in Investment Activity*, League of Nations, Geneva, 1939.

Togati, D.T., *Keynes and the neoclassical synthesis: Einsteinian versus Newtonian macroeconomics*, Routledge, London and New York, 1998.

Tronti, M., *Operai e capitale*, Einaudi, Torino, 1966.

Tsuru, S., 'Business Cycles and Capitalism: Schumpeter vs. Marx', *Annals of Hitotsubashi Academy*, 1952, vol.2, 2.

Tully, J., *A Discourse on Property*, Cambridge University Press, Cambridge, 1982.

Turco, L., *La prima "Inquiry" morale di Francis Hutcheson*, Rivista critica di storia della filosofia, 1968, vol.23, 1 and 3.

—— *Dal sistema al senso comune*, Il Mulino, Bologna, 1974.

Urbani, G., 'J.A. Schumpeter e la conoscenza empirica dei fenomeni politici', in Filippini, Porta 1985.

Vadée, M., *Marx penseur du possible*, L'Harmattan, Paris, 1998.

Varese, F., 'Keynes "apostolo" della probabilità', in Rossini Favretti 1989.

Vaughan, Ch.E., *Studies in the History of Political Philosophy before and after Rousseau*, Russell & Russell, New York, 1960.

Vaughn, K.I., *John Locke Economist and Social Scientist*, The Athlone Press, London, 1980.

Vercelli, A., 'Equilibrio e disequilibrio nella Teoria Generale di Keynes: il ruolo dei salari monetari e le difficoltà di un metodo di puro equilibrio', in Graziani, Imbriani, Jossa 1981.

—— 'Peso dell'argomento e decisioni economiche', Marzetti Dall'Aste Brandolini, Scazzieri 1999.

Vianello, F., 'Plusvalore e profitto in Marx', in Sylos Labini 1973.

Vicarelli, F. (a cura di), *La controversia keynesiana*, Il Mulino, Bologna, 1974.

—— *Keynes*, Etas, Milano, 1977.

—— 'Dall'equilibrio alla probabilità: una rilettura del metodo della *Teoria generale*', in Id. (a cura), *Attualità di Keynes*, Laterza, Roma-Bari, 1983.

Villani, A., *Gli economisti, la distribuzione, la giustizia. Adam Smith e John Stuart Mill*, F. Angeli, Milano, 1994.

Viner, J., 'Adam Smith and Laissez Faire', *Journal of Political Economy*, 1927, vol.35, April.

Virno, P., *Il ricordo del presente. Saggio sul tempo storico*, Bollati Boringhieri, Torino, 1999.

Vivenza, G., *Adam Smith and the Classics: The Classical Heritage in Adam Smith's Thought*, Clarendon Press, Oxford, 2001.

Vopelius, M.E., *Die altliberalen Ökonomen und die Reformzeit*, Fisher, Stuttgart, 1968.

Vygodskij, V.S., *Geschichte einer großen Entdeckung*, Verlag Die Wirtschaft, Berlin, 1967.

Walch, J., *Bibliographie du saint-simonisme*, Vrin, Paris, 1967.

Warriner, D., 'Schumpeter and the Conception of Static Equilibrium', *Economic Journal*, 1931, vol.41, 161.

Weintraub, E.R., '"Uncertainty" and the Keynesian Revolution', *History of Political Economy*, 1975, vol.7, 4.

Welzel, H., *Naturrecht und materiale Gerechtigkeit*, Vandenhoeck und Ruprecht, Göttingen, 1962.

West, E.G., *Adam Smith. The Man and his Works*, Liberty Fund, Indianapolis, 1976.

—— 'Adam Smith's Economics of Politics', in O'Driscoll 1979.

Willey, B., *The Eighteenth Century Background*, Chatto and Windus, London, 1940.

Wilson, T., Skinner, A.S. (ed. by), *Essays on Adam Smith*, Clarendon, Oxford, 1975.

Winch, D., *Economics and Policy*, Walker & Company, New York, 1970.

—— *Adam Smith's Politics*, Cambridge University Press, Cambridge, 1978.

—— 'Adam Smith and the Liberal Tradition', in K. Haakonsen (ed. by), *Tradition of Liberalism. Essays on J. Locke, A. Smith and J. Stuart Mill*, The Center for Indipendent Studies, Sidney, 1988.

Winslow, E.G., 'Organic Interdependence, Uncertainty and Economic Analysis', *Economic Journal*, 1989, vol.99, 398.

Wolfe, Ch.T., 'Smith's Crypto-Normativity', *Fenomenologia e società*, 2000, vol.23, 2.

Wolin, S.S., *Politics and Vision*, Little, Brown & Co., Boston, 1960.

Wright, H., *Die Bevölkerung*, Springer, Berlin, 1924.

Wright, D.M., 'Schumpeter's Political Philosophy', *Review of Economic Statistics*, 1951, vol.33, May.

Yolton, J., *John Locke and the Way of Ideas*, Blackwell, Oxford, 1956.

—— 'Locke on the Law of Nature', *The Philosophical Review*, 1958, vol.67, 4.

Young, W., *Interpreting Mr. Keynes. The IS-LM Enigma*, Polity Press, Cambridge, 1987.

Zamagni, S., 'Sui fondamenti metodologici della scuola austriaca', *Materiali filosofici*, 1983, 7.

Zanini, A. *Keynes: una provocazione metodologica*, Bertani, Verona, 1985.

—— *Schumpeter impolitico*, Istituto della Enciclopedia Italiana, Roma, 1987.

—— 'Schumpeter e la crisi del fondamentalismo razionalistico nella economia neoclassica', *Quaderni di storia dell'economia politica*, 1987, vol.5, 1–2.

—— 'La questione della "politics" in Adam Smith. Un commento a Donald Winch', in Geuna, Pesante 1992.

—— 'The Individual and Society: On the Concept of "Middle Conformation" in Adam Smith's *Theory of Moral Sentiments*', *History of Economic Ideas*, 1993, vol.1, 2.

—— *Adam Smith. Economia, morale, diritto*, B. Mondadori, Milano, 1997.

—— *Joseph A. Schumpeter. Teoria dello sviluppo e capitalismo*, B. Mondadori, Milano, 2000.

Index

Aaron, Richard I., 26n, 29n
Acham, Karl, 248n
Adam, Charles, 56n
Aglietta, Michel, 164n
Ahmad, Syed, 101n
Albani, Paolo, 290n
Albertone, Manuela, 213n
Alembert, Jean-Baptiste Le Rond d', 56n
Alessandrini, Pietro, 326n
Allen, Peter, 285n
Allen, Robert L., 210n
Althusser, Louis, 140n, 162n
Anscombe, Gertrude E.M., 299n
Anspach, Ralph, 99n
Appleby, Joyce, 126, 126n
Arago, François, 33n
Arena, Richard, 211n, 212n, 224n
Arendt, Hannah, 10, 10n, 128, 131, 134, 134n, 136n, 137–8, 138n
Arestis, Philip, 11n
Arrow, Kenneth J., 332n, 352n
Ashcraft, Richard, 26n, 27n
Ashley, William J., 138
Asimakopulos, Athanasios, 355n
Assézat, Jules, 56n

Backhaus, Jürgen G., 213n
Bacon, Francis, 58
Baczko, Bronislaw, 33n
Bagolini, Luigi, 67n, 73, 73n, 78, 78n, 87n
Baird, Robert M., 67n
Baldini, Artemio E., 27n
Baldwin, Stanley, 326
Balibar, Étienne, 140n
Barber, William J., 331n
Barotta, Pierluigi, 309n
Barral, Robert, 32n

Bastiat, Frédéric, 102, 143
Bateman, Bradley W., 284n, 285n, 288n, 303n, 358n
Bayle, Pierre, 57
Becattini, Giacomo, 212n, 311n
Becker, James F., 62n
Begg, David K. H., 11n
Beinsen, Lutz, 271n
Belaval, Yvon, 45n
Bellamy, Richard, 126n
Bellofiore, Riccardo, 139n, 157n, 165n, 187n, 234n, 312n
Benetti, Carlo, 132n, 164n
Bentham, Jeremy, 26n, 77, 77n, 79n, 322
Berkeley, George, 47, 47n
Bernard, John H., 42n
Berti, Lapo, 234nm 240n
Biasco, Salvatore, 188n
Bishop, John D., 101n
Bitterman, Henry J., 62n, 73n
Blaug, Mark, 141n, 331n
Bobbio, Norberto, 26n, 27n, 141n
Boenigk, Otto von, 236n
Böhm-Bawerk, Eugene von, 212, 212n, 219n, 233n, 236n, 261
Bologna, Sergio, 151n, 153, 153n, 154n, 155n, 160, 160n, 188n
Borkenau, Franz, 36, 36n, 113n
Braithwaite, Richard B., 296n, 302n
Braverman, Harry, 192, 192n
Breicha, Otto, 210n
Breton, Yves, 265n
Brown, Maurice, 21n, 24n, 62n, 73, 74n, 75n, 101n, 102, 109n, 119n, 133n
Brozen, Yale, 265n
Brunner, Otto, 79n
Brunschvicg, Léon, 31n
Buchanan, James M., 352n

414

Oakley, Alley, 233n, 239n, 240n
Olson, Richard, 55n
Opie, Redvers, 225n
Orlean, André, 164n

Paley, William, 322
Panzieri, Raniero, 140n, 180n, 182n
Parsons, Talcott, 107, 107n, 247n
Pascal, Blaise, 31–2, 31n, 32n, 34
Pasinetti, Luigi, 188n
Pateman, Carole, 251n
Patinkin, Don, 326n
Peacock, Alan, 326n
Pearson, Karl, 306
Perlman, Mark, 265n
Perri, Stefano, 188n
Perroux, François, 153n, 233n, 239n, 265n
Persky, Joseph, 101n
Pesante, Maria Luisa, 27n, 51n, 99n, 112n, 119n, 326n
Pesaran, Hashem, 287n, 288n, 358n, 368n
Pesciarelli, Enzo, 23n, 79n, 265n
Petry, Franz, 166n
Petty, William, 142n
Pietranera, Giulio, 29n, 140n
Pigou, Arthur C., 332n
Plamenatz, John P., 251n
Plessis, Alain, 153n
Pocock, John G.A., 112
Pöggeler, Otto, 128n
Poincarré, Henry, 228n
Pollard, Sidney, 327n
Pollock, Frederick, 26n
Pope, Alexander, 33n, 34, 34n, 45n
Popper, Karl, 298n
Porta, Pier Luigi, 129n, 218n, 233n, 250n
Portinaro, P.P., 8n
Presley, John R., 314n
Preti, Giulio, 21–2, 22n, 67n, 73, 73n, 87–8, 87n,

Pufendorf, Samuel, 26, 28–9, 40

Racinaro, Roberto, 283n
Rae, John, 66n
Raffaelli, Tiziano, 22n, 308n, 309n
Ramsey, Frank P., 296n, 302n
Rancière, Jacques, 141, 141n
Raphael, David D., 21, 21n, 22n, 52n, 62n, 66n, 68n
Rawls, John, 16, 17n, 69, 69n
Realfonzo, Riccardo, 139n
Reichelt, Helmut, 142n, 213n
Reid, Thomas, 29, 67n
Renault, Emmanuel, 141n
Restaino, Franco, 29n
Rhees, Rush, 293n
Ricardo, David, 20, 111n, 112, 119, 201–3
Riedel, Manfred, 114n
Robbins, Lionel, 125, 125n, 233n, 271n
Robertson, Dennis H., 313, 314n
Robertson, John C., 126n
Robinson Edward A.G., 314n, 334n
Robinson Joan V., 53n, 190n, 245n, 252, 252n, 273, 285n, 288n, 308n, 312n, 324n, 355n, 369, 369n
Rodezno, Veronica, 216n, 271n, 276n
Roncaglia, Alessandro, 219n, 277, 277n, 312n
Roscher, Wilhelm, 143
Rosdolsky, Roman, 139n, 151–2, 151n, 152n, 153n, 159, 159n, 160n, 178n, 183n, 190n, 201, 201n
Rosenbaum, Stanford P., 201n
Rosenberg, Nathan, 129n, 237n
Ross, Ian S., 31n, 70n
Rossi, P., 56n
Rossini Favretti, Rema, 288n, 291n
Rothschild, Emma, 101n
Rousseau, Jean-Jacques, 29n, 45n, 80n, 119n, 321–2
Roversi, Antonio, 214n
Rubin, Isaak I., 163n, 166n

417

Winters, Carl, 35n
Wittgenstein, Ludwig, 14, 210n, 289–90,
   290n, 292n, 293, 293n, 299n, 300,
   302–3
Wolfe, Charles T., 75n
Wolin, Sheldon S., 128, 133, 133n
Woolf, Virginia, 284
Wright, David M., 251n
Wright, Georg H. von, 290, 299n

Wright, Harald, 282n

Yeager, Leland B., 234n
Yolton, John W., 26n, 27n
Young, Warren, 281n

Zamagni, Stefano, 98n, 212n, 286n
Zanini, Adelino, 19n, 81n, 252n, 304n